QUALITATIVE RESEARCH IN EDUCATION

An Introduction

to the

Major Traditions

DAVID F. LANCY

UNIVERSITY OF TOLEDO

Longman
New York & London

Qualitative Research in Education: An Introduction to the Major Traditions

Longman, 10 Bank Street, White Plains, N.Y. 10606

Associated companies:
Longman Group Ltd., London
Longman Cheshire Pty., Melbourne
Longman Paul Pty., Auckland
Copp Clark Pitman, Toronto

Acquisitions editor: Kenneth Clinton
Sponsoring editor: Ray O'Connell
Development editor: Virginia L. Blanford
Production editor: Marcy Gray
Cover design: David Levy
Production supervisor: Richard Bretan

Library of Congress Cataloging-in-Publication Data

Lancy, David F.
    Qualitative research in education: an introduction to the major
traditions / David F. Lancy.
        p.   cm.
    Includes bibliographical references and index.
    ISBN 0-8013-0309-5
    1. Education-Research. I. Title.
LB1028.L243 1992
    370'.78—dc20   92-20128
                                                        CIP

1 2 3 4 5 6 7 8 9 10-AL-9695949392

For my parents, Alice and Leslie Lancy

Contents

CHAPTER 9 HISTORICAL INQUIRY
by John L. Rury   **247**

Preface

This text is designed as an introduction to the field of qualitative research. There is a small but growing number of graduate students and more established scholars who are choosing to utilize a qualitative approach in their research. This approach is moving from the status of a rather specialized alternative to a place of legitimacy alongside the quantitative approach to educational research. As a consequence, there is growing consensus that a thorough grounding in qualitative research should become the *sine qua non* for all professional educators inside and outside of academe. This book is aimed, then, at a large and diverse audience. It is primarily aimed at students enrolled in a graduate level, introductory class in qualitative research. It is also aimed at scholars and practitioners who completed their graduate education without having had such a course and who would now like an opportunity to rectify that omission.

Unlike typical introductory research texts, this work presents the substance of qualitative research as well as its methods. One reason to focus on substantive issues is that qualitative research is inductive. That is, unlike quantitative research, which is deductive, in qualitative research one observes reality, the particular, and extrapolates to the general. Hence, the general principles are *induced* from an examination of particular examples of qualitative research. Another reason to focus on substantive issues is that qualitative research is more than a collection of techniques. It often addresses different issues and incorporates different assumptions about reality than quantitative research.

This argument applies to those who would do qualitative research as well as to those whose goal is only to be able to read these studies with a critical and discerning eye. I will lead the reader through a representative sampling of work in the field, and, along the way, point out critical features that make a work qualitative, I will also note features that can be considered strengths or benefits of this approach as well as weaknesses or liabilities.

Another reason for offering the reader a chance to sample a rather extensive catalog of discrete studies flows from my desire to forgo paradigmatic purity for pragmatic utility. Many research texts focus exclusively on what should be—and this may be defined very narrowly—rather than on what is. Among my early mentors were Mike Cole and Millard Madsen, two experimental psychologists who introduced the study of culture into their work, and Jack (John W.) Roberts, a cultural anthropologist who used experiments, questionnaires, and other quantitative data collection techniques. Hence, I willingly err on the side of being overinclusive and include work that might be considered only marginally qualitative. This eclecticism permits me to stress "crossing points" between qualitative and quantitative methods. Ultimately, my aim is to promote the development of resourceful investigators, who use whatever means at their disposal to pursue interesting questions and pressing problems.

Another aspect of this text that reflects my interest in addressing the needs of a large and diverse audience is my inclusion of several distinct "traditions" of qualitative research. Many qualitative research texts focus exclusively on the ethnographic method, and most exclude such robust traditions of qualitative research as biography, history, and cognitive studies. By relying on a traditions framework, however, I eschew any lengthy consideration of newer, less well-established perspectives such as connoisseurship, deconstruction, critical theory, feminist theory, hermeneutics, post-structuralism, post-modernism, in short, what Fred Erickson, in a 1992 AERA address, referred to as "post-everything."

I would like this work to fill what I see as a wide gulf between the very brief treatment of qualitative research presented in the typical introductory research methods text and the very thorough treatment of specific areas of qualitative research characteristic of the current library of qualitative research texts. An instructor could, in theory, cover the material I review here but she would have to require her students to purchase several separate texts to do so—or use no text at all, which is what I've done until now.

This volume is exclusive in the sense that it focuses on research in education. Previous texts have had to draw on a variety of fields in the social sciences for illustrative examples. Because of the explosive outpouring of qualitative research in education during the last decade, I am able to pick and choose from a rich store of cases within my own discipline.

Chapter 1 consists of an in-depth introduction to the field of qualitative research. It is designed to make the reader aware of critical issues that will be raised again and again throughout the text, such as what role the qualitative researcher should assume. The chapter also delineates areas of widespread agreement in the field regarding the identifying features of qualitative research. These features will then be instantiated with numerous examples throughout the text, for example, deriving theory from data.

The following six chapters each deal with a distinct "tradition" of qualitative educational research. Many would argue that unlike quantitative research, qualitative research cannot be viewed as a unitary, monolithic body of shared assumptions and tools. Rather, it has evolved in the context of the more narrowly focused and discipline-based traditions such as anthropology, sociology, and history. Uneven chapter lengths reflect the varying popularity of these traditions. There are literally hundreds of published scholars in the field of educational anthropology, for example, while there are only a dozen or so active ecological (educational) psychologists. Each chapter reviews several studies on particular topics in considerable depth. This review permits an examination of the kinds of issues that unite scholars in this particular tradition as well as the development of a more discerning and critical approach to the research literature. An underlying premise here is that one must first read and digest a fairly large body of qualitative research before attempting to do it oneself.

In the penultimate chapter of the book, the practical problems involved in getting started on a qualitative research project are discussed. Finally, in the last chapter, John Rury offers the reader the unique perspective of the historian of education.

ACKNOWLEDGMENTS

Jim Cangelosi and Ray O'Connell stimulated the development of this book and kept a watchful and nurturing eye on me as I wrote it. Lynne Hudson and Joyce Kinkead both contributed to the creation of splendid thinking and working environments. This work is the product of many hands. Sandy Gee oversaw many production details and typed large sections of the manuscript, ably assisted by Jodi Eneper, Chris Muffaletta, Marge Richmond, and Patricia Dunaeff, who constructed the figures and tables. Charles Carter, Sarah Evans, and Jackie Harrah provided research assistance at critical junctures.

Several colleagues, including David Bergin, Gary Knowles, Annette Laureau, Bud Mehan, Tony Pellegrini, Peter Smith, and the following reviewers, reviewed and critiqued one or more chapters:

Carol Edelsky, Arizona State University

David Fetterman, Stanford University

Michael S. Meloth, University of Colorado

Geoff Mills, Southern Oregon State College

Petra Munro, Louisiana State University

Jim Sanders, Western Michigan State University

Carl Summers, The Ball State University

Bruce Uhrmacher, Denver University

Harry Wolcott, University of Oregon.

Their comments enhanced the text, although I was not always capable of responding to the challenges they set me. To all these individuals, and to my many co-investigators over the last twenty-five years, I am exceedingly grateful.

CHAPTER 1

Introduction

You know my method. It is founded upon the observation of trifles.
—Sherlock Holmes in The Boscombe Valley Mystery *by A. Conan Doyle*

Ten years have passed since the first broad overview of *Qualitative Research for Education* (Bogdan and Biklen 1982, 1992) was published. In their preface, the authors claim that qualitative research is growing in respectability and in sheer volume. Despite the fact that most qualitative research is still tagged in scholarly journals and forums by a kind of warning label (e.g., "qualitative" used as a modifier in labeling a qualitative study, where "quantitative" is *not* used to label quantitative studies), I would have to agree with these claims. Qualitative research now has its own journal (*Qualitative Studies in Education*), several book series (Falmer's *Social Analysis Series;* Longman's *Research on Teaching Series;* Methuen's *Contemporary Sociology of the School Series*), and growing acceptance within the American Education Research Association whose flagship journal recently issued a call for articles based on qualitative research methodology (Richardson-Koehler 1987). This volume also joins a veritable flood of texts on the subject (one publisher, Sage, has at least 40 separate titles related to qualitative research). Finally, more and more colleges of education are balancing quantitative with qualitative research by designating faculty slots for experts in the field and offering qualitative research methods and epistemology courses to complement existing courses in research methods and statistics.

However, proliferation and acceptance has been accompanied by considerable confusion as to what truly constitutes qualitative research. Eisner and Peshkin (1990), for example, claim: "There is . . . no general agreement about the conduct of . . . qualitative inquiry; perhaps there never will or can be consensus of the sort that is embodied in the standardized procedures of quantitative research . . ." (p. 1). Evelyn Jacob (1987), in a very influential article suggests an inductive approach to the definition problem, in effect that qualitative research is what those who consider themselves qualitative researchers do. She rejects the search for a consensual definition and instead sees "a variety of alternative approaches . . .'' (1987,1). At the other extreme are Yvonne Lincoln and Egon Guba, whose ''definition,'' in effect, runs to 414 pages because, as they point out, ''. . . it is not possible to provide a simple definition . . . Instead a proper impression . . . can be gleaned only as an overall perspective'' (p. 8). Lincoln and Guba's treatment (1985) is comprehensive, coherent, and compelling but, alas, very few actual studies are cited, and virtually none in education seem to meet the criteria for ''naturalistic inquiry.'' The way out of this dilemma taken by many writers is to define qualitative research by listing its characteristics, particularly as contrasted with quantitative research.

Table 1.1 is typical and can be helpful in giving the reader a quick sense of what qualitative research is about. Its principal limitation is that it oversimplifies and distorts both qualitative and quantitative research.

What I would like to attempt in this book[1] is to navigate the shoals of Scylla and Charybdis so to speak. I would like, particularly in this first chapter, to present a parsimonious set of ideas, constructs, proposals . . . which together emphasize the unitary nature of qualitative research. Rather than skirt controversy, I hope to identify some major points of contention so you can see where consensus

TABLE 1.1 Characteristics of Qualitative Contrasted with Quantitative Studies

Qualitative	Quantitative
The investigator has chosen a topic or issue to study. Task is to discover, hypotheses emerge	Investigator goes much further, delimiting the study, selecting variables, making predictions, etc. His/her task is to verify or refute. Hypotheses are stated in advance
The sites/individuals chosen for the study governed by topic . . . sites/individuals/cases relatively few in number	Sample size is governed ideally by considerations of statistical ''power.'' ''N'' is preferably large
The investigator is the principal ''instrument'' for data collection	The investigator should remain anonymous and neutral vis-a-vis the research site/subjects. He/she gathers data via intermediary instruments like questionnaires, tests, structured observation schemes, etc
The research process is designed to intrude as little as possible in the natural, ongoing lives of those under study	Intrusion may be extreme in that *subjects* may be *paid* to participate in a *laboratory simulation.* At a minimum those being studied will be aware that they are part of an ''experiment''
Investigator aware of his/her own biases and strives to capture the subjective reality of participants	Investigator assumes an unbiased stance; safeguards are employed to maintain objectivity
Investigator uses ''wide-angle lens'' to record context surrounding phenomena under study. Focus may shift as analytical categories and theory ''emerge'' from the data	Context is seen as potentially contaminating the integrity of study. Procedures employed to reduce extraneous factors
Typical study lasts some months, perhaps years	Typical study lasts some hours, perhaps some days
Report utilizes narrative format, there is a story with episodes	Report is expository in nature, consisting of a series of interlocking arguments

has broken down. However, in subsequent chapters, I intend to celebrate the incredible diversity of qualitative research manifested in various "traditions" (Kuhn 1970).

TRADITIONS

In quantitative inquiry there is, in theory, if not always in practice, a clear separation between the issue studied and the methodology used to conduct the study. The sensorimotor development of infants, the effect of gender on math achievement, and the side effects produced by a new drug can all be studied via experiments. Thus quantitative methodology, along with its handmaiden mathematics (including, but not limited to, statistics), has developed as a loosely united and relatively independent field of endeavor. There is a large cadre of "research methodologists" whose intellectual investment is made not in answering questions or solving real world problems but in trying to improve the tools employed to do these things. Thus quantitative research methodology grows and expands much like new limbs on a mighty oak tree. It is possible to connect every little twig, eventually, to a single trunk. Some limbs cease to receive nutrients or are storm-damaged, die and fall off. Newer limbs, their leaves reaching for the sun, grow vigorously.

By contrast, topic, theory, and methodology are usually closely interrelated in qualitative research. Following Kuhn (1970), Jacob (1987) has chosen to discuss qualitative research as manifested in the differing guises of several scholarly traditions. For her, a tradition is established when ". . . a group of scholars . . . share . . . assumptions . . . about the nature of the human universe, theory, legitimate questions or problems, and appropriate methodologies" (1987,250). I would add that many, if not most, practicing qualitative researchers learned their "craft," not from a text, but primarily by studying under a recognized "master," again, reinforcing the notion of tradition. For example, I studied the tradition of *educational anthropology* under John Singleton, the first editor of what was to become the principal journal in the field (*Anthropology and Education Quarterly,* see Singleton 1984). Singleton, in turn, studied (see Singleton 1967) under George Spindler, one of the acknowledged founders of this particular tradition (Spindler 1955).

Examined within the traditions framework, qualitative research more closely resembles a "mixed forest" than the "mighty oak" of quantitative research. While there is some cross-pollination, by and large these traditions are like distinct trees representing different species or, at least subspecies. In many cases their growth has not been spectacular and some trees appear to be almost moribund. That is, whole traditions seem to spring up ("critical ethnography," Anderson 1989) while others slowly die out ("ecological psychology," Barker and Gump 1964).

The chapters that follow correspond, to a great extent, to these different traditions. In Anthropological Perspectives in Chapter 2, I will focus on one of the oldest and certainly one of the most prolific, in terms of number of distinct studies, traditions of qualitative research in education. I will trace this history showing that the earliest educational anthropologists sought to fill holes in the ethnographic documentation of non-Western peoples by describing indigenous patterns of education, *enculturation,* as well as the initial impact of introduced, European-style schools. Underlying concerns will be identified such as a preoccupation with culture—the rules that underlie the patterned behavior of people who've lived together and interacted long enough to have reached consensus about what those rules should be. I will discuss two of the three different traditions which Jacob (1987) isolates, which grew from anthropology, namely, "wholistic ethnography" and "cognitive anthropology." The former is more concerned with a full description of culturally patterned behaviors while the latter is more concerned with the rules as "natives" see them.

The kinds of assumptions educational anthropologists hold, the methods they use, the controversies that divide them will be examined in the course of describing several noteworthy research studies. These studies contribute to our understanding of prominent topics that have preoccupied many educational anthropologists, namely, "school-community relations" and "the nature of the student culture."

Where the anthropologist employs the *ethnographic* method to study *culture,* the sociologist conducts a *field study* to document a *community.* These community studies had their origins in the Department of Sociology at The University of Chicago in the 1920s and, as early anthropologists brought back the first sympathetic, non-ethnocentric portraits of the culture of peoples in Africa, Asia, Oceania, etc. (as contrasted with the reports of missionaries, soldiers, capitalists, and bureaucrats) so, too, sociologists trained at Chicago provided relatively sympathetic portrayals of ghetto dwellers, bar patrons, gang members, and so on. These researchers have a common view that communities are created and held together by the interaction of their members. The most visible group of scholars practicing in this tradition in education are in the United Kingdom (Burgess 1985; Walford 1987).

Another tradition which one can identify as fundamentally sociological is *ethnomethodology.* The ethnomethodologist is especially concerned with the relatively unnoticed, routine, informal interactions that take place in human communities. The studies we will examine in Chapter 3, Sociological Perspectives, will address stratification in education and society.

The researchers whose work I will review in Chapter 4, Biological Perspectives, share a concern for documenting *universal* aspects of human behavior and human institutions. With intellectual roots in natural history, these scholars have a close affinity with modern field biologists who meticulously record the behaviors of a particular species over prolonged periods of time (McGrew 1972a). *Human ethologists* (Hutt and Hutt 1970) constitute one biological tradition that has produced work of importance to education. Their "field" is the nursery school, the playground, the summer camp; their species human beings, especially younger members of the species. *Ecological psychologists* use biological constructs and assumptions in an analogous rather than literal manner. They treat culturally patterned behavior as if it were species-specific in order to get at some of the ways that the environment might influence behavior such as Barker and Gump's

(1964) study of the influence of school size on student behavior. This chapter has three themes: dominance hierarchies, rough-and-tumble play, and the effects of density on behavior.

Case Studies, our focus in Chapter 5, deviates from the pattern established so far, in that people who do them probably do not have a sense that they are carrying on a "tradition." I would argue that, despite this, case studies do have one vital feature in common, they all address very directly the improvement of practice, all are designed to influence educational policy (Stenhouse 1985).

The traditions discussed to this point all promote "basic" research, the accumulation of findings that gradually give us a better understanding of some educational or psychological phenomenon. However, any given finding from a single study may not lead directly to a recommendation or conclusion. In the case study, however, a problem is either identified in advance or the investigator proceeds on the assumption that problems will be uncovered in the course of the research, obligating him/her to look for possible solutions. The case study literature reviewed in this Chapter ranges on a continuum from small scale projects involving a single case (e.g., an elementary school classroom, Edelsky, et al. 1983) to large-scale evaluation efforts with multiple cases (study of educational innovations, Huberman and Miles 1984). The theme we will address in this chapter is instructional innovation.

The "traditions" framework will again have to be stretched a bit to accommodate the material gathered together in Chapter 6, Personal Accounts. It is argued that many disparate strands of scholarship, are just now coalescing or being woven into what I believe is an emerging tradition. Anthropologists have used biography to illuminate enculturation processes (Simmons 1942); Wolcott conducted an "ethnographic-type account" (1974,176) of the daily life and work of an elementary school principal that has become a classic; teachers' diaries have been used to illuminate the history of schooling (e.g., Kinkead, in preparation); and teachers are now being trained to observe and record life in their own classrooms. It has only been recently, however, that contemporary and archival personal accounts, as well as concurrent in-depth studies of individual actors on the education scene, have been viewed as having unique properties that set them apart from other traditions (Bruner 1986). Among the topics which we will treat in this chapter is the process of becoming a teacher.

One of the characteristics often noted for qualitative research is a focus on the group as the unit of analysis as opposed to the quantitative researcher's use of the individual as the unit of analysis. As is demonstrated in Chapter 6, Personal Accounts, and Chapter 7, Cognitive Studies, this distinction may not be very helpful. Researchers interested in discovering the "universal in the particular" utilize qualitative methods. The sine qua non of the work presented in the Cognitive Studies chapter is the use of relatively open-ended, lengthy interviews with a single individual which focus on the solution of a particular problem. The goal of the interview is to discover how the individual (as representative of a class of similar individuals) represents and solves this particular problem (as representative of a class of similar problems). Substantively, two themes dominate this chapter: the teaching of mathematics and composing processes.

In Chapter 8, Decisions, Decisions, I walk with the aspirant qualitative researcher through the decisions that will be made in the course of planning and executing a qualitative study.

Those who do historical research in education have a unique problem—they cannot, as a rule, observe or interview the subjects of their study. Historians are, therefore, extremely adept at extracting meaning from unpublished documents, diaries, and other archival material. Their methods are collectively described as *historiography.* One theme in Chapter 9, Historical Inquiry, will be school attendance and class, ethnicity, and gender.

Table 1.2 provides a convenient summary of these various traditions.

TABLE 1.2   Qualitative Research Traditions

Tradition	Principal Methods	Research Techniques	Typical Foci
Chapter 2 Anthropology	Ethnography	Participant observation . . . collect artifacts . . . unstructured interview	Enculturation . . . student culture . . . school-community relations
	Ethnoscience Cognitive anthropology	Ethnosemantic interview	World view . . . members' perceptions
Chapter 3 Sociology	Field study	Participant observation . . . semi-structured interview . . . document analysis	Stratification in school and society . . . socialization
	Ethnomethodology, Sociolinguistics	Discourse analysis . . . breaching experiments . . . member check of videotape	Participation structures . . . socially constructed situations
Chapter 4 Human Ethology	Field study Natural experiment	Codes for behavior . . . direct observation . . . tallies and statistical analyses . . . audio-recording of observations . . . multiple observers	Documenting universal aspects of human behavior . . . children's play . . . social relations . . . gender-specific behaviors
Ecological Psychology	Field study Natural experiment	Codes for behavior . . . direct observation . . . tallies and statistical analyses . . . audio-recording of observations . . . multiple observers	Effects of physical environment and instructional constraints on behavior . . . school size . . . playground space . . . seating arrangements
Chapter 5 Case Study . . . of programs	Case study	Multiple cases . . . multiple investigators . . . mixture of qualitative and quantitative techniques . . . structured interviews . . . document analysis	Policy-related analyses of educational programs, including, especially, innovative programs May have an explicit evaluative purpose—summative . . . may have an explicit developmental purpose—formative

TABLE 1.2 continued

Tradition	Principal Methods	Research Techniques	Typical Foci
Chapter 6 Personal Accounts	Autobiography, biography, oral history	Long-term interview . . . diary . . . journal . . . content analysis	Process of becoming a teacher . . . relation of teaching to other aspects of life cycle
		Memoir, chronicle, confession	Expose injustice . . . describe unusual assignment
	Case study or "ethnographic-type account" (c.f. Wolcott 1973)	Shadowing, long interview, collecting written material	Study of actor as representative of a class of similar actors . . . (e.g., "elementary school principal," "school board member")
	"New journalism"	Investigative journalism . . . prose style more characteristic of fiction	Vivid portrait of individual actor
Chapter 7 Cognitive Studies	Clinical interview	Use of standard problems to elicit responses . . . think-aloud . . . introspection . . . use of computer to present material and monitor subjects' reaction time, pattern of responding . . . content analysis of written, verbal protocols	Study individuals' representations of academic problems . . . (e.g., in math, science, composition, etc.) . . . steps to solution . . . comparison of subject experts vs. novices. . . .
Teachers' Thinking	Case study	Video-taping and use of video tape to elicit participant's schemas and stimulate recall . . . model-building	Description of cognitive processes related to teaching . . . comparison of expert with novice teachers
Chapter 9 History	Historiography	Document collection and analysis . . . use of first-person accounts.	Development of institutions, practices over time . . . search for origins of key ideas . . . discover patterned relationships among social forces

EPISTEMOLOGICAL ISSUES

Distinct traditions aside, trying to determine the essence of qualitative research has been complicated by the fact that the term and its putative synonyms (ethnography, naturalistic inquiry, case study, field study) have at least three distinct referents.

Qualitative research is most commonly (e.g., Bogdan and Biklen 1992) thought of as a *method,* a program or set of procedures for designing, conducting, and reporting research. However, Lincoln and Guba (1985), among others, see it "... defined not at the level of *method* but at the level of *paradigm*" (p. 250). This distinction is captured in the anthropologist Ray Rist's lament over the increasing popularity of ethnography: "The term ethnographer is now being used to describe researchers who neither studied nor were trained in the method ... the traditional 'rite of passage'—a prolonged field study—has now been bypassed ... the idea of going into the field and allowing the issues and problems to emerge ... has ... given way to the preformulation of research problems, to the specifying of precise activities that are to be observed, and to the analytic framework within which the study is to be conducted. And all of this prior to the first site visit" (1978,9). At the level of paradigm, qualitative research is distinguished from quantitative research in terms of their respective underlying *epistemologies*. That is, they differ in basic assumptions made about how one derives truth, the purpose of inquiry, the role of the scientist/investigator, what constitutes evidence, how one evaluates the quality of a given study, and so on. Some scholars (e.g., Phillips 1983; Eisner 1983) have even gone so far as to declare that a paradigm "shift" (cf. Kuhn 1970) has occurred in education whereby *positivism* is no longer considered a defensible stance in conducting inquiry but has been replaced by *naturalism* (cf. Lincoln and Guba 1985).

Given the legions of still active quantitative methods users and the many scholars who see themselves as using qualitative methods but who are not necessarily prepared to abandon what they see as the scientific method, this declaration of a paradigm shift is premature. In particular, those who conduct case study research (Chapter 5) and cognitive studies (Chapter 7) do not completely adhere to the epistemological canons associated with the qualitative paradigm. In all likelihood they would agree with Michael Quinn Patton, author of the definitive text on the use of qualitative research in evaluation, who prefers "... pragmatism to one-sided paradigm allegiance" (1990,38).

As if two levels were not enough, I must warn you that many omnibus research methods texts (e.g., Borg and Gall 1983) consider qualitative research to be no more than a set of otherwise unrelated *techniques* such as "content analysis," "open-ended interviews," and "behavior observation" where the subject's possible responses are relatively unconstrained, compared to say, multiple choice tests, rating scales, and the like (but see Borg and Gall 1989). Hence, before one discusses what is or is not qualitative research one must first establish whether the discussion is occurring at the level of paradigm, method, or technique. To sum up: When one follows the qualitative paradigm, one buys into an entire philosophy of inquiry (see next section) that stands in sharp contrast to the tenets underlying quanitative research; one may follow a particular qualitative research method (e.g., case study) that deviates somewhat from the purest form of the paradigm and; one can work entirely within the quantitative paradigm and yet, occasionally, use a qualitative technique such as conducting open-ended interviews as a preliminary step in the design of a standardized survey instrument.

PHENOMENOLOGY AND THE
QUALITATIVE PARADIGM

Those who subscribe to the qualitative paradigm conduct their work within a phenomenological framework. Phenomenology has been variously characterized as a method, a philosophy, and a theory. Its wellsprings are found in the earliest writings of Edmund Husserl (1859–1938) (see especially Husserl [1913] 1962). As a method, phenomenology has been most fully elaborated by the ethno-methodology school in sociology; as a philosophy by the French existentialist school; and as a theory, by the Gestalt and symbolic interactionist schools of social psychology. Certain cherished tools of the scientist are abandoned or at least handled with caution. Thus a researcher taking a phenomenological approach avoids, as much as possible, the use of *assumptions* about the phenomenon under study; avoids *reducing* complex reality to a few "variables" and minimizes the use of instruments that are *reactive* and that greatly influence the reality she or he is trying to study. Such a researcher tries to go into the field with an open mind, to carry out investigations in which the conclusions are post hoc rather than a priori. Operating like the natural historian, the researcher observes, records, classifies, and concludes, seeking, wherever possible, to capture the reality of the *subjects* and not only her or his own reality.

Reality, however, is constantly changing. This change process may be described as "progress," as "evolution," as "entropy," or in any number of ways, but the researcher who employs the phenomenological perspective will be aware of it. Subjective realities are therefore often studied comparatively and historically to determine the kind and rate of change that affects them.

Obviously, there is a need for openness to afford the investigator the opportunity ". . . to be impressed by recurrent themes . . ." (Diesing 1971,145). The phenomenological researcher is open to alternative constructions of reality; open to many possible explanations for observed phenomena, few of which, in the absence of hypotheses or assumptions, can be ruled out in advance of the study; and open to a variety of data from many sources because no specified set of research techniques follows from the paradigm. Finally, the openness is demonstrated in the open-ended time frame in which change becomes part of the study rather than invalidating it.

Hence, the qualitative paradigm is ideal for phenomena that are patently complex and about which little is known with certainty. For less complex topics, phenomenology captures too much; it is wasteful (e.g., a phenomenological study of hiccupping). For phenomena about which a great deal is known, it would again be wasteful to throw away the known, to start from scratch as a phenomenological study would do (e.g., a phenomenological study of maze learning in the Norway rat in which nothing is assumed about the effects of handling, reward, or punishment). The phenomenological researcher is, above all, opportunistic. By being on the scene, the researcher observes and collects incidents, artifacts, and quotations that illuminate the phenomena. For this reason, phenomenology is best employed in situations that have relatively confined temporal and physical boundaries.

Another fundamental element in the qualitative paradigm is the use of "grounded theory." The concept was developed and elaborated in a book by Barney Glaser and Anselm Strauss entitled *The Discovery of Grounded Theory* (1967), undoubtedly the most influential work published to date on qualitative research. Glaser and Strauss were seeking a compromise between the relatively atheoretical community studies of the *Chicago School of Sociology* and the hypertheoretical, reified formulations of scientific sociologists like Merton and Parsons. They argue that theory should be grounded in the data. It is wrested from the data in the course of research rather than being imposed in a preordained fashion: "Theory should emerge . . . it should never just be put together" (1967, 41). They describe the "constant comparative" method where potential categories are identified, tried, and discarded until a "fit" between theory and data is achieved.

I sought to ground my theory in a study of parental influence on children's reading of storybooks, in which Kelly Draper and I videotaped 32 parent-child pairs as they read to each other. We had few if any preconceptions about what we would find, only that we hoped that distinct patterns would emerge and that these would be associated with the children's evident ease/difficulty in learning to read. I spent literally dozens of hours viewing these videotapes; developing, using, and casting aside various categories until I found two clusters of characteristics, which I called "reductionist" and "expansionist," which accounted for a large portion of the variation among parent's reading/listening styles. I was, of course, guided in my search for appropriate categories by my " . . . experience with the setting . . ." (Patton 1990,14) and by the transcripts of our interview with each parent (Lancy, Draper and Boyce 1989).

Bronislaw Malinowski (1922) discovered anthropology's version of grounded theory nearly 50 years earlier when, stranded by the outbreak of World War I, he was forced to spend much longer doing field work in the small Pacific community of the Trobriand Islands (just off the eastern tip of New Guinea) than he had intended. His prolonged stay had several consequences. He got to know the islands much better than he might have and was able to " . . . grasp the native's point of view, his vision of his world (1922,25)."[2] And his prolonged stay permitted him to develop and test a variety of explanations for the elaborate *Kula* ceremony which was practiced in the area before arriving at an account consistent with his observations and the natives' beliefs. Malinowski's method is still held up today as the ideal for anthropologists, in general, and educational anthropologists in particular (Goetz and LeCompte 1984).

THE RELATIONSHIP BETWEEN QUALITATIVE AND QUANTITATIVE RESEARCH

Given that qualitative and quantitative research clearly have different means and, perhaps, different *raisons d'etre,* what should be the relationship between the two?[3] Lincoln and Guba (1985), who have done a thorough job of building a rationale for the naturalistic paradigm by attacking positivism, see qualitative research as utterly antithetical to quantitative research (see Table 1.3). "The design specifications of the [quantitative] paradigm form a procrustean bed of such a nature as to make it impossible for the [qualitative researcher] to lie in it—not only uncomfortably, but at all" (p. 225). Meanwhile, "Critics of qualitative inquiry have charged that the approach is too subjective, in large part because the researcher is the instrument of both data collection and data interpretation, and because a qualitative strategy includes having personal contact with and getting close to the people and the situation under study" (Patton 1990,54).

This mutual antagonism has been played out many times in the pages of *Educational Researcher* (Gage 1989; Howe 1985; Howe and Eisenhart 1990; Eisner 1983; Firestone 1987; Miles and Huberman 1984a; Phillips 1983; Smith 1986; Smith and Heshusius 1986) whose editors strive to keep it abreast of the latest research trends. For our purposes, we should note that as the polemical debate heats up, there is also increasing evidence of rapprochement.

Rury's (1991) study of nineteenth century women's participation in high school is but one example in this book (see page 263) of many studies where qualitative data are used to complement quantitative data. Qualitative and quantitative methods may be combined in a single study, or a qualitative researcher

TABLE 1.3 Relationships between Qualitative and Quantitative Research

Relationship	Examples	Comment
Antagonistic	Sociology Chapter 3	Those who adhere rigidly to one paradigm or the other, reject the truth or evidential worthiness of research conducted within the opposing paradigm
Complementary	Case study, Chapter 5, Cognitive Studies, Chapter 7, History, Chapter 9	View is that both qualitative and quantitative research has the potential to contribute vital information bearing on a question or problem
Antecedent	Sociology, Chapter 3, Biology, Chapter 4, Case Study, Chapter 5	There is an exploratory or natural history phase to identify issues and variables and to better understand the setting or the population. Qualitative inquiry precedes quantitative
Encapsulated	Case study, Chapter 5	Embedded in a large-scale quantitative study, a few in-depth case studies are done to provide added context for and checks on the validity of the quantitative procedures
Primary/ Secondary	All	The research is primarily qualitative but quantitative data is used for background— demographics, for example. Quantitative data, as in interviews, may be collected near the end of the study to test the representiveness of the sample
Independent	Anthropology, Chapter 2, Biography, Chapter 6, History, Chapter 9	Essentially the qualitative researcher studies issues that may not attract the interest and attention of a quantitative researcher and vice-versa

may rely heavily on previous quantitative research on the topic in constructing his/her literature review and rationale.

Patton (1990) describes using qualitative research as, essentially, the "natural history" stage of a quantitative study. He and his colleagues were to carry out a summative evaluation of a "leadership program." Before designing the study they became participant observers in the program, which was essential as ". . . the program . . . bore little resemblance to our expectations, what people had told us, or the official program description" (p. 202). We must be very cautious in promoting this antecedant use of qualitative research, as Glaser and Strauss (1967) indignantly point out, it suggests that "real" research must be quantitative. Perhaps the most-noted example of the antecedant relationship in the literature is Jake Kounin's (1970) work on classroom management processes.

Another possible relationship (Table 1.3) occurs when investigators imbed qualitative case studies in an, essentially, quantitative study. Sylvia Hart-Landsberg (1982), for example, conducted a case study of one classroom's use of *Think-About,* an instructional television program, that was also evaluated by more conventional means. The "real world" material she gathered from the single classroom was used to flesh out the bare skeleton of achievement test and opinionnaire data from the larger study (Sanders and Sonnad 1982).

As the mirror image of quantitative researchers engaging in an initial natural history phase to identify variables, formulate hypotheses, etc., it has become extremely common for qualitative researchers to utilize various quantitative techniques, especially experiments and attitude surveys at the end or near the end of their study. They do so for several reasons, but one of the most common is to determine that the views they have obtained from a small sample of informants, who they have interviewed at length, are consistent, in the main, with those held by the larger group to which their informants belong.

> A ten-page questionnaire designed for the study was distributed to all the faculty and staff at the end of the fieldwork. The questionnaire was particularly valuable in enabling me to obtain systematic data about the staff, as I could see no point in holding a long taped interview with each of the twenty-nine members of the regular and part-time staff. This questionnaire provided standard census data and information concerning each teacher's perceptions of the school, community, and classroom. It also provided an opportunity for all staff members to state their feelings about an "ideal" principal. (Wolcott 1974,182)

Another possibility occurred in my ethnographic study of Kpelle children's play. I had formulated some ideas about the way in which children learn folk tales which I proceeded to "test" using standard experimental procedures (Lancy 1977).

Finally, we should consider the possibility of qualitative and quantitative researchers working in parallel. Educational anthropologists see themselves as focusing on different issues than educational psychologists, for example. That is, the ethnographer seeks to capture "the big picture," "culture," "surrounding context," and so on, or the ethnographer looks at what lurks in the interstices of the setting, finding "hidden curricula" (Gearing and Epstein 1982). At the time I undertook an ethnographic study of "Longbranch," many aspects of the innovative instructural program used in the school had been extensively evaluated (Glaser 1976). However, by taking a phenomenological perspective on the views and experience of pupils in the school, I addressed issues, questions, problems which no one had looked at before (Lancy 1976 a, b, c). The study was not, however, designed to complement, in any direct sense, the previous quantitative research.

Ultimately, of course, to understand the nature of education, we will need much additional research of all stripes. Consider trying to characterize someone's "quality of life" without reference to quantitative data of any kind, e.g., age, income, family size, etc., or only with reference to these various quantifiable criteria. Clearly either extreme is unsound. Table 1.3 presents a summary of these differing relationships between qualitative and quantitative research.

SHARED ELEMENTS OF METHODOLOGY

The Researcher as Instrument

A primary distinction between qualitative and quantitative research relates to data-gathering instruments. Let me describe two extreme scenarios. There are two researchers who are interested in a similar issue, how do students interpret and respond to feedback in class on their academic performance (e.g., teacher's comments, graded tests, papers). One researcher chooses to use "attribution theory" (Bar-Tal 1978). Essentially this theory specifies that each student has an attributional tendency which governs the way in which he/she will respond in feedback situations. That is, one student may attribute his B grade to his having studied carefully, another to his good fortune, and a third, may conclude that the teacher likes him. Our researcher wants to know if giving all students consistently high grades will change their attribution patterns. A random sample of students is drawn from several high schools. Half are assigned to a treatment condition where the teacher has agreed to give them high grades regardless of their performance. Our researcher sends a graduate assistant to the various schools to administer his attribution instrument (25 statements regarding feelings towards evaluation that students are to rate on a 5-point scale from "Strongly Agree" to "Strongly Disagree") before and again after the experimental manipulation to all of the 240 subjects. These instruments are scored by machine and the data are run through a statistical package to determine the level of significance of the change scores. . . .

Our qualitative researcher is a participant observer in Lincoln High School. She has become, over the last six weeks, closely associated with a couple of the tightly knit cliques that make up the student community including the "skaters" and the "fluff chicks." She has been zeroing in on their reaction to "grades." She's recorded numerous spontaneous remarks about grades in the cafeteria, in the stands during football practice, and so on and has interviewed several of her key informants at length on the subject. Finally, she has held focus group interviews (relatively unconstrained discussion, guided by a series of questions, such as, "Do students ever complain about grades?") on this subject with a group of teachers, she's gotten close to. Poring over her notes and transcribed interviews, she teases out a distinct pattern. . . .

I make no claim that the information the qualitative researcher obtains is any more true, valid, or generalizable than the quantitative researcher's data, just that the conclusions the two will draw from their research may be quite different, and that the qualitative researcher, who is herself the principal research instrument, will certainly feel much more confident about her conclusions having got it all straight from the horse's mouth, so to speak. The point here is that qualitative researchers, regardless of the tradition they adhere to, regardless of the degree to which they adhere to the paradigm, must experience the phenomenon first hand, in order to, at the least, develop what Hemingway called a "crap detector" (Baker 1969). Like Malinowski in the "Trobes," the ideal participant observer becomes intimately involved in the life of the "tribe" under study.[4]

Guba and Lincoln (1981) suggest that the many disadvantages of participant observation are ". . . offset by the flexibility, insight and ability to build in tacit knowledge that is a peculiar province of the human instrument" (p. 113). Of course, defining precisely how this human instrument is supposed to function is far from straightforward. (See Bogdan and Biklen 1992, 79–105 on procedures for doing fieldwork.) The ideal would be when the investigator can play a legitimate role within the setting. Note-taking and interviewing occur during natural breaks from one's "duties," or after school is out. Annette Lareau functioned as an instructional aide in her comparative study of two elementary schools.[5] I was the computer lab supervisor in several studies of children's adaptation to this new medium (Lancy, Forsyth, and Meeks 1987; Lancy and Hayes 1988).

One can become a participant by just being there, until gradually one is accepted (Cusick 1973). However, non-participant observation is also extremely common (Stodolsky 1988; Green, Harker and Goldin 1987), and as Goetz and Le Compte (1984) point out: "Nonparticipant observation requires a detached, neutral and unobtrusive observer. The researcher's objective shifts from a central concern for participant meaning to focus on participant behavior" (p. 145). Further, they advise that "nonparticipant observation rarely is used as the initial, exploratory technique . . . it is more appropriate for refinement and verification stages of the research process" (p. 145). In my study of students at Longbranch Elementary School, I derived behavior categories (e.g., "goofing off," "making contraptions" "passing out folders") and their definitions from several months of participant observation and student interviews. I then used them to construct a "Behavior Observation Checklist," which I used, with the aid of an assistant, as a non-participant observer in several classes to code the stream of behavior and thereby obtain a sense of the frequency of these various student-identified activities (Lancy 1976a). Clearly there are a variety of roles open to the qualitative researcher and Table 1.4 illustrates several.

To be a participant observer means working in the field and . . . "Field work involves getting one's hands dirty" (Patton 1990,47). Pursuing one's quarry

TABLE 1.4 Role of the Investigator (I) Vis-a-Vis the Informant

Role	Examples	Comments
Interviewer	Case study: Chapters 5, 6 Cognitive Studies: Chapter 7	Importance of rapport between researcher and subjects. . . . Audio recording essential . . . May be formal, distant from subject . . . Observation as data-gathering tool is minimal.
Nonparticipant observer	Human ethology, ecological psychology: Chapter 4	Generally more distant and structured than participant observation, but I. may have conducted prior P.O. . . . use of predefined categories for behavior . . . video-audio tape recording likely . . . use of one-way mirror . . . remote T.V. camera.
Participant observer	Case study: Chapter 5	Degree of participation generally low. I. maintains a degree of detachment.
	Anthropological . . . Sociological perspectives: Chapters 2 and 3	Degree of participation varies a great deal as does the degree of detachment . . . I. may identify with one set of participants (students) to the exclusion of another (teachers). High degree of participation implies a formal role assignment, such as teacher's aide.
Collaborative partner	Teacher-researcher collaboration: Chapter 6	I. identifies completely with the people she/he is working with and functions as their equal . . . Perspective of I. and participant are complementary.
Teacher/researcher	Teacher as researcher: Chapter 6	Primary function is that of participant, observation and/or other forms of research are secondary.
Historian	Historian: Chapter 9	Little or no relationship between researcher and the subjects of the research. Personal documents are relied upon.

through the corridors, on the swings, in the board room is unpredictable and complex; there are numerous blind alleys and wasted initiatives; one's motives are suspect; one's allegiance is questioned; one learns about proper etiquette after committing the *faux pas*. And, if we are very successful; if everyone cooperates; the tape recorder works and we don't run out of tape; there is still the risk that ". . . the quantity of interview data . . . collected [is] almost unmanageable; we collected so much data that we left ourselves too little time to reflect on and analyze it" (Scott 1985, 119). Compared to working in the lab or conducting research via standardized instruments, working in the field is messy! Sue Scott's candor is unusual, most published accounts leave out the false starts, the self-doubt, the errors of judgment, and so on (see Wax 1971; Lareau 1989).[6]

But the arguments which dictate that a good researcher get in direct touch with the phenomena apply with equal force to the need to get into the field. The volume of *prescriptive* literature on educational administration, the role of the principal, school governance, and so on, is voluminous. But in these thousands of pages about what the elementary school principal should or shouldn't do, hardly a line had been written about how a real, live, principal actually functioned until Wolcott (1973) undertook his two-year-long study of *The Man in the Principal's Office.*

Two issues arise in connection with fieldwork: sampling, where does one go to do one's research, and gaining entry, how do you get admitted and maintain your research role? In quantitative research (and assuming one intends to use inferential statistics), the ideal sample is a random sample; any other kind opens the possibility that the researcher's bias might influence the selection process. In qualitative research, the bias becomes purpose, as in *purposive sampling* (Bogdan and Biklen 1992). One chooses the site(s) that will yield the maximum information regarding the specific topic/issue one is investigating. Similarly, "sampling [adding sites, interviewing more informants, taking additional field notes] is terminated when no new information is forthcoming from newly sampled units . . ." (Lincoln and Guba 1985,202). Hence, one chooses sites which are somehow "representative" for the phenomenon of interest. Peshkin studied "an exemplary Christian school . . ." (1986,12) and Wolcott an "average American Elementary School Principal" (1974,176). At the same time, qualitative researchers are supposed to be opportunistic. Everhart (1983), on a team evaluating a federally funded instructional innovation in a junior high school, took the opportunity to pursue a topic (student resistance) largely unrelated to the evaluation. Some years ago, just prior to the onset of a new quarter, I noted with great interest an announcement for a "Rodeo Queen Clinic." Recalling that a horse-loving friend of mine intended to take my qualitative research course, I convinced her to do an ethnography of the clinic for her "class project." She started immediately under my supervision and was well into the study by the time the class started. Unorthodox perhaps, but I believe the results (Raitt and Lancy 1988) were more than satisfactory.

Margaret Raitt's affinity for horses gave her a considerable advantage in gaining entry as an otherwise obvious outsider in the "clinic," and this problem is one of the most widely discussed in the methods literature (e.g. Beynon 1983; Fetterman 1989; Marshall and Rossman 1989). Educational research often takes place in institutions that are "under siege." Schools and families have, of late, been closely scrutinized for failing to live up to public expectations. This sense of vulnerability can throw up a wall of resistance to the qualitative researcher (e.g., Weiss 1985) who'd like "free access" but is unprepared to specify in advance what the findings might be. In fact, the researcher's careful speech to the contrary, most people assume that research equals evaluation.

And yet, despite this, I am always amazed at how welcoming students, parents, teachers, and school administrators are to my initial overtures and later queries. While much has been written on the subject of entry, perhaps the best advice is to "be prepared," as Fetterman (1989) notes: "The ethnographer enters the field with an open mind, not an empty head. Before asking the first question in the field, the ethnographer begins with a problem, a theory or model, a research design, specific data collection techniques, tools for analysis, and a specific writing style" (p. 11). Each situation is different, of course, and no matter how well prepared one is, being intrepid is an asset in the pursuit of one's research topic. Alan Peshkin, a professor at the University of Illinois and a Jew, set himself the task of conducting an ethnography of a fundamentalist Christian school. Before eventually succeeding, he knocked on many doors and was repeatedly denied entry to study such schools, e.g., "You're like a Russian who says he wants to attend meetings at the Pentagon—just to learn . . . no matter how good a person you are, you will misrepresent my school because you don't have the Holy Spirit in you" (1986,12).

Interviewing Informants

Once data-collection begins, the researcher has three principal data sources: observation, interviews, and artifacts. Observations are recorded in field notes; which can be free-form jottings that one takes down, on the spot, or lengthier, but perhaps less detailed, reconstructions after the fact. They are often written on two levels: the facts, very direct descriptions of what was observed and/or verbatim recording of what was overheard and; the observer's comments to provide context for the raw facts; and/or to speculate on what it all means; how what was just observed relates to earlier observations, and so on. Aside from the blank note page, some studies call for more structured, precise observations which will be facilitated by the use of specially developed forms.[7]

One has several distinct interviewing formats to choose from, beginning with the "non-interview." Margaret Raitt didn't formally interview any of the Rodeo Queen Clinic participants, except the director, but she created many opportunities to engage students, instructors, and parents in conversations which she led around to the issues she was interested in. Individuals one is studying will often express more candid thoughts in a conversation than in an interview, though they are aware they are the object of a research study. One can conduct a formal interview in a largely informal manner by using a series of very broad guiding questions. Lynn Meeks and I (nd) used such a strategy in interviewing ninth graders in an experimental composition class. We used such questions as "What is writing?," "Tell me about this class." Although we had a list of "probes" which we each used, we varied the order, and if a student spontaneously mentioned a topic we were interested in, we did not feel compelled to ask that particular question. One's goal in this type of interviewing is to obtain information, but also to remove any constraints on the interviewee's responses so that her conceptualization of the phenomena emerges rather than having her fit her views into the investigator's framework. Often one is rewarded by the interviewee presenting a view or using a type of phraseology which is completely unexpected (see Whyte 1984,97–101). In this particular study, Meeks and I were not expecting students to tell us as much as they did about their previous writing experiences in and out of school.

These unanticipated forays provided us with the strongest analytical angle on our data.

Group interviews have their place. I found in my field work in Liberian (Lancy 1980a) and Papua New Guinean (Lancy 1979) villages that group interviews were more natural than the typical face-to-face interview. Indeed, my informants often felt reluctant, as individuals, to respond to my queries about general aspects of their society as they felt they lacked sufficient authority to speak on these matters. Also in schools, one can quickly dispel any mystery about one's role and purposes via a semi-structured group interview with teachers.

Then there are at least two highly structured interviewing procedures that qualitative researchers use, the open-ended questionnaire where respondents have a great deal of latitude in composing their responses and which can be presented in verbal or written form, and the ethnosemantic interview (Spradley 1979). The latter will be explained in some detail in the next chapter. Pre-constructed interview questions are incompatible with a phenomenological stance. However, there are strategies we can employ to increase the naturalness of this procedure (what Gorden [1980] calls "facilitators of communication"). For example, I recently completed a study of Running Start, a parent involvement/reading promotional program for first graders sponsored by the Chrysler Corporation with Ann Zupsic, the teacher whose class constituted the research site. One item in the kit sent home to parents was a checklist of 10 activities the parent could initiate to promote literacy. We were, in fact, interested in the role parents play in promoting reading acquisition, so we used this list as a basis for asking parents about their practices. The list was, of course, familiar to them and, with it in front of us, I asked, for example, "What do you think about item eight: *Share family stories with your children?*" (Lancy and Zupsic, 1991).

Another interesting aspect of this particular case study was that, having spent a great deal of time interacting with the children in Ann's class, I was able to offer several observations about the child before beginning the interview with his/her parent. This helped to break down what was, in many cases, evident fear/hostility on the part of some parents. There are a number of comprehensive reference works available on the subject of interviewing (Gorden 1975; McCracken 1988; Churchill 1978; Whyte 1982) but the best designed interview is useless if the interpersonal "chemistry" isn't working. A slim volume by Jack Douglas (1985) is particularly helpful regarding the human side of this endeavor, a sample: ". . . small talk and chit-chat are vital first steps on the way to intimate communion" (p. 79).

Gathering Artifacts

The third major data source in field research are "artifacts." Typically they encompass various pieces of printed material.

> Thanks in part to the accountability movement, social institutions have become paper mills. Organizations produce written budgets, interoffice memos, market surveys, transcripts of meetings, personnel files, statements of policy or

philosophy, and newsletters. Schools produce these and more: pupil case files, curriculum guides, test score reports, needs assessments, disciplinary codes, teachers' planning books, grade books, pupil essays, and student newspapers. Every piece of paper represents a potential source of data for the qualitative researcher. Added to the official records and archives of the organization are the writings of individuals—letters, diaries, autobiographies, and the like. (Smith & Glass 1987,269)

During Everhart's (1983) study he ". . . asked for and was assigned a mailbox in the school office, and received all announcements and material normally received by teachers" (p. 285). Another example is drawn from Leacock's (1969) study of racially segregated Elementary Schools in New York City: A study of twenty-three social studies texts that were being used at the time of the study

> . . . shows how serious were both the omissions in these books and the direct statements they made about other nations and racial and religious minorities. . . . Missing from the texts was any mention of the consistent fight for freedom engaged in by the Negro people, or any discussion of the moral and physical injustices of slavery. . . . Several books repeated the myth that Negroes were well suited to hard work in the hot sun. (p. 76–7)

I asked for, and was given, the "New Year's Resolutions" just after they were taken down from the bulletin board in one fifth grade class because I felt they revealed something fundamental about gender stereotyping in the school. A sampling from the girls:

> I resolve to brush my teeth four times a day. (several of these)
> I resolve to stop biting my nails. (several)
> I resolve to do better in my math and reading.
> I resolve to do better in my school work.
> I resolve to stop fighting with my brother.

The boys' New Year's resolutions were different:

> I resolve to stop talking. (several of these)
> I resolve not to get any sentences. (as punishment)
> I resolve to do my work and quit fooling around. (several)
> I resolve not to play games before I am done with my work.
> I resolve I shall not bug Thy [sic] teacher. Lancy (1978,121)

Ray Rist (1978) conducted one of the earliest (1973–74 school year) studies of busing to achieve school integration (in Portland) and made extensive use of printed material, including newspaper articles, to provide a historical perspective on the problem. Whereas these artifacts are usually given less attention than one's observation and interview records, they may become central to the aims of the study. Johnson (1980) used artifacts exclusively to study ". . . public schooling

[as] . . . a mechanism for socialization and enculturation into *national* society and *culture"* (p. 174). Objects (*material culture*) in classrooms, especially posters and other wall decorations, were coded as reflecting local or national cultural values. Johnson found a near total absence of locally relevant material and concludes, "The nature of the setting in which elementary school children spend over 7,000 hours of their lives is primarily influenced by national rather than local mandates" (p. 185).

Triangulation

Printed material and other artifacts are combined with observation and interview records in a process that is widely known as *triangulation.* The qualitative researcher's most effective defense against the charge of being subjective is to buttress what she has observed with material that reinforces these observations from other semi-independent sources. Also, "The rationale for this strategy is that the flaws of one method are often the strengths of another" (Denzin 1970,308). Gibson (1987, 1988) creates a tightly woven net to support her argument that immigrant high school students from the Punjab were able to accommodate to the demands of the school and achieve success without necessarily "becoming American." The net was made up of her notes from two years of participant observation; lengthy face-to-face interviews with students, parents, and teachers; test scores and report cards, etc. The major theme, "accommodation without assimilation," occurs throughout these materials. Contrariwise, she looked for and could not find material to support alternative themes, such as, that the evident racism directed at the Punjabis had a depressing effect on their self-esteem and academic motivation.

Using multiple data sources also allows one to fill in gaps that would occur if we relied on only one source. For example, Peter Woods (1986) discovered that ". . . *punishment books* may not reflect all the punishment that has been administered . . . [a variety of minor punishments go unrecorded and] the 35 strokes of the cane administered to Stephen Winters by Mr. Gordon for persistently and deliberately refusing to bring his games kit omits to say that the boy had to be held down shouting and struggling" (p. 91, italics added).

Analyzing the Data

Regardless of his tradition, the qualitative researcher faces the problem of systematically analyzing what is usually a substantial body of data. Unlike the quantitative researcher, however, he has relatively little idea at the outset how to partition this continuous mass into discrete, perhaps even countable, categories. For example, with my colleague Steve Zsiray, I developed a microcomputer based robotics curricula for an eighth grade class. Students worked their way through a series of interactive microcomputer programs that became increasingly challenging. The curriculum was trialled with a sample of 12 students who were "shadowed" and encouraged to "think-aloud" (Ericsson and Simon 1984) as they explored each program. I read and reread the think aloud/interview transcripts trying to find an analytical framework that best captured the patterns that emerged. Obvious candidates (computer phobic vs hacker; smart vs dumb) weren't useful. Ultimately, I found a developmental "stage" framework to be most effective (Lancy 1991a).

Reviewing the transcripts and assigning students to stages based on their varied reactions to the programs didn't take very long at all compared to the lengthy time spent in creating the analytical framework. "There are no formulas for determining significance . . . no . . . tests for reliability and validity. In short, there are no absolute rules . . . [only] guidelines" (Patton 1990,372). Perhaps the best single source for such guidelines is Miles and Huberman's (1984) handbook (see Chapter 5). By contrast the quantitative researcher usually begins the data analysis phase with categories, coding systems, operational definitions, in hand.

However, before one plunges into the nitty gritty of content analysis, coding field notes, preparing case records, etc., one must consider what the appropriate *level of analysis* should be. One can envision two extremes. At one extreme there is relatively little analysis per se. The object is to provide a straightforward description of the phenomenon. DeWalt and Troxell's (1989) ethnography of an Old Order Mennonite school is a case in point. Their goal was to provide a concise portrait of an unusual school. This is not to say that the task of summarizing their undoubtedly voluminous material in 17 pages was an easy one, but at least they didn't have to agonize over whether their interpretation of what they observed will seem credible. It may be that most people who are unfamiliar with qualitative research assume that these documentary pieces are its primary raison d'etre, but as Schofield (1990) ascerbically notes: "Unless the researcher chooses a very atypical site or presents an unusually insightful analysis of what is happening, the purely descriptive value of the study may be . . . discounted" (p. 205). Mischler (1979) discusses the other extreme, analysis to the nth-degree.

Very precise and detailed methods for analyzing qualitative data, especially naturally occurring discourse, are sometimes referred to as microanalysis (Green, Harker, and Golden 1987) or microethnography (Goetz and LeCompte 1984). As we will see, the level of analysis[8] varies widely among the different qualitative research traditions, among cultural anthropologists, description may predominate with relatively little analysis beyond what is necessary to prepare an organized and coherent report. By contrast, those engaged in cognitive studies may develop extremely elaborate schemes for organizing and representing their data (e.g., Leinhardt 1989). Finally, we can make a distinction between two different strategies (or two poles on a continuum) for analyzing qualitative data. On the one hand, classics in the field like Becker et al. (1961) and Glaser and Strauss (1967) suggest that one works from the bottom up, breaking the data into the smallest pieces possible, then systematically coding and collating all the lower level (grounded) categories, and then moving upward to seek meaningful, larger aggregates. This contrasts with Lou Smith's (1978) "skimming the cream."

During our last week of data collection we had to make a brief presentation of results to the several parties of the larger project we were investigating; these individuals were making decisions regarding the form the project would take in the succeeding years. The tactic we adopted was a simple one. In a local coffee shop, for a period of a couple of hours, we asked ourselves: "What are the major things we have learned from our year in the field?" As we brainstormed these ideas, with no reference to our file drawer of notes, interpretive asides, or summary interpretations (some of which were still untyped on tapes because of organization resource problems), we gradually accumulated a list of ideas, findings. We pushed and pulled on these until they gradually fell into reasonable, broader topics and differentiated outlines (p. 337).

Reporting the Study

While it is easy now to find reports of qualitative research that resemble comparable reports of quantitative research, they more commonly employ a narrative format as opposed to a strictly expository format. Because of the enormous importance of description and context, as well as the growing importance of describing in very personal terms the researcher's history vis-a-vis this particular topic, the qualitative research report is written as a story. And, according to Van Maanen (1988), one expects the qualitative researcher to use a ". . . literary style that is . . . evocative and graceful" (p. 22). Also the field worker disappears. He may introduce himself in a footnote or appendix, reappear in an occasional "cameo" role but "The voice assumed throughout the tale is that of a third-party scribe reporting directly on the life of the observed" (p. 64). Use of the vernacular, verbatim quotes, and precisely detailed observations all serve to convey that the author is merely a "translator," and that the story is the natives' own.

However, if one goes too far in this direction, one ends up writing what VanMaanen calls "Literary tales [which] are meant to provide an emotional charge to the reader. The reality is not sliced, diced, and served up analytically . . ." (p. 132). He refers specifically to authors Tom Wolfe, John McPhee, Joseph Wambaugh, and Peter Mathiessen, whose books ". . . are not written for tenure, grants or a Ph.D . . . ." (p. 134). Certainly the work that is most germane here is *Among Schoolchildren,* a recent best seller by Tracy Kidder (1989). This is a very vivid portrait of a year in Chris Zajac's fifth grade classroom. Kidder is certainly all but invisible, his prose is graceful and there is much we can learn from reading about Mrs. Zajac. However, *Among Schoolchildren* is not a report of qualitative research, but a journalistic account.[9] It is almost purely descriptive and when some kind of conclusion is drawn—"It is remarkable how much of the time of how many adults in a school a child can command simply by being difficult." (p. 166)—no empirical basis is provided to support it.

One of the essential problems that a qualitative researcher faces is to combine description which is engrossing and convincing with analyses that go to the heart of the phenomenon. And the analytical procedures must be made sufficiently clear so that the reader can follow the steps from evidence to conclusion. One can err on the side of too much description, such that the reader asks "Where is this leading?" or too much analysis, such that the reader says, "I don't believe this, show me the evidence." or inadequate presentation of method, such that the reader responds: "I don't follow this, how did we get to this particular conclusion?'' Wolcott (1990, see also Delamont 1992) focuses on these kinds of issues in his recent book, e.g., ''. . . qualitative studies in education . . . reveal a tendency towards heavy-handed or intrusive analysis . . .'' (p. 29). He describes the writer's block that can occur when the author has a large volume of material, field notes, transcribed interviews, printed matter—and a weak or nonexistent analytical framework. It is this framework which guides one in deciding where to begin, how to organize the presentation of material, and what to put in and what to leave out.

Wolcott would also argue, and I agree with him, that one's framework should always be made explicit to the reader. As we will see, this dictum is not always followed. Indeed, far from reporting on their methodology for data-gathering and analysis, some authors eschew the very idea of methodology (Suransky 1982). Among the items to be noted in the methods section, appendix, or chapter, Wolcott (1990) includes: the duration of the study, the setting, details about who was interviewed, the circumstances surrounding the interview as well as how questions were phrased, details on the use of recording equipment, and so on. The overriding issue here is to provide sufficient information for the reader to judge the author's credibility as a research instrument and his/her astuteness as an analyst of social scenes.

A final note on writing it up contradicts, somewhat, what has just gone before. I have noticed a laudable increase in the number of books being published in education which report in-depth on particular qualitative research projects. However, you should recognize that you are far more likely to be able to publish your work as an article or chapter than as a book. Here one has several choices. One can write-up a mostly descriptive piece devoid of analysis and conclusions; these are extremely hard to get published. One can write a piece that is long on conclusions and short on description. This is most commonly done but it is a practice that throws away what is most valuable about qualitative research—the ''believability'' that comes from obviously thorough familiarity with the phenomenon. Or, and I think this is the preferred route, one can, like a gem cutter, fracture one's study along natural division lines and provide several reasonably complete accounts of these separate pieces (see, for example, Leinhardt and Smith 1985; Leinhardt, Weidman, and Hammond 1987; Leinhardt 1988, 1989).

THE RISING POPULARITY
OF QUALITATIVE RESEARCH

At the American Education Research Association in 1988, I noticed a strange thing happening, as I went from plenary session, to invited speaker, to featured speaker, I sat in amazement as this parade of luminaries whose names are enshrined in the ''quantitative research hall of fame'' got up to the podium and . . . told stories. Some illustrated their tales with videotape clips from the classrooms they were ''studying,'' none offered tables, graphs, or grids. This stands in sharp contrast to the first conference I ever attended where I tried vainly to summarize in 12 minutes, a paper which itself had been shrunk from an extra large to a petite, as I tried to reduce several months of full-time data collection and analysis down to 20 pages! Qualitative research has gone from being fringe, marginal, unscientific, to fashionable and I will try and detail some of the reasons in this section. I begin by describing my own conversion process.[10]

My undergraduate degree is in psychology, with an emphasis on experimental design. My senior thesis was an experimental study comparing hunger and aggression drives in Siamese Fighting Fish (Fantino, Weigele, and Lancy 1972). Shortly after commencing graduate school, my advisor offered me an opportunity to go to Liberia to work on a National Science Foundation-funded research project for which he was principal investigator. From 1967 to 1970 we developed and supervised the conduct of dozens of tests/experiments designed to elucidate the impact of culture on the cognitive development of children (Cole et al. 1971). In the process, we discovered that without a better understanding of the culture of our subjects it was difficult to make sense of some of the results, indeed we weren't sure that we were even asking the right questions. I tried my hand at some observation in the local elementary school (Lancy 1975) and we gradually learned enough about local ways of thinking to permit the design of more culturally sensitive tests. For example, one cognitive test I devised used material from and was based on the underlying structure of traditional Kpelle riddles (Cole et al. 1971,195–7).

By the time I returned to Liberia in 1973, to carry out research for my dissertation, I had accumulated more than 30 graduate hours in anthropology and had read widely in the ethnography of West Africa and especially the Kpelle. While the topics to be addressed were quite similar in this second study, the primary approach was qualitative with quantitative techniques being used as a supplement to test the grounded theory that emerged during the ethnography (Lancy 1977). My subsequent research has followed one or another of the models depicted in Table 1.2.

Validity and Qualitative Research

A prime reason, therefore, for the growing interest in qualitative research is the growing disenchantment with an exclusive reliance on quantitative methodology. As McDermott and Hood (1982) point out, a major problem with many experimental tests of intellectual functioning is that even when we carefully select materials and language which are familiar to our subjects (e.g., Lancy, Souviney, and Kada 1981), the nature of the task environment itself is foreign in the sense that it does not represent a microcosm of real-world problem solving. In other words, humans use one set of reasoning strategies for everyday situations and another set for critical, test-like situations. When subjects use everyday problem solving in a test or laboratory problem solving task, they will inevitably do poorly (Lancy 1989). The same arguments have been applied to standardized tests administered in schools (Cicourel et al. 1974). Cicourel (1968), McDermott and Hood (1982), and Hammersley and Atkinson (1983), are three of the best sources for critical analyses of the limitations of quantitative methods.

Another and closely related problem is the "definition of the situation." During my study of *Longbranch,* I spent a great deal of time observing in the "science lab" which housed probably the most elaborate (and expensive) science curriculum ever developed for the elementary grades (e.g., Champaign and Klopfer 1974). A culminating activity in the program was the SIIA or "Self-Initiated Independent Activity." Students were to apply the methods they had learned during the structured lessons in framing and carrying out their own investigations. Evaluated quantitatively, the SIIA's were a total failure and cast doubt on the success of the entire program. However, when we look at the SIIA from the student's point of view a different picture emerges:

> Because they must initiate the projects themselves, and because there are relatively few constraints on what they may do, they have redefined the SIIA so that it bears little resemblance to the curriculum developer's and teacher's model. A fourth-grade girl was interviewed about recent SIIAs she had done.
>
> SALLY: Well, sometimes I make an experiment. Like my girlfriend and I once maked an experiment. We put 1/3 dixie cup of lemon juice and sugar in it and we stirred it and then we put it in the freezer.
>
> D.L.: And what happened?
>
> SALLY: Then in three days we came back and it was frozen.
>
> This is a description of a fairly typical "mixture" and mixtures are the most common experiments. Girls seem to prefer mixtures that "turn out nice." When there was snow on the ground, a frequent activity was collecting a beaker full of snow and then adding various food color dyes until a pleasing effect had been achieved. Boys prefer making mixtures that either look or smell "awful." They delight in pouring unlikely materials (baking soda, honey, soap powder) together and then heating the whole thing until it boils. They also seem to relish in heating things, in general, because they get to wear asbestos aprons, gloves and goggles. (Lancy 1976b,18)

Quantitative research may oversimplify what is patently complex. And although one can detect a clear trend in educational research to move from simple univariate or bivariate designs, to complex multivariate, non-linear models (Barr & Dreeben 1983), all these procedures require variables that can be scaled, that is, numerically scored or rated in some way, whereas the qualitative researcher insists that not all of the reality that constitutes education is in fact reducible to variables.

Lincoln and Guba (1985, see also Edelsky 1990) provide a thorough analysis of perhaps the most damning charge against the dominance of logical positivism. They argue that, to a considerable extent, the persistence of bottom-up (phonics, vocabulary drill, syllabication) methods in teaching reading in schools, as contrasted with what appear to be much more appropriate and natural "whole language" methods, is attributable to the fact that the former isolates skills which can be measured by quantitative means. What they argue, in effect, is that research methodology cannot be opaque with respect to, especially, theories of education.

Put differently, researchers are being held to account for the over-reliance on what may turn out to be a misguided and potentially very damaging instructional technology (Hirsch 1987).

What many of the recent methods debates suggest, therefore, is that quantitative research (sometimes, often, always) obscures the very phenomena under investigation. However, I cannot endorse the extreme position taken by some (Lincoln and Guba describe "science" in the past tense, "Science was thought to be . . ." 1985,92) who would, I believe, throw the baby out with the bath water. Along with Mehan and Wood (1975), I am troubled by those who reject the scientific method because while they ". . . disparage science's absolute validity, they continue to embrace science's accomplishments in their daily lives. They reject science's philosophy but continue to turn to physicians when they are ill, to machines when they wish to travel. . . . Few . . . have attempted to build alternative 'societies' " (p. 211).

The Transparency of Qualitative Research

Another major set of arguments in favor of qualitative research concerns its transparency, ". . . since the categories are discovered by examination of the data, laypersons involved in the area to which the theory applies will usually be able to understand it . . ." (Glaser and Strauss 1967,3–4). Woods (1986) talks at length about the value of ethnography to teachers, seeing them as "natural" ethnographers, and this seems borne out by the easy collaboration between Lou Smith—a university researcher and Bill Geoffrey—the classroom teacher (Smith and Geoffrey 1968). Patton (1990) reports on an evaluation of an "accountability system" in Kalamazoo, Michigan, in which the open-ended responses of the teachers, detailed, heartfelt, and poignant carried far more weight with Board members than the systematically tabulated results of the closed-questions on the opinionnaire.

There are several reasons we can identify for this transparency. First, qualitative researchers eschew variables and abstruse constructs (e.g., secondary circular operations; attention deficit disorder, learning styles) that only a specialist can be expected to understand. They usually speak and write in plain English rather than "statisticese." They engage in face-to-face interaction over a prolonged period with "informants" whose opinions they value, thus building trust and credibility for their eventual findings. We are committed to suspend judgment, hence rapport and cooperation may be more easily achieved. However, our proximal audience of teachers, students, and so on are often disappointed when they find we have little practical advice to offer as we attempt to describe "how" things happen rather than "how well." Another source of disappointment lies in the relatively long time between the completion of a study and the appearance of the report. Ball's study of "Beachside" was done in 1973 and when his book appeared in 1981, several teachers were upset because it no longer accurately portrayed their school, viz, "we don't do that anymore" (1984,90). On balance, however, the qualitative project should correspond much more closely to the lived reality of the individuals the research is designed to portray.

And, we need to consider that, especially for the case study, a small-scale qualitative investigation of the problem may serve not as an alternative to a large-scale multivariate evaluation, but as an alternative to "expert opinion." Or as Lawrence Stenhouse (1985) put it so well: ". . . the case study tradition may be seen as a systematization of experience within which interpretations are critically handled in the interest of preventing experience from becoming opinionated" (p. 266).

Undoubtedly, the apparent ease of doing field work also contributes to the increased interest/volume of studies. One does not need to run the gauntlet of statistical hazards which confront most doctoral students to do an ethnography, for example.[11] More importantly, it is, I believe, much easier for a student to acquire a sense of "ownership" of a qualitative project. I have encountered many students who were never sufficiently proficient with quantitative techniques to move their work beyond the "follow the recipe" stage and/or to escape from the ever-watchful eye of their major professor. At the same time, this very ease of access to qualitative research (especially if one finesses one of the "traditions") leads us to consider some unresolved problems.

SOME UNRESOLVED PROBLEMS

"Ethnography is becoming a mantle to legitimate much work that is shoddy, poorly conducted, and ill conceived" (Rist 1980,8). "The popularity of qualitative research . . . threatens to trivialize the approach. Researchers rush to join the bandwagon . . . without conceptualizing a sound research design . . ." (Noblit & Pink 1987, xiv).

Strong words perhaps, but very timely. The major problem we face is not that there is poor work being done under the auspices of qualitative research but that we still have no widely shared language to use in discussing the worth of a piece of qualitative research. Indeed, as Rist (1980) sarcastically notes: ". . . it is inappropriate for an outsider to challenge what, in the final result, was phenomenological and very personal experience" (p. 9). In Hammersly and Atkinson's (1983) text on qualitative research, for example, the authors take over 260 pages to review dozens of studies without writing a single critical word about a single one of them (but contrast Delamont's just published [1992] broadside). There is, therefore, a pressing need to develop a set of standards which can be used to evaluate completed studies, to guide neophyte researchers, and to stimulate improvement in the quality of research. One standard to apply is that the research should be unselfish. That is, it must satisfy something in addition to the author's own selfish purposes. A doctoral student once came to me for guidance in carrying out a "History of the Deseret Alphabet." I asked him what purpose this work would serve, what question it would answer, what educational problem it would solve? He responded that its purpose was to fulfill degree requirements and that historians don't need a rationale for doing history. I said that I doubted the latter claim but that, in any event, the dissertation was being conducted in a College of Education. I further pointed out that as there were dollar costs associated with his dissertation (committee members' time for starters) and that taxpayers had a right to expect at least the attempt to relate the research to some practical matters. My pleas fell on deaf ears and he carried on as planned.

Then there is the "soapbox" problem which occurs when the data are not commensurate with the analysis, that is, either there simply isn't enough data presented to carry the elaborate analyses and conclusions or the data seem to have been selectively arranged to support what appears to be a preexisting thesis. Bengston's (1988) critique of Gershman's (1988) study of a high school drama production meets this issue head on: "Her focus is more in keeping with non-qualitative research which obscures contextual variation in its effort to find a superordinate principle that can be shown to operate across contexts. Had she been more qualitative, had she looked more precisely at what went on, we would have had a more accurate and substantial account of the proceedings" (p. 343).

Despite what I said a few paragraphs ago, the qualitative research literature is not devoid of convoluted language which, perhaps inadvertently, serves to shelter the author's work from critical scrutiny. For example:

> At certain times, it may be useful to gloss over a description of the work people do with each other in social events. In fact, the bulk of sociology does exactly this in centering its attention on social facts as adequate accounts of the constraints people have available in ordering their relations with one another. Such glosses can never be adequate, however, to the specification of how situations might operate to encourage the development and display of cognitive practices. (McDermott and Hood 1982,240)

Recent recruits to the qualitative fold can also be faulted for too readily applying the term "ethnography" to their work. As several authors (e.g., Wolcott 1980; Rist 1980; Howe and Eisenhart, 1990), point out, ethnography is the methodology associated with the discipline or tradition of anthropology and carries with it a number of epistemological caveats which are blindly ignored by many who use it to describe their work (Miller, Leinhardt and Zigmond 1988; Turkle 1984). Much the same can be said about the term "case study." More refined and restricted definitions for these terms will be presented in Chapters 2 and 5 respectively.

The Need for Standards

The field is slowly beginning to recognize the need for critical standards. Howe and Eisenhart (1990), among other things: would like there to be a good fit between questions asked and methods applied; they would like to see the author relate his/her current study to previous research in the area and to attack previous arguments and offer new ones; and they are concerned about the trade-offs between the quality of the data versus risks to informant confidentiality. Goetz and LeCompte (1984) have an excellent discussion of the problem with respect to ethnography but which can be applied, in the main, to all qualitative research.

For example, they call attention to the length and intensity of the author's stay in the field as a check on the credibility of the findings. The investigator should demonstrate a high degree of self-awareness, so that he neither loses empahy for his informants nor "goes native." The investigator must also balance the demand for fully describing the setting/culture under investigation without distortion while, at the same time, applying appropriate universal or pan-cultural constructs in the process of analyzing this material and constructing a theoretical model.

These authors are all striving to create a set of standards unique to qualitative research, however there is now a lively debate as to whether the tools used to evaluate quantitative research can or should be applied to qualitative studies. Kirk and Miller (1986) do an excellent job of defining "reliability" and "validity" in terms used by qualitative researchers. They argue, for example, that one way to assess internal consistency might be to have an outsider read the report and compare his/her conclusions with those of the original author. Unfortunately, field notes are not very accessible.[12] Wolcott (1975) suggests that enough raw data needs to be included in a report to permit a reader to form his or her own conclusions. Mehan (1979) makes a very strong case for the use of videotapes in qualitative research, which permits an independent investigator (or the original one, for that matter) to easily reanalyze the data.

Other writers seek to create alternatives to reliability and validity. Lincoln and Guba (1985) use "credibility" and "trustworthiness," Patton (1990) would substitute "neutrality" for "objectivity": "The neutral investigator enters the research arena with no axe to grind, no theory to prove, and no predetermined results to support" (p. 55). Cronbach and Associates (1980) offer "extrapolation" in lieu of "generalization." The issue of generalizability indicates just how difficult it will be to establish firm criteria for determining the value of a qualitative project.

> What are the grounds—if any—for generalization? And if no generalizations are possible, how can knowledge accumulate? Thus, what does one make of an approach to the study of the educational world that depends on the unique aptitudes and proclivities of the investigator, that possesses no standard method, that focuses upon non-randomly selected situations, . . . indeed, are we justified in referring to the use of such a collection of procedures as "research"? (Eisner and Peshkin 1990,10)

Schofield (1990) argues that qualitative researchers are obligated to consider the generalizability of their results and suggests a number of steps, mainly revolving around careful sampling, to enhance generalizability.

I expect the "standards" problem will continue to receive a great deal of attention but, on a cautionary note, I'll let Phil Smith (1980) have the last word: "While methodology should always be as rigorous as possible, it can be no more rigorous than the subject matter permits. A methodology might be extremely rigorous, but if it is not suited to the subject matter, it will not aid our understanding" (p. 6).

The Perspective Problem

Another persistent, but in many ways fascinating, problem is represented by the question "Whose perspective should the qualitative researcher adopt?" It obviously should not be highly personal and idiosyncratic but this is, unfortunately, often the case.[13] Dobbert (1982) comments on the field work report of one of her students done before the student had worked with her: ". . . she was not trained and not objective about her individual and cultural style . . . the data she could gather were merely personal and impressionistic. She could not achieve a cultural, holistic perspective . . . [but used] an approach [that] was deductive and predefined" (p. 18). But not only students go into the field with an ax to grind. James Spradley, who was one of the most widely respected methodologists in the social sciences, describes his own agenda for "strategic research" (1980,18–19) that would certainly flunk Patton's test for neutrality.

One of the most useful concepts in anthropological research has been the distinction between an emic (from phone*mic*) and etic (phone*tic*) perspective. Emic represents the insider's perspective, etic, the outsider's (or objective). It is indeed a hallmark of qualitative research that the investigator must be able to describe the phenomena under study from an actor's (syn : native, participant, member) point of view, and Lincoln and Guba (1985) offer as one test of the "validity" of a study, the "member check" (p. 314), where one's conclusions must be screened by members of the group one has been studying. This strategy has been widely adopted in field studies of various kinds.

Taken a bit further, some authors (Woods 1986) state or imply that the only legitimate purpose of educational research is to work with teachers to resolve what they perceive to be problems. This is called "participatory research" (Lather 1986).

> Participatory research brings outside researchers and local participants together in joint inquiry, education, and action on problems of mutual interest. Ideally, all parties become learners: they share control over the research process; they commit themselves to constructive action instead of detachment; their participation promotes empowerment, as well as understanding. Outside researchers who undertake participatory research projects join with local participants to define problems, design data-collection methods, analyze results, and utilize research outcomes. Commitment to the interests of local participants often requires challenging oppressive political and social arrangements, so outside researchers often take political positions beside their local colleagues. (Brown 1985,70)

Fetterman (1989), on the other hand, makes the case that ". . . good ethnography requires both emic and etic perspectives" (p. 30).

Most qualitative researchers maintain a stance best described as "investigative" where "It is taken for granted that many of the people [the researcher] deals with . . . have good reasons to hide from others what they are doing. . . ." (Douglas 1976,55), and that the investigator ". . . learns things about the people he studies that may harm them, if made public . . .'' (Becker 1970,105). One evident example of this stance is McPherson's (1972) study of teachers in a small town in New England. She herself was a teacher in the school, but she never made her fellow teachers aware of the fact that she was studying them for her dissertation. The resulting portrait is, perhaps, less flattering and more candid than had she done so.

The crux of the matter lies in the question of whether in order to achieve an insider's perspective, one must personally adopt that perspective? In Everhart's (1983) ethnography of a junior high school, the principal and the teachers are presented in unrelieved negative terms, while students, especially those who engage in creative and extravagant displays of what they call "goofing off," are portrayed sympathetically. Everhart (see also Willis 1977) clearly became "one of the boys." However, I would argue that this extreme identification with one's informants is neither necessary, nor even desirable.

As we have seen, Malinowski has been held up to generations of student anthropologists as the model of the scientific, insightful participant observer, yet in his own diary (1967) he disdains any show of positive feeling for the people he'd lived with, as other equally talented scholars have done since (e.g., Hallpike 1977). Alan Peshkin's (1986) rejoinder to the quote on page 17, was: "It is absurd to think that only insiders can truly understand" (p. 18). His study of Bethany Baptist Academy represents a fine balance between etic, and emic perspectives. In the first chapter he lays out clearly his own, etic perspective but also details his manifold strategies for suspending it while capturing the perspective of the school's participants. For example, he actually set up house in the community for 18 months and returned to his own home only one day a week. Then in Chapters 2 to 10, he describes Bethany Baptist almost entirely in its own . . . terms, using lengthy quotations. Hence, one is almost shocked when, finally, in Chapter 11, Peshkin reemerges and is ready to ". . . analyze the meaning of what I saw there from my own . . . perspective" (p. 270) and this perspective is extremely critical.

Ultimately an adroit student of the educational enterprise must deal with a multiplicity of perspectives.[14] First, there is one's own perspective which reflects personal training and experience (e.g., allegiance to a tradition, prior experiences as student and teacher) and one's underlying philosophy of schooling (as a litmus test what one thinks of people like Paulo Freire and E. D. Hirsch). Then there is the scientific perspective, where "science" here means the accumulated wisdom on one's topic and not "positivism." Third, there are the obviously differing perspectives of teachers, parents, students, and administrators (Lightfoot 1978). Fourth, no one of these groups' perspectives can be described as monolithic. Cusick (1973) was one of the first to demonstrate how varied the high school student's perspective could be. Ball (1984) discusses at length the problem of overly relying on the information supplied by a very cooperative but, perhaps, unrepresentative and even marginal teacher. But, to represent these various perspectives is an ideal, something we should strive for but which has, in the literature published to date, been rarely achieved.

NOTES

1. Parts of this chapter were taken from D. F. Lancy, "The classroom as phenomenon," in D. Bar-Tal, & L. Saxe, eds., *Social Psychology of Education,* New York: Wiley, 1978: 111–132.
2. There's a certain irony in Malinowski's use of the male pronoun as Weiner (1976), in subsequent research, found that he had ignored or distorted the role of women in Trobriand Society.
3. For a longer and more elegant answer to this question, see Smith (1980).
4. When I lived in Gbarngasuakwelle (Lancy, in prep) I had to repeatedly fend off offers of marriage. It was unseemly for a man of my age and obvious means (I supplemented the local diet with canned corned beef and had a radio) not to take a wife; in this polygamous society the fact that I had already had a wife "at home" made no impression. This "breach" caused no problems, fortunately, because I always felt I was among friends. I felt the same way in the Trobriand Islands, incidentally, unlike Malinowski (1967).
5. As Lareau indicates, being a participant observer can be a two-edged sword: "The few times when I forgot about note-taking and observing and just enjoyed being there, I felt a tremendous sense of relief . . . [but] the cost was a lack of carefully collected information" (1989b,207).
6. In quantitative research one is cautioned to exclude this kind of material. "Discuss . . . difficulties encountered in executing your study only if they might effect the validity or the intepretation of your results. Otherwise spare us your tales of woe" (Bem 1987,182).
7. For a lengthy and thorough treatment of note-taking strategies see Dobbert (1982).
8. Level of analysis is not synonymous with unit of analysis (see page 41) although there is a tendency to use broader, less precise analytical tools in working with larger units (eg. school, community, district) and more precise, refined tools when working with smaller units (e.g., lesson, reading group, Sheila).
9. Yin (1984) makes much the same point about Kidder's (1981) earlier work *Soul of a New Machine,* "Because the book is not an academic study, it does not need to . . ." (p. 32).
10. For a much lengthier and more detailed intellectual biography of another "convert" see Smith (1978).
11. But I am in complete agreement with Eisner and Peshkin (1990): ". . . future scholars may find that being 'bi-methodological' is the true mark of scholarly sophistication" (p. 7). The authors acknowledge that this term was coined by Linda Grant at the University of Georgia.
12. And this may not be all bad, Spradley (1980) tells of an ethnographer studying a school who was worried that his field notes would be subpoenaed in a lawsuit filed by the teacher's union against the district—they weren't.
13. Among Smith and Glass's (1987) eight . . . issues to be raised about the qualities of [qualitative] studies: "Researcher self-criticism. The researcher's preconceptions and biases can influence and perhaps distort the data. There should be evidence that these were acknowledged and controlled. If prior hypotheses or biases were evident, were they compensated for by the introduction of alternative hypotheses, multiple sources of evidence and observers, and a disciplined search for disconfirming evidence?" (p. 278).
14. A wonderful piece from Sara Delamont (1984a) gives substance to this assertion: "I had a special gray dress and coat, the days when I expected to see the head [principal] and some pupils. The coat was knee-length and very conservative-looking, while the dress was mini-length . . . I would keep the coat on in the head's office and take it off before I first met the pupils" (p. 23).

CHAPTER 2

Anthropological Perspectives

FIRST MAN: A child who has good ways will imitate his father. If his father is a trapper, he will learn to make a trap. If his father is a palm-wine maker, he will learn how to make palm-wine.

SECOND MAN: As the way I play "Fanga" [a type of drum] my children will learn it. If I'm cutting brush, I give him the machete for him to know how to cut brush. If work becomes hard, I'll show him how to make it easier.

FIRST WOMAN: The work I do she will do some of it. She will plant rice, beat rice, and draw water. . . .

SECOND WOMAN: A girl who is trained will take her mother's steps. If her mother can make fish net or spin thread, she will learn it from her mother. She won't leave the house while cooking to go and play. . . .

FIRST WOMAN: What makes a child good? If you ask her to bring water, she brings water. If you ask her to cook she cooks, if you tell her to mind the baby, she does it. When you ask her to plant rice she doesn't complain. . . .

FIRST MAN: "A bad child shows his mother's buttocks." [Proverb meaning that a bad child is born from his mother's anus rather than her vagina.]

THIRD MAN: If a child is very bad, it is hard for his father to eat. You can't go among your friends with a bad child because you will be ashamed. Such a person's ways follow him forever.

FIRST MAN: It is the devil . . . that put these ideas in his head, for such a person, you will go to a sand cutter to find out what makes this boy so bad. The sand cutter will tell you what to do about the child.

This discussion was recorded in Gbarngasuakwelle, a village in the hinterlands of Liberia, as part of a project to document the process of education in a society without schools (Lancy, forthcoming). Living in the chief's home, I gradually learned the ways of the village, experiencing the anthropologist's traditional rite of passage.

But the image of the anthropologist immersing him/herself in a foreign society, for a prolonged period of time to soak up the ambiance and then prepare a "verbal photograph" (Goetz and LeCompte 1984,238) of these obscure people and places resides more in the public imagination than in reality. For one thing the world is fast becoming homogenized, with wealth as the principal force that differentiates people's lifestyles rather than the diversifying effects of culture. Second, it is no longer considered sensible or useful to try and study a people's entire way of life. One does topic-centered (Spradley 1980) studies of economy, kinship, or, perhaps, education. Third, there has been a marked shift in the attitude of the discipline to the conduct of inquiry.

As Van Maanen (1988) points out: "Until the 1960s, field work was with few exceptions, simply done and not much written about or analyzed" (p. 96). Perti Pelto (Pelto and Pelto 1978) echoes this refrain on a more personal note: "When I embarked on my first major anthropological research venture—the field work for my Ph.D. dissertation—I had had no formal training in the logic and structure of social sciences research" (p. xiii).[1] The aims of the ethnographer have remained relatively constant:

> If it is our serious purpose to understand the thoughts of a people, the whole analysis of experience must be based on their concepts, not ours" (Boas 1943,314). ". . . an interpretation of the way people live which is neither imprisoned within their mental horizon, an ethnography of witchcraft . . . by a witch, nor systematically deaf to the distinct tonalities of their existence, the ethnography of witchcraft . . . by a geometer. (Geertz 1974,30)

Yet the methods employed to achieve these aims have received increased attention. The Peltos (1978) criticize much early anthropology on the grounds of "the lack of specification of research operations that another investigator could use to replicate. Definitions and key terms are lacking, and the precise modes of observation (interviewing format, . . . etc.) are not generally specified by the ethnographer" (p. 34). What we see here is an interesting irony where anthropology, chastised by its own (e.g., Harris 1968), has sought to shed its image as a highly personal, almost ad hoc endeavor; (Eisner and Peshkin referring to qualitative research: "There was about it almost a back door sense" [1990,1]) while, in the field of education, we seek to embrace the indeterminate, phenomenological stance (Lancy 1978) that has traditionally been associated with research in anthropology.

Hence, it is important to recognize that while anthropology moves toward greater rigor, "a discussion of operationalism . . . is an indication of the direction ethnography is taking . . . [it] means defining one's terms and methods of measurement" (Fetterman 1989,40); some would see it moving backwards: ". . . operationalism is too shallow . . . and . . . results in a meaningless splintering of the world" (Lincoln & Guba 1985,26–7).

THE UNDERLYING TENETS OF ETHNOGRAPHY

Ethnography is or should be the principal method of anthropologists and, as such, the ethnographer seeks to describe the culture of a particular group of people: "A culture is an historically developed, patterned way of life which includes beliefs and ideologies; formally and informally established interrelationships between persons and groups; and material goods and technologies, all of which are systematically related so as to form an integrated whole" (Dobbert, 1982,10). But "culture is never observed directly; it can only be inferred" (Wolcott 1987,50). The ethnographer must be prepared to interpret what she sees and hears and "anyone who has ever mistaken a blink for a wink is fully aware of the significance of cultural interpretation" (Fetterman 1989,28).

In Longbranch, fourth and fifth graders loved gym—it was one of their favorite subjects. I was therefore stumped by their furious reaction to the first classes with a new gym teacher who arrived late in the year. But when the students said things like, "We have to learn skills . . . yeah, she makes us take tests!" I realized that what had happened, in their view, was that a set of activities had been transformed from a rare and welcome commodity, "play," to a plentiful and unwanted commodity, "work," thus substantially effecting their enjoyment of school (Lancy 1976b).

The ethnographer gains increased confidence in her ability to interpret a particular culture if she has learned the native language or dialect; has spent an extended period of time in the field; has systematically gathered materials, including notes from her observations, transcripts of conservations and interviews, and artifacts; has sought to, occasionally, broaden her focus to achieve a holistic perspective that includes contextual information surrounding her topic; and has established sufficient rapport with some participants so that they become key informants, virtual collaborators on the project. This enables her to capture their *emic* perspective to set alongside an *etic* perspective (Pike 1954) derived from the data and/or the scholarly literature dealing with this topic.

As readers of her report, we are inclined to find her interpretations credible to the extent that she shows evidence that she has done the above. We seek evidence of her training and experience, and of her beginning the study without a lot of preconceptions about what she could expect to find.

> If a man sets out on an expedition, determined to prove certain hypotheses, if he is incapable of changing his views constantly and casting them off ungrudgingly under the pressure of evidence, needless to say his work will be worthless. (Malinowski 1922,331)

On the other hand, we would like to see that she was systematic in seeking information regarding her topic, and that she sought evidence to support her interpretation as well as evidence that might support alternative interpretations. Her report should resemble Geertz's (1973) "thick description." "In order for a reader to see the lives of the people [she studies, she must show them through particulars] . . . i.e., not merely talk about them in generalities" (Spradley 1980,162). The reader ought to be able to second guess the author by reinterpreting the data in the way a well-written report of a quantitative study permits another scholar to replicate accurately the original study. But as I have stressed, we want to focus here not on what the novice qualitative researcher should do but on what real field workers do before, during, and after their encounter with an alien culture.

OUTLINE OF THE CHAPTER

In this chapter we will look at some of the major educational themes or topics that have energized anthropologists, and examine in depth several studies which address these themes. The reader should come away with a sense of the field of educational anthropology, both its substantive and methodological accomplishments. The first theme we consider is enculturation, the process by which culture is transmitted from one generation to the next in societies without formal schooling, in this case the Sisala and Kpelle societies of West Africa. We also look at societies that are just acquiring schools as a transition to a consideration of school-community relationships.

Another major concern of educational anthropologists has been the relationship between the public school and the surrounding community. In many cases, this relationship is a dysfunctional or hostile one, however, I go on to review, in depth, three societies where the relationship is more cordial, where communities have successfully adapted to formal education. These are the Amish; a Punjabi immigrant community in California; and a fundamentalist Christian community in the midwest.

A major concern of educational anthropologists has been student culture or the way in which students create their own society within the larger society of the school. We first review studies of student culture in the high school, including a mainstream school in the midwest, a rural school in the southwest serving a multiethnic population, and then studies in schools serving younger children. We review Corsario's very thorough ethnographic studies of American and Italian nursery schools and then an ethnography of student culture in an experimental elementary school. This last study incorporates a special type of ethnographic methodology called cognitive ethnography or ethnoscience.

EDUCATION AND CULTURE

The Study of Enculturation

Perhaps the earliest and, still one of the most compelling, topics in this field is the study of enculturation (see Middleton, 1970, for a representative collection of studies). We've just had a definition of culture—enculturation is the process whereby this "patterned way of life [and these] . . . beliefs and ideologies" are transmitted to the next generation. Margaret Mead, herself a student of Franz Boas at Columbia, made several extensive trips to the South Pacific to examine the experiences that children had from birth through adolescence; she was particularly interested in the role that parents and other adults played in guiding children's behavior (1928; 1930; see also Dennis 1943; Dubois 1944). As she made clear in her lectures, as well as her writing, she had been heavily influenced by prevailing Euroamerican theories of child development, especially B. F. Skinner's learning theory (as a student in her undergraduate Introduction to Anthropology class, I was assigned Skinner's *Walden Two*) and Freud's theory of child/adolescent sexuality. However, heavily influenced by Boas, she sought to demonstrate that these theories did not hold up particularly well outside the culture that spawned them. (This also happened years later when Piagetian theory was applied in Papua New Guinea: Lancy & Strathern 1980; Lancy 1983.) For example, she argued contra Freud, that adolescence was not inevitably a period of stress, especially vis-a-vis sexual activity. She based this on her observations and interactions with, primarily, female adolescents on Samoa and the picture that she painted (Mead 1928) was of an almost idyllic life highlighted by open sexuality.

As we shall see, a hallmark of anthropological work in education and child development has been the "debunking" of prevailing wisdom. However, this study was later to come under attack (Freeman 1983), shortly after Mead's death. The ensuing debate at conferences and in print totally preoccupied anthropology for years. Without taking sides, it is clear that Mead was determined to prove Freud wrong, and that she probably was selectively attentive to evidence that supported her thesis. The debate about Mead's work notwithstanding, encul-turation is still a lively topic of study, and Guilford Publications has recently announced a new book series on culture and human development that will be at least party devoted to this topic. Like Mead and others, current students of enculturation are heavily influenced by a theoretical framework borrowed from psychology, namely Vygotsky's social constructionist theory of child develop-ment (Wertsch 1985). However, unlike Mead, Rogoff (Rogoff and Gardner 1984) seeks to support Vygotsky's theory through the study of enculturation in non-Western societies.

Bruce Grindal's study (1972) in rural Ghana represents a fairly typical example of what was a real "growth spurt" in enculturation studies during the 60s and early 70s (see also Howard 1970; Jocano 1969; Leis 1972; Peshkin 1972; Read 1959; Williams 1969). He begins his account with a description of Sisala birth customs. This is a period that is fraught with danger and must be ringed around with precautionary practices and ceremonies, including *wencheming* or "meeting on the road," which is described at length. In the next section, Grindal continues a stage-like description of development. His preoccupation with the details of toilet training belies the influence of Freudian theory; however, he, like others before and since who have studied village childhood, finds toilet training to be a rather casual affair. Indeed the very term "training" has no real meaning in this society. "This emphasis upon situational observation and the lack of formal or structured learning is characteristic of all aspects of the enculturative process" (p. 31). Grindal does not report any sort of lengthy "bush school" which is found widely in West Africa and is associated with formal training designed to prepare young men (and, less often women) and indoctrinate them into adulthood (Lancy 1975). Throughout, Grindal uses a Western lens to view his subjects, in that he makes statements that could only have been motivated by implicit comparisons with "normal" practice in the West, viz: ". . . the value often attached to children is based almost solely upon the criterion of usefulness" (p. 32).

Given the time frame of the study, it is not surprising that Grindal also had an opportunity to study "adaptation to formal schooling," another theme in the anthropology and education literature which we will take up shortly. Unfortunately, due to the slimness of his book, also characteristic of the majority of the works just cited, Grindal has no space to tell us about methodology.

My study of enculturation in a West African community was undertaken a few years after Grindal's but in a more remote and less acculturated area. In 1973, Gbarngasuakwelle had no school or very many other "benefits" of modernization. An occasional corrugated iron roof replaced the traditional thatch, and Western, store-bought clothes and cooking utensils were seen here and there. Although there were a few Christian converts in town, the traditional *Poro* secret society held sway as masked figures literally terrorized the town twice during my stay.

Although a major objective of my (dissertation) study was the unadorned description of childhood among the Kpelle people, the largest of several tribes in Liberia, another prime objective was to explore an idea about child development that had its origin, in studies of non-Western societies that play contributes in significant ways to enculturation (Roberts, Arth, and Bush 1959; Lancy 1980a). Hence, I narrowed my observational focus from the start to activities which people (children themselves or nearby adults) would point to and label *pele* or play. I also used a special set of interviewing techniques collectively known as *ethnoscience,* to elicit the entire taxonomic domain of *pele.* In this way I could either observe activity X and ask what was going on, or in the case of more complex play forms like *Malang,* I could ask to be included as a novice player. I could also take a named playform from my interviews and ask to have it demonstrated. These procedures yielded a total of 101 distinct playforms. I also reasoned that there might be links between particular play activities and particular work activities. I used the same observation and interview procedures to elicit descriptions/demonstrations of *tii,* yielding a total of 128 *work* activities (Lancy, forthcoming).

I used a variety of procedures to probe links between play and adult skills, values, beliefs, etc., including, on several occasions, learning-type experiments (Lancy 1977). Not surprisingly, among the richer areas for exploration proved to be *neé pele* or make-believe (see also Lancy 1982). Because Kpelle adults conduct their work outdoors, for the most part these activities serve as a prolific source of themes for *neé pele.*[2] One of the most elaborate episodes I witnessed was a make-believe enactment of the work of the blacksmith.

> Several children were gathered in an open square in the town, an area designated as the "mother ground" because children habitually play there. A boy of nine fulfills the role of blacksmith. Sticks of varying lengths and thickness represent the tools. He has a rock to use as an anvil and a piece of bamboo that has been

partially split along its length serves as a pair of tongs. Two other boys of approximately the same age act as clients bringing scraps of wood and iron and carrying away flat pieces of wood, which are finished machetes. A boy of seven is the assistant; he fetches wood chips for the fire. Two girls, younger than ten, prepare and bring make-believe food for the blacksmith to eat at regular intervals. In addition to reproducing the tools and roles associated with the blacksmith, the children also employ the appropriate vocabulary to designate the tools and the actors; that is, the blacksmith is referred to as "smith" or "old man," the girls as "wife," the assistant as "boy" or "son." (Lancy 1980a,271)

This put me on the alert for similar episodes and I also conducted a rather thorough analysis of the process whereby a youngster eventually becomes a blacksmith. I hung out at the forge and informally interviewed two elderly blacksmiths and their helpers (Lancy 1980a).

These studies of enculturation have immensely enriched our understanding of the nature of child development (Cole and Cole 1989). In general, we find that in non-Western, nonindustrialized societies, there is little formal teaching. Much learning may occur in play and parents don't "push" children. Children are expected to observe the behavior of those older than themselves and, when the time comes, glide easily into more responsible roles in the community. The guidance and nurturance of one's biological parents is supplemented by the watchful eyes of the entire community which shares child-rearing responsibilities. This literature provides a corrective to our Eurocentric view of children and suggests that there are different endpoints to development, and different pathways to get to those endpoints. However, the spread of formal, western education provides a common endpoint. There is growing consensus, internationally, on the need for universal literacy and numeracy. The intrusion of elementary schools into villages has, therefore, provided a challenge to traditional enculturation practices.

Schooling and Transition

The *U.S. Agency for International Development* was busy building rural schools in Liberia in the 1960s. They were staffed by U.S. Peace Corps volunteers until Liberia could train its own teachers. This pattern prevailed throughout much of what came to be called the third world and many researchers studying enculturation also availed themselves of the opportunity to study the impact of recently introduced public schools. Grindal's (1972) work is representative. The one-room schoolhouse in "his" village is crowded and ill-equipped. The teacher is rigidly authoritarian, instruction is teacher-centered. This heavy-handed approach is reinforced by parents (see also Wolcott 1967) because: "The . . . villager who sends his child to school regards education as an investment. A child who attends school will someday be able to earn good wages with which to help his father . . ." (p. 81). The informal, casual nature of instruction, characteristic of the village, no longer applies in school. Now, in a relatively short period of time, about six years, (rather than the life-long education of the village) students must master whole volumes of new information in a foreign language. The result,

I argued from observing in a school similar to the one Grindal observed in, was "indoctrination without education." Students become indoctrinated with Western values and aspirations, reject the traditional values of the village, but the quality of instruction is so poor, they don't learn enough to succeed at increasingly higher levels in the education system (Lancy 1975). Interestingly, a similar process occurs in a totally different educational milieu: ". . . for the vast majority, the West Point education is what it is meant to be, a socialization process. Most cadets have been trained rather than educated . . ." (Ellis and Moore 1974,121).

This scenario was repeated a decade or so later in Papua New Guinea, where Australia played the patron's role: building and initially staffing rural schools throughout the country. My colleagues and I had an opportunity to observe this process first-hand in several different villages (e.g., Carrier 1979; Cheetham 1979; Grieve 1979; Lancy 1979; Wohlberg 1979). Unlike studies of enculturation, these studies of villages in transition (see also King 1967; Modiano 1973) forced ethnographers to become cognizant of government policies and initiatives, and to take into account the multi-tribal, multi-cultural nature of these post-colonial "republics," as the school teacher was often (in Papua New Guinea always) from a different ethnic group than his/her students. In short, the patterns established by Malinowski, Boas, and Mead for conducting ethnography would no longer suffice.

The added burden of taking these multiple perspectives into account also yielded a valuable dividend. We were able to compare the dynamics of adaptation to schooling cross-culturally. Ali Pomponio and I took advantage of the fact that, in Papua New Guinea, the spread of formal education had been gradual, thus permitting us to look at three communities that had, relatively speaking, long, medium, and short histories of Western-style formal education. What we found was that community support, while initially quite high (with consequently high levels of academic investment on the part of students), dropped precipitously after a five- to eight-year period if the expected economic returns were not forthcoming (see also Hanks 1973). That is, villagers expected that students, who completed their six years of schooling in the village, would continue their education in boarding schools in urban centers. The goal was for them to eventually land high-paying, white-collar jobs and remit funds home regularly. These expectations were, increasingly, unfulfilled as the white-collar work-force became saturated, and the central government shifted to a policy of "education for rural development." Under this policy school leavers were (unrealistically) expected to work to transform the subsistence-based local economy via cash-cropping and various entrepreneurial schemes (Pomponio and Lancy 1986). Our study fell under the heading of *ethnology,* where we took three separate ethnographic studies and compared them. Although ethnology has a long and respectable history in anthropology (e.g., Frazer [1900]1922; Murdock 1967); it has not been particularly popular in educational anthropology. However, Noblit and Hare (1988) have recently introduced the concept of *meta-ethnography* to describe research that involves the comparison or synthesis of two or more ethnographies (see below p. 55).

These studies of adaptation to public schooling in Africa and Papua New Guinea were paralleled by studies of schooling among Native American and Black communities in the United States (e.g., King 1967; Wax, Wax and Dumont 1964; Collier 1973; Rosenfeld 1971; Ward 1971). Some of these ethnographies focused exclusively on the school or even on the classroom, and relied on the pre-existing ethnographic record to flesh in details of the culture of the surrounding community (e.g., Gallimore, Boggs, and Jordan 1974), while others were more truly holistic and extended the study to the community (e.g., Ogbu 1974; Phillips 1983; Wolcott 1967). All document persistent "failure" in the sense that one sees little pleasure in either the teaching staff or the children. There is no evidence that students are making satisfactory academic progress, enabling them to "climb out of the ghetto," "leave the reservation," or "become self-sufficient." Increasingly, anthropologists who study minority education now take student failure as their point of departure (see special issue of *Anthropology and Education Quarterly* on "Explaining the School Performance of Minority Students," Volume 18, Number 4, 1987).

Dysfunctional School-Community Relations

One obvious explanation for these students' lack of success can be located in the differing values, beliefs, and practices (e.g., culture) of the community and those of the school. A recent statement of the culture-conflict theory has been provided by Trueba (1988), but it was a central issue in Howard Becker's dissertation study in Chicago in 1951. "We had one of the girls [first year teacher] who came to school last year . . . she'd never had anything to do with Negroes . . . almost in tears she said, "But they don't even want to learn. Why is that?" (p. 148)

Similarly, Chilcott (1962) saw trouble looming ahead for immigrant children from rural Mexico. "Transferred from the rural villages to the United States and placed in the modern classroom, the children . . . appear frightened, bewildered, and quiet" (p. 46). As he noted, the experiences of a child growing up on a *rancheria,* ill-prepare her for the hectic, information-rich life of the modern classroom. Again, we see evidence of relaxed child-rearing practices. "The [toilet training] methods are as variable as the starting age . . . [also] . . . a child may eat whenever he gets hungry" (p. 43). "Toys and games are rare, . . . a girl is 9–10 years old before she is assigned definite duties . . ." (p. 44). On the other hand, "Usually, by the age of 13–14, a girl will have learned all the household skills . . ."(p. 45). There is no formal education and little emphasis on, say, oral history: "The history of the Rancheria is learned mostly through listening to the conversations of parents. Few children, however, could give an accurate account if asked" (p. 46).

Erickson and Mohatt (1982), Heath (1983), Phillips (1983), and others have shown that children acquire communication styles at home which are different than those expected in the classroom. For example, Sarah Michaels and Courtney Cazden have made videotapes of and studied "Sharing Time"—that part of the kindergarten to first-grade class called "Show and Tell," "Sharing," "News," etc. These narratives have distinctive patterns, they are topic centered, there is an opening with information about time, setting and central actions, and the child uses rising intonation. However, only about 1/4–1/3 of African-American children's sharing narratives look like this, they are more often "episodic." They find that teachers are less accepting of episodic narrative, and try to steer children around to topic centered narratives. Cazden (1988) argues that teachers use sharing time as an opportunity for students to ". . . construct an oral text that is as similar as possible to a written composition, . . ." (p. 14). Aside from problems with the form, episodic stories don't have natural stopping places and tend to "run on" which provides further frustration for the teacher.

Not surprisingly, educational anthropologists have contributed to two notable attempts to reconcile these differences, and thereby enhance children's chances for a successful schooling experience by adapting instruction to the local culture. These are the Kamehameha (officially: Kamehameha Early Education Program or *KEEP*) School for native Hawaiian children on Oahu, and Rough Rock Community School located in a remote and sparsely inhabited area of the Navaho reservation. KEEP has experienced an absolutely unprecedented research and development effort[3] due to its very generous endowment from the Bernice Bishop Trust. Researchers attached to the school and/or the University of Hawaii, have focused on ways to structure classroom interaction which are more in keeping with social interaction patterns found in traditional Hawaiian society. They had not been able to show significant improvements in "test scores" for many of their innovations until the development of a reading program that, among other things, emphasized the interaction and cooperation of children across a broad age range (Au 1980; Weisner et al. 1983). However, there were at least two problems with the claim that instruction had been successfully adapted to the local culture. First, the reading program was based on the assumption that "sib-care," an apparently important factor in traditional Hawaiian culture, was still applicable today. Weisner et al. (1988) decided to test this assumption and found it wholly unwarranted. Not only were large numbers of children not cared for by sib-lings, parents weren't even sure that sib-care was an unquestionable good. "The picture of sib-care and shared management that emerges from these interviews and observations poses a fundamental challenge to earlier interpretations of the connections between sib-care and peer teaching in the learning centers at KEEP school" (p. 336). The authors do a major retreat from their earlier position, (e.g., Gallimore et al. 1974). They now say that trying to closely match class-room practices to those of the child's home experience ". . . would lead to segregation on an unimaginable scale. It could also promote rigid teaching, based on a stereotyped and romanticized vision of minority culture" (Weisner et al. 1988,345).

A second problem with the widely-cited curriculum and instruction develop-ment effort at KEEP is that it is not at all clear that the beneficial changes to the reading program were not ". . . simply features of good teaching for all children . . . [that] can be universally recommended" (Cazden 1988,72). In my terms, the program (Au 1980) looks like "language experience in a grass skirt."[4]

The Rough Rock program has also failed to show lasting benefits from a "culturally adapted" instructional program. As Collier (1988) in his careful and poignant history says, it was ". . . an innovation in community-directed and culturally determined education that caught the attention and imagination of educators and anthropologists . . ." (p. 253). Rough Rock was the first school to be "turned over" to the local Navajo Council by the Bureau of Indian Affairs. Its initial success at attracting attention as a "model" school was due in large part to Robert Roessel; a former teacher, fluent in Navajo and married to a Navajo woman. He was a tireless and charismatic organizer and promoter. Initially, the (elementary) school was extremely well staffed. There were special staff for the library, TESL, arts and crafts, guidance, etc. In addition, community leaders were paid to visit the school and lecture the students about and/or demonstrate Navajo traditions. Navajo and English were the languages of instruction. Collier, visiting the school during this initial period, noted that students seemed self-confident as contrasted with Navajo children at "contract" schools, however, Rough Rock received ". . . poor academic evaluations" (p. 262). A high school was built on the grounds which, in Collier's view, was a mistake and following Roessel's retirement in 1968, there was a persistent leadership crisis. The federal government became increasingly disenchanted with the school, as it was costing far more per student than comparable schools and test scores continued to lag behind "regular" BIA schools. As the school could no longer afford to pay them, the Navajo adults refused to continue to present lessons on traditional culture, and as the direct economic impact of the school declined, community support dried up.

Meanwhile, there has been a discernible backlash against the kind of "applied" anthropology seen at KEEP and Rough Rock. This sign hangs in the Alaska Department of Education: "We don't need any more anthropological explanations of school failure," which means, according to Kleinfeld (1983), "cultural differences are replacing cultural deprivation as the fashionable excuse for school failure" (p. 283). In other words, educators are expressing some skepticism about anthropological attempts to account for and/or remedy the problem of underachieving minority youth.

Adaptive Strategies in School-Community Relations: The Amish

When a community finds its values in conflict with those of the school, open hostility and "failure" is not inevitable, as shown in three studies to be reported in this section on Punjabi immigrant, Amish/Hutterite/Mennonite, and fundamentalist Christian adaptations to public schooling. All three studies show again the anthropologist's penchant for studying the culture of people who are perceived as "different."

The first study is actually a composite of several studies, stretching over several years, on relations between North American descendants of radical Swiss Protestants and public schools. One of the first reports on enculturation and education among these people appeared in 1971 as *Children in Amish Society* (Hostetler and Huntington). The "Old Order Amish . . . reject much of modern technology and new cultural developments" (p. 2); further they espouse "separation from the world" (p. 5). Their dress is distinctive, they practice "shunning" and arranged marriages, and speak a distinct language. Throughout this report, the authors adopt a normative stance. "Amish babies are rarely alone . . . During the first year of life, the baby receives solicitous care from a large number of Amish of all ages" (p. 17) and the ethnographic present is used throughout. There is the assumption of a relatively unchanging world, reflective of the anthropologist's interest in small-scale, isolated, and essentially conservative societies like the Amish, as well as an interest in documenting those particular aspects of culture that seem most resistant to change.

However, in this and other works (Hostetler 1974), the authors describe the growth and resolution of conflict between the Amish and related groups and the *in loco parentis* authority of the public school system. "Acquiring literacy and skills for their young, without subjecting them to a change in world view, confronts the Amish community with a fundamental problem" (p. 124). The Amish have fought court battles to win exemptions from mandatory schooling laws, and migrated to other states when these were not successful. "The high school is viewed as a system that prepares the individual for living in the 'world' not in the Amish community" (p. 127). Today, no Amish child is required to attend school beyond the eighth grade.

A second problem arose during the 1960s, with the wave of school consolidation, which wiped out one-room, locally-controlled schools and replaced them with large, modern schools whose curricula were set by anonymous committees. The response to this problem was typically forthright, the Amish and similar groups opened their own local schools. The curriculum range was narrow and conservative. "Some . . . schools substitute agriculture for history and geography" (p. 44). *McGuffey Readers* over 100 years old are still used. The Amish object to fairy tales, fantasy, abjure stories from other countries, cultures, and so on. Children are expected to become fluent in High German, the language of their religion, Pennsylvania Dutch, the language of the home and, less importantly, English, the language of the outside world. Teachers are called from the community. They seldom have more than an eighth grade education themselves, and no teacher training. Teachers are inevitably female. One notable difference in instructional practice is that accuracy and thoroughness are emphasized over speed. A final contrast between Amish educational philosophy and that of the public schools is "education for persistence" versus "education for change" (p. 106).

These observations, about early attempts by the Amish to establish their own schools, were nominally based on a study of one school that had been in operation just three years, but Hostetler and Huntington have devoted their entire professional lives to the study of these people. Hence, it is often difficult to trace in their writings the origins of a particular insight. This sort of blurring of various distinct bits of "data" is commonplace in much anthropology. It is not uncommon for an anthropologist to invest his/her entire career in the study of one particular society; towards which he/she may show a proprietary attitude, such that other investigators may be reluctant to "invade" that territory.

Hence, a more recent account (DeWalt and Troxell 1989), represents an interesting contrast methodologically. It is a study of a single "old-order Mennonite," one-room school, one of approximately 750 operating in the United States. Not only are the authors quite explicit about their methods, but create a convincing rationale that these methods contributed to enhanced "rigor."

Rigor was incorporated into this . . . study in four ways: triangulation, peer debriefing, member checks, and prolonged engagement. Student interviews, parent interviews, and classroom observation served as triangulation of the data obtained from each source. Interviews of the local public school superintendent, school nurse, and attendance officer also served as triangulation for the data obtained. Peer debriefing occurred as the researchers shared the observations with colleagues. Member checks were evident when the researchers returned to interviewees to confirm or follow up on questions of interest. Prolonged engagement was evident because one of the researchers has been conducting research in this community for over ten years. The final member checks occurred when the teacher and the bishop reviewed a draft of this case study. (p. 311)

The essential theme of the DeWalt and Troxell study parallels the work done 25 years earlier[5] by Hostetler and Huntington. Namely that, in this case, Mennonite communities reduce the conflict between their own and the values normally associated with public schools by vigorously managing what goes on in the school. The only unusual subject is German. As noted, texts are often cast-off public school texts valued as much for the absence of modern information as for their obvious economy. In social studies, references to war and environmental problems are acceptable. They provide a positive contrast with the pacifist, environmentally conservative practices of the Mennonites. However, references to television, evolution, and other seductive topics are taboo. New "Text books in use are written for old order Mennonite and Amish Schools, and are designed to portray the ethnic values of hard work, anti-materialism, nonviolence, and honesty" (p. 322). The teacher upholds community values. Her salary is $22.00 a day, which she considers "too high" (p. 320). She ". . . teaches as she was taught. Innovative ideas are not expected or encouraged" (p. 215). Students rarely leave their seats for any purpose, and are rarely off task. "Student work habits are automatic. They know what to do and when to do it" (p. 317). Not surprisingly, parents visit the school often, and are responsible for cleaning and maintenance.

Adaptive Strategies in School-Community Relations: Bethany Baptist Academy

Interestingly, as Hostetler observes, when the Amish established their own schools, "The intent was not so much to teach religion, as to avoid the 'way of life' promoted by a consolidaled school system" (p. 125). This provides a nice point of departure as we turn to look at Alan Peshkin's (1986) brilliant study of Bethany Baptist Academy. The Baptist congregation in Bethany faced some of the same problems faced by the Amish, but their conflict with the public schools was, if anything, more acute. This, because, unlike the Amish, they do not live in complete isolation from modern society. They, and more importantly, their children, interact daily with the mass media and others, who don't share their culture. The Amish economy revolves totally around nonmechanized agriculture, so they have no compelling need for higher or vocational education. Bethanyites don't have this luxury; their children must be educated in order to insure themselves gainful employment. Hence, one of the primary themes of Bethany Baptist Academy, the school that the community established to insure that their children do not stray from the faith, is that the curriculum is not only heavily censored, as it is in Amish schools, but that both teachers and the curriculum actively proselytize the students at all times. For example, in an interview the librarian said: "I look for evolution . . . I look for swear words. . . . We take those out . . . I just sealed the pages together and it didn't bother the reading on the other side . . . If I find a naked person, I draw a little bathing suit on them. . . . One of the books sort of made light of discipline and so we, instead of having a little frowning boy . . . that had been punished and he didn't accept it, we put a sticker on there with a smiling face" (p. 263). But, also we learn that the goals of the science class are: "To develop a Christian mind so that kids see everything from God's viewpoint . . . *Speech and Drama*. It's not to put students on the stage, but to get them to be more effective witnesses for the Lord" (p. 80). All of the teachers quite consistently infuse Christian dogma into their classes at every opportunity.

Peshkin's study of Bethany Baptist Academy is noteworthy in two respects. First, it represents an extraordinary level of commitment. He actually moved to Bethany for the duration of the project (18 months), commuting home to visit his family one day a week. In addition to his own extensive participant observation in school, church, and community, he was assisted for a good bit of the time by two graduate students who independently collected data. Finally, he had to invest a great deal of time just finding a Fundamentalist school that would admit him as a researcher. The second extraordinary aspect of *God's Choice* is Peshkin's handling of his own perspective vis-a-vis that of the pastor, the principal, teachers, etc. He spends most of the first chapter delineating these differences, revealing a great deal about himself, arguing that the ". . . more he reveals of his personality and motives, the better able readers will be to . . . make their own judgements about what I saw, what I missed, and what I misconstrued" (p. 15). Using very long verbatim transcripts of his interviews, Peshkin lets members of the Bethany community speak for themselves, even quoting the pastor's attempts to convert him. In Chapters 2 to 10, Peshkin presents a thorough description of the Bethany Baptist Academy and, convincingly, from an emic perspective. Finally, in Chapter 11, Peshkin sheds his participant observer cloak in order to ". . . analyze the meaning of what I saw there from my own [subjective] perspective" (p. 276). Clearly Peshkin has found a way around the perspective controversy I discussed in the previous chapter (pp. 30–1).

The school is remarkably successful in its own terms. "If most school statements of philosophy and goals are misleading guides to what actually happens in schools . . . the converse is true at BBA" (p. 38). Students do well on standardized tests. Enrollment is stable and the budget is balanced. Staff turnover is light, and their dedication to the school phenomenal. More importantly, raising children to be "true believers" is clearly the primary aim of the school; secular education is secondary. Teachers' fondest hope is that graduates will become preachers. "We think of scholarship as an avenue of service [to Jesus], as opposed to scholarship for its own sake" (p. 58). Peshkin's (1986) research shows that the school is very successful at enforcing conformity of dress, behavior, beliefs, politics, specific attitudes about gender roles, racial separation, and so on. The reader is convinced that Peshkin and his students were sufficiently immersed in this setting to allow them to penetrate the "facade" if any. Moreover, they also used "anonymous" questionnaires. Hidden opposition or nonconformity on the part of either teachers or pupils is almost nonexistent. Further, like the Amish practice of shunning, students are summarily removed from school for offenses and the principal brooks no interference from individual parents. ". . . when parents send a check to us each month they feel they're buying a service. This makes them think they can criticize us, just like they would poor service at Kroger's . . . They either accept our view or remove their child" (p. 95).

The fact that Peshkin presents what is, essentially, a sympathetic[6] portrait of BBA is all the more remarkable given the very grave reservations he has about the school as we learn in his concluding chapter. In the first chapter he notes the steadily rising enrollment of students in Christian Academies (as contrasted with the steady decline in traditional parochial schools), and the rising influence of the religious right on public schools (e.g., school prayer, creationism, book censorship). He considers BBA an ". . . exemplary Christian school" (p. 14) and is troubled by what he has seen there. Peshkin decries the hypocrisy of BBA's support for notions like diversity and pluralism when it comes to arguing for freedom from interference by government agencies seeking to regulate or control them (e.g., unsuccessful attempt to deny tax exempt status to schools that practice racial segregation), while teaching students that diversity and plurality are inherently wrong, evil (e.g., "We are the way. Mormons don't have it" [p. 133]). "Thus while Supreme Court judgements secure their right to exist, their own doctrine does not move them to protect and preserve that network of ideas and practices which support these judgements" (p. 293).

Peshkin is also disturbed by the inroads that the emphasis on indoctrination makes into the student's education (see also Ellis and Moore 1974). "Christian students reside in a cognitively limited environment . . . The price they pay is what they do not become, what they cannot enjoy, what they fail to comprehend" (p. 286). Peshkin concludes, "I confess to seeing Bethany's doctrinal yardstick poised like a guillotine to lop off dissenting heads, mine and others" (p. 290).

Adaptive Strategies in School-Community Relations: The Punjabi

The third ethnographic study of successful community/school adaptation we will review contrasts with the previous studies along several dimensions. Margaret Gibson (1983, 1987, 1988) undertook to study the process whereby a recent and still very poor, immigrant community manages to socialize its children for success in a typical American high school. Sikh immigrants from the Punjab (Northern India) experienced a great deal of conflict with the schools but did not, or could not afford to, establish their own school. Like the Baptists and Amish, this conflict centered on religion, values, dress, customs, or life-style, but they also experienced overt racism and had to communicate and learn in what is for them a second language. In other words, Gibson confronted a considerably more complex nexus of social and cultural issues than is typical.[7] The "community," in this case, consists of at least two minority "subcultures" (Punjabi and Mexican American) and a white, largely agrarian majority. Furthermore, among the Punjabi, she found that girls experienced schooling in ways very different from boys. She also found herself ". . . in the midst of Punjabi community factionalism, with one group trying to oust my co-investigator and, to bolster its position, sending letters to the funding agency to say that we were misappropriating money" (personal communication 9/9/90).

To present a complete and credible account of this complex phenomenon, while at the same time addressing a theoretically important question, took an enormous amount of time. Gibson spent two years in "Valleyside" (Stockton, California) as a participant observer, and rarely missed an important school or community event, even if it meant bringing along her nursing infant. She was aided by three assistants, two of whom were hired from (and one paid for by) the local community (Gibson 1985). Among other things, the assistants carried out interviews (in Punjabi when necessary) with the parents of the 44 seniors who were the focus of the study. Typical questions included:

A. View of school (20 minutes)
    1. How is _____ (twelfth grade child) doing in school? OK
    2. How did _____ (child) do in school? PROBE (Try to get at positive, negative, any difficulties, ways to overcome difficulties; what the child is actually getting out of school.)
    3. In your opinion, what are the most important subjects for _____ (child) to take in high school? PROBE (academic versus vocational) (Gibson 1983, Appendices, p. 4)

Similar structured interviews were conducted with students and Valleyside educators, and Gibson (1983) reported that: "Altogether the data base for the project exceeds 5,000 typed pages, plus computerized data on school achievement" (p. 16). Finally, and I think this is remarkable, Gibson and her family also spent a year in the Punjab region of India where she gathered additional background material that she makes extensive use of in her analysis (Gibson 1987,1988).

She draws on this material to trace the cultural "roots" of the Punjabi community in California and to illustrate their motives for immigrating. The Sikh reputation for aggression, for example, stems from the fact that Sikhs were originally a group of Hindus who eschewed a passive response to Mughal invaders in the sixteenth and seventeenth centuries. Initially, immigrants have to work just as hard as they did in India as farmers. However, in California they can acquire farmland (particularly orchards) with their savings, there are opportunities for factory employment, and students who proceed with their education often end up in high-paying jobs in technical fields.

The study demonstrates that adaptation to the demands of formal education is not easy for these students. Their English is often very poor and ESL classes appear to be a mixed blessing. They look and act differently and are the subject of racially motivated harassment. Their society teaches them to respect authority, and yet teachers demand that they express and defend their own opinions. This is just one of the many, subtle and not so subtle, ways that teachers and students attempt to force the Punjabis to conform to "American ways" (Gibson 1988,142). And yet, on a variety of measures of academic success, Punjabi students do better than Anglo students. The parental/home/community view of what it means to be a student appears to be a major factor. Among Anglos, only 12% take college prep courses and parents and students seem to share a low estimate of the value of schooling. Similarly, ". . . principals observed that the Mexican American children seemed to have less sense of purpose and direction in school than the Punjabis . . . Mexican American parents . . . looked to the schools for assistance in helping children develop and maintain their Spanish skills, while the Punjabi parents favored all-English instruction" (p. 107). This, and other evidence from her study, suggest that parents in the three groups view schooling quite differently. They convey their differing values to their children and to the school authorities, and that these values significantly influence student/school interaction patterns. (See also Chapter 3.) On the other hand, in rural Punjab there continues to be a feeling that too much education can 'spoil' a girl ". . . Valleyside Punjabis were worried, too that if a daughter went away to college she might . . . wish to arrange her own marriage or . . . find it difficult to take up her proper role within her future husband's family. She might say . . . 'I've just finished college; how can I make the roti?' " (p. 112)

"Parents were not naive about the difficulties their children faced in school. They simply brooked no excuses for poor performance" (1989,293). They couldn't blame their failure on teachers or the "system." If students fell out of line, they were forced into early marriage and/or put to work in fruit orchards. The primary method by which Punjabi parents facilitate their children's success is by insisting that they conform rigidly to the academic demands imposed by the school. They ". . . directed their children to do as teachers [say], to follow the rules . . . to acquire the skills and credentials necessary for competing in mainstream society, but warned them at the same time to do nothing that would shame their families" (p. 128). And, like students at Bethany Baptist Academy, the Punjabis implicitly accept their parent's views. They work hard, do homework before watching T.V., stay out of fights, and obey and respect their teachers. Students do not want to follow their parents into the orchards, but aspire to well-paid white-collar occupations. The Punjabis feel that "American" kids have too much freedom and too little responsibility. Punjabi students don't engage in extra-curricular activities, sports, or jobs; they don't date, and marriages are arranged.

Gibson argues that the Punjabi community, (in direct contrast to the "indoctrination without education" mentioned earlier) has achieved "accom-modation without assimilation." They have managed to transmit their culture intact to the next generation, while insuring that their children acquired sufficient education to permit them to participate in the economic mainstream. Unlike the Amish and the Bethany Baptists, they have done so without being able to exercise any control over the teachers or the curriculum. One wonders how long this can last, and whether there might not be a Punjabi private school in Valleyside's future.

A second major issue which she deals with at length is cultural discon-tinuity. "The comparative success of American-educated Punjabi Sikhs and other immigrant minorities forces us to take a fresh look at some of our theories and assumptions regarding the school performance of minority students. Many of these theories have originated in an effort to explain minority failure and have been generated without sufficient attention to cases of minority success" (p. 168). Arguments that minority student failure can inevitably be traced to the fact that children who are poor, don't speak English, or are culturally different are inevitably given prejudicial treatment by public schools must be reexamined. One compelling theory is offered by John Ogbu, and I refer the reader to a recent expression of this theory (Ogbu 1987).[8]

A third, and related theme in Gibson's work, is the proccss whereby the Punjabi students band together to reinforce for each other their community's model for appropriate action in the high school. "There is increasing evidence that the peer group can act as a force for resistance to school authority, but among immigrant students the peer group more frequently serves to reinforce a positive school adaptation pattern and to support compliance with school norms" (p. 178).

The peer group has attracted the persistent attention of qualitative researchers, including ethnographers. Scholars have been particularly interested in the way in which youth create their own society that stands in contrast (or outright opposition) to the dominant or adult sociely. Prominent consideration should be given to Gary Fine's (1983) study of *Dungeons and Dragons* players, Frederick Thrasher's (1927) early study, and Ruth Horowitz's (1983) more recent studies of adolescent gangs. However, our focus in the next section will be on ethnographic studies of the operation of the peer group in school, or student culture.

Student Culture in High School and College

Willard Waller's (1932) somewhat misnamed *The Sociology of Teaching* is perhaps the first descriptive work on the high school, which evinces understanding and sympathy for high school students.[9] Waller had trained at Chicago, where some 25 years later a group of the faculty (Becker et al. 1961) went off to Manhattan to study the student culture of the students at the University of Kansas Medical School. They also ". . . used an interview guide, asking each student 138 questions . . . but we left room for the free expression of all kinds of ideas and did not force the student to stick to the original list of questions or to answer in predetermined categories" (p. 29). They followed students from class to class, and dictated their observations at the end of the day. What they found was that the student culture was organized around the requirements for succeeding in medical school. That is, students used whatever freedom and autonomy they were granted by the school to develop their own institutional practices which, while self-serving, also served the ends of the school. This finding is very consistent with the Punjabi students studied by Gibson (1988) and the West Point cadets in Ellis and Moore's (1974) study, but strikingly at odds with many studies of student culture, as we shall soon see.

Historically, a third benchmark was established by Phil Cusick's (1973) ethnography, done while he was a faculty member at Chicago, *Inside High School*.[10] Cusick (1973) very clearly played a participant's role without actually trying to pass as a student. In his study of a midwestern high school, he found that school life was organized almost entirely around several well-recognized student groups, including "athletes," "power clique," and the "music-drama group." Every classroom situation was filtered through the particular group one belonged to and defined accordingly. For the "hood" group, to which Cusick attached himself, all classes were profoundly boring, and members put forth as little effort as possible. They tried to get away with as much as they could, and they constantly trod the borderline of expulsion. The loyalty to one's group and its view of the school was unswerving: "I asked one of the athletes, Greg, about associating with those not in his group. The thought just did not make sense to him. 'You know, like if you came here and didn't hang around with us, I wouldn't even know you' " (1973,67).

Cusick's use of student argot and his ability to view the school through their eyes, goes far in convincing the reader that he is describing student culture. However, it is likely that by overly associating with one group (compare Varenne 1976, 1982), his portrait may be unbalanced—something that Deyhle (1986) freely acknowledges in her study of ethnically mixed "Border" High School. "I also marked myself . . . by publicly identifying with a particular group, and perhaps forfeited access to the 'opposing' student groups" (p. 115). She vividly describes the work she does to "present herself" and "manage the impression" (cf. Goffman 1959) students have of her.

> During my first few weeks students were polite, curious, but hesitant about my presence. I was clearly an adult (I did not try to act 15), but I was also somehow different from the other adults in their school. I dressed closer in style to the students, they called me by my first name, and they could use "slang" and profanity around me without fear of repercussion. I did not judge their academic work, nor did I interfere with 'fights' in the class, and they often interacted with me out of school, in the local teenage fast food restaurant, and on the town streets. (p. 114)

Deyhle (1986) carried out her ethnography of student culture during intermittent (and often lengthy) visits to the school in 1984 and 1985, facts that we don't learn at the outset. Very effectively she arouses the reader's interest by beginning with a lengthy anecdote, and it is only in the middle of the second page that she tells us, "I had come to this border community to do a study of . . ." (p. 112). This strategy is not at all uncommon in writing ethnography. The crux of the opening anecdote is summed up in the following quote from one of the students: "Yeah, we don't hang out there; it's for the jocks and preps. Us breakers don't hang out at the end of the hall" (p. 112). This is a study of student cliques in a high school, and of one low status, marginal clique in particular, Ute and Navajo "breakers."[11]

Deyhle goes on to analyze the purpose of break dancing. "Break dancing formed a powerful support group for these Indian students. The clique dictated clothing and social stance. It offered its members both self-confidence and a means for expressing success in an otherwise indifferent or negative school and community environment'' (p. 112).[12] However, her ''telling'' the reader would have been far less believable if she had not also ''shown'' us using quotes like the one above.

As Gibson, Deyhle faced an extremely complex social scene at Border High School. She uses quantitative data very effectively to help ''set'' this scene.

> Border High School is nestled in the center of a small rural town of approximately 4000 people, and draws its student population from the town and the nearby Ute and Navajo reservations. At the time of my study the school population, grades 7–12, was 560, of which 40 percent were Ute and Navajo students. Almost half of these Indian students were bused from their homes to school and back every day. The average commute was an hour and a half round trip, but some spent as much as four hours a day traveling to and from school. . . . Academically, the school average was at the national norm according to the California Test of Basic Skills. The Indian students' scores, however, were an average of two to three grade levels behind those of their Anglo peers in both reading and math. (p. 113)

Since her focus is on a group of students, her observations don't end at school. For example, she notes that break dancers offer a defiant ''side-show'' at football games, demonstrating simultaneously their indifference to one of the more cherished rituals of the popular students, while also showing off their own formidable physical/athletic skills. Indeed, she clearly shows that school is not one but several different places, depending on the perspective of a particular group of students. Indian students: ''. . . were academically marginal, finding very little in the classroom that was of interest to them or relevant to their lives out of school . . . [they] . . . saw school as a place to organize socially, . . . class activities . . . interrupted the pleasant times with their friends'' (p. 117). As Michael Agar (1986) points out, however, this is the essence of ethnography: ''Ethnographers set out to show how social action in one world makes sense from the point of view of another'' (p. 12).

A study by Lois Weis (1985), of the black student culture[13] in an urban community college makes me wonder about Ute and Navajo students at Border High School who didn't associate with the ''breakers.'' Weis (1985) adopts a critical theory perspective (see also Willis 1977; Everhart 1983; McLaren 1989) to argue that the Community College, ostensibly established to open additional avenues for upward mobility, instead aids in reproducing the existing social order (see Chapter 3). Weis had to overcome a great deal of initial hostility to gain access; the college had been experiencing a run of bad press, not an uncommon situation in urban schools. Eventually she was able to play a participant-observer role. Her observations were complemented by open-ended interviews and a highly-structured student opinionnaire. Not surprisingly, Weis found hostility between different student groups. In particular, white students wanted ''efficiency,'' maximum learning or career advancement for the dollars and time they invest, and, therefore, resented black students' efforts to make classes more casual and informal: ''rapping,'' bringing along their children, eating, and socializing. The black student culture is cohesive. There is a high degree of conformity because it is a culture that has been incorporated almost unaltered from their own community. This culture promotes active resistance to the norms of the school, and attempts by the school to change student language use, reading, study, and attendance patterns. Thus we see this student culture operating in a manner quite different from that of the Punjabis at Valleyside High; but quite consistent with Border's "breakers." Where Weis breaks new ground is in her analysis of the few black students at "Urban College" who are academically successful. These students forgo membership in the black student culture and embrace mainstream values and habits. They "act white" (Fordham & Ogbu 1986). They actively seek out faculty support. And the faculty respond in turn, almost without exception. They seem willing to spend an inordinate amount of time assisting Blacks who demonstrate that they are willing to begin learning the dominant culture.[14]

Student Culture: Some Methodological Issues

The study of student culture presents several interesting methodological paradoxes. We can clearly see the potential value of close identification with the "natives" in a study of student culture. Moffatt (1989), who conducted a field study of student culture at Rutgers while on the faculty, offers a convincing defense of participant observation:

> Questionnaires usually require their subjects to respond to predetermined topics, however; with students, they are about what adult investigators have decided should be relevant to youths in advance. Interviews give students a better chance to talk and think in their own terms. But interviews with adolescents, especially with glib college adolescents, also encourage subjects to talk in their most formal, adult-sounding ways. Participant observation with the undergraduates, on the other hand, amounts to hanging around with one's subjects for a long enough time to start hearing them in their own natural adolescent tones . . . and to start sensing their own priorities. . . ." (p. xv)

He then attempts to take on a full participant's role: "In 1977, on a whim, I decided to try passing as an average, out-of-state freshman for the first few days of the fall semester at Rutgers College" (p. 1). The facade, however, cracked after a few days. For example, his roommate told him that his ". . . vocabulary had been too advanced . . . and he had thought it odd that I read the *New York Times* every day . . ." (p. 11). Nevertheless, his "discovery" of the overwhelming preoccupation that Rutgers' students have with sex suggests the depth to which he was able to penetrate the student culture.

And yet one must ask, if the goal is to maximize one's similarity to and affinity for one's informants, how can one "make the familiar strange" (Erickson 1973,1984). Harry Wolcott, widely regarded as the authority on the ethnographic method, has written about this problem as faced by his students.

> Requiring my students to select informants or scenes from societies radically different from their own . . . enhances the likelihood that the differences students identify will be associated with aspects of culture . . . On a grander scale, that

same argument has obtained in the strongly voiced preference for having anthropology (and anthropology and education) students do their first major fieldwork—typically the dissertation study—in a distant society, or at least with a dramatically different microculture (e.g., migrant workers, gypsies, an ethnic minority, a religious sect), rather than in the all-too-familiar 'culture' of the school or classroom.

That raises another of the issues that make school ethnography so difficult and even so unlikely. The people interested in doing it are, for the most part, individuals who have invested virtually their entire lives in school, first as students, then as students of the teaching process, and finally as professional educators. Being so totally immersed in and committed to formal education, they are as likely do "discover" school culture as fish are likely to discover water. The cross-cultural and comparative basis that helps ethnographers identify something they are tentatively willing to describe as culture in someone else's behavior—because it is readily distinguishable from their own—is lacking. These hopelessly enculturated insiders accept as natural and proper the very things an ethnographer from another society—or even an ethnographer from our own society not so totally familiar with schools—might want to question. (1987,50)

A potentially more serious problem stems from the over identification with one's informants noted by Deyhle. Willis's (1977) *Learning to Labor* is a widely admired (e.g., Everhart 1983; McLaren 1989) description and analysis of the pattern whereby the working class (male) student culture in a *comprehensive* high school in Britain actively "resists" school authority. It demonstrates an extraordinary degree of rapport with a widely scorned and misunderstood group. However, as Davies (1985) points out, Willis so fully accepts the "lads" perspective that his work comes across as blatantly sexist and anti-female. Hymes (1977) suggests that "the conditions of trust and confidence that good ethnography requires (if it is to gain access to . . . meanings) make it impossible to take . . . the role of impartial observer . . . [but] since impartiality cannot be avoided, the only solution is to face up to it, to compensate for it as much as possible, to allow for it in interpretation" (p. 21).

A second paradox stems from Wolcott's lament that school ethnographers in the United States lack a comparative or cross-cultural perspective, rendering it all the more unlikely that the investigator will experience what Agar (1986) calls "breakdown." This occurs when something unexpected happens, it doesn't make sense, and the ethnographer has to talk to his/her informants seeking "resolution." Ideally, the ethnographer should read other ethnographies dealing with his/her topic to gain a comparative perspective. But they often fail to do this and the following "pledge" by Ellis and Moore (1974) indicates why this might be so: "The purpose of this book is to describe and analyze the operation of the United States Military Academy . . . Our research was begun as a concentrated effort to withhold judgement until we felt that we understood how West Point viewed itself" (Ellis and Moore 1974,vii). Moffatt's (1989) work is one of the most recent studies of student culture, and yet he cites only one (Varenne 1982) of the many antecedent studies cited here. Like Ellis and Moore, Moffatt wanted to see how Rutgers' students view themselves, and evidently they do not feel they are participating in a student culture. Hence, he saw no need to review literature on the topic. On the other hand, by not reviewing this growing body of work, he may have missed a chance to make the familiar seem strange.

We have then this double paradox. Ethnographers are urged to take great pains to identify with and blend into the culture they are studying, while also being urged to study that which is most foreign and strange. Likewise, they are advised to tease out unique aspects of the culture, and to adopt a posture of cultural relativism. At the same time, they are advised of the value of a comparative perspective and exhorted to conduct a thorough review of prior research on their culture/topic. There are other conundrums for the novice ethnographer.

The growing popularity of qualitative research has meant that the researcher is faced with a new and fortuitous problem—how to review and synthesize several ethnographic studies on his/her topic. One problem associated with this enterprise we have just identified, namely the emphasis on the uniqueness of culture precludes the use of etic terms and categories. Hence, while a quantitative researcher interested in student "motivation" can quickly find a welter of current and appropriate sources through ERIC, searching for qualitative studies on "student culture" would have turned up less than half of those cited here. Indeed I would still be ignorant of Moffatt's work if my colleague David Bergin hadn't called it to my attention.

A second problem is that a large number of ethnographies written every year never see the light of day. Most of the major treatments of ethnographic methodology (e.g., Dobbert 1982; Goetz and LeCompte 1984; Smith 1978) cite numerous dissertations (e.g., costly and hard to get) from the last 20 years, that I was unable to find later appearing as articles or books in the published (e.g., cheap and easy to get) literature. Undoubtedly, one reason for this problem has been the reluctance of journals to publish qualitative studies. The editors of the modal journal in the field of educational research, *American Education Research Journal,* felt compelled in 1987 to issue a statement that said in effect: "although the journal has slighted ethnographic research in the past, in the future it will be welcome" (Richardson-Koehler, 1987; see also Templin and Griffey, 1987). However, another factor may be that doctoral students who opt to do an ethnography have career paths that lie outside academe and thus have little incentive to publish their work.

Still another problem is identified by Noblitt and Hare (1988) in their innovative work on meta-ethnography. As they point out, ethnographers use a wide variety of analytical frameworks from the traditional structural/functional analytic approach (e.g., Burnett 1969) to the more recently employed Marxist or critical theory framework (e.g., Everhart 1983), thus making it difficult to compare across studies. Agar (1986) also addresses this problem: ". . . ethnographies of similar groups, or on similar topics, differ from one another. They differ because of differences in the audience addressed, in the background of the ethnographers, or even the groups themselves" (p. 15). Nevertheless, if one focuses on the descriptive part of the ethnography, as Noblit and Hare (1988) advise, one can carry out a ". . . reciprocal translation of studies into one another . . ." (p. 11). They have done this for several studies of school desegregation (Collins and

Noblit 1978; Metz 1978; Rist 1979; Schofield 1989) and as I have done here for student culture.

Student Culture: Nursery School Ethnography

While the ethnographic study of student culture has been dominated by works which focus on adolescents, there have been a few studies of younger children. These illustrate several noteworthy aspects of epistemology and methodology (e.g., Tammivaara and Enright 1986).

William Corsario (1985) conducted an extremely thorough analysis of student (or peer) culture in American, and, more recently (1988a; and Rizzo 1988), Italian nursery schools. Corsario faced a number of methodological challenges, at least partly because, unlike Phillip Cusick (1973) in Horatio Gates High School, he could not ". . . easily check his perception by asking [students] to describe and explain a particular event or asking them to verify his perceptions for accuracy" (p. 5). Here is a transcript of one of Corsario's attempts at entry.

Two 4-year-old girls (Betty and Jenny) and adult researcher (Bill) in the nursery school:

BETTY: You can't play with us!

  BILL: Why?

BETTY: Cause you're too big.

  BILL: I'll sit down. [*Sits down*]

JENNY: You're still too big.

BETTY: Yeah, you're "Big Bill!"

  BILL: Can I just watch?

JENNY: Ok, but don't touch nuthin'!

BETTY: You just watch, okay?

  BILL: Ok.

JENNY: Ok, Big Bill?

  BILL: Ok.

  [*Later Big Bill got to play.*] (p. 269)

Further he tells us that ". . . it was essential that the children perceive me as different from the teachers and other adults in the nursery school setting, so that they would not suppress certain behaviors for fear of negative reactions" (p. 27). He also needed to be sure not to act like other adults; he noticed that adults were active, they initiated contact, so he decided to be reactive: ". . . of all the many hours observing in this setting, these were the most difficult for me. I wanted to say something ('anything') to the children, but I stuck with the strategy and remained silent" (p. 28).

Although he is eventually granted full access to the student culture, getting an emic perspective was difficult. He explains that it took him a very long time to notice: ". . . how deeply concerned the children were for the physical welfare of their playmates" (p. 177), and that: ". . . young children are deeply concerned with physical size" (p. 179).

Hence, most of his constructs are etic, derived from the literature, (e.g., *secondary adjustment* from Goffman 1963) or grounded in his data: "I have used the term initial resistance because attempts to gain access did not always result in permanent exclusion" (p. 128). He began with nonparticipant observation, observing through a one-way mirror, a common feature of the kind of university sponsored nursery school (or child study lab) he worked in. He worked back and forth between his notes and the literature, to gradually sharpen his focus until he had a workable unit of analysis, the *interactive episode.*

> *In the nursery school, interactive episodes are those sequences of behavior which begin with the acknowledged presence of two or more interactants in an ecological area, and the overt attempt(s) to arrive at a shared meaning of ongoing or emerging activity. Episodes end with physical movement of interactants from the area which results in the termination of the originally initiated activity.* (p. 24)

I have reproduced below a typical interactive episode in order to illustrate Corsario's very interesting note-taking scheme.

Date: October 29

Morning—Episode #5

Scene: Outside Sandbox

Participants: Rita (R), Barbara (B), Jack (J), Bill (Bi), Linda (L), Richard (Rich)

FN—Field Note; **MN**—Methodological Note; **PN**—Personal Note; **TN**—Theoretical Note

N: Five children (R, B, J, Bi, and L) are playing around the outside sandbox. The children are pretending to make cakes, pies, etc., by placing sand in pans and other cooking utensils. There is a toy sink with faucet and a toy oven near the sandbox. Most of the time the children seem to be involved in parallel play, but there is verbal negotiation when the children need to share utensils or props.

B-Bi: I need to get some water. [*Bi is standing near front of sink and moves to one side as B approaches.*]

Bi-B: There's no water in there. [*Referring to fact that faucet is not real.*]

B-Bi: Well, it's pretend water.

Bi-B: Ok.

B-J: Jack?

J-B: What?

B-J: I'm putting this in the oven.

J-B: Ok. [*B puts pan in the oven.*]

B-J: Here, this is mine, J. [*J now holds pan as B puts sand in it. J now reaches for a scoop in the sandbox.*]

J-B: Mine.

B-J: No, you can have this. [*B hands a spoon to J.*]

[*Shortly after this exchange B leaves the area with no verbal marking and goes inside the school. Now only R, J, and L remain playing around the*]

sandbox. Rich now approaches and watches the other children for a few minutes. Rich then walks near J and says:]

RICH-J: It's clean up time! [*Richard then reaches for Jack's pan filled with sand and tries to dump it out.*]

PN: I found earlier that any attempt to record everything the children said was fruitless. As a result, I often relied on summaries here. It seemed Richard said it was clean-up time, so that he could dump Jack's sand, but it was apparent that Jack did not fall for his ploy.

MN: I will want to observe interaction around the outside sandbox when I begin participant observation. This should not be difficult, since I could sit down by the sandbox and be at the same height as the children. Obtrusion would be less of a problem around the sandbox than in the playhouses or climbing bars.

TN: The fact that the children moved from seemingly parallel play, to social interaction, to negotiate sharing of objects is interesting and should be investigated further. It suggests the importance of contextual factors in the children's use of social and egocentric speech. (pp. 25–6)

Once he was confident that he had a workable strategy for making sense of activity in the nursery school, he negotiated entry into the student culture. Later still, after he had been accepted, he began videotaping.[15] The videotape recording would permit him to achieve a more fine-grained analysis (he describes his method as "micro-ethnography"). He goes so far as to identify quantifiable variables, e.g., "coefficient of variation" (V), which ". . . is a way of estimating how widely each child spreads his contacts" (p. 156), and uses inferential statistics to compare "V" for the morning and afternoon nursery school sessions.

Data collection and analysis proceeded simultaneously within a "constant comparative" (Glaser and Strauss 1967) or "reflexive" (Mehan and Wood 1975) framework.

The initial phase of data analysis involved three processes: (a) the identification of consistent patterns in field notes, (b) the generation of working hypotheses, and (c) the theoretical sampling of additional field observations and videotaped episodes. Once participant observation began, I reviewed theoretical notes once a week and isolated a number of patterns regarding peer interaction and culture. . . . Once patterns were identified, I documented their consistency, frequency, and distribution across participants and interactive settings. (p. 39)

The reader is made aware of these shifting hypotheses: ". . . children were primarily concerned with control over play areas, and used friendship as a device to gain control and exclude others" (p. 39). A further analysis of field notes in initial videotaped episodes suggested that, they were more concerned with *maintaining the stability of the interaction than with the control of territory or play materials* (p. 40).

Among his major findings is a vivid picture of the emergence of the concept of "friend," which we see when children ". . . used the *denial of friendship* as a basis for exclusion [from interaction]" (p. 150, italics added). He also observed the beginnings of "resistance" (cf. Willis 1977; Everhart 1983). ". . .one of children's most cherished desires: *to defy and challenge adults, share the experience, and not be detected"* (p. 261). Also, "In collectively resisting adult rules, children develop a sense of community and 'we-ness' " (p. 267). However, the study is also interesting for what he failed to observe, viz: "I did not find any clear dominance hierarchies in children's play groups . . . [however] dominance hierarchies . . . may be related to size of the school" (p. 127) and ". . . there were very few stable core groups or cliques in the nursery school" (p. 40).

George Spindler (1983) is critical of studies of "youth culture" in the United States because ". . . there is no explicit and very little implicit cultural comparison" (p. 71). Corsario (1988a) remedies this problem with his study of a *scuola materna* in a major North Italian city, using nearly identical methods as in his initial study. In this article, he focuses his attention on several recurrent "routines," such as the construction and maintenance of an interactive play area:

> The routine normally involves two phases. First, the children discuss and eventually make a joint claim to a specific area of play. The claim often involves the physical movement of objects, as well as verbal descriptions of activities. In some cases, the first phase may also include discussion of anticipated attempts by other children to gain access. The second phase involves active attempts to protect ongoing interaction from the intrusion of other children. (p. 8)

In general, there were many commonalities between the two peer cultures. "The fact that there were so many analagous routines in the two data sets provides some evidence for the possible 'universality' of certain elements of the peer culture of young children" (p. 5)[16] However, he found that this routine differed in important ways in the Italian and American children's peer culture. The Italian childrens' fantasy play is much more "permeable" than the Americans'. They are more tolerant of children joining their play activity, even if just temporarily passing through. They seem able to maintain the fabric of their play activity intact despite interruptions. Corsario relates this to the northern Italian's noted ability to maintain several conversations at once.

> In many ways, these patterns of peer play were similar to everyday "relations in public" among adults in the city, where the scuola materna is located. Brief visits and short exchanges and greetings with a wide range of acquaintances were often interwoven within more intense and involved discussions with a smaller subset of friends. On some occasions, several conversations would seem to be occurring at once, but there was no apparent problem in maintaining social order. (p. 12)[17]

Student Culture: Ethnoscience in the Elementary School

As documented by the Peltos (Pelto and Pelto 1978) anthropology in the 1960s was shaken by an epistemological earthquake. A number of scholars, notably Frake (1969) and Goodenough (1971), challenged the accepted view of both the purpose and methods of ethnography. The focus should shift from documenting the patterns of human behavior and interaction, and interpreting their meaning to discovering culture as manifested in the learned and ordered beliefs of members. Methods would change from the relatively unstructured and ad hoc participant observation, key informant interviews, and the like, to highly structured and precise "elicitation" procedures labeled, among other things, ethnoscience. Adherents were not modest in their claims: ". . . ethnoscience shows promise as the New Ethnography required to advance the whole of cultural anthropology" (Sturtevant 1964,101). This new ethnography is widely employed in non-Western societies, while the late James Spradley stands out as the dominant force in the application of ethnoscientific methods in the study of U.S. urban culture (Spradley 1979, 1980; Spradley and McCurdy 1972). Not surprisingly, not all anthropologists have "heeded the call," and there have been vigorous counter-proposals (Harris 1968), so that today we can identify a materialist stance associated with those "materials," including human behavior and speech one can observe and record. Then we have a cognitive stance that treats as primary data the schemas people use to make sense of their social world.

It is rare for an ethnographer to maintain one stance to the exclusion of another; however, sometimes there are special circumstances. Often, the group of interest presents formidable problems as potential informants, forcing one to focus more exclusively on behavior and achieve a primarily etic description. Such certainly was the case in Corsario's work, as we have seen, but was also the case in Gleason's (1989) long-term study of a residential facility for severely retarded individuals (see also Bogdan 1980).

Another special circumstance occurs, I would argue, in studying the student culture in an elementary school. For 18 months, during the 1974–75 school year, I conducted an ethnography of Longbranch, an otherwise typical elementary school that had been used for nearly ten years as an experimental school, to field-test the federally-funded curriculum projects developed at the Learning Research and Development Center (LRDC) in Pittsburgh. Two issues led me to employ the ethnoscientific (Jacob, [1987], refers to this tradition as cognitive anthropology) methods. First, I was very concerned that my familiarity with American elementary schools would blind me to taken-for-granted aspects of the student culture. This method forces the investigator to act as a stranger, asking naive questions. Second, the student culture in high school is readily apparent in dress, speech, seating, and class participation patterns and so on, I assumed that elementary student culture would be at least partly hidden to conventional participant observation. As I will show, ethnoscience specifies a set of interviewing and analysis techniques (Spradley 1979) that greatly increase one's chances for getting an emic or, in this case, the students', rather than teachers' or the participant observer's view of this experimental school. Indeed, researchers had already gathered a great deal of test data on these schools, and had also interviewed teachers regarding their attitudes towards the (individualized) curricula (Glaser 1976).

Before beginning ethnosemantic interviews with students, I did spend four months conducting more conventional participant observation.[18] As much as anything else, this period allowed participants to get to know me. I also began learning the students' "language." I did this by openly eavesdropping, but also by listening to tape-recordings I made in areas where students habitually gathered. One such place was a large metal storage cabinet in the hall, which contained hundreds of audio cassettes used in language arts lessons. Students would go and get the appropriate tape when instructed to do so in their individualized lesson; permission from the teacher was not required. When, as frequently happened, two or more students arrived to get or return a tape at the same time, a conversation would take place, recorded by the machine sitting plainly in view on top of the cabinet. These conversations were invaluable in helping me to create an initial portrait of the student culture and, more importantly, teaching me the appropriate vocabulary to use in talking about it.

Following this initial period, I conducted ethnoscientific interviews with several fourth and fifth graders.

> D.L.: What else do you do in the library?
>
> JOHN: We throw things.
>
> D.L.: What kinds of things do you throw?
>
> JOHN: Oh, spit balls, pencils, paper airplanes.
>
> D.L.: What kind of activity is it when you throw things?
>
> JOHN: That's when we're fooling around.
>
> D.L.: How else do kids fool around in the library?
>
> JOHN: They bug people.
>
> D.L.: What does that mean?
>
> JOHN: Well, when someone is working, you bother them. You steal their pencil, or call them names. Anything to get 'em upset. (Lancy 1976a,15–6)

Earlier I had determined that "library" was indeed a term students used, ditto with the term "activity." Notice that "What else . . ." elicits additional terms at the same level in the taxonomy (or "cognitive map" as I referred to it in this study), while "What kind of . . ." elicits subordinate categories. I continued in this vein until I had an exhaustive taxonomy.

The division between working and playing was quite striking, and came up again and again.

> . . . all the categories seem to depend on or revolve around work. Work is primary, in belief, if not in fact. Other activities are contingent upon work. A pupil explains: ". . . you work, then you take a break for ten minutes and you fool around or build a puzzle." All other activities serve as either a break from work, or as a reward for having done one's work . . . Art and music classes . . . aren't work, they're fun." Play also follows work, or, for students who regularly meet their goals, serves as a break between work activities. (Lancy 1976a,44)

Students' view of school was organized around activities and not "groups." They more closely resemble nursery school children (Corsario 1985) than junior high students (Davis 1972; Everhart 1975). I will come back to this issue shortly.

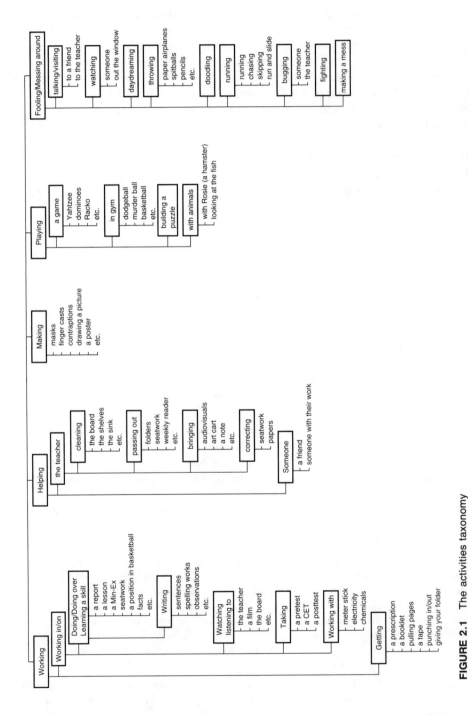

FIGURE 2.1 The activities taxonomy

SOURCE: Lancy, D. F. (1976). "The Beliefs and Behaviors of Pupils in an Experimental School: Introduction and Overview." *Learning Research and Development Publication Series* No. 3, p. 39. Reprinted by permission.

One of the grounds on which ethnography, in general, and ethnoscience, in particular, has been criticized is that we generalize about an entire society on the basis of intensive study of only a few informants (Harris 1968). As the Peltos' (1978) point out, studies show that core values and beliefs may be widely shared, but one must be extremely skeptical of the cherished assumption in anthropology of cultural homogeneity (for an early, critical, study of the homogeneity principle see Roberts 1951). Consequently, techniques were developed that permitted me to measure, quite precisely, the degree to which this particular world view is shared. In this study (1976a), I:

> . . . designed a *similarities judgement* instrument . . . I wanted a device that would tap the relationships among activities, but which could be standardized and economically administered to all 80 fourth and fifth graders. I composed 25 phrases, each of which had been a part of a pupil's response in [an] interview, but selected so that the main (taxonomic) categories would be about equally represented. Each of the 25 phrases was paired with every other phrase, and pupils were given a five-point similarity scale, and told to rate the degree of similarity of each pair. This yielded a total of 300 judgments made by each pupil. (p. 23)

Without going into details, these instruments can be easily scored and analyzed by a process called multidimensional scaling. The analysis yields a taxonomy that displays the distance (very similar, very different) between any two activities, and provides a measure of consistency. In this case, the taxonomy generated from data on 80 students very closely resembled the taxonomy elicited from the few students I had interviewed at length.

Another concern has been the failure to relate the participant's thoughts about the situation or setting to their behavior in that setting. Ethnographers are exhorted (Fetterman 1989) to seek both etic and emic perspectives. Hence, I used my interview material to construct "a behavior-observation checklist" to use in conducting systematic observations of the children's behavior throughout the school. Each of the 80 students was observed in six different settings in the school, and observations were distributed so as to obtain a representative sample of all combinations of students/settings/activities. I (and a second observer) had no difficulty identifying each of the activities, and only one activity not supplied by students, "waiting," had to be added to the checklist in order to make it exhaustive of all observed activities. This suggests that the "cognitive ethnography" I had obtained was accurate and comprehensive.

In still another procedure designed to corroborate the cognitive ethnography I had elicited from students, I conducted in-depth interviews with the six teachers who had the greatest contact with my fourth and fifth grade informants. Although there were elements common to both teachers' and students' views, there were also striking differences. For example,

> . . . teachers were less likely than pupils to supply a commonly used term to describe a class of activities. What all pupils call simply "working" is described by one teacher as "contract work," by another as "doing prescriptions," and

by a third as "on task". . . . Pupils talk a great deal about activities and, in the process, a mutually intelligible dialect has evolved that facilitates such discussion. Teachers (at least in the teachers' lounge) spend little time talking about pupils' activities, so they . . . use terms which are not shared with other teachers. (Lancy 1976b,30–1).

Despite differences in terminology, there was a great deal of consistency in teachers' responses; that is, it was clear that they were talking, roughly, about the same things. Some of the categories that emerged are analogous to student categories, but have different meanings for teachers than they have for students. For example,

> A striking difference between the teachers' and the pupils' view of fooling around is that where pupils see it as a normal manifestation of their own exuberance (fooling around is bad only if you get caught), teachers see it as a symptom of some underlying "problem": "The children might be trying to goof off in school because they know when they go home they have to do such and such as punishment." Another teacher said, "A pupil fooling around in the bathroom is a signal to me that the pupil is having difficulty in the classroom." [At least one teacher category, "socializing," has] . . . no direct counterpart in the pupils' description of their activities." (Lancy 1976b,34)

Hence, I concluded that:

> The teachers' view of pupils' activities is different from the view that pupils themselves hold. Pupils do play a role in the management of their school life. They do not always behave in conformity with the expectations of the teachers or the planned agendi of various school settings. (Lancy 1976b,35)

At the time the Longbranch study was conducted,[19] there were relatively few extant studies of student culture. Cusick's (1973) study suggested that student groups or cliques were central to understanding student culture. Davis (1972), in a study of a junior high school, also found cliques, viz. "Troublemakers," "Goody-goodies," "Brains," "Cool Kids," "Colored Kids," "Loners," etc., although these were probably less stable than those in the high school. She also found that junior high students, unlike students in "Horatio Gates" (Cusick 1973), were extremely conscious of the adults in the school, especially teachers. They talked about them a lot, and had shared views on everything from their "strictness" to their "picking on kids." Finally, and again unlike the high school students, "activities" occupy a prominent place in the view of school held by junior high students. Many of their activities are analogous to those I found at Longbranch, but there are interesting additions; including "trying to act cool."

With this background, I probed for evidence of these additional elements in Longbranch students' view of their school. Students utterly refused to acknowledge that there were different groups or kinds of kids in school. They freely used epithets with each other, but were unable to generalize a trait or collection of traits to a group. And, indeed, aside from loose-knit, small, and shifting friendship clusters, this school did not have cliques. Nor did I find any evidence that the "teachers" or "types of teachers" figured prominently in this student culture. Obviously, they were present in the school, but they must have been as static and unremarkable as items of furniture. Whether this is a function of the unusual curriculum, or characteristic of student culture in the elementary school is an open question. However, one thing does seem clear, and that is, while activities dominate the student culture in nursery, and elementary school, gradually student groups appear and, increasingly, occupy the dominant position. The few studies of post-secondary student culture suggest a weakening of the clique system in many cases and a reassertion of "activities" as the principal organizing rubric for student culture.

In the Future

Despite the decline in opportunities to study enculturation and acculturation in non-Western societies, the field of education and anthropology is thriving. Membership in the Council on Anthropology and Education has climbed steadily, and CAE is now one of the largest subdisciplines of anthropology. At the American Anthropology Association's annual meeting, December 1990, CAE sponsored numerous sessions at which scholars presented papers. Some prominent topics were: "Closing the educational access gap"; "Taboo topics and unheard voices: Women's stories"; "Literacy issues in a minority setting: An ethnographic perspective"; "Play across home and school contexts"; and "Competing discourses on school violence."

What I find interesting is that it has become harder and harder to identify educational anthropology on the basis of topical foci. Educational anthropologists now study issues that have historically been the provenance of sociologists, social psychologists, and political scientists. Increasingly, it is the ethnographic method (an all-encompassing concern for the entire culture of a group of people) that serves as the hallmark of an anthropologically-oriented study.

Nevertheless, the topics identified in this chapter deserve continued attention. The study of enculturation has received a boost from renewed interest in the developmental theory of Lev Vygotsky. His work directs our attention to the role of parents and the larger social group in assisting the child to become a competent member of society. Rogoff (1990) reviews recent research on enculturation that is informed by Vygotsky's theory. Another robust source of inspiration for enculturation studies is the voluntary organization, such as the street gang, 4-H, catechism class, Karate lessons, learning to manage a paper route, and so on.

While globally more and more children are becoming "schooled," and the culture of the school is becoming more standardized, in the United States, interest in alternatives to regular schools is growing. Home schooling and magnet schools are two recent alternatives but there are many others. We very much need ethnographies of these new schools which, among other things, relate their programs and practices to the culture of the community that sponsored them.

Studies of student groups show no signs of abating. A very recent example challenges the accumulated wisdom on the very nature of black student culture.

Jay MacLeod (1987) identifies two groups, the "hallway hangers" and the "brothers" in a working-class urban high school. The former closely resemble Cusick's "hoods" and Willis' "lads," but the latter, although black, are pro-school. The brothers attend class, obey the rules, work hard, avoid drugs, are active in sports, and so on. Indeed, the brothers and their parents bear an uncanny resemblance to the Punjabis in Valleyside. They believe that education will now open doorways for the youth that were not open for their parents.

There are as yet manifold opportunities to document the culture of student groups. Students groups in vocational schools and community colleges are underrepresented in the literature, and I would like to see us rapidly rectify the relative neglect of female student groups at all levels of the education system.

Reconstructing the Web

Most anthropologists use the ethnographic method, which, in many ways, is the prototype for the qualitative method. However, anthropologists have a unique concern for culture, a term subject to a variety of interpretations. Think of it as a spider web—as this strong, multifaceted, but nearly transparent structure. Classical anthropologists attempted to capture the entire web, while modern anthropologists focus on a particular topic or section. However, the key is that they are bound to trace, at least cursorily, all the silk threads leading away from the little area they've chosen to work in. They do this in order to get some sense of what the total web looks like, but also in order to hazard a guess as to what happens in other parts of the web when there are perturbations in their area. Notice the way Corsario traces aspects of Italian children's play to adult communication patterns. Notice the way investigators consider the impact on culture of foreign elements like the school. For some societies, schools are like juicy new bugs that are pounced on with relish by the spider, for others the school is an inedible, even destructive substance that disrupts the delicate harmony of the web.

Tracing the patterns formed by all these filaments takes a great deal of time. Hence, ethnography is characterized first and foremost by prolonged engagement and participant observation. As the chapter progressed, we moved from the relatively unstructured and intuitive methods of the traditional ethnographer, to the more and more refined, precise, and redundant (or triangulated) methods of the contemporary ethnographer or ethnoscientist. It's as if the modern ethnographer wants to move beyond describing the surface appearance of the web and examine its molecular structure. Now participant observation is supplemented by systematically interviewing samples of informants, casual observation is buttressed by structured observation procedures, and computer programs aid in the analysis of massive amounts of text—notes, interview transcripts, and printed materials. One reason for this escalation in the use of a greater variety of techniques, and the supplemental use of quantitative data to enhance credibility, is the need to capture several different perspectives on the phenomenon of interest. It is not enough to study and report what we think the spider's web looks like, how it is structured, and how it functions. We must also describe it from the spider's point of view, from that of its victims, and from the perspective of the birds which prey on the spider. Is it any wonder that anthropologists return again and again, over the course of their careers, to study the same people, as Deyhle has done with Indian adolescents in Southwestern Utah?

However, as we attempt to enhance reliability and become more focused, more rigorous, and more precise in analyzing specific aspects of culture, there is the danger that validity will be sacrificed, that we will fail in our mission to adequately describe the culture with all of its fascinating nuances. After all, most spider webs command respect for their sheer beauty. Ethnography, without rich narrative description, isn't worthy of the name. This detailed, recorded-for-posterity quality of ethnography comes through in the use of the present tense and the use of a static framework—Grindal describing the *wencheming* ceremony, and in the tendency to offer a collective portrait of group members—Gibson's Punjabi—and gloss over inter-individual variation.

The best time to view the spider's web is in the morning as heavy dew throws it into sharp relief. Otherwise the web, like our own culture, is all but invisible. This is the primary reason anthropologists study societies markedly different from their own as Peshkin did at Bethany Baptist Academy. One can also contrast two or more distinctive cultural responses to a particular situation as Pomponio and I compared Ponam, Mandok, and Imbonggu adaptation to government schools. One can contrast what one observes with descriptions of the same or similar societies in the extant literature. One must somehow make the familiar strange, as my pat understanding of what a spider's web should look like was shaken upon moving to Arizona and encountering the black widow's "web."

Ultimately, the anthropologist's primary identification is not with a particular research methodology (psychology departments advertise for *experimental* psychologists, anthropology departments do not advertise for *ethnographers*); nor, usually, with a specific topic, but with the culture associated with a particular group of people. The anthropologist represents a living archive of material on these people (all-knowing, like E. B. White's Charlotte) capable of speaking authoritatively on many aspects of their culture. She continually adds to her archive through reading other's research reports and returning to the field to collect additional data. Even in the absence of new data, she will reanalyze old data in the light of new theoretical ideas. Painstakingly, sometimes over many years, the anthropologist studies the web of culture by reconstructing it over and over, getting it better each time, until, even the spider herself would be fooled.

NOTES

1. "I really did not know much about field work. The course on methods that Professor Boas taught was not about field work . . . ." (Margaret Mead 1972,147). ". . . training has been very much a matter of the transmission of a craft and of learning by doing . . . it has not helped that some people talk as if the key to ethnography were a personal psychological experience, rather than the discovery of knowledge" (Hymes 1977,5).
2. However, I must agree with Corsario (1985) that: ". . . role play is not simply imitation of adult models, but is often an innovative expansion of the adult model" (p. 105).

3. KEEP has sponsored extremely important basic research on the social context of child development (Roberts, in press).

4. If KEEP success can be more parsimoniously attributed to the use of enlightened, progressive curricula and good teaching, then perhaps we can see the obvious failure so often documented by anthropologists as attributable less to racism or cultural differences than to the use of outdated instructional practices and bad teaching. Ray Rist (1978) certainly expected to find a racist reaction to the integration of an elementary school via busing in 1973. Instead he found ". . . a situation where it was more the academic performance of the black children than their skin color that defined their experiences at Brush" (p. 195). He argues that the pattern, whereby black students eventually found their way into the lowest reading groups, labelled as behavior problems, referred for testing, held back, etc. was not due to racist attitudes on the part of teachers. Rather it was because their store of strategies for dealing with students who might not be bright, well-adjusted, highly motivated and academically attuned, was extremely limited.

5. About as close as we get to "replication" in anthropology.

6. Fred Erickson (1973,1984) much earlier had argued that ". . . much of the ethnography of schooling in our own society has fallen short on this point . . . we give in to our rage too self-indulgently and present schools, teachers, and students as essentially . . . inhuman . . ." (p. 61).

7. Ogbu (1982) argues that many cultural discontinuities are "natural," learning in context vs decontextualized learning, for example. Or, Corsario's (1988b) observation that, at home, toys, etc. are owned, whereas in nursery school they must be shared. Ogbu's point is that not all cultural discontinuity is bad. Also he identifies "primary" discontinuities, of the sort I found in Papua New Guinea between the indigenous counting system and that taught in school (Lancy 1983), for example. Then, there are "secondary" discontinuities associated with caste-like minorities, such as blacks and Indians in the U.S., Bunraku in Japan, and Maoris in New Zealand. Members of these groups and their children actively resist conformity to the norms of the public school, which is seen as an extension of the dominant, oppressor society.

8. No doubt this study also benefitted from her work on a very similar project, a comparison of native and immigrant student adaptation patterns in a high school on St. Croix (Gibson 1982).

9. "The present writer feels that the gang makes an indispensable contribution to personality, and a contribution which adults sometimes overlook. One learns morality in the gang and one learns to take punishment. Even a vicious gang is better than no gang at all" (Waller [1932]1961,180).

10. Notice that the term "ethnography" is used to describe a particular kind of methodology, as well as the end product of the study that used the ethnographic method. This, as well as the title of his book, convey the kind of finality and completeness that anthropologists strive for in their work. It implies that they tend to view the world as rather static, it also suggests a degree of arrogance, or at least great self-confidence. Further, Cusick (1973) has almost no discussion of methodology. However, subsequent studies (Palonsky 1975; Eckert 1989) have added to, but not substantially challenged, Cusick's ethnographic portrait.

11. Interestingly, Varenne (1982) did not find students using clique labels to refer to themselves in their own group, only to others.

12. While Deyhle can see the importance of break dancing for these students, she frequently makes the point that teachers/administrators utterly fail to see how important break dancing is to Indian students. They fail to understand or acknowledge what it says about the Indians' "attitude" toward school.

13. It says something about the "culture" of the anthropologist tribe that none of us has seen fit to do an ethnography of a country club. When educational anthropologists do an ethnography in a school, they rarely study those in positions of authority like teachers, administrators, and high status student cliques.

14. An interesting confirmation for this finding comes from the University of California at Berkeley. A mathematics instructor was puzzled as to why Asian students did so well in his calculus class, while black students did so poorly. He discovered that the Asian students studied in groups, while black students studied alone. Probing further, he found that these academically successful black students had had to divorce themselves from black student culture, in order to succeed in high school. While being a loner was an adaptive strategy in high school, it became dysfunctional in college. The professor helped the black students form mutual support groups, and achieved the hoped-for effect on their calculus grades (Treisman 1983; Watkins 1989).

15. Actually he had a research assistant do the videotaping, so he wouldn't have to step out of character. He signaled to her what to record, and when to start and stop taping.

16. We will take up the universality issue in Chapter 4.

17. I can personally verify this pattern, as I vividly remember having a heated interchange with a submanager at the Fiat factory in Torino (as to why my new car wasn't ready), while he kept three other conversations going—two via telephones and a third with one of his office assistants.

18. The reader should be aware that this study, like many others in this chapter, including Corsario's initial study, were generously funded by organizations like the National Institutes of Education. During the 18 months that I worked on this project, I had virtually no other assignments (the salary was commensurate), and I had access to computer-assisted data analysis, graduate research assistants, audio and video recording equipment, typing, and so on. While straightforward participant observation may be relatively "inexpensive," assuming the researcher has some source of salary, as soon as one complicates the research by trying to triangulate field notes with more systematic data collection and analysis, the costs for human and machine "assistance" can quickly become prohibitive for the "unfunded" or "small grant" researcher. Compare these remarks to Lareau's (1989b) discussion of the difficulties encountered in doing an unfunded field study (p. 208–9).

19. As an aside, about a year after I completed my study, management of Longbranch was turned back over to the local school district. They refused to provide funds to continue purchasing the consumable lesson materials, hence the entire individualized curriculum was dropped in favor of traditional textbooks and whole class instruction. The fate of similar educational innovations will be discussed in Chapter 5. I should also note here that Everhart's (1983) study of student culture in a junior high school in "Jefferson" district was initiated as part of an evaluation of a federally-funded program to individualize instruction, however, he concludes ". . . student life was not significantly altered by the project" (p. 279).

CHAPTER **3**

Sociological Perspectives

Twenty-two of 37 of the East Asian parents reported that they had spent time teaching their children reading, writing, and simple arithmetic skills before entering kindergarten. Four out of 25 Anglo parents indicated that they engaged in similar types of activities . . . the effects of this instruction were evident in the results of the *Metropolitan Readiness Tests* . . . East Asian students had higher mean test scores than Anglos in all areas, with the exception of language skills . . . [where they] were at a disadvantage, because their parents did not speak English . . .

East Asian parents reported . . . that teachers usually did not give homework in the primary grades, so to compensate for this, they made sure their children studied for more than one hour per day, by giving them extra homework problems from workbooks purchased outside of school . . . East Asian parents establish a specific period of time for study . . . and also limited the time spent playing with friends or watching TV.

In comparison to Anglo parents, more East Asians paid tuition for . . . private lessons in music, computer science, martial arts, or languages. [Many] East Asian children took more than one of these types of lessons per week . . . [and they tended to be] . . . school related and required practice at home. . . .

Study habits of East Asian students were reinforced at school . . . [where they] tended to be grouped in top-level classes. . . . Teachers ended to challenge students with interesting, exploratory topics in the top-level classes, while in the low-level classes they concentrated on mastery of basic skills and on disciplining students. Moreover, teachers gave more creative and interesting homework assignments to the top-level students [who] tended to distract each other much less often than those in the low-level classes. (Schneider & Lee 1990,372–3)

What we have here is a meticulous point-by-point comparison of the support structure for academic achievement provided by East Asian immigrant and native Anglo parents. Schneider and Lee (1990) were interested in the role that parents might play in accounting for the greater academic success (as measured by grades, test scores) of East Asian students. In effect, what they are asking is how children from poor, low-status families gain high status in school. Their theme is *stratification* in school and society. From an initial pool of 30 schools, they selected a suburban and an urban school in the Chicago area, and studied 46 East Asian and a matched group of 49 Anglo students from the sixth and seventh grades. Families in the two groups had similar income levels, but East Asians had lower occupational status; they made up the income differential by working longer hours, or holding multiple jobs as compared to the Anglos. They described their data base as follows:

> Five methods of data collection were used: (1) student census, (2) review of school records, (3) participant and nonparticipant observations, (4) semistructured, in-depth interviews with students, parents, teachers, and administrators, and (5) collection of student essays. . . . From September 1982 through June 1983, 90 days of participant and nonparticipant observations of school activities were conducted. On the average, four hours per day were spent observing in classrooms, talking (informal interviewing) with teachers and students during recess and lunch periods, and participating in special school activities. Observations were conducted for all subjects in both schools at least once. However, focused observations were conducted in reading, language arts, mathematics, and social studies. . . . For the first three months, the observations were primarily descriptive. However, over time, several key areas emerged, which seemed appropriate for more intensive focused observations. These areas included teacher and student use of time, student attentiveness to class tasks, and interactions among students and teachers. Beginning in December, focused observations were conducted. . . . Interviews with teachers, administrators, parents, and children were also conducted. . . . Teacher and school administrator interviews [12 teachers, 4 administrators] were conducted in classrooms, offices, and occasionally in the teachers' lounge. Most of the parent and student interviews were conducted at home, however, several parent interviews were conducted either at work places or over the telephone. Each interview lasted at least an hour. . . . The total number of East Asian students and Anglo-American students interviewed was 73. . . . The interviews were free-flowing and as informal as possible. . . . (pp. 365–6)

The very thorough description of their methodology and the precision with which they report the results: "80 percent . . . of the East Asian parents compared to 13% of the Anglo parents stated that their children studied at home at least an hour a day . . ." (p. 372), should alert us that, in sociological studies of education, there is a blurring of the distinctions between qualitative and quantitative research. At least one reason for this is that, in contrast to the anthropologists' wide compass, sociologists are concerned with a narrower range of issues. Educational sociologists, in particular, are united in their pursuit of the following set of interlocking questions: (1) How does schooling affect one's economic and social status (stratification)? Is status enhanced or, do students end up with roughly the same status as their parents?[1] (2) How do class, ethnicity, and gender interact with schooling to create stratification in society? (3) What role do parents, students, and teachers play in creating stratification within schools? The lengthy excerpt which opened the chapter clearly resonates to all these questions.

Of these three general questions, researchers interested in pursuing the first tend toward the quantitative end of the continuum, the last question is more often studied qualitatively, while the second gets attention from scholars of both persuasions. Furthermore, how one approaches these questions, and the range of answers considered reasonable depends on which of several grand theories[2] one has chosen to embrace. We turn now to a brief discussion of these theories.

GRAND THEORIES

Schneider and Lee (1990) relate their findings to Ogbu's (1987) education and caste model, which posits that members of minority groups in the U.S., who have suffered a history of economic discrimination, withhold their investment in education because they believe it will not pay off. They see this theory as inadequate because "Even though East Asians receive relatively low economic returns from additional schooling, they encourage their children to acquire more education . . . it would seem that non-economic cultural values, such as self-improvement and upholding family honor, may mediate the perceived economic benefits of education" (p. 362 see also, Caplan, Choy, and Whitmore 1989). Mikelson (1989) also challenges this "investment" theory of education. Based on their far lower return, women should invest far less in education than men, but just the reverse is true. She says "Abstract attitudes . . . cannot predict achievement behavior . . . [all groups of students hold positive attitudes toward school and believe] . . . that schooling is a vehicle for upward mobility and success" (p. 48).

In Ogbu's theory, some groups (see discussion of Punjabis in previous chapter) do take advantage of opportunities for upward mobility, which schooling may provide. But, in classical Marxist (now called *critical* theory) such mobility is just not possible. ". . . power is in the hands of dominant classes or groups, who control all wealth and capital, and who maintain and reinforce traditional class, ethnic, and gender inequalities" (Bennett and LeCompte 1990,14). The best known application of Marxist theory to education in the U.S. is *Schooling in Capitalist America* (Bowles and Gintis 1976). However, in this chapter we will review works by Anyon and Suransky, which are written from the Marxist perspective.

Like Marx, Bourdieu (1977) sees schooling as serving primarily to reproduce the existing social order.

> Bourdieu's main thesis is that since what is being taught is the dominant cultural arbitrary, excellence and scholastic achievement will naturally be defined in terms of that arbitrary cultural paradigm. Those pupils whose familial socialization bestows upon them greater amounts of cultural capital, i.e. familiarity with the cultural arbitrary, will necessarily achieve more academically than those

whose relationship to the cultural arbitrary is more distant. Furthermore, the sub-culture of the subordinated class will, in legitimizing their class position, serve to inhibit their demands for access to the higher reaches of the education system. (Jenkins 1983,4)

However, the theory of cultural capital goes much further in explaining what it is about schooling that leads to reproduction. And, in Lareau's (1989) view:

> The concept of cultural capital has the potential to produce significant improvements in conceptual models of the linkages between social structure and individual biography. . . . It retains a notion of individual variability: while individuals possess capital, they must 'invest' these class resources to yield social profits. Privilege associated with class does not automatically yield benefits, for individuals must 'activate' those resources. This approach is an improvement over existing models, which often posit an association between class position and behavior without addressing the notion of human agency or the pattern of internal variation within social classes. . . . By highlighting the intersection between social structure and biography, cultural capital has the potential to provide a conceptual bridge . . . as sociologists move between "macro" and "micro" levels of analysis. (p. 177)

Juxtaposed to these reproduction theories is the theory that drives much of the quantitative research in the sociology of education. In this view, schools are charged with the responsibility of developing human capital. Students show up on the school's doorstep possessing various resources, knowledge, intelligence, "educability," and so on, and schools aid the student to make the most of these resources. Along the way, schools also evaluate students' worth in human capital terms, by awarding symbolic capital, grades, diplomas, placement (e.g., high reading group, vocational track), and designations (gifted, learning disabled). Finally, once the student leaves the education system, she/he has an opportunity to convert this symbolic capital into "real capital": in a wage earning job, marriage to a wage earner, welfare, and so on.

Mehan (1979), in reflecting on these theories linking schooling and stratification, is critical of the over-reliance on the quantitative paradigm used to evaluate them:

> While schooling is recognized as an intervening process between background and social context, and later economic and academic attainment, the school has been treated as a "black box" in between input and output factors. *Indices* of schooling have been examined, such as the number of books in the school library, the amount of equipment in science laboratories, and the opinions of teachers and administrators toward the school. But what actually happens inside schools, in classrooms, in educational testing situations, at recess, in lunchrooms, and in teachers' lounges, on a practical everyday basis has not been examined. . . .
>
> If we want to know whether student-teacher ratios, classroom size, teaching styles, and all the rest actually influence the quality of education, then we must be able to show how they operate in pragmatic, educational situations. Likewise, if we are to understand how so-called input factors, like social class, ethnicity,

or teachers' attitudes, influence educational outcomes, then their influence must be shown to operate in the course of interaction among participants in actual educational environments. (pp. 4–5)

Qualitative researchers in sociology, not surprisingly, focus, therefore, on "descriptions of actual processes." But before we turn to these descriptions, it would be instructive to consider what implication each of these theories has for improving education. The strong version of Marxist or critical theory would posit that nothing can be done about education, until the class system itself is dismantled by changing the relationship between society, capital, and the means of production. A weaker version (e.g., McLaren 1989) posits the need for a redistribution of resources. That is, schools for the poor must receive drastically more resources than schools for the rich, in order to achieve equity. Additional resources could be invested in shrinking class sizes, improving physical facilities and the supply of materials, attracting better teachers via higher salaries, and so on.

Those who base school reform on considerations of cultural capital have proposed two drastically different alternatives. Hirsch (1987) would insist on the infusion of "high culture" throughout the curriculum, and would hold schools accountable for all children regardless of race, class, or gender becoming *culturally literate.* By contrast, here is a proposal circulating in England (Hargreaves 1982): "A grammar school academic and cognitive-intellectual curriculum, which is partly defined as 'high culture,' is not suitable for . . . working class pupils. Instead, they must be provided with a 'popular education' which is closer to their own culture, life style, and capacities; it will be a curriculum which is oral rather than literary, concrete and practical rather than theoretical and abstract" (p. 118).

Followers of the human capital model would embrace any proposal which promised to make schools more "efficient" at evaluating and developing students' potential. Obvious contenders are those who labor to improve the validity of I.Q. and other tests to measure "capacity," as well as standardized tests of achievement and other measures of "competency." Indeed, the I.Q. test was developed in the first place as a means to make selection for schooling more efficient (Gould 1981). Currently, popular constructs such as *Effective Schools, Academic Learning Time, Magnet Schools, Career Ladders,* and *Voucher Systems* all derive from an underlying model of the school as searching out, developing, and certifying human talent. This lengthy discussion on theory and application, as regards the relationship between schooling and stratification, is necessary to drive home the point that some sociologists do not necessarily acknowledge the virtue of "neutrality" (see page 29), on the contrary.

OUTLINE OF THE CHAPTER

Thus far we have seen that sociologists are typically concerned with the study of how society comes to be stratified. Qualitative sociologists may use quantitative indices in their pursuit of this issue, and they tend to invoke broad, all-encompassing theories to account for this phenomenon. In the remainder of this chapter, we will see these issues addressed in the course of reviewing research under several major themes. First, we will consider the role of the family in mediating the child's relationship with his/her school. Then, we move from the home to the pre-school, contrasting the pre-school curricula available to children from different social classes. A similar comparison is undertaken for the elementary school, and then we review "tracking" in the secondary school, another pervasive form of stratification in education.

In the second half of the chapter, our focus shifts more drastically. We now zoom in to scrutinize, very closely, the ways in which social structuring actually happens. We consider the interactions among participants in social settings. A pervasive feature of educational institutions is the task of testing, selecting, and placing students. We review several studies of these processes from intelligence testing, to selection into first grade, to designation as learning disabled. We then move into a regular elementary school setting, to observe the way classroom social competence is defined and developed in the interactions among teacher and pupils. Our lens moves into even closer range, as we consider a very special, and highly stratified, area of the elementary school classroom—the reading group. Investigators have carefully revealed the very subtle, prosodic, and semiotic cues which structure interaction in the reading group. Then, we zoom in to look at power relations displayed in the interaction between pairs of individuals, students, and guidance counselors and students and writing center tutors.

In the remainder of the chapter we return to the wide angle setting, to consider some more general issues raised by this body of scholarship.

THE ROLE OF PARENTS: PRESCOTT AND COLTON

As much as anything else, growing interest in the role of parent/family in facilitating/hindering school success stems from the disappointing results of numerous government-initiated intervention efforts in the 1960s and 1970s. However, as McNeil (1988) suggests, it is not family background per se that determines a student's "career."

> Thus, a child *becomes* an upper-class, prep school graduate, with medical school aspirations; or a lower-class, teenaged mother about to drop out of school, not just because they were born into a particular kind of family. Family background sets up a set of expectations for present and future behavior, as well as influencing how other people will react to and interpret the consequences of that type of background. (p. 157)

We must look beyond simple markers of ascribed status (e.g., parental education, family income, number of bathrooms in the home), and study more dynamic and instrumental aspects of parental influenee of the sort identified by Schneider and Lee (1990).

This was precisely Annette Lareau's (1989) objective in her two-year-long study (her doctoral dissertation) of working class and middle class communities in Northern California.[3] As her goal was to study the impact of social class on family/school relations, she chose her two schools and two first grade teachers carefully. Both Colton and Prescott were considered to be "good" schools, as were the teachers. While Prescott served a mainly white, upper-middle class community; Colton served a working class, ethnically mixed (50% Anglo, 33% Hispanic, remainder African- and Asian-American) community. However, the Colton community was not troubled by massive unemployment, widespread drug abuse, violent crime, and the like.

Lareau acted as participant observer in the two first-grade classes the first year, and selected five children from intact families, and one from a single-parent family in each school, for in-depth study during the second year. She indicates the "typicality" of her sample with statements like: ". . . the Colton families I interviewed were somewhat more active in their children's schooling than the average parent" (p. 199). Also, "There were no glaring omissions in terms of discipline problems, achievement levels, temperament, popularity, and parent involvement in schooling" (p. 200). Lareau shares precise details reflecting the quality of her data base, e.g. ". . . I succeeded in interviewing only three of the five fathers . . . because of . . . I only interviewed . . . once rather than twice" (p. 201).

She encountered numerous minor problems, like the fact that with working class parents she had great difficulty defining herself. "Graduate school," "research," "field study" were all foreign terms to them. They thought she was studying to become a teacher, or working for the school. Also she confesses:

> I made one very serious mistake in the field; I fell behind in writing up my field notes. Writing up field notes immediately is one of the sacred obligations of field work. Yet, workers I have known well, all confessed that they fell behind in their field notes, at one time or another. Researchers are human: We get sick; we have an extra glass of wine; we get into fights with our spouses; we have papers to grade, due the next day; or we simply don't feel like writing up field notes immediately after an interview or a participant-observation session. On top of that, at least for me, writing field notes is both boring and painful. Boring, because it repeats a lot of what you just did, and it takes a long time to write a detailed description of a fifteen-minute encounter/observation. Painful, because it forces you to confront unpleasant things, including lack of acceptance, foolish mistakes in the field, ambiguity about the intellectual question, missed opportunities in the field, and gaping holes in the data. To be sure, there is a tremendous sense of satisfaction, in having placed on paper, the experiences of the day, and then adding these to the top of a neat and growing pile. But the time! Initially, one hour in the field would take me three hours to write up. Missing sessions of writing field notes can, like skipping piano practice, get quickly out of hand . . . exponentially, in fact. (p. 206)

None of these mistakes were fatal. After she began the study, she discovered that straightforward descriptions are unlikely to lead to answers to the question: "How does social class influence children's schooling?" She had to actively pursue specific pieces of information in order to answer a ". . . more conceptual question: Do these data support one interpretation, and suggest that another interpretation is not as useful?'' (p. 211) Fortunately, she was taking a research methods class at the time, and her instructor's comments on her initial write-up ''. . . made it clear that I could not continue to conduct a study that posed no problem, and articulated no argument . . . an unfocussed 'thick description' would not do'' (p. 212).

Lareau describes, at length, her procedure for analyzing interviews. Each interview was transcribed, a process that could take up to fifteen hours depending on tape quality.[4] Interviews were segmented, with each segment cut out and pasted on cards. The cards were ''. . . sorted by basic category . . . 'parents' views of their role' . . . 'teachers' expectations of parents'. [She] . . . ended up with over a thousand cards . . . all over the living room floor'' (p. 205).[5] She made ''data displays'' (see discussion p. 157, Chapter 5), for example ''. . . matrices, with the children listed in rows and various types of parental involvement in columns (i.e., reviewing papers after school, reading, attending open house, . . .'' (p. 206). All this effort pays off, as Lareau achieves a balance between analysis and data—at no time does one feel that her interpretations are unsupported by evidence, nor does she provide excess description that goes unanalyzed.

The value of long-term, painstaking, qualitative research is borne out by the ''cumulative nature'' of Lareau's findings. No single factor sharply differentiates between Colton and Prescott. For example, ''When I went into the field, I thought I would find evidence of institutional discrimination . . . I thought . . . that the teachers were going to differ significantly in their interaction with parents of different social classes. I did not find evidence to support this position'' (p. 218). While, there were differences in the expected direction in parental participation in school-orchestrated events, some Colton parents attend parent/teacher conferences (60 percent), open house (35 percent), and volunteer in the classroom (3 percent).

Prescott parents were conscientious about reading to their children. They also helped them see the practical value of their education by integrating ''. . . educational goals into virtually all aspects of home life'' (p. 74). Toys and presents were all selected with a view toward their education value, and they enrolled children in ''. . . supplementary enrichment activities, including art and French classes, soccer, and Indian guides'' (p. 67). On the other hand, Mrs. Morris is typical of Colton parents, in that ''When Tommy entered first grade, she turned over responsibility for his education to the school'' (p. 41). Teachers resist taking 100 percent responsibility for children's education: ''During this twenty-minute conference, Mrs. Thompson suggested at least five times that Tommy's mother keeps her son reading during the summer'' (p. 21). Colton parents have only a vague idea of what goes on at school, and Mrs. Morris is surprised when Mrs. Thompson recommends that Tommy be retained in first grade.

Prescott mothers, without exception, are intimately aware of their children's progress in school. Mrs. Harris observes Alan's (lack of) progress in spelling as she serves a volunteer stint in the classroom. She asks for, and is granted, spelling materials to (successfully) work with Alan at home. As Lareau notes, ''. . . parents' activities shaped the degree to which children received a 'generic' or a 'customized' educational experience within schools" (p. 123). Another family found out that their son needed occupational therapy for fine muscle control, which they willingly paid for and the child experienced ". . . dramatic improvement in his posture, his handwriting, and his motor coordination in soccer" (p. 117). Indeed, this is one of Lareau's most striking findings, that ". . . the most intense family-school relationships were not for the highest achieving students in upper-middle class families. These occurred in families whose children were at the bottom of their class" (p. 129).

Shortly, we will consider Mary Lee Smith's study (1982), of how students come to be designated "learning disabled" in a suburban Denver district. Her study seems to offer additional support for this finding. She reports several cases at length. For example, John was not doing as well in school as his parents thought he should, his mother bought him educational games, drilled him with flash cards, and observed in his classroom . . . "she was . . . frantic . . . she said . . . 'reading is so *central,* . . . if you can't read, you can't learn anything' " (p. 38). Despite his teacher's claim that, "I'm not worried . . . he is a little behind grade level. There are several children lower than he is in this class" (p. 40), his mother asked to have him "referred." The evaluation and placement process determined that he was not qualified for special education services. The parents hired a tutor for the child, and continued to press the school to have him placed in the resource room. They threatened litigation, and, finally, the school acquiesced to their wishes.

Prescott parents' high status and substantial education give them the confidence and resources to intervene very directly in the school experience of their children. They address teachers on a first-name basis, enter classrooms without preamble, freely criticize teachers among themselves and to the administration. "Parents felt that Mrs. Walters' expectations were too low, the discipline was lax, the class was too noisy, and the children were not required to work consistently, or finish their projects" (p. 79). They could speak knowledgeably, in *academese,* about their children's problems: "His attention span is short. He has auditory reception problems . . ." (p. 77). Furthermore, parents gained information relevant to their child's academic career, through frequent interaction with other Prescott parents, whose acquaintance they actively cultivated. Colton parents, by contrast, felt inferior to teachers—"If they start using big words, you think, 'Oh God, what does this mean?' You know, it is just like going to the doctor's. And it makes you feel a little insuperior [sic] to them. But I don't have the education they do" (p. 108). "Colton parents lacked educational *competence,* and they were aware of their shortcomings" (p. 107). "A lot of the mothers [who came to school] felt they would grade a paper wrong . . . , even in the first grade level, to even spell the words" (p. 109). One Colton parent, ". . . a high school graduate, . . . found that her reading started to improve as she read pre-school books to her son . . ." (p. 120). They feel particularly inadequate at E and P conferences: "She put that paper in front of me with all this stuff, and you know, half of it I didn't understand" (p. 108). While some Prescott parents had used schooling as a means to dramatically alter their social status (son of barber to Harvard M.B.A.), Colton parents had less positive experiences. Several had not graduated from high school, and some claimed to have reading problems.

While Colton teachers continued to solicit parental involvement and assistance at every turn (and there was evidence of a positive relationship between student achievement and parental involvement), Prescott teachers were sometimes resentful at the lack of respect offered them by parents. Clearly, the ideal is high parental involvement that is directed by the teacher (see also Van Galen 1987).

A final note; Lareau did not find major differences in patterns of instruction in the two schools—something that is reported often in the literature, as we shall see. In fact, the only observation that stands out was Mrs. Thompson's (Colton) abandonment of using manipulatives to teach math. On the one hand, the kids were too unruly to be left alone to work in groups, and, on the other, she was unable to get enough parent volunteers to assist her in supervising these groups.

THE ROLE OF PARENTS: SOME OTHER EVIDENCE

Because of shared views on the nature of the "problem space," and a relatively ecumenical attitude toward methodology, sociologists are more likely to draw on both qualitative and quantitative studies in synthesizing material on a topic.[6] I will briefly review three studies that extend and support Lareau's work, but which lay closer to the quantitative end of the continuum. An interview study in Israel (Ninio 1979) compared high and low SES mothers developmental time tables for their offspring. Higher-class mothers saw their children as passing various perceptual and cognitive (but not sensorimotor) milestones earlier than lower-class mothers. They were also much more likely to intervene in their children's development with cognitively stimulating activities, such as storybook reading. Very similar findings were obtained in a comparison between Anglo and Lebanese mothers in Australia (Goodnow, Cashmore, Cotton, Knight 1984). Approximately 40 mothers in each group were given open-ended, semi-structured interviews.

> The Anglo mothers were far more likely to describe themselves as actively teaching school-related skills before school. Earlier expected ages tended to parallel areas of teaching (p. 197) . . . For example, 84 percent of Anglo mothers taught their child the alphabet at home, only 37 percent of Lebanese did; 82 percent 'days of the week' vs. 40 percent. The Lebanese mothers simply did not appear concerned with a possibility that seemed pervasive in the 'Anglo' mothers' thinking about young children, namely that one might leave instruction until it was too late. (p. 203)

A study by Baker and Stevenson (1986) extends Lareau's concern for parental management of their children's school careers to ". . . the transition from middle school to high school" (p. 157). Forty-one mothers, randomly drawn from an initial sample of all mothers of eighth graders, in a middle school, in a small town were interviewed. Most families ". . . are between the upper-middle and upper-lower range of occupations" (p. 157). Two data sources were used: Student records and 45–90 minute interviews with the mothers. Questions focused on ". . . knowledge of and contact with schools . . . knowledge of their child's school performance; their suggested and implemented homework strategies, their suggested solutions to school problems, their solution to hypothetical academic and in-school behavioral problems, specific actions they have taken in the last year . . ." (p. 158).

Their results indicate that higher SES mothers ". . . have more knowledge of their child's schooling . . . they are more likely to be able to name their child's teachers, identify their child's best and worst subjects, and offer an overall evaluation of their child's performance . . . are more likely to have had contact with the school . . . to have attended parent/teacher conferences . . . when their child has a problem, they are more likely to know about the problem, and to use the school's resources to respond to the problem" (pp. 161–2). Like Lareau, they find that the effects of social class are most pronounced in cases of children who are not outstanding academically. For example, the more highly ". . . educated mother is one likely to override the school's recommendation and increase the number of college-preparatory courses for her child, irrespective of the child's performance" (p. 161).[7]

Taken together with Lareau's (1989) study, this research suggests the need to modify Bourdieu's theory of cultural capital, at least as applied in the U.S. The transmission of knowledge about "high culture," appears not to be sufficient to insure the academic success of one's offspring. On the contrary ". . . not all resources associated with upper-middle class life were salient. Teachers appeared to be relatively indifferent to the size of the children's homes, the quality or quantity of house furnishings, the distribution of family vacations, parents' taste in music, and the style of clothing worn by children and parents" (Lareau 1989,145). Rather, it is the middle-class parents' vigorous monitoring of the child's at-home and in-school learning environments, and knowledge of strategies to enhance and modify those environments when needed, including a willingness to purchase materials and supplemental educational services, that explains why schools reproduce social class.

While these preceding studies have tended to focus on the parents, in the next section we will review two very similar projects, which consider the ways in which the very character of a school might reflect the sorts of expectations held by parents from varying socioeconomic strata.

SOCIAL CLASS AND CLASSROOM
INSTRUCTION: PRESCHOOL

Lubeck (1984) carried out parallel field studies in an all-white preschool and an all-black Head Start program, located about one mile apart, in an integrated suburb of a major midwestern city. Although her study lasted only two months, she had previously taught in a pre-school and was easily accepted as a participant observer. She freely shared her notes with the staff, who ". . . found it remarkable that [she] could record information they thought trivial" (p. 221).

Differences between the two programs were pervasive. In the preschool, the curriculum was richer and more varied. It included science, and there was much discussion and several activities to teach "raw" vs. "cooked," for example. On the other hand, in Head Start ". . . school days were composed of activities that were repeated day after day . . ." (p. 224). At Head Start, a great deal of time was taken up with catering to the nonacademic needs of the children ". . . van regularly picks up groups . . . during the school hours for their medical, dental, and lead poisoning check-ups" (p. 22). Children are served two meals a day, there are many holidays, and sessions are held on only four days per week. "The sum total of these policies, procedures, and contingencies means that the Head Start children have considerably less school time than their preschool peers" (p. 222).

At the same time, in Head Start but not preschool, there was a lengthy period each day for "group time," where children learn how to behave in a group. They are taught their names, addresses, the calendar, and the alphabet. Group time is seen as ". . . getting the children ready to listen to the [kindergarten] teacher" (p. 223). In other respects, there was a clear demarcation of the children's space/activities, from the staff in Head Start; whose ". . . primary focus of attention appeared to be on other adults . . ." (p. 225) and, during free play ". . . teachers tend to other duties" (p. 268). By contrast, the white preschool teachers interacted directly with children in the various centers, and assisted them in carrying out chosen activities, in a process referred to in the child development literature as "scaffolding" (Rogoff 1990). Lubeck (1984) creates a "local" as opposed to "grand" theory, and relates the teaching/learning environments in the respective programs to home life/parenting styles associated with white middle class and black underclass (see also Heath 1983) culture.

A book by Valerie Polakow Suransky (1982), entitled *The Erosion of Childhood,* provides some interesting points of comparison with Lareau and Lubeck's work. Suransky, as her title suggests, is concerned with the tendency to overly structure and regiment children's lives in preschools, in the name of academic preparedness. Furthermore, she adopts a critical theory perspective, not as something to be tested or modified as we have seen above, but as a given. As Patton (1990) notes, scholars like Suransky and Anyon (see below): ". . . aim to describe and explain *specific* manifestations of already presumed general patterns . . . confirmation and elucidation, rather than discovery" (p. 86). There is, characteristically, no presentation of methods. Indeed, Suransky dismisses the very notion of methodology, labeling her work a "hermeneutical undertaking."

She provides brief portraits of five centers for the care of preschool-age children. The "Golda Meir Nursery School" and "Busy Bee Montessori Center," most closely resemble Lubeck's preschool. However, where others might see the continuous pressure on children, scaffolded by adults, to develop cognitive and social skills and a sense of efficacy in a positive light, Suransky sees teachers "interfering" with children's natural tendencies. The "Martin Luther King Child Care Center" and "Pinewoods Freeschool" (mixed race, but taught by black mother of five), closely resemble Lubeck's Head Start program. Here children are left alone to do their own thing. Fighting and rough play are not tightly controlled and, like Lubeck, Suransky sees the extended family style of parenting, characteristic of the black community, at work in these programs. As contrasted with Colton and Prescott (Lareau 1989), these preschool centers observed by

Lubeck and Suransky are much more differentiated one from another, and much more adapted to the child development philosophies (and financial resources) of their clientele.

SOCIAL CLASS AND CLASSROOM INSTRUCTION: ELEMENTARY SCHOOL

Much the same can be said of the elementary schools observed by Jean Anyon (1980). Anyon also incorporates a critical theory perspective in her work, but is careful to specify the particular interpretations which guide her thinking. Her central thesis is that elementary school programs of instruction are geared to preparing students with a view of themselves in relationship to work, authority, and means of production. Here is how she describes these schools:

> In the working-class schools, work is following the steps of a procedure (p. 73). The control that the teachers have is less than they would like. It is a result of constant struggle with the children. The children continually resist the teacher's orders and the work itself . . . Very often the work that the teachers assign is "easy," that is, not demanding, and thus receives less resistance. Sometimes a compromise is reached where, although the teachers insist that the children continue to work, there is a constant murmur of talk. The children will be doing arithmetic examples, copying social studies notes, or doing punctuation or other dittoes, and all the while there is muted but spirited conversation . . . (pp. 76–77)
>
> The *working-class* children are developing a potential *conflict* relationship with capital. Their present school work is appropriate preparation for future wage labor that is mechanical and routine. . . . However . . . they are also developing abilities and skills of resistance. These methods are highly similar to the "slowdown," subtle sabotage and other modes of indirect resistance, carried out by adult workers in the shop . . . . (p. 88)
>
> In the executive elite school, work is developing one's analytical intellectual powers. Children are continually asked to reason through a problem, to produce intellectual products that are both logically sound and of top academic quality. . . . School work helps one to achieve, to excel, to prepare for life . . . (p. 83). The teacher of math and science explained to the observer that she likes the ESS program because "the children can manipulate variables. They generate hypotheses and devise experiments to solve the problem. Then, they have to explain what they found." (p. 86)
>
> The *executive elite* school gives its children . . . the opportunity to learn and to utilize the intellectually and socially prestigious grammatical, mathematical, and other vocabularies and rules by which elements are arranged. They are given the opportunity to use these skills in the analysis of society, and in control situations. Such knowledge and skills are a most important kind of *symbolic capital*. They are necessary for control of a production system. (p. 89)

Anyon (1980) concludes ". . . school experience, in the sample of schools discussed here, differed qualitatively by social class. These differences may not only contribute to the development in the children in each social class of certain types of economically significant relationships and not others, but would thereby help to *reproduce* this system of relations in society" (p. 90).

While the credibility of Anyon's (1980) work is heightened by virtue of its compatibility with much of the work discussed in this chapter, it is undermined by various lapses. The qualitative differences between these five schools seem extreme, especially in view of the fact that they share district and state curriculum mandates. All five schools draw on a common pool of teacher-training programs for their employees, have excellent teachers, are governed by democratically-elected school boards, etc. Her rather superficial treatment of methodology does nothing to lessen one's skepticism. For example, she says ". . . the fifth grade in each school was observed . . . for 10 three-hour periods" (p. 68), but later we learn that there are several fifth grades in each school. It is not clear whether she means 30 hours per school or per fifth grade. She makes no mention of using videotape or audiotape records, or of sharing her notes with teachers. There are ". . . interviews of students, teachers, principals, and district administrative staff . . ." (p. 68), but no indication of how many, how structured, how analyzed, etc. She does not claim to have been a participant observer. There is no discussion of her sampling decisions.

Another troubling aspect of the Anyon report is the lack of consideration of what we might call "directionality." She implies that "society" creates these varying school environments via the expectations teachers have about what is appropriate instruction for children from different classes. However, an equally compelling alternative, as we have seen, is that parents both directly in their contacts with the school, and indirectly through their socialization practices, "determine" what goes on in schools. Could it be, for example, that the highly routinized instruction, characteristic of the working class school, occurs as a response to the children's lack of self-discipline and short attention span? (See the discussion of "Kensington" school in chapter 5, p. 144.) Barr and Dreeben (1983) conclude from a large scale classroom observation study, that ". . . the less tractable the class—the more children with low ability, who are immature, and who are disruptive—the fewer viable forms of instructional organization that become available" (p. xi). Unlike Lareau (1989, and see Gibson 1987, 1988), however, Anyon (1980) does not discuss any search for alternative sources of explanation for the variation she observes. But as Anderson (1989) points out, critical theorists are not seeking explanations, rather they are ". . . concerned with unmasking dominant social constructions and the interests they represent, studying society with the goal of transforming it, and freeing individuals from sources of domination and repression . . ." (p. 254).

SOCIAL CLASS AND TRACKING
IN THE SECONDARY SCHOOL

Willard Waller ([1932]1961) is widely acknowledged as the first educational sociologist and, not surprisingly, class and stratification attracted his attention: "Many children attain an easy and unhealthy leadership through the use of economic resources of their parents. . . . It is upon the basis of such distinctions, that many of the cliques and social clubs of high school children are formed . . ." (p. 37). However, another University of Chicago sociologist, A. B. Hollingshead ([1949]1975), conducted the first true field study[8] of stratification in the public school. Hollingshead and his wife (who evidently was a co-investigator, although not a co-author) lived in Elmtown, a medium-sized midwestern town between 1941 and 1942. Their goal was to study the ". . . relationships existing between the behavior patterns of the 735 adolescent boys and girls who lived in the community, and the positions occupied by their families in the community's social structure" (p. v). Simultaneously, they studied families and student culture. They became extremely active in various community organizations, viz. "I was invited into the rotary club and attended all meetings . . . I taught the men's and women's Bible classes in . . ." (p. 13). Their "entry" tactic with students was different: ". . . we approached the high school students informally through our Dachshund. For several days we took him for walks around the school buildings during the lunch hour, and many students became interested in him and his antics . . ." (p. 14). "Most of our time was spent around the high school . . . we skated and bowled with them, shot pool, . . . our policy was to be with them whenever and wherever possible" (p. 15).

Their notes from field work were supplemented by lengthy "schedules," such as ". . . *the family schedule* was filled out during home visits, in the presence of the person giving the information . . . all homes were visited once, 84 two or three times, and 67 four or more times" (p. 17).

The study had two parts. In the first part it had to establish that there were "classes," in an emic sense.

> . . . within three months after the field work was started, evidence accumulated which indicated that Elmtowners divided the social structure into several strata. They spoke of each other as members of "the aristocracy," "the 400," "the society class," "our community leaders," "the class below the society class," "the little business people," "the hard-working people who pay their bills, but never get any place," "the ne'er-do-wells," "the canal squatters," "the river rats," "the criminal class."
>
> . . . people identified the same families with particular status groups . . . some half-dozen family names were used as examples of people who belonged to "the upper class" or "the aristocracy." Other families appeared to be notorious for their "criminal records," "dependence upon welfare," and generally low status . . . Gradually, the tentative conclusion was reached, that families who were repeatedly cited as occupants of a given status position functioned as reference points when [people] thought about . . . the social structure. (p. 20)

Then they had to determine which class each adolescent belonged to. In the second part of the study, the Hollingsheads attempted to determine how a student's social class influenced her high school experience (including those who had dropped out). There were, for example, college prep, general and commercial tracks; and "Enrollment in each [track] is related very significantly to class position" (p. 122). Parents acted to guide children into what they considered to be appropriate tracks. For example, Nellie, whose family occupied class IV, or second from the bottom, had enrolled in the college prep track because a member of her clique had done so. As a result,

Nellie's mother was explosively angry with Nellie, and with the high school authorities for allowing Nellie to enroll in the college preparatory course. She immediately told Nellie that she must change to the secretarial course. Nellie cried most of the night, but her mother went to school the next morning and changed Nellie's course herself. Nellie continued in school for a year and a half, but dropped out of her old clique, and then left school to work in the "dime" store. (p. 124)

The upper class parents extended subtle pressure on the school, and their children were treated deferentially. They were more likely to get scholarships, and less likely to get detention.

Reaction to the publication of *Elmtown's Youth* was quite sensational, despite Hollingshead's attempts to conceal the town's identity. It attracted national media scrutiny, and he was the recipient of angry letters from townspeople and educators, who felt the book had tarnished their reputation. Nevertheless, the Hollingsheads found a welcome on their return for a lengthy "restudy" in 1972. Although the town's population had grown by a third, it was still ethnically homogeneous, and the class structure very much intact. A great deal of additional money was being spent on schooling and school governance appeared to be much more democratic.[9]

Metz (1978) examined tracking in two junior high schools during the 1967–68 school year. The schools were located in a suburban fringe area of a medium-sized city. Metz spent the year as a participant observer in the eighth grade classes, collecting written materials and interviewing teachers and students. She operated under a number of self-imposed restrictions.

I have taken a number of precautions to minimize subjectivity. First, I tried throughout the field work to be aware of my own pedagogical prejudices and personal likes and dislikes, and to lean over backwards to see what they would tempt me to deny. More formally, I made a rule not to accept even small conclusions without data from several sources and preferably data of several different varieties. . . . I do not use information obtained from just one or even just two or three informants, without giving the reader specific warning of the slim data base. Since I did not draw random samples of either events or persons, I cannot generalize from the frequency of any event or characteristic in my sample to its frequency in the school . . . I intentionally use such phrases as "few teachers said this" or "most students did that. . . ." (p. 13)

There were four tracks (1 being the highest), and students were placed in tracks according to their academic achievement. Not surprisingly, track placement reflected social class, elementary school attended, and race. However, teachers were rotated among tracks to insure everyone was exposed to the best and worst, and there was a great deal of upward and downward mobility on the part of students. For example,

. . . officially, a child's academic achievement in the classroom was the only criterion for his track placement. But since teachers were given wide discretion in judging whether a child's achievement warranted a change in track, some rid themselves of disruptive children by moving them down a track. The lower tracks, therefore, consisted of a mixture of children who were actually slow to learn, children who were capable but did not try, and children who were able but also rebellious, disruptive, and spotty in their academic effort. (p. 70)

Metz (1978) goes well beyond establishing that social class and tracking are linked, however, she studies the process whereby teachers and students collaborate, to create distinctly different educational climates in the different tracks.

> High track students wanted "liberal" teachers, who would provide opportunities for discussion where students could express themselves. When a teacher simply expected the students to incorporate the contents of a textbook, to "memorize" as some of them complained, these students could become angry and withdrawn . . . they characterized these teachers they liked least and learned least from as those who taught 'straight from the book,' who would not allow students to ask questions on related topics not included in the lesson, and who would not allow them to discuss their own understandings of the matter (p. 75). [They] . . . were quite capable of carrying on debates with teachers who disagreed with them about educational goals (p. 76). [They] . . . were emphatic in their belief that, as students, or as eighth graders, they were not *qualitatively* different from teachers." (p. 78)

> [Their] . . . parents, were, for the most part, of higher status than the teachers. At the least, they were not awed by teachers, and they communicated their feelings to their children. At the most, they questioned the teachers' capacities and judgment, and did not hesitate to believe that their child might be right and a teacher wrong . . . parents had accustomed their children to asking for explanation and justification when adults asked them to do something they did not want to do. (p. 80)

On the other hand, lower track students,

> . . . took the school as they found it, and did not question the administrators' and teachers' right to define what they should learn, how they should learn it, or how they should behave. However, . . . they frequently failed or refused to cooperate in the activities the definitions implied. They did not question the school's proper character, but they held themselves apart from it . . . When asked in their interviews which teachers they liked best or least, these students preferred teachers who were not "mean" or "always hollering" at you, who treated everyone alike (did not play favorites), who made accusations of misdeeds only when justified, and who explained the material so the student could understand it. Unlike the students in the top tracks, these students considered adults to be people really very different from themselves. (pp. 81–2)

> It is important to note that while this passive and alienated attitude was clearly linked with the racial and socioeconomic backgrounds of these students, . . . it was not shared by all children from these backgrounds. Some black children were in upper track classes. Other less sophisticated black children, many from the poorer parts of the city, did their academic work well enough to qualify for Track Two, some moving out of lower tracks as they caught on to required skills and behavior. And they were sufficiently diligent and cooperative to remain

in Track Two, or to move up. But for those who remained in the lower tracks, not only the content of the curriculum in fields like English, social studies, and the arts, but also the full range of skills to be learned seemed alien and of little use. (pp. 83–4)

Not surprisingly, "In the daily rhythm of classes, the lower track groups were far more restless, and subject to collective activity, distracting from the lesson at hand, than the top track ones were. . . . It was harder for the teacher to simply get their attention" (p. 96). And, the teachers respond in kind, a black teacher acknowledges ". . . as far as discipline is concerned. You have to yell and scream and hit them over the head and kiss them" (p. 97). This from a social studies teacher:

> I think that maybe the clue would be in the way I conduct a class. Groups One and Two . . . I try to conduct as oral discussions, interaction with students, you know, "express your own idea." And everybody, I hope, if they want to, has a chance to talk. Because they seem to be able to handle it without getting too far out of line. I think that's really important in social sciences that people be able to talk and discuss things. But in Threes and Fours, I find it very difficult to do it that way. I use a worksheet and work around this, and this keeps the kids more in control. I don't use the discussion methods a lot because it seems to really get out of hand then. A little bit at a time I do, and then I'll cut if off and we'll do the worksheet. (p. 102)

and an English teacher:

> I have found, of course, that dictionary work with Threes, particularly, has been successful. They love it. They like to be busy. Isn't that strange? They like to be able to sit down, open a book, and work on something. . . . Discussion— they have not been able to handle too well. (Hesitation) Because it's still, "Let's outshout one another," I tried discussions with them and found them unsuccessful. I keep trying a little of it but cutting it down, making it pretty short, to get kids to express their ideas. But never anything more than five minutes, because they go *completely* up and they won't relate to the subject material at all. They will relate particularly on a personal basis. And, of course, this is part of the difficulty anyway. What I did in connection with such and such a thing, or what my mother did, or my girlfriend or boyfriend, or something of this nature. They cannot state a situation where they are not directly involved. (p. 102)

Metz's (1978) findings regarding differences in the nature of instruction in the various tracks are supported in large-scale observational studies of secondary schools (Goodlad 1984). One of the investigators (Oakes 1986) reports "Students in high track classes were exposed to 'high status' content, literature, expository, and thematic writing, library research, and mathematical ideas. Students in low track classes were not expected to learn these topics and skills. They rarely, if ever, encountered them. They worked in workbooks and kits, and practiced language mechanics and computation" (p. 63). A review of these and other studies on tracking appeared recently (Gamoran & Berends 1987). The authors note that qualitative studies consistently find differences in the way instruction is organized in different tracks, however, quantitative analyses suggest that the actual effects of tracking on achievement may be minimal. One ". . . possible explanation for weak and inconsistent tracking effects is that although instruction varies between tracks and ability levels, the instructional differences may actually be small when compared to the overall similarity of instruction at all levels" (p. 425). Indeed, as we shall see in Chapter 5, Linda McNeil (1986) finds a watered down, unchallenging curriculum is pervasive at all levels in contemporary high schools. A second reason for the lack of effects, overall, is that in parochial schools students in all tracks make substantial gains in achievement (see Hoffer, Greely, and Coleman 1985). As Gamoran and Berends (1987) point out, these schools ". . . make greater academic demands of students, especially of students in noncollege programs" (p. 427). So, depending on the school, lower track students may make greater achievement gains than high track students. Finally, and most importantly, most quantitative studies control for initial achievement levels, so tracking has to exert an influence over and above the influence of the student's knowledge base, his/her commitment to school, parental influence, and so on. The peer group is also a factor. Hollingshead ([1949]1975) discovered student cliques do not cut across tracks to any appreciable degree. Indeed, as we have seen in the last chapter, the influence of the student culture in high school may be so pervasive, that it can create a "track-like" experience for students, even in the absence of a formal tracking system (e.g., MacLeod 1987).

We turn now to a major divide in the sociology of education landscape. To this point, the unit of analysis or object of focus was the school or several schools. Although we have seen researchers peering inside the black box, their middle range focus has allowed them to see the results of stratification, but not to really capture the processes that operate to create stratification in the school. In the research to be reviewed in the remainder of the chapter, investigators have zoomed in on the single classroom, or, even more narrowly, on testing, tutoring, and counseling sessions involving only two individuals. Where earlier we saw authors using snippets of interviews to illustrate a particular point, in the work that follows, natural language samples as well as interview transcripts will be the subject of intense analysis.

ETHNOMETHODOLOGY AND THE STUDY OF ROUTINE ACTIONS

Ethnomethodology[10] has a somewhat similar history to *ethnoscience* (Leiter 1980; see also page 60). It developed in California as a reaction against the mainstream of the discipline of sociology: "Early ethnomethodologists claimed that sociologists, in their search for regularities in social structures, had ignored participants' structuring activities . . ." (Mehan 1978: p. 60). Ethnomethodology was originated by Harold Garfinkel (1967) to describe the ethnographic study of the methods people use to accomplish everyday tasks. Garfinkel's earliest studies were concerned with how juries reached verdicts, and how medical decisions were made: ". . . my coworkers and I undertook to analyze the experience of the UCLA outpatient clinic, in order to answer the question 'By what criteria are its applicants selected for treatment?' " (p. 18)

As Mehan (1978) notes: ". . . one of Garfinkel's seminal contributions was to . . . exhort . . . researchers to find in the interaction between people, not in their subjective states, the processes that assembled the concerted activities of everyday life" (p. 60). What Garfinkel and his followers discovered is that, contrary to the Aristotelian view of man and society, there are few hard and fast rules, people do a great deal of "ad hocing." And, so-called objective criteria, like test scores and grades, are always subject to interpretation, they are social accomplishments. Furthermore, "Ethnomethodologists stress that the social world is made up of shared meanings and shared viewpoints. So much so, that if actors changed places they would quite likely see the world in much the same way, and that our knowledge of the world is generated through interpretations" (Hitchcock and Hughes 1989,158).

I now want to provide a brief illustration of ethnomethodology. This is George Payne's (1982) analysis of how a secondary history teacher "puts down" a late comer. First, a transcript of the episode:

118. T: . . . Ethelwolf—father, himself a famous warrior, he himself fought a lot of the Danish invaders now where have you been?
119. P: Sir ma bags broke ink (went) all over me books so I (had to dry them all out).
120. T: Oh and did it have to be in my lesson—um.
121. P: Don't know sir (   )
122. T: Go on sit down—expect you've nowt—to do—show a lot of er—answering a lot of the questions now—you've got a lo—you've go—five minutes work to catch up on haven't you—what were we talkin about last week.—um/
(2.0)   [*General background noises*]
123. P: Er—Alfred the Great.
124. T: No that's what we're (just goin to) talk about now.
125. P: (   )
126. T: The Vikings lad the Vikings—an you'd better concentrate (pp. 90–91).

Then, excerpts from the analysis, showing the "interpretive work" of the teacher in explicating and reaffirming the power relations inherent in the classroom.

. . . although the late arrival has gone to some trouble in producing his response, the teacher does not readily accept his attempt to exonerate himself. . . .

T: Oh and did it have to be in my lesson—um.

In this utterance, the teacher does not, in any way, indicate that the pupil's absence has been for a worthy cause. Rather, he responds to the pupil's effort to excuse himself with a measure of sarcasm, as he 'puts him on the spot' in front of the class by asking him a second question, which is practically unanswerable. . . . The teacher is making it clear to the pupil and to the class—who are an audience to the interaction—that pupils should not come late to lessons. (pp. 94–5)

If Garfinkel (1967) invented ethnomethodology, Aaron Cicourel and his students deserve credit for applying it in education. But in considering their contribution, we immediately encounter a serious difficulty in trying to make sense of it all. We have almost the opposite problem of the overuse of the term ethnography to describe studies that bear little relation one to another. Here, the problem is that a great many studies, which I see as sharing a common concern for the description and analysis of reoccurring social situations, are identified by a great variety of different labels. Cicourel (1974), while freely acknowledging his intellectual debt to Garfinkel, refers to his work as cognitive sociology, to show a parallel perhaps with cognitive anthropology (see page 60). Bud Mehan, Cicourel's student, close colleague, and co-author of the definitive text on ethnomethodology (Mehan and Wood 1975), calls his own work constitutive ethnography. Among the scholars Mehan (1978) cites as sharing his view of methodology is Fred Erickson (1982a), who refers to his own work as micro-ethnography. Others (e.g., Cazden 1988) refer to this tradition as sociolinguistics. Finally, in Jacob's (1987) article on traditions, she uses ethnography of communication and symbolic interaction to refer to work which I argue shares a single tradition. To be sure, some of these terminological differences do reflect important epistemological and/or methodological differences. But, I hope to show that the similarities outweigh the differences and that, in time, scholars will see the need to unite under a common banner, and "ethnomethodology" would get my vote.

HOW EDUCATORS MAKE PLACEMENT DECISIONS: GRADES AND TEST SCORES

Cicourel and Kitsuse's (1963) *The Educational Decision Makers* is widely cited as a classic in the field, and provides a bridge between the community oriented research of Hollingshead and others, and the more narrowly focussed studies of Mehan and his colleagues. Done in 1958, the study was designed as an antidote to quantitative studies that sought to relate collections of "background variables" to the decision to attend or not attend college. Working in Lakeshore, a large high school serving predominantly white, middle-class Evanston, Illinois, it was their ". . . wish to investigate how the *routine decisions* of the guidance and counseling personnel within the high school are related to the college/non-college decisions and, by implication, to the occupational choices made by students" (p. 6 italics added). They provide a virtual definition of the "unstructured" interview.

In questioning parents concerning their knowledge of college requirements, therefore, it is important that the questions do not present the respondents with the very knowledge that is being investigated. If parents were presented with forced choices between specific items about college requirements (e.g., four years of English, two years of a foreign language, two years of mathematics, etc.), the form of the questions would obscure the common-sense character of parental responses regarding entrance requirements. The social distribution of knowledge documented by such a method would attribute to parents a greater knowledge and awareness of the importance of the organizational processes of the high school for college admission than may in fact be the case. We asked parents the following question: "What sorts of requirements does he(she) have to meet for college entrance?" (pp. 37–8)

And, while they did not find such knowledge to be particularly thorough (in contrast to Baker and Stevenson 1986), they did note that: "Among the middle and upper social classes, parents routinely expect their children to go to college, and their children consistently reflect such expectations . . . independent of whether the students tested capability is high or low, and irrespective of his prior school performance as recorded in his grades" (p. 35).

While Cicourel and Kitsuse (1963) relied primarily on interviews, most subsequent studies have used more direct observation. Cicourel and his students (Cicourel et al. 1973) undertook a series of studies of educational testing and the ensuing placement decisions, utilizing videotape recordings and interviews, to capture with fidelity the "methods" people used in "constructing" test scores and grade placements, in order to demonstrate that these ". . . are institutional facts and not brute facts" (Mehan, Hertwig, and Meihls 1986,85). Mehan (1978) videotaped five sessions, where a psychologist administered the Wechsler Intelligence Scale for Children (WISC). On 21 of 65 questions the tester deviated from standard procedure. He ". . . either repeated the question or prompted the student with cues: . . ." (p. 52). Analysis showed that ". . . a student's score could increase as much as 27 percent as a result of the tester's cueing" (p. 53). "The testers' puppeteering practices contribute to the assembly of student answers . . . Testers may emphasize key words, compliment correct replies, or cut off students after they have completed an answer . . . [and] these . . . are not the result of sloppy test administration, but are inevitable aspects of the social interaction that comprises testing encounters" (p. 55).

Roth (1973) also focused on intelligence testing, but his attention was drawn to the way the tester adapted to the behavior of the testees. The testees were African-American children, who had not yet learned the "proper" way to behave in such situations: "Pe was as difficult to work with in the testing situation as An was. He was playful and talkative, though much less noisy than An, and never defiant. The main trouble with Pe was how easily he reached the verge of tears . . . the tester couldn't probe as deeply as she wanted, for fear Pe would break down" (p. 205). Roth observes "It is unreasonable to expect that a tester or teacher can maintain a strictly standardized procedure, while probing children's unstandardized background knowledge, and while managing the children's feelings" (p. 215).

Leiter (1976), as part of the same project, interviewed kindergarten teachers as to their reasons for placing students in first or "junior first" grade. Among the background information teachers used, was information on the child's language. An Hispanic girl got a better evaluation than her placement test score warranted: "Now on the phonemes, the auditory part, she was low, but a lot of this could have to do with language, you know" (p. 61). A black child, with low scores, was given a higher placement because ". . . the mother wants badly for her children to achieve" (p. 62), indicating the importance of perceived family background. Finally, teachers take into account emotional handicaps, as with an immature, inattentive child: ". . . he answered the questions by himself. I didn't answer them for him, but I had to sit there and point my finger just to keep his attention on the right line, and to make sure he was in the right place" (p. 63).

SPECIAL EDUCATION PLACEMENT DECISIONS

Mary Lee Smith (1982) undertook a study of the evaluation and labelling of elementary students as "learning disabled." She spent three months negotiating access to Belleview, a suburban district near Denver, then "Six months were spent full time in direct observations of staffing conferences, meetings, and other relevant interactions, in-depth interviews with . . . [all participants] . . . and analysis of documents, such as files of pupils identified as learning disabled. Two months were spent analyzing the data and writing the preliminary report for the district" (p. 230).

An ethnomethodological study allows one to compare informal, socially-constructed practices with the formal procedures and criteria that are to be followed. Prior to the enactment of PL 94-142 in 1975, the determination of assignment to special education was subject to the whim of the principal. "The laws were intended to make the decision making process—the "staffing" process—as it is called, standard throughout the nation. They have taken the powers of decision out of the hands of teachers and principals, and turned these powers over to staffing committees . . . " (p. 3).

It is not clear how many "staffing" meetings Smith attended all together, but she presents three cases in some detail, one of which, "John," we have already encountered. The staffing draws on a large (6–18, average 10) cast of characters—the teacher, nurse, special education supervisor, the principal, speech therapist, psychologist, and parents. Not all of the people are present at every meeting, and no one role holder dominated consistently, although, "The wishes of the parents were powerful, and only resisted when the data and wishes of the staff were extreme in the opposite direction" (p. 100). Meetings lasted about 90-minutes, longer when parents were present (75 percent of the time), as more "explaining" was necessary, and circumlocution was used ". . . so that feelings could be spared" (p. 96).

Smith makes clear that the underlying premises of PL 94-142, indeed the premises underlying the entire field of special education, are faulty,[11] and that this is a major reason for the protracted meetings and complex negotiations: "It was almost possible to see alliances building, as one person's eyes sought those of another. There seemed to be a need for each side, not just to present data, but to build a case and sell the others on it" (p. 24).

She points out that: "The handicap of learning disability has always been controversial, and difficult to define. . . . Diagnosing a learning disability always requires an inference, a leap, based on several separate characteristics [however] these same characteristics are shared by many normal children" (p. 5).[12] Furthermore, the "medical" model that serves as a foundation for special education ". . . the concept of handicap becomes equivalent, sociologically speaking, with that of disease" (Mehan et al. 1986,85) means that "The clinicians have a vocabulary and implicit definitions about learning disabilities that invariably locate the problem in the child . . ." (p. 25).

As a consequence of this lack of fit between the rational, medical model PL 94-142 imposed on special education and the complex lived reality of teachers, students, and their families, less than half of those designated learning disabled actually meet the official criteria. Instead, there was an "implicit definition," namely

> . . . children [who] needed more help than a teacher could give and were behind their peers [however] . . . what constituted the need for help was variable from school to school. . . . For the many children identified, but not matching the official definition, a variety of ploys were used to hold to the local implicit definitions and finesse the official one. Outside experts were brought in to attest to the child's need for services. Data were twisted, in some cases, using age norms instead of grade norms to "establish" a significant discrepancy. (pp. 232–3)

Put differently, Smith (like Cicourel and Kitsuse 1963) found that "data" like test scores and grades, far from being the determining factor, were used selectively to justify a decision that had been reached on other grounds. Furthermore, the federal dollars allocated to the district to pay for these special education services were fixed, so there was an optimal number of cases that could be handled and ". . . definitions of learning disabilities seemed to be loosened or tightened to maintain this steady state" (p. 100).

Smith's (1982) initial report was filed away and forgotten (". . . a fate common to many evaluation reports . . ." p. 234), but it found its way into the hands of a state legislator who successfully pushed for a ". . . statewide evaluation of identification practices" (p. 234). Smith (1982) conducted this study as well, which included a total of 790 cases, 10 of which were examined in-depth. She was, essentially, able to replicate her initial study:

> . . . the existing differences between Belleview and the rest of Colorado are those of degree rather than kind. . . . One can see the same ritualistic procedures operating, the same tests of dubious validity used, the same implicit personal definitions overriding the legal and professional ones, the same 'mistakes' made in identification, the same desire to help children rather than match children to definitions, the same tendency to expand the roles until resources are exhausted, the same growing bureaucracy. (pp. 216–7)

Mehan and his associates replicate and extend the study of Belleview in their analysis of the entire cohort of 157 students referred for (special education) evaluation, and placement in one school year in a working class district in Southern California. Like Smith (1982), Mehan, Hertwick, and Meihls (1986) find that:

> Disability, we conclude, exists neither in the head of educators nor in the behavior of students. It is, instead, a function of the interaction between educators' categories, institutional machinery, and students' conduct. That is, designations like "disability" and "handicap" do not exist apart from the institutional practices and cultural-meaning systems that generate and nurture them. (p. 164)

They also describe the formal, impossible to fulfill, procedures mandated by PL 94-142, and the informal practices the district employed to remain "in compliance." For example, they were unable to process referrals within the government's mandated time frame, so they "stopped the clock." ". . . the clock did not start until the case had actually been heard by the committee" (p. 64). The main reason the process dragged on is because the law requires the presence of a number of designated individuals at SAT (School Advisory Team) and E&P (Evaluation and Placement) committee meetings, making them extremely difficult to schedule. Teachers were reluctant to be gone from their classrooms, or to prolong the school day by coming early or leaving later. Hence, ". . . they just tried to get meetings over with—an attitude that is not conducive to careful and reasoned consideration of complicated referral cases" (p. 59).

In addition to studying the entire process, Mehan's team conducted a fine-grained analysis of three points in the decision making process, the initial referral by the teacher, the testing by the psychologist, and the E&P meetings. In the case of referrals, they videotaped 55 referred children in their classrooms, and asked the 27 teachers to review the videotapes. These viewing sessions were conducted as follows.

> While they viewed the videotaped classroom event, the teachers were first asked for general information about their classrooms, then to recount the reasons they referred each student, and finally to comment upon the student's behavior on the videotape. They were invited to "stop the machine whenever something interesting that you want to report on appears on the tape." Teachers were also given the following specific instructions for asking the interviewer to stop the tape: (1) "when the child who was referred is doing something about which you would like to comment"; (2) "when you or the children, other than the referred, are doing something about which you would like to comment"; (3) "when you see a comparison between behavior and/or ability of the child referred and other members in the group"; (4) "when you see some of the behavior on the tape that could have caused you to refer the child." In our analysis, we shall distinguish the stated "interview reasons" from the "official reasons" for referrals that we obtained from the students' school records . . . teachers' identification of referral behavior during viewing sessions were juxtaposed to an independent analysis of taped classroom events. . . . (pp. 72–3)

The "reasons" for referral did not completely correspond to the "reasons" listed on the referral form. Also, there is a blurring of the distinction between a referral category and examples of behaviors that fit the category. This is borne out by the fact that the behaviors, which teachers noted as being linked to referrals, were not noted when they were displayed by children who had not been referred. "Because the teacher is attending to organized configurations, and not discrete elements, a piece of behavior is not the same when it is conducted by different people in different contexts" (Mehan, Hertwick, Coombs, and Flynn 1982,313).

The team also videotaped 20 testing sessions. It was immediately apparent that the tests were not administered according to the manual or in a standardized manner. Aside from the referral and the test results, other issues came into play in E&P meetings. Again, as in Belleview, there was an optimal number of children that the system could handle so, early in the year, ". . . teachers reported to us that they received strong recommendation to find more children in order to meet the quota" (p. 61), while, later in the year, they were discouraged from making referrals. However, unlike Belleview, or perhaps because they were able, with the aid of videotape records, to make more careful analyses, they did find evidence of an authority hierarchy in the E&P meeting. High status participants—psychologist, nurse—have technical expertise and "present" their information, whereas low-status participants—teacher, mother ". . . had information *elicited* from them" (p. 126). What is especially interesting, is the apparently more passive role of parents, as contrasted with Belleview. ("This is a school district with sophisticated parents who know their rights and demand them." [Smith 1982,9]) Taking the Mehan et al. and Smith studies together we can, again, see the influence of social class and parental involvement in children's educational careers.

What the Mehan et al. (1986) study does not show is any evidence of systematic bias or prejudice, such that children are selected for special education (about 2/3 of those referred are actually placed) on the basis of race, ethnicity, or social class. On the contrary, they found that Mexican-American children, who exhibited referral behaviors, were not referred because they were in bilingual education classes and their teachers felt they could better deal with the students' problems in the regular classroom. Indeed, as Palincsar (1986) points out in her review of *Handicapping the Handicapped,* "the serious indictment implicit in the title is never actually supported in the book" (p. 192). In other words, while the special education system undoubtedly does contribute to stratification within the schools, it is not clear, from this study, whether it alleviates or exacerbates stratification in the society at large. However, as Lareau (1989) points out ". . . with a few dramatic exceptions, research has found little evidence that teachers apply standards unequally" (p. 104).

PARTICIPATION STRUCTURES IN THE CLASSROOM

While academic achievement, or underachievement, does entail quite open labeling of children with self-evident consequences for their status, classrooms provide other, less obvious opportunities to rank students vis-a-vis one another. An earlier, ground-breaking study by Mehan (1979) explored something called *participation structure* (cf. Phillips 1972). In this book he makes a case for the use of video and audio tape recording in qualitative research. As we will soon see, the fine-grained analysis that a videotape record affords is absolutely essential in studying something as subtle as participation structure.[13]

> Field studies of the school have a number of difficulties. As is so often the case, the strengths of an enterprise are also its weaknesses. First, conventional field reports tend to have an anecdotal quality. Research reports include a few exemplary instances of the behavior that the researcher has culled from field notes. Second, these researchers seldom provide their criteria or ground for including certain instances and not others. As a result, it is difficult to determine the typicality and representativeness of instances and findings generated from them. Third, research reports presented in tabular or summary form do not preserve the materials upon which the analysis was conducted. As the researcher abstracts data from raw materials to produce summarized findings, the original form of the materials is lost. Therefore, it is impossible to entertain alternative interpretations of the same materials.
>
> Audiovisual equipment has been employed as a data gathering device in order to overcome some of these shortcomings in conventional field studies. . . . Videotape and film are helpful in field research because they preserve research materials in close to their original form. . . . [they] also serve as an extrasomatic "memory," that allows researchers to examine materials extensively and repeatedly. Furthermore, basic materials can be presented, along with an analysis to document conclusions, and to allow alternative interpretations. . . . (pp. 15–16)

Mehan (1979) studied an ungraded primary classroom in a school serving a poor African- and Mexican-American neighborhood in San Diego. He and his team ". . . videotaped the first hour of school every day for the first week of school, and one hour a day approximately every third week until April" (p. 25). They had a total of 13 hours of tape to work with, not all of it usable because much student talk was lost, but they ended up with a corpus of six complete lessons. Their general focus was on the ". . . socialization of students into the academic and normative demands of the classroom" (p. 26). However, Mehan is particularly interested in *social competence* ("the skills and abilities that people must employ to be effective as members of a particular community can be called their social 'competence'" (1978,48). As he points out:

> Success in educational settings has often been gauged entirely in terms of academic knowledge, while social behavior has been assigned residual status. I will show that participation in classroom lessons involves the integration of academic knowledge and social or interactional skills . . . since we find inter-actional competence to be a necessary companion to academic knowledge in classroom participation, it is important to know whether students give evidence of learning the skills necessary for interaction through time as well (p. 34).

Mehan's (1979) analysis reveals that virtually all teacher and student talk during lessons fall into three categories: (I) initiation (usually the teacher), (R) reply (the student), (E) evaluation (usually the teacher). Figure 3.1 shows a schematic diagram of one common IRE pattern.

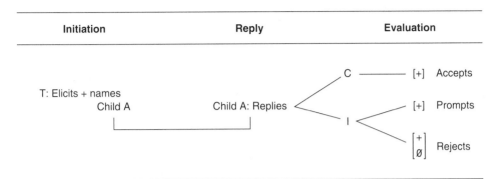

Key: C = correct reply; I = Incorrect reply; Ø = no evaluation   (p.87)

FIGURE 3.1   The initiation/reply/evaluation sequence
SOURCE: Mehan, H. (1979). *Learning lessons.* Cambridge, MA: Harvard University Press, p. 87.
Reprinted by permission.

Table 3.1 shows the way in which the audio portion of the videotape is segmented for analysis. It illustrates a case where Audrey has successfully participated:

> When the teacher initiates action, she allocates the floor, the students reply,
> and the teacher takes the floor back again as she evaluates the reply (p. 140).
> [she] . . . provides information to the students, elicits information from them,
> and directs their actions. Certain replies are called for and others are denied
> by these initiation acts. Effective participation in classroom lessons involves

TABLE 3.1   Sample IRE

Initiation	Reply	Evaluation
3:41		
T: What else, what else, Edward, what do you think we could put here that starts with an *m?*		C: (raises hand)
3:42		
T: Somebody in your family, Edward?	E: (shrugs shoulders no)	
3:43		
T: All right, Jerome (raises hand)	A: I know, I know	
3:44		
T: What?	A: Man	T: Man, good for you, Audrey, that is a good one for here. Very good.

SOURCE: Mehan, H. (1979). *Learning lessons.* Cambridge, MA: Harvard University Press, pp. 58–59. Reprinted
by permission.

providing the kind of reply that is consistent with the teacher's initiation . . . [and it] involves distinguishing between directive, informative, and elicitation speech acts as providing the proper replies. . . . (pp. 134–5)

Of course the participation structure also allows for social *incompetence,* such as calling out answers without raising one's hand, being called on and not having a response, raising one's hand to provide a response before a response has been called for, and so on. And, as Mehan notes ". . . there is not a one-to-one correspondence between everyday conversation and classroom conversation . . ." (p. 196).[14] Furthermore, "Because classroom procedures are not stated in so many words, students must infer the appropriate ways to engage in classroom discussion from contextually provided information" (p. 163).

> There are practical consequences for students who misinterpret these subtle cues. If a student replies when a bid is expected, that student will be sanctioned. A history of such inappropriate behavior can lead the teacher to treat the student negatively. If a student bids when a reply is possible, that student loses an opportunity to express knowledge. A history of lost opportunities can lead the teacher to believe a student is inattentive, unexpressive, and the like. (p. 168)

However, in this classroom the teacher seems to be adept at socializing children so they learn the proper rules for participation. For example, in the six lessons there were no examples of negative evaluations, the teacher provided either a positive evaluation or no evaluation at all. The transcripts are coded using variables like "accepts," "prompts," "ignores," and so on. Frequencies are tallied, allowing Mehan and his team to show that while 70% of student initiatives in early fall were ignored, suggesting that they were inappropriate, by mid-January the figure drops to 30%. Unfortunately, Mehan (1979) does not indicate whether this improvement in social competence was true for all students. Again, while we can see that the participation structure has the potential to contribute to stratification, there is no evidence presented to affirm that it actually does so.[15]

Another study of participation structure (Morine-Dershimer 1983, 1985) more directly addresses the stratification issue. Methodologically, this work, conducted in 1978–79[16] is quite similar to the study just described. Morine-Dershimer video-taped six classrooms (grades 2–4) in an urban, ethnically mixed, working-class school in the San Francisco Bay area. Twelve minutes (beginning, middle, end) of each of 36 language arts lessons were taped. Morine-Dershimer also interviewed a sample of the children she had videotaped. The results indicated that, by the third grade, students not only know and can follow (but they may choose not to, see Hanna 1988) participation rules, but can articulate them as well.

> INTERVIEWER: How are kids expected to talk in your classroom? When do they talk and what kinds of things do they say?
>
> MANUEL: We're supposed to talk properly—the right way. Whoever says bad words, they're gonna get their mouth washed out with soap.
>
> INTERVIEWER: What else can you tell me about how kids are expected to talk in your room?

MANUEL: You're supposed to raise your hand in the classroom when you're gonna say something.

INTERVIEWER: Anything else?

MANUEL: You should not shout out. (Morine-Dershimer 1985,211)

She treated participation rate as a dependent variable and looked at how it was effected by several independent variables, including the students' reading achievement scores at the beginning of the year, which was the only variable that seemed to effect participation. Anglo children did participate more, but they also had higher reading scores. Mexican American children had lower scores, but

Their evident deficit in entering reading achievement was not reinforced by concomitant deficits in status with teacher (teacher expectations) or participation in class discussions, and they did not fall significantly further behind in reading achievement as the school year progressed. . . . What they . . . demonstrate is that ethnic (cultural) difference, in and of itself, does not (need not) lead automatically to school failure. (p. 166)

Another of the numerous analyses Morine-Dershimer (1983) undertook using her videotaped records was to compare participation structures in classrooms reflecting three different models of instruction. Mrs. Estes was one of the weakest teachers in the school in terms of her classes' reading achievement gains during the year. She used a "textbook" based instructional strategy. Mrs. Flood used an experience-based approach: ". . . almost invariably her lessons involved discussion of pupils' actual experiences, and these experiences were related to the material presented in the textbook" (p. 652). Mrs. Brown used a "models-based" approach to instruction, in which pupils were encouraged to think critically and creatively about the lesson. Furthermore, Mrs. Estes used very little praise compared to the others. Mrs. Brown used praise in a discriminating manner, helping to more sharply define the conditions for successful participation.

In Mrs. Estes' room, where participation was the task, the high status group (high participation) was composed of an almost random assortment of pupils. Practically anyone who chose to participate could become high in participation status. In Mrs. Flood's and Mrs. Brown's classrooms, however, the basic classroom tasks were cognitive, and . . . to be high in participation status in these classrooms, one had to have some academic standing. (p. 655)

As a corollary, in Flood's and Brown's classrooms, all students attended to and learned from high participation students. This was not true in Mrs. Estes' room.

PARTICIPATION AND READING

Reading groups are to elementary schools what tracks are in the high school, an instructional "adaptation" to differing levels of skill and interest that also confers social status. As such, interaction in the reading group has attracted a great deal of attention from those interested in stratification (McDermott 1976; Piestrup 1973). A study (Eder 1982) closely paralleling the two just reported, compared participation by students in four ability-linked reading groups in a single first-grade classroom. This time four lessons in each group were videotaped at intervals during the year. These data showed that the teacher used a much stricter regimen in the high-ability group. ". . . When students in the high group talked or read during another students turn, they were often reprimanded . . . when students spoke out of turn in the low group, however, the teacher did not reprimand their interruptions, and often acknowledged them" (p. 256). Eder argues that "If teachers perceive academic tasks as being more difficult for low group members, it is not surprising that they allow more turn-taking violations" (p. 262). However, a consequence of this was that while interruptions declined drastically from fall to spring in the high group, they stayed constant in the low group. Hence, children in the low groups will fail to learn "proper" participation rules and will appear "less competent."

James Collins (1988) analyzed 16 lessons (part of a larger corpus). Five were drawn from the high, and 11 from the low reading group in a first grade class-room. His report indicates just how versatile videotape is in terms of affording the opportunity to conduct multiple analyses on the same data base. Collins first shows how "type of instructional activity" varies with reading group placement (Table 3.2).

These types are widely recognized (e.g., emic) categories of reading instruction. The table indicates that the low group is given primarily low-level, decontextualized "skills" instruction, whereas the high group gets more opportunity to interact with real text (cf. Edelsky and Draper 1989). ". . . the different instructional emphases were evident in the first weeks of school, and continued throughout the year" (p. 315). Collins then proceeds to the next level of analysis.

> The texts were transcribed with a detailed prosodic notation, which enabled us to analyze how different readers divided the text into 'information units' . . . the staccato quality was more noticeable with low group readers. They read with pauses between words . . . high-group readers, on the other hand, were more likely to have some of the intonational characteristics of a fluent, adult reading

TABLE 3.2 Instructional Activity in Two Reading Groups

	High Group		Low Group	
	Minutes	Percentage of Total Time	Minutes	Percentage of Total Time
Dictation	0	0	24.5	16
Sound-word identification	10.5	17	48.5	31
Sentence completion	8.0	13	24.5	16
Passage reading	29.5	49	49.0	31
Comprehension questions	13.5	21	9.0	6

SOURCE: Collins, J. (1988). Language and class in minority education. *Anthropology and Education Quarterly, 19,* p. 315. Reprinted by permission.

aloud . . . There were other differences, including more use of Black English in the low group, who were less likely to use falling intonation and sentence boundaries. These tendencies in children tended to be exacerbated by the teachers . . . [who] focus on surface features of reading, on 'how it sounds' rather than 'what it means'."

With the low group, corrections concentrated on low-level linguistic instruction about phoneme-grapheme correspondences [and "correct pronounciation"]. With the high group . . . information about clauses, sentences, and textual inferences were also brought into play. (pp. 316–17)

The following illustrates the way in which the audio portion of the tape is transcribed to reflect speech patterns.

1. C: And then . . . he . . .   ⌐ threw his
2. T: sound it out . . . threw: ⌐
3. C: bu-boat . . . into the . . .   ⌐ gahbage can
4. T: guh ⌐
5.   garbage. Say garbage.
6. C: gahbage.
7. T: Don't say gahbage, look at me, say ga:r:bage, gar:, say it. Everybody say it (p. 317).

It also illustrates the way well-intentioned teachers, imbued with a bottom-up view of reading acquisition, keep dragging poorer readers down to lower levels by focusing their attention on sound-letter correspondence and correct pronunciation, thereby denying them the scaffolding effects of story, picture, and syntactic cues to aid decoding. Far from being enabling, bottom-up instruction becomes crippling. Collins suggests that children come to school with varying levels of reading "readiness," but also ". . . prior tendencies to focus on reading as an exercise in meaning extraction or an exercise in correct utterance" (p. 320).

Indeed this is precisely what my colleagues and I are finding with parent-child interaction in early reading (Lancy, Draper, and Boyce 1989). We videotaped 32 parents (in two cases, grandparents) reading to their children and listening as their children read to them for thirty-minute episodes that were designed to simulate or reconstruct what happens at home during "bedtime stories" (Heath 1982). Like Collins, we "passed through" the data several times, each time seeking a more fine-grained view. We found parents of early fluent readers acting much like the teacher in the high reading group. They emphasize context, meaning, pictures; they enhance fluency by assisting children with words they hesitate over, making it fun and not a chore. We called their general strategy "expansionist" (Lancy et al. 1989). By contrast, the parents of late non-fluent readers used a "reductionist" strategy, they read straight through the book, and when listening to their children read, they provided little help beyond reminding the child to "sound it out." They reduce fluency by forcing the child to stop and correct minor errors that do not affect meaning. In a second pass through the data, we developed a measure of fluency (Bergin and Lancy 1991, 1992), and we were able to show that, for example, the parents of fluent readers encourage questions, whereas non-fluent readers tend not to ask questions and/or are discouraged from asking questions.

These last studies move the zoom lens in close, to focus on interaction in a dyad, or "face-to-face interaction." Here the videotape comes into its own, so to speak, as one does not so easily lose children's voices as in a classroom setting. One can also capture subtle aspects of communication, body position, gesture, and other forms of nonverbal communication.

FACE-TO-FACE INTERACTION

As indicated in the introduction, many sociologists are concerned with the way in which class, ethnicity, and gender interact with schooling processes to effect the nature of one's education, or career as a student. The studies reviewed to this point have been primarily about class, these last two investigations looked at ethnicity and gender, respectively.

Erickson and Schultz (1982) filmed (using both 16 mm and videotape) a series of counseling sessions at a community college in Michigan. Prior to filming, they spent ". . . 3 or 4 days . . . sitting in the counselor's office doing interviews with students, having lunch with the counselor and asking about his work—the organizational routines involved in it . . ." (p. 55). Within two weeks of filming, they found an opportunity to have counselors and students view the videotapes and identify points that were salient. For example, often as the counselor or student watched their videotape ". . . it was at moments of conversational stumbling that the counselor or student would stop the videotape and say that something had gone wrong in the interview" (p. 104). Even though one of the counselors was female, they decided not to include cross-sex interviews because ". . . intuitively those cross-sex encounters seemed to be qualitatively different from the others. Sex differences seemed to make a difference, but that issue was not part of the original design, so we decided not to include those interviews in the sample of those we analyzed most closely" (p. 54). Instead, they concentrated their analysis on what they came to call co-membership, and its role in structuring the counseling session. To begin with, they looked at ethnicity. Among the 25 sessions, they had at their disposal various combinations of Italian-American, Irish-American, and African-American counselors, with students of the same ethnicity, as well as Polish-American students.

The conversation began by attempts to establish co-membership. While this process was clearly facilitated by similar ethnic background, high co-membership was not synonymous with shared ethnicity. For example, an Italian-American counselor, who was a former coach and used sports as a basis for constructing co-membership, had no luck establishing rapport with an Italian-American student who was overweight and a music major.

In general terms, they find that the counseling interview ". . . is *socially organized* in that actions taken by a speaker and listener together are actions taken on account of what the other is doing . . . and *culturally organized* in that the options people choose in their ways of . . . [communicating] . . . and interpreting . . . are . . . learned from and shared with others . . . cultural conventions . . . provide definitions of what is appropriate and intelligible in communicative action" (p. 7). When things are going smoothly (the norm for high co-membership), there is a great deal of synchrony: ". . . conversational partners are literally completing one another's action in and across time; they are forming behavioral environments for one another in real time" (p. 96). The audio portion of the tapes was subject to a voice print analysis, and the video portion studied for nonverbal and kinesic patterns. These analyses ". . . show clearly . . . extreme points of emphasis—those points marked by both volume and pitch shifts on the verbal channel, and also by simultaneous kinesic shifts in a number of body parts on the nonverbal channel . . ." (p. 92). Also, arhythmia or asynchrony occurs during "uncomfortable moments," which occurred in some of the sessions of low co-membership.

In cases where counselors were able to establish co-membership, they accepted the student's goals and did what they could to facilitate, including suggesting courses the student should take that would transfer to program X at college Y. Therefore, "In the high co-membership context, solidarity with the student and distancing from the official role of counselor was appropriate. . . . [However] in the low-co-membership context, less solidarity with the students was found and the counselor embraced the official role of institutional gate-keeper" (p. 161). Gatekeeper here refers to the counselors imposing the school's goals on the student, urging him to complete course work in the most expeditious manner, to earn an associate degree and graduate.

As Erickson and Schultz (1982) note, gender seemed to play a role as well, in that cross-sex sessions seemed different than same sex sessions. A study in progress, undertaken by Joyce Kinkead and I, looks at the role of gender in the writing conference, a common feature of college composition classes. And, with the provision of a campus Writing Center, students can bring their early draft essays for critical analysis and assistance to a peer (advanced undergraduate or graduate student) tutor. There is wide consensus in the field on general principles that should prevail in the writing conference, which are heavily emphasized in the training the tutors receive (Meyer and Smith 1987). There is an emphasis on letting the writer maintain "ownership" of the paper and control the direction of the conference. Among the more specific injunctions, tutors are taught that they should not write on the paper; not tell the writer how to change it; and to leave the paper positioned in front of the writer. Kinkead believed (and pilot work with four tutors bore out) that these injunctions were more readily taken to heart by female than male tutor trainees, and speculated that stereotypical patterns of conversational style associated with gender (Edelsky 1981) was a major factor. We are now analyzing a corpus of 16 videotaped writing conferences with four male and four female tutors, each with four male and four female student writers. Somewhat to our surprise, we are finding that idiosyncratic or life history (see Chapter 6) and situational factors seem to override the effects of gender. One of the female tutors is older and very conservative—she is very controlling. One of the males, both of whose parents are college English teachers, is a model tutor. And, several tutors, male and female, sit across from the student (in direct violation of the model presented during their training), thus almost necessitating that they take ownership of the paper in order to read it.

This study, like many others reviewed in this chapter that involve the analysis of discourse and kinesic patterns, is characterized by an enormous imbalance between the resources required in collecting the data and those required to analyze them. In this case, obtaining permission and cooperation, gathering up the drafts of student papers, tutor diaries, student evaluations of the writing conference, as well as making the videotapes, was relatively inexpensive in terms of researcher time and dollar costs associated with the purchase of material and employment of technicians and research assistants. Getting the data analyzed requires employing someone to transcribe the tapes; developing and refining a coding scheme which will take a big chunk of the researcher's time (see Speier 1973); and employing assistants to carry out the coding. Two are required, for at least some of the tapes, to establish that the coding scheme is straightforward and unambiguous, e.g., that independent coders see the same thing (see Chapter 4). Finally, these data require analysis via the computer, a two-step process where first the coded material is entered into a data file, and then various statistical manipulations are carried out on the data. This particular project has limped along with the aid of mini-grants and free labor, but its actual cost will easily run to $150,000. The tighter one zooms in the lens to focus on more finely detailed aspects of behavior, the costlier will be the analysis and the longer it will take to complete. Hence, my last word of advice is, don't do it unless you are reasonably certain you'll find something worth writing about. Many topics in the sociology of education can be adequately covered by thorough and meticulous participant observation, without the need of audio or videotape recordings.

PERSPECTIVE-TAKING

One of our themes has been that qualitative research must be viewed as emerging through various distinct "traditions," e.g., anthropology, sociology, biology, history, etc. However, within each of these traditions there is considerable diversity as well. In anthropology, we have seen that the emic-etic distinction[17] is helpful in understanding some of this diversity. In sociology, this dimension also holds true, but it is cross-cut by another dimension, what we might call description vs. interpretation. This second dimension is nicely illustrated by a selection from a group discussion that Willis (1977) had with some of the "lads"— working class youth—after they'd had a chance to read a draft of his report on their adaptation to school and work. They understood and agreed with the descriptive material, it was the "analysis" they couldn't follow.

> BILL: The bits about us were simple enough.
> JOHN: It's the bits in between.

JOEY: Well, I started to read it, I started at the very beginning, y'know I was gonna read as much as I could, then I just packed it in, just started readin' the parts about us, and then little bits in the middle [. . .]

SPANKSY: The parts what you wrote about us, I read those, but I was, y'know, the parts what actually were actually describing the book like I didn't . . . (p. 195).

JOEY: Well, I can tell yer now, straight from the fuckin' knuckle, none of it was med up.

CHRIS: Almost 90 per cent of what I've read in there was, I can actually remember.

PERC: O yeah I can remember a lot of things what I read . . . (p. 196).

BILL: You were staff (at first), you were somebody in between, later on I took you as one of us.

JOEY: [. . .] you were someone to pour our hearts out to. You were obviously as old as most of the staff, . . . they were so far apart from us. They used to sit with us at dinner table but you couldn't really talk to them just 'cos of the fact that they were staff. . . .

JOEY: When you first started asking questions something illegal must have come out and we'd told you things we'd done wrong and we never got any backlash off other members of staff which obviously meant you hadn't told anybody. . . . (p. 198)

From this discussion, Willis is able to confirm that he was not viewed as an authority figure, he was seen as being sympathetic towards the lads' lifestyle and was, therefore, deserving of their trust. His descriptive material is accurate from their point of view (or emic). On the other hand, it is equally clear that his interpretation was externally imposed, as the lads were unable to penetrate his analysis.

Willis (1977) does not conduct a parallel "member check" with teachers and/or figures of authority. He is apparently unconcerned as to the accuracy of his description from their point of view. Furthermore, other critical theorists (Anyon, Suransky, Everhart), while obviously attuned to the students' perspective, give no indication that either their interpretation or description had been subjected to members' scrutiny.

While Beynon (1983) makes much of his previous experience and credentials as a teacher to break-the-ice and increase the candor of his teacher-informants in a London High School, Metz (1978) and Lareau (1989) attempt to distinguish their role from the teacher's. "I also had the status of a sociologist. Here it was more important that I *lacked* certain other statuses. I had never taught in elementary or secondary school, and I was not in the field of education. I also was not (yet) a parent. All of these nonstatuses made me credible as someone who came without an ax to grind" (Metz 1978,257). However, she is careful not to set herself above the teachers. "Since I genuinely needed a good deal of basic information about the functioning of school, I embraced the role of learner. In my observing classes and interviewing teachers, more than one person who was initially wary grew comfortable in undertaking to inform me" (p. 258).

Lareau (1989) draws another distinction. "Educators are trying to change social behavior; sociologists are trying to understand it. As part of this investigation, sociologists have a duty to examine a wide array of social variables, including those that cannot be easily changed through school programs and policies" (p. 13). This view contrasts with that held by those conducting case studies (Chapter 5), who do make common cause with educators.

Metz and Lareau count on their long-lerm residence and interpersonal skills to gradually disarm members and encourage them to speak freely and act naturally. Smith (1982), who did not spend years in the field, uses a more direct approach:

> The reader should know that this study originated as a commissioned study, an evaluation that the school district wanted me to undertake. My consent to doing the study was conditional on their permission to let me do a case study with no hypotheses, and with a role and methods of my own choosing. Thus I was able, for the most part, to avoid the evaluator's usual role as judge. I could promise confidentiality and offered control over the information to any parent, teacher, or clinician who provided it. Thus, any data that might be associated with the individual who gave them were shown to him or her before the report was submitted. In no case was information suppressed as a result of this clearance policy, but having it probably gave me access to data that I would not otherwise have had. (p. 234)

Lareau (1989) also quite explicitly rejects the obligation to cast her interpretation within an emic framework. " . . . I do not want to restrict myself to 'folk explanations.' It does not trouble me if my interpretation of the factors influencing their behavior is different from their interpretation of their lives" (p. 213). Silverman (1985), provides a very neat analysis of the problem, " . . . second-order sociological accounts will have an analytic purpose that may be irrelevant to members' first-order concerns. Instead of relying on direct comparison of these two accounts, the aim is to discover whether members understand and accept the researcher's account" (p. 44).

Mehan's work exemplifies the way in which the researcher can move back and forth between the scientific and the participants' perspectives, slighting neither. In his analysis of classroom lessons, the IRE model is clearly etic in the sense that neither the model nor its constituent parts are supplied by the teacher. Indeed, as Courtney Cazden, a Harvard professor on leave who served as the teacher in this study, observes in her forward to Mehan's (1979) book: "Where the researcher sees order [e.g., IRE], the participant may have felt impending chaos . . ." (p. ix). Mehan (1979) constructs his interpretation with the assistance of participants, the aim being to describe " . . . the social organization of classroom lessons in such a way that the researcher's model captures the participant's actual practice [in a way] . . . the participants themselves already know, but may not have been able to, articulate . . . [revealing] . . . patterns of interaction that surprise participants or scientists" (p. 173).

Sociologists appreciate the value of an emic perspective but, as their goal is to elucidate the workings of society and not just a description of culture, their analyses will, ultimately, reflect a commitment to a universal or an etic framework.

ISSUES FOR THE FUTURE

Mehan (1978), in reviewing his own and other ethnomethodological work says, that these ". . . studies point to stratifying practices within schools that produce differential treatment, and may result in differences in later life (p. 671)." Yet, with the possible exception of the reading group studies, there is little evidence that links stratifying practices in schools to one's later socioeconomic status. That schools are suffused with opportunities to classify, rank, and differentially treat students is clear. But, we simply don't know whether such actions are a help or a hindrance or neither. Again, we turn to Mehan (1979) for suggestions.

> One way to determine the influence of schooling on students would be to study the processes by which educators make decisions about students' careers as they progress through school. . . . While we have substantial evidence from these separate studies of counseling sessions, tests, and classroom events that educational outcomes are structured in interaction, we do not yet have information about the treatment of the same students in these different, though interrelated, school situations. It would be informative to follow the same group of students through the maze of the school, conducting a constitutive analysis of their treatment by teachers, testers, and counselors. By linking the study of these encounters together, we would be better able to make informed statements about what does make a difference in students' lives in schools. (p. 201)

This is an excellent idea but it doesn't go far enough. It is unidirectional, looking only at the way students are "treated." Also, it ignores the very potent role of parents and community. The "maze" must be lengthened to include interactions with family and peers. Compelling as this issue is, the costs of conducting such a study over an extended period of time—careers aren't built in a year—would be nearly prohibitive. We might be able to turn to recent technological innovations to make the task of following students through the maze a little easier. I'm referring to cellular phones and palm corders. The researcher would make periodic phone calls to the student, soliciting a description of the upcoming day's events, current activities, direct the student to make a brief video recording of newsworthy events, and so on.

Could it be that we have been looking at the wrong end of the stick, as far as the effect of stratifying practices in school is concerned? There are hints throughout the literature in this chapter (and in studies reviewed in Chapter 5) that, such practices primarily serve teacher's needs. The entire special education apparatus may function as a safety valve, "bleeding off" students a given teacher can't cope with. Grades, differentiated assignments, reading groups, retention, tracking, etc., may all serve in one way or another as tools to manage the behavior of students. We very much need research which compares across a number of teachers (the Morine-Dershimer 1983 study comes closest), at the same grade level, working with students from similar backgrounds, but who appear to differ in the degree to which they actively sort and label their students.

I anticipate great interest in magnet schools (e.g., Metz 1991), and voucher and other choice systems on the part of sociologists. Given what we have seen here, we could expect such systems to accentuate the influence of parents on schooling practices. We should expect to find that schools that serve children of active, concerned parents will focus their energy on enhancing each child's potential, whereas schools that serve the remainder will fulfill a largely custodial function.

The influence of community on the character of schools might also be fruitfully investigated within a contrasting qualitative research tradition, via personal accounts (Chapter 6). It would be fascinating to interview experienced teachers who have taught in different communities (urban vs suburban) and get them to reflect on how their classrooms differed in the different circumstances.

Finally, the concept of cultural capital suggests a related notion that bears investigation, namely the redistribution of cultural capital. One example of this phenomenon is taken from Lareau (1989). Another project, to be described more fully in Chapter 5, had parent volunteers, who read storybooks to their children at home, come daily to kindergarten classes and read storybooks to pairs of students, including, inevitably, many who were not read to at home (Lancy and Nattiv 1992). These examples only suggest what may be a widespread and under-studied phenomenon.

DECODING THE COLONY

If anthropologists study the spider's web of culture, the ant colony with its workers, slaves, soldiers, and queen provides a model of the sociologist's domain. Sociologists are interested in how society comes to have these different "types," how people in different roles or classes relate to each other, how rank, status and power are manufactured and displayed during these encounters, and how individuals go about constructing and maintaining their own "face" or status in their own and other's eyes. And, as we have seen in this chapter, they're particularly interested in the way in which social status is transmitted from one generation to the next.

To be sure, there is much overlap between the anthropologist's and sociologist's perspectives. For example, sociologists study the culture of working class youth, while Ray McDermott, trained under educational anthropology founder George Spindler, was the first to study stratification in the reading group. And there is much overlap in methodology, ethnography being almost indistinguishable from field study. Ultimately, however, their foci are different. American anthropologists have tended to document the unique culture of particular student groups—Deyhle's breakdancing Utes, whereas sociologists like Jenkins, by contrast, have focused on the interactions of varying status student groups in the secondary school.

This concern for interaction has led to the growth of a distinctive methodology. The interview is far more central in sociology than in anthropology, because the private, face-to-face interview is the most direct way to elicit a member's views of the other parties in a social setting. While the anthropologist studies the tightly scripted routines of the ritual or ceremony, the sociologist studies informal encounters where social ends are negotiated. Even when studying supposedly routine events like the E&P meeting, the sociologist seeks to discover the ad hoc, unscripted activities that actually structure the meeting. For this reason, audio- and videotaping can be essential. Otherwise it would be impossible to capture the moment-to-moment unfolding of the event to discern, for example, the way high status persons manage the meeting, or to establish that the nature of counselor-student interaction varies as a function of shared ethnicity. Furthermore, because language is so central in human interaction, the ethnomethodologist is, almost by definition, a sociolinguist. That, in addition to the mechanical tools of videotape recorder and word processor, he must draw on a panoply of conceptual tools, as well, such as the analysis of prosody, turn-taking, notation systems, backchanneling, and so on.

Of course not all sociologists choose to focus on the interaction process itself. Their attention may be drawn to more stable and static aspects of inter-group relations, such as family-school ties. Here, participant observation is the preferred technique, because it is necessary to obtain a large quantity of basically descriptive material to provide sufficient context, to turn social class from an abstract label or category into the lived reality of a group of people. Hollingshead and Lareau provide hundreds of details to illustrate the distinct lifestyles and values of Elmtown, Colton and Prescott residents. Metz offers a comparably rich description of life in a junior high school, and shows, compellingly, the way in which the curriculum and the atmosphere changes across the various tracks. These field studies are most closely parallel to ethnography in method and substance.

Sociologists, to a much greater extent than anthropologists, tend to draw on quantitative data in their analyses. This occurs in one of two ways. In the field studies of social class, they may collect various quantitative indices to buttress the normative portraits achieved from the fruits of participant observation. Schneider and Lee's comparative study of Asian and Anglo-American parental investments is a case in point. A second source of quantitative data are the audio and videotape records made in the course of doing ethnomethodology. These qualitative data can be converted to quantitative indices by partitioning the behavior stream using a code derived from grounded theory. These variables can be aggregated and used descriptively, as when Mehan compares indices of classroom competence at the beginning and in the middle of the year.

Lastly, there is a pronounced tendency in sociology to locate one's study within the framework provided by one or another grand theory. This is especially so in the sociology of education. Schools in the U.S. operate implicitly from the theory that their role is to aid in the location and development of human capital, which is distributed randomly throughout the population. Each student should be afforded the opportunity to develop inherent abilities and talents to their fullest. An individual born into an impoverished family, but with talent and drive, should be able to use the school as an avenue of upward social and economic mobility. Most sociologists would agree that this scenario is idealized. There is disagreement over just how often it happens and, more importantly, why the school is unable to achieve this ideal. It is in the ferment regarding these issues that theories are constructed, modified, and brought into contention. For some theorists, human society is dynamic, under the right circumstances, the pauper can become a prince.

But, for others, it is analogous to the ant colony, where it is as unlikely for someone born into the working class to ascend to middle-class status, as it is for a soldier ant to become a worker ant.

NOTES

1. "One perspective views schooling as the central channel of social mobility. Evidence in support of this position is obtained from intergenerational mobility studies . . . which show education is largely independent of social origins and is a strong determinant of occupational status . . . the other perspective puts more stress on schooling as a transmitter of the existing status advantages of a group from one generation to the next. Support for this position comes from studies that claim attained socioeconomic status can be predicted better by background socioeconomic variables than by education achievement. . . ." (Cicourel & Mehan 1983,5)
2. Grand theory here means a theory that goes beyond trying to account for why it is, say, that children from a particular ethnic group do well or poorly in school. Grand theories take in all members of society and all of society's institutions, the family, the schools, places of employment, government bureaucracies, etc.
3. Lareau's 1989 effort is also noteworthy because she offers one of the most detailed and honest accounts of methodology in the literature. Methodological issues are discussed throughout the text, but there is also a lengthy appendix entitled "Common problems in field work: A personal essay." She discusses aspects of her own background, including a long-standing interest in education (both her parents are teachers) and her qualifications to do this research (lengthy apprenticeship as a paid interviewer). We also learn a great deal about her sampling procedures.
4. Based on painful prior experience, I recommend against using "built in" microphones on either audio- or videotape players. Hock your pearls if you have to but get a lapel pin wireless microphone.
5. Specially designed word processing programs for analyzing qualitative data (Pfaffenberger 1989) would facilitate this process.
6. Annette Lareau herself suggested I review the Baker and Stevenson article in this chapter, which prompted a discussion as to whether it was qualitative (Lareau) or quantitative (Lancy).
7. It is worth noting here that Punjabi parents in Valleyside (Gibson 1988) do not want their children placed in ESL classes, even though they may be struggling with English because they realize that while in ESL classes they will miss out on critical academic courses, without which, they will not qualify for college admission.
8. What makes this a field study rather than an ethnography is more its purpose than its methods. Hollingshead is very clearly motivated by specific theoretical concerns and he seeks to answer a very specific question. Yet, his thoroughness, lengthy residence in the field, and willingness to let his informants and events guide his inquiry make clear the fundamentally qualitative nature of the study. And, although the methods may be similar, the sheer volume of, especially interview, data collected is noteworthy.
9. Hollingshead ([1949]1975) never quite comes out and says this in so many words, but he suggests that in the 1940s the upper classes maintained a stranglehold on school finances to keep it from functioning effectively in enabling children from lower classes to get a "good" education and enhance their status. The high school lost its state

accreditation, for example, but even this drastic blow failed to convince community leaders to spend money on the school and its underpaid staff.

10. Despite the *methodology* in ethnomethodology; scholars working in this tradition exemplify use of the qualitative paradigm (see Chapter 1, p. 9).

11. Indeed, Smith uses an even broader brush; ". . . those who advocate centralized programs to reform education and those who preach positivist social science find common cause. . . . Federally-imposed programs, no matter how well conceived, are inevitably modified by local circumstances. Positivist research and evaluation models designed to study these programs overlook these local circumstances and therefore are bound to fail" (p. 229).

12. The same is true for most special education categories, Conrad (1981) writes about the "social construction of *hyperactivity*:" "*Data* consist of all . . . information on the school and parents' forms, the total medical and developmental history that is generated, the physical exam . . . observations of . . . behaviors, . . . performance on . . . the . . . exam. . . . *Evidence* on the other hand, is data made meaningful . . . the physician is central in constructing the evidence; he or she selectively gives data meaning, hence creating evidence" (pp. 203–4).

13. *Learning Lessons* is an excellent source of ideas for researchers interested in videotaping classroom activities. However, quite recently scholars have begun to debate (Raymond 1991) the need for constraints on the use of videotapes obtained in a research study. Often tapes are used subsequent to the original research without the consent of the research participants.

14. As mentioned in the previous chapter, Susan Phillips' (1983) study shows that Indian-American children are placed at a distinct disadvantage because of their lack of competence in what to them are alien participation structures in the public school classroom.

15. Note the "production cycle" from the onset of research in 1978 to publication of the report in 1985. The time involved in developing and applying a coding scheme, using it to code thousands of discrete behaviors on the videotape, transferring these coded data to the computer for analysis and so on means that "micro" ethnography takes even longer from start to finish than "regular" ethnography. This study was one of several studies of language use in the classroom funded by the federal government in the late 1970s (Wilkinson, 1982). A study by James Collins, to be discussed later in the chapter, is another.

16. Erickson and Schultz (1982,57–8) have an excellent description of the origins of the emic/etic contrast.

17. For similar methodology see: Csikszentmihalyi, M., & Larson, R. *Being Adolescent: Conflict and Growth in the Teenage Years.* New York: Basic, 1984.

CHAPTER **4**

Biological Perspectives

'Rough-and-tumble play', as I shall call it . . . consists of seven movement patterns which tend to occur at the same time as each other, and not to occur with other movements. . . . These are running, chasing, and fleeing; wrestling; jumping up and down with both feet together ('jumps'); beating at each other with an open hand without actually hitting ('open beat'); beating at each other with an object but not hitting; laughing. . . . There seems to be a common facial expression in this play . . . an open-mouthed smile with the teeth covered which morphologically resembles the 'play-face' of *Macaca* and *Pan* . . . [primate species]. . . .

Most of the rough-and-tumble play consists of behaviour which on the surface looks very hostile: violent pursuit, assault, and fast evasive retreat. However, the roles of the participants rapidly alternate and the behaviour does not lead to spacing out or capture of objects; the participants stay together even after the chasing ends. Also the movements involved are quite different from those involved in fights over property. Facial expressions and vocalizations, and the motor patterns involved, separate out into two quite different clusters. Thus, beating with clenched fist occurs with fixating, frowning, shouting, and not with laughing and jumping . . . (pp. 357–9).

In the age group studied, rough-and-tumble play seems to be more clearly differentiated from hostile behaviour than it is in any other species. . . . The comparison suggests that rough-and-tumble play has a very important function in man, if there are so many signals to indicate its difference from serious hostility. (pp. 364–5)

The quote is taken from a landmark study carried out by Nick Blurton-Jones (1967), while a student of Tinbergen's at Oxford (he is now a professor of education at UCLA). Tinbergen, along with Konrad Lorenz, had been the founder of the field of ethology—the naturalistic study of animal behavior. Two hallmarks of the field are the use of the qualitative paradigm—"Lorenz had always argued that to understand a species you must go through a prolonged period of acclimatization, 'just watching,' leaving behind one's preconceptions and entering into the *Umwelt* of the species being studied" (Smith 1990,192), and a concern for what Tinbergen (1951) called the "four whys." Like sociologists, ethologists are preoccupied with a limited set of questions, for any piece of behavior, they would like to know what its proximal cause was, what released or triggered it? In a broader sense, they would like to know what the function of this behavior is, how does it help the animal in its fight to survive and reproduce? Finally, how did this behavior develop over time in the species (evolution), and how does it develop in the life cycle of the individual (ontogeny)?

But Tinbergen and Lorenz had limited their research to animals with relatively simple behavioral repertoires, dumb creatures with neither speech nor "intelligence." Blurton-Jones originally studied birds, specifically the great tit (Blurton-Jones 1968), when in 1963 he began the first study of human—British nursery school children—ethology. As he says, "My approach is best described by reference to ethological studies of bird behaviour . . ." (1967,348). Beyond this he ". . . used no special observation techniques, but simply visited the school repeatedly, and sat on a chair in the corner with a notebook" (p. 349).

Several things are worth noting in the opening passage. First, there is the focus on easily observable behaviors—"running, chasing . . . open-mouthed smile with teeth covered" (pp. 357–8). Ethologists avoid making inferences based on the animal's imputed cognitive or affective state, e.g., "angry," "sad," "eager." Second, one object of this open-ended, descriptive stance is to uncover sets of behavior that go together in some integrated, purposeful fashion. Here Blurton-Jones teases apart rough-and-tumble play from aggression, a very similar complex. Imagine the proverbial traveller from Mars visiting an elementary school classroom and gradually distinguishing "math" and "reading." Third, note Blurton-Jones comparing what he observes with what is reported in the literature for other primate species. This comparative perspective is essential in addressing the perennial questions already alluded to, as well as the question as to whether the behavior at issue is instinctual or learned—an issue we will take up shortly.

OUTLINE OF THE CHAPTER

The first section is an overview of the basic techniques employed by a human ethologist, especially the various sampling procedures available. Then we consider several prominent themes in the human ethology literature, including, rough and tumble play, the dominance hierarchy and density, with one short digression to discuss "natural experiments." Density is also a theme one encounters within the tradition of ecological psychology, an area of scholarship in which the physical spaces that constrain human interaction are a paramount concern.

CONSTRUCTING THE ETHOGRAM

Blurton-Jones (1967) moved from relatively unconstrained observation to a more systematic system where he tallied the occurrence of specific behaviors. In this fashion he could look at his record sheets and determine with some conviction that "wrestling and open-handed beats occur with jumping and laughing and not with frown, fixate, and closed beat" (p. 358).

McGrew (1972a, b) following closely on Blurton-Jones's heels, conducted a series of ethological studies in nursery schools between October 1966 and September 1969. He identified many of the topics which have held investigators' interest to the present, including the response of the group to the addition of a new member, dominance heirarchies, and the effect of varying density. But his most significant contribution was the development of very precise definitions of commonly observed behaviors, which have since become part of the basic tool kit of ethologists who study children. In Chapter 4, Elements of Behavior, which runs to 76 pages, McGrew (1972a) identifies over 100 distinct behaviors, including the *eyebrow flash*.

> . . . a rapid raising of the eyebrows, which remain elevated for 1/6 second, followed by a rapid lowering to the normal position. It may occur singly or in short series, and it results from the contraction of the frontal belly of the occipito frontalis muscle. . . . Like adults, children appear to use eyebrow flashing in friendly greeting, for example, when glancing up at passing and approaching individuals (p. 43) . . . and . . . *snatch:* After grasping a small object, the arm is suddenly flexed, thereby pulling the object away from another individual and toward the actor's body or above the head. Turning away often accompanies the snatch. Snatching of objects is a common cause of agonistic interactions among nursery-age children. (p. 85)

The first human ethologists saw themselves as radicals in methodology— "At that time [early 1960s] simply watching and recording behaviors seemed a dangerously new idea compared with the laboratory traditions in which we had both been educated" (Smith and Connolly 1980,xi)—and in theory. McGrew (1972a) boldly challenges the prevailing wisdom of the behaviorists who ". . . held that the origins of behaviour could be wholly accounted for by post-natal individual experience" (p. 18), in arguing for the importance of the genetic blueprint. His goal in this series of studies is ". . . a tentative attempt at defining an ethogram for the young *Homo sapiens*" (p. 36). An ethogram is the behavioral equivalent of anatomy and physiology. That is, it is a description and mapping of the behavioral repertoire of the species, where the frequency of behaviors and their temporal relationship (two behaviors occur simultaneously, sequentially, are unrelated, etc.) are depicted. McGrew (1972a) finds, for example, that most interaction occurs in pairs and that the mean length of an interaction is 12.9 seconds. Many of these interactions share a common pattern—they are "posses-sion struggles." Not only do these have clear winners and losers, but over time a pattern emerges: ". . . most interactions involve the more dominant males engaging in possession struggles with each other . . . [others have obtained] similar findings for adult male langurs . . .'' (p. 122).

Keeping this catalog of behavior in mind, McGrew (1972a) unobtrusively ''. . . recorded observations on a portable tape recorder. Observations were later transcribed, timed by stopwatch, and coded onto a standardized sheet. Two percent of the data were rejected because of equipment failure, restriction of a subject through adult intervention, or observer error. The data were punched onto cards and analyzed using conventional electronic data processing methods'' (p. 178).[1] Indeed, high-speed electronic data processing is virtually a prerequisite to the attempt to produce a human ethogram. The outcome of the analyses are tables of figures which permit various comparisons among the behaviors of interest.

McGrew (1972a) demonstrates his skill as a natural historian or field biologist by taking advantage of climactic conditions to conduct a natural experiment (Tinbergen and Lorenz were also masters of this). He wanted to know how density would affect behavior. Three differing conditions were possible: during bad weather, children had to play indoors producing high density; just after it had been raining, the children could play indoors or on the paved areas producing medium density; and during fine weather, play could extend from these areas onto grassy areas producing low density. Many changes were noted, this was typical: ''The amount of time children spent in arm movements increased significantly with higher group densities . . .'' (p. 179). We shall return to the topic of density shortly.

As comprehensive as McGrew's (1972a) lexicon of behaviors is, there is an interesting omission, namely speech. Ethologists are primarily concerned with non-verbal behavior because of the desire to make cross-species comparisons, and because they are interested in universal or pan-species aspects of behavior and the content of conversations is likely to be heavily influenced by the child's experience. With an exception to be noted below, ethologists don't talk to their subjects, either, at least partly because to do so would interfere with the naturally-occurring behaviors they are trying to record.[2] Instead, they have devised a variety of means to observe and record the behavior of individuals in groups. The major problem to be faced, of course, is that the observer can't possibly record everything. She must sample from the available behaviors. Janet Altman (1974), a primatologist, has prepared the definitive work on the subject. She describes seven basic sampling procedures.

Ad libitum: Informal, nonsystematic observations—as in participant observation in ethnography.

Sociometric matrix completion: This complements ad libitum; where certain specific behaviors are observed for certain specific individuals in order to provide a quick test or a check on a pattern one has observed more informally.

Sequence sampling: One observes a lengthier sequence of interactions and the ''sample'' includes all those individuals who participated in the sequence.

Focal-person sampling: An individual is selected and all his/her behaviors are observed for a specified length of time.

One-zero sampling: Like focal-person, but here the observer works with a check-list noting only if specific behaviors occur during the observation period.

Sampling all occurrences: The whole group is observed for a period and the observer looks for and notes all occurrence of a particular behavior in the entire group.

Instantaneous scan sampling: The whole group is scanned very quickly, one individual at a time, and the observer notes the presence in each individual of some set of salient behaviors. Virtually every study done since 1974 has drawn on this set of techniques.

ROUGH-AND-TUMBLE PLAY

As we have seen (Blurton-Jones 1967), children's rough-and-tumble play was one of human ethology's discoveries and it remains an extremely popular object of study. Pellegrini (1988, 1989) and his students observed kindergarten, second, and fourth graders from a public elementary school on the playground during recess.

> . . . observers used scan sampling techniques to observe each child, in pre-determined counterbalanced order, for 5 seconds. Each observer recorded the following information (by whispering into an audio recorder) for each scan: the target's name; the location of the behavior; the numbers of boys, girls, and adults present; target's behavior, and reactors (peers and the adults). Each child was observed at least 100 times across the school year. . . . The information from each taped scan was recorded on coding sheets. The behaviors making up the [r/t] category included: tease, hit and kick at, poke, pounce, sneak up, carry child, play fight, pile on, chase, hold, push. Aggressive behavior was defined according to both topographical dimensions—hit with closed hand, frown, take, grab, push, fixate, swear at, insult . . . and outcome dimensions—whether children separated after the act. (Pellegrini 1989,249–50)

Tabulations were made of r/t and aggression as a function of grade level, location on playground, and gender. Of the behaviors noted, about 11 percent could be reliably coded as r/t, but boys were three times more likely than girls to engage in r/t. Aggression occurred very rarely. Furthermore, ". . . popular boys often engage in r/t. They do so to have fun and to interact cooperatively with peers . . . aggressive behavior . . . was negatively correlated with popularity . . ." (p. 257).

Peter Smith and his colleagues have also conducted a thorough investigation of rough-and-tumble play in children. They note the distinctiveness of play and aggression: "Twelve out of 325 rough-and-tumble bouts observed (3.7 percent) led to an injury. In eight of these, the partner comforted the hurt child . . . only three fights were seen throughout the whole study . . ." (Humphreys and Smith 1987,205). In this research, observers often work from videotape recordings of school children on the playground.

Videotaping of live playground action preserves maximum information about the structure of the behavior. Thus, absolute frequency scores and absolute duration scores are available as is information concerning temporal sequences. Moreover, by reducing the playback speed or even analyzing the record frame by frame, a rich source of information concerning the detailed structure of the behavior emerges. This method is so powerful that even aspects of structure, which are not immediately apparent at normal speed, may reveal themselves. The rich detail it provided was used by us early on in our project, in developing the taxonomy. Furthermore, through analyzing recorded sequences it is possible to achieve very high reliability, both within and between observers. By using the consensus coding method . . . two or more researchers can review the tape until they agree that the behavior fits one or other category. (Boulton and Smith 1989,65)

Two methodological issues are raised here which pervade the human ethology literature. First, there is a concern for the quality of one's operational definitions. To the naive observer, behavior occurs in a continuous stream. The challenge for the researcher is to partition this stream in sensible ways, that is, in ways that correspond to some objective reality (e.g., chase vs flee) and that, taken together, reveal predictable patterns. A videotape record allows one to continuously rework these definitions, so that particular segments of behavior can be reliably coded as one thing and not another (e.g., flinch vs duck). A second problem concerns the perceptual filter of the observer. Despite training, different observers will still see different things. Consequently, all studies that involve the analysis of observational data mandate multiple observers. Disagreements are handled in one of several ways. If there is consistent disagreement between two observers, a third observer analyzes, independently, the same material. If this third observer is in general agreement with one of the first two, the discrepant observers will be retrained or excused from further coding duties. More commonly, the observers will agree on most items, but there will be some areas of disagreement, in which case the researcher will need to further refine his definitions to eliminate ambiguity. The level of agreement among observers is called *concordance,* which is the ratio of agreements to agreements plus disagreements. Generally speaking, a concordance rate above .70 is considered satisfactory; there would be no need to retrain the observers and/or rework the coding scheme.

An exception to the rule noted above, that ethologists do not interview the individuals whose behavior they have recorded, occurred when Smith and Lewis (1985) had eight (of 26 in the study) nursery school children view videotapes made on the playground. The children were asked to judge whether a given episode was playful or aggressive. The children's judgements corresponded closely to that of the researchers, demonstrating the congruence of emic and etic views—although Smith and Lewis do not use these terms.

Empirical study of rough-and-tumble play is invariably accompanied by speculation on its function. Smith (1974—see also Smith 1982), reflecting perhaps on the pervasiveness of r/t reported for juvenile canids and felids (Aldis 1975) as well as human r/t, offers " . . . it would seem that the forms it takes . . . are such as to provide practice for adult hunting activities" (p. 108). More recently,

Pellegrini (1989) has sought to test the proposition that r/t contributes to the individual's development of social competence. I have argued (Lancy 1980) that play might simultaneously serve two distinct functions, first to maintain an optimal level of arousal—e.g., to stave off boredom and, second, perhaps to aid the individual in perfecting skills that will be critical later in life—such as hunting,[3] escaping from predators, or participating in a dominance hierarchy.[4] The point to be made here is that ethologists are as committed to grand theory as sociologists, which imposes constraints on what they choose to study, as well as how they go about it.

THE DOMINANCE HIERARCHY IN PRE-SCHOOL

Biologists have had a long-standing interest in formal, structured dominance hierarchies that arise in social groups. One of the earliest studies, characteristically, was an analysis of the pecking order among barnyard fowl (Schjelderup-Ebbe 1922). During the early 1960s numerous studies were conducted with captive and free-living primates, which established the pervasiveness of the dominance hierarchy, as well as providing descriptions of how individual members gain and lose rank (Chance and Jolly 1970).

Among primates, rank is gained and displayed in several ways. One of the most common is the very straightforward "property fight," another is "proximity," and a third is "attention structure." This last grew out of research (Omark and Edelman 1976) which showed that members of the group are more likely to glance at high ranking as opposed to low-ranking members.[5] A study by Abramovitch (1976) was one of the first of dominance relations among *homo sapiens*. She and her assistants observed four preschool classes. One can't help but note the great care and precision with which she describes the physical setting of the nursery school classrooms—a hallmark of the biological perspective.

An observer dictated into a cassette recorder every instance of a property fight and indicated a winner and a loser. In addition,

> Proximity, in this study the neighbor relationship between individuals, was recorded by "instantaneous" or "scan" samples. . . . Scale drawings had previously been made of all of the nursery school rooms. At 1–15 minute intervals the position of every child in the room was noted. The code initials of each child were recorded on the scale drawing, in the position corresponding to the child's actual position in the room. These proximity scans provided an estimate of the amount of time each child spent as the first, second, third, or more distant neighbor of every other child. . . .
>
> The method of estimating proximity relations used in this study, the "nearest neighbor technique," was based on methods used by plant ecologists. . . . Attention, or more precisely, glance rate, was recorded through a focal animal sampling technique. . . . In a focal sample, the observer recorded every occurrence of the focal child's glancing at every other child, as well as the name of the recipient of the glance and the neighbor relationship, i.e., whether the focal child glanced at his first nearest neighbor, second nearest neighbor, etc. The observer recorded a 1-minute focal attention sample after each proximity scan. (pp. 160–1)

Winners/losers, proximity, and glance rate are all low inference behaviors. They do not require that the researcher interact with the child or draw inferences about the child's mental state. Not surprisingly, agreement between observers was high. These data were then analyzed with the aid of the computer, and the aggregated results showed, among other things, that children who consistently won property fights were observed by other children more than twice as often as children who lost such fights. Proximity data showed that high ranking children tended to place themselves in proximity to higher ranking children and move out of range of low ranking children. Abramovitch (1976) concludes:

> Perhaps the most interesting thing which this study demonstrates is the degree of sophistication in the organization of the social behavior of preschool children. Status relations were fairly stable and . . . spacing and attention behaviors are part of an ongoing system of social relationships. The comparative aspect of this study is also of importance. Visual attention and spacing are related to rank in similar ways for both non-human primates and human adults. This study indicates that similar relationships also exist for at least this sample of preschool children. (p. 174)

Strayer and Strayer (1976) used another one of the methods recommended by Altman, matrix completion. ". . . The observer scans the immediate environs for episodes of behavior defined in the . . . inventory. . . . If two episodes occur simultaneously, the one involving a child who has not been previously observed in conflict, is videotaped. Toward the end of the observational period, greater attention is given to those children who have participated in the fewest number of agonistic episodes" (p. 982). Their focus was on various behaviors that corresponded to either aggression or submission. They first analyze their data to determine whether there is, indeed, a recognizable dominance hierarchy in this group of 18 preschoolers. They look for evidence of the ". . . linear transivity rule [which] . . . states that, if individual A dominates B and individual B dominates C, then A should also dominate C" (p. 984). In this case, 98 percent of all interactions were in the expected direction. Next, they look at relationships within the data, for example, ". . . Furthermore, the low incidence of counter attacks . . . suggests that the dominance structure of these preschool children may function to minimize intragroup aggression just as it does in other primate groups" (p. 987). Another interesting finding is that higher ranking children initiate agonistic encounters far less frequently than lower ranking children. ". . . frequency of initiated aggression does not determine dominance status . . . a relatively low aggressive girl was the most dominant individual in this group" (p. 988).

THE DOMINANCE HIERARCHY
AMONG ADOLESCENTS

Scholars have built on this foundation, and gone on to probe developmental aspects (Melson and Dyar 1987) of the dominance hierarchy, and such things as leadership style (Hold 1976). Rich Savin-Williams (1987) has conducted several noteworthy studies of adolescents within the human ethology tradition, in particular, dominance hierarchy formation in a coed summer camp where cabin residence was unisex. Although not strictly an educational study (Savin-Williams 1979), it has a number of illuminating features. University of Chicago graduate assistants, with experience as camp counselors, were trained via joint (with Savin-Williams) observation of volley-ball games prior to the summer. For this study,

> A premium was placed on unobtrusively observing naturally occurring behavior in the ongoing life of the group. While it is likely that some instances of social competitive behavior were not noted, especially subtle ones, other means of gathering data commonly used in child studies (video-tape, film, nonparticipant observers) were either not feasible or inappropriate with adolescents in a camp setting.
>
> For 3 hours per regular day of the camping session, cabin counselors (observers) recorded all episodes of social dominance which occurred between members of each cabin group (total hours observed, 692). Observations entailed the use of an event-sampling technique, "all occurrences of some behavior" . . . and were made during five behavior settings: (1) rising from and going to bed (rest periods), (2) meals, (3) cabin cleanup, (4) cabin discussions and meetings, and (5) athletic activities. (p. 926)

The observers were able to disguise their note-taking as score-keeping during athletic contests, minute-recording during cabin meetings, writing letters during rest periods, and so on. Campers were, hence, unaware that they were the objects of a research study as were their parents.

> The approval of the executive director of the camps had been procured prior to the collection of data. This approval was received only after the following human subject conditions were guaranteed: (1) the study would in no manner interfere with normal camp procedures or camper behavior; (2) confidentiality of the participants would be strictly maintained by coding all behavioral records to mask the identity of the adolescents, and by eliminating all personal references from subsequent oral and written presentations of the data; and (3) each participant would be debriefed, in language appropriate for his level of understanding, as to the nature and purposes of the project and his role in the project, and would be also given the option of having his data deleted from the study (all willingly participated). (p. 926)

In view of the fact that a permanent record was being made of "undesirable" behavior—"Some, cabin bullies, physically threatened and fought . . . to assert their dominance" (p. 932). I would guess that this study would encounter heavy sailing through the University Human Subjects Research Review Committee. On the other hand, it is also not clear that Savin-Williams could claim to be observing "naturally occurring behavior," if he had fully informed campers of their subject status and the purposes of the study to obtain their *prior* consent.

Weisfeld and Weisfeld (1984) took advantage of the creation of an intramural volleyball league to study dominance-hierarchy formation among upper-middle-class ninth graders. Twenty-four players, six per team, played a round robin tournament following two weeks of practice. Where the nursery school studies recorded nonverbal behaviors exclusively, and Savin-Williams (1979) used a mixture of verbal and nonverbal behaviors, in this study relatively high inference, verbal behaviors are simultaneously noted on audio tape by two observers. Specifically: ". . . The identities of evaluator and recipient were recorded, along with the nature of the comment: *praise* (containing rewarding content), *criticism* (containing punishment), or *instruction* (neutral). Any verbal response to the evaluation—accepting it (*acknowledgement*) or rejecting it (*protest*)—was noted" (p. 93).

Tallies were made of praise, criticism, and so on for each player and these were analyzed for evidence of rigidity and linearity:

> Rigidity refers to consistency in the outcome of . . . interactions. It is simply the percentage of dominance encounters that the dominant individual wins. Linearity refers to transivity in the dominance relations of members of the group. (p. 91)

> Hierarchies were constructed for each team on the basis of the direction of instruction, praise, and criticism. For example, if Player A instructed Player B more often than the reverse, A was said to dominate B, and was placed ahead of B in the instruction hierarchy. Rigidity was generally high: large percentages of the evaluative comments were given by the more dominant individual to the subordinate. For instruction, rigidity for the eight teams averaged 85 percent. For praise, mean rigidity was 91 percent. For criticism, mean rigidity was 84%. . . . Likewise, linearity was nearly perfect; only three reversals, or violations of transitivity, occurred. The mean linearity for instruction was 95 percent. For praise, mean linearity was 99 percent. For criticism, mean linearity was 100 percent. (p. 94)

> A single hierarchy seemed to emerge that was relative to volleyball ability. This hierarchy formed in the virtual absence of acts of physical aggression. The best players hit the ball frequently and instructed, praised, and criticized their teammates. (p. 96)

This mention of the absence of aggression is echoed throughout the ethology literature on the dominance hierarchy. Aggression steadily declines with age, and as one rises in the hierarchy. Savin-Williams (1982) compared eighth and tenth grade intramural volleyball teams using a similar approach to the Weisfelds.

> When the participants were early adolescents the frequency of physical contact, teasing, boasting, and criticism rose precipitously. On the other hand, middle adolescent participants were more prone to encourage teammates, even when the team was losing, and to give positive and neutral instructions and advice. These findings are similar to those on dominance relations in adolescence: early adolescents were more apt than middle and late adolescents to be physical and overt when dominating campmates. (p. 208)

Indeed, Savin-Williams (1987) and others argue that the reduction of intra-group conflict (over scarce resources) is the primary function of dominance hierarchies.

NATURAL EXPERIMENTS

Ethologists make great use of comparative data to determine whether a particular pattern of behavior is true only for one species or is more widely found. For example,

> A newborn langur's experiences with its mother vastly differ from those of a baboon. Baboon infants usually do not leave their mothers arms during the first month of life, and baboon mothers are reticent about allowing other females to touch their offspring. But the newborn langur is passed about to other females . . . while the infant langur matures in almost a matriarchal society, baboon . . . infants mature amid a mixed society of males and females. (Poirer 1972,21)

Human ethologists and developmental psychologists also record and compare patterns of behavior in different societies, especially those that have not yet experienced the homogenizing effect of public schooling and the mass media. Their goal is to determine what aspects of human behavior or human development are universal, true for all humans or culture-specific, true only for certain societies.[6] Eibl-Eibesfeldt (1983) for example, has spent a lifetime trying to address the following question: "Do universal patterns of mother-child interactions exist, which can be considered as a shared phylogentic heritage of *homo sapiens?*" (p. 179) He has made extensive film and audio recordings from unacculturated peoples around the world. Careful observation is made of such things as the amount of time the baby remains in physical contact with the mother, the time spent with mother as opposed to others, and so on. He concludes that the mother-infant bond is universal—common to all human societies.

These cross-cultural scholars also use strange devices (e.g., Lancy, Souviney, and Kada, 1981; Lancy and Strathern 1981) to control for the effects of prior experience, and also to make more visible and easier to record behaviors which are often hidden from the participant observer. The late Millard Madsen developed a number of extremely ingenious game-like devices to probe the degree to which interpersonal cooperation was biological or cultural. We (Lancy and Madsen 1981) used one such device with children in several Papua New Guinea societies.

> For all of the procedures the children are seated opposite each other across a table. . . . The first task is the "coin-pull." A 62-cm × 15-cm board, raised 7 cm off the table, is placed between the [children]. Lying on the board is a rectangular block of plexiglas with a hole in the center into which a . . . [coin] is placed. Attached to both ends of the block are cords which run through eyelets at each end of the board. Each child holds the end of a cord. As the child pulls on the cord, the block moves towards the child's end of the board and, just before it reaches the edge, the . . . coin will drop through a 3-cm hole in the board. In order for members of the pair to draw the block to their end, and thus drop a coin through their hole, the other member must relax the grip on his or her cord. This procedure is demonstrated to [them], each being given an opportunity to pull the block to his or her end and gain a [coin], during an initial practice phase. The task is, then analogous to a tug-of-war, with one difference. The

plexiglas block is actually split in half, the two halves being held together by magnets; thus, when each [child] pulls simultaneously, the block splits and neither wins a [coin]. This feature is *not* demonstrated during the practice phase. The [children] are told they will have 10 [coins] to win and these are lined up on the table in plain view . . . a [coin is placed] in the block and [they are told] to begin. If [they] take turns pulling they will win [coins] and these moves are recorded as cooperative; if they tug simultaneously, the block breaks, . . . the [coin is taken] back and the move is recorded as competitive). (p. 204)

One of the most widely cited studies in the field of human ethology is Hutt's (1971) landmark work on exploration and play in nursery school children. She developed a strange device and then let nursery school children have access to it.

The object consisted of a red metal rectangular box on four brass legs. On the top was mounted a level, at the end of which was a blue wooden ball. The four directional movements of the lever were registered by four Post Office counters which could be made visible to the child. It was also possible to allow the child differential auditory feedback contingent upon specific manipulatory movements (a bell in one of the horizontal directions and a buzzer in one of the vertical). (p. 236)

She found that children first explored the novel device, trying out various movements of the lever, then they began to play with it, repeating certain movements over and over for effect, or using it in novel ways like riding it as if it were a horse. On subsequent opportunities to interact with the device, children explored it much less indicating that they had learned all they needed to learn about it, however its value as an object of play remained high.

Hutt (1971) was intent on asking fundamental questions about the relationship between exploration and play, but was confronted with a difficulty as far as conducting a fully naturalistic study. Namely, she had no way of assessing children's prior experience with a particular object. Even were she to introduce a new toy into one of the nursery classrooms, there would remain the possibility that some children had had prior exposure to it outside the school.

Charlesworth and his associates were faced with a similar dilemma in their attempt to study how gender and the dominance hierarchy influenced problem-solving in the nursery school. He, too, developed a novel device that created a reasonably authentic representation of problem-solving situations that occur in the nursery school.

The apparatus (hereafter movie viewer) consisted of a Fisher-Price toy movie viewer mounted on a plexiglas panel fastened to a welded steel frame. The viewer itself consisted of an eyepiece (mounted 96.5 cm from the floor), a cartoon cassette, and an electric bulb to illuminate the cartoon strip. The plexiglas panel was so constructed that it was impossible for the child looking through the eyepiece to touch a crank (located to the right) that was connected to gears that moved the cartoon. If the child looking through the eyepiece wished to view the cartoon in motion, another child would have to turn the crank. To the left of the viewing child, and also out of reach, was a light switch that controlled power to the electric bulb. If the viewing child wanted to see the film, another child would have to press continuously down on a lever controlling the light switch. (Charlesworth and Dzur 1987,193)

Prior to children being introduced to this apparatus, the dominance hierarchy had been fully documented. Children were then video taped as they used the movie viewer. High-ranking children were much more likely to gain early access to the viewer and had no difficulty in coercing others to turn on the light and turn the crank. However, one way they did this was by offering to help while others used the viewer.

> While high ranking children had priority of access to the viewer, middle ranking children were often no less competent than their high ranking peers in actually using the resource. However, children of low dominance status were strikingly ineffectual in negotiating an equal turn with their peers. These children often assumed roles marked by passivity in the face of a challenging and stimulating social situation and compliance to higher status peers. Occasionally, a dominant child would arrange for a low status peer to take a turn at the viewer, but in most cases these children remained on the periphery of the activity, demonstrating an interest in the viewer (by approaches and indirect requests), but not the ability to take their place in the centre of activity. (LaFreniere and Charlesworth 1987,355)

These are hybrid studies. While they use variables and experimental manipulations, they may incorporate qualitative elements. For example, great care is taken to accurately replicate the features of naturally occurring problem-solving situations in the design of these devices. Children do encounter strange things that they have to figure out, and they do need to enlist each other's cooperation in order to share resources and accomplish a goal like playing a game. Second, these devices all permit the unambiguous coding of low inference behaviors, it is quite clear, for example, when one of the children in Charlesworth's studies has successfully negotiated an opportunity to view the film. Third, most of these investigators conduct relatively unconstrained observation of their eventual "subjects" before, during, and after the experiment to verify the validity of the procedures. With the Madsen procedure, pairs of children who are bent on competing, try to get the jump on their opponent and pull the rope before the signal is given to begin; cooperative pairs are more cautious, they negotiate turn-taking and indicate by word or gesture that it is the other's turn to pull the block and retrieve the coin. Although badly dated, the Hutt's (1970) guide, entitled *Direct Observation and Measurement of Behavior,* is still one of the best references available for naturalistic and hybrid studies of human ethology (see also Sackett 1987).

ETHOLOGICAL RESEARCH ON DENSITY

The study of group size and density will allow us to explore the relationship between two distinct traditions which share a biological perspective, human ethology and ecological psychology. An experiment by Calhoun (1962) caused an enormous stir as he documented that rats (highly social creatures) lost all social restraint when forced to live in overcrowded conditions. Positive social behaviors like grooming, nursing, and nest-building were attenuated or disappeared altogether. Peter Smith and Kevin Connolly (1980) of Sheffield University collaborated on the major study of group size and density in nursery school. Their general approach follows the r/t and dominance hierarchy studies; in particular they draw on McGrew (1972a) and Altman (1974).

Their discussion of methodology is revealing.

> There is a myriad of ways of categorizing the flow of a young child's behaviour, and many recording systems have been developed. . . . We did not have preconceived ideas as to what the effects of the environmental changes would be; this was a fact-finding research programme, rather than the testing of specific hypotheses about particular behaviours. This suggested using quite a large number of behaviour categories, reflecting different facets of the behaviour flow such as social contacts, object use, body posture and locomotion, and so on. Alternatively, fewer, more complex categories could have been used, such as measures of a child's cooperative behavior or attention to tasks . . . [but] more complex [high inference] categories involve larger inferences on the part of the observer. It requires more time to decide whether a child has shown 'cooperative behaviour' or 'sustained task attention,' than to record 'gives object to child' or 'manipulates' object'. . . . These [categories] . . . were influenced by ethological methods and by the approach to behaviour categorization developed by researchers in animal behaviour. The animal ethologists, faced with the task of describing the behaviour of a species with which they could not communicate directly, attempted to delineate relatively invariant units of behaviour, described and defined in largely physical terms. In this way anthropomorphic interpretation by the observer could be minimized. (pp. 37–8)

Ultimately they defined and used over 100 distinct categories of behavior.

They worked in several nursery schools over an extended period of time. With the cooperation of school authorities, they combined smaller groups into larger groups to study the effects of group size, and also altered the size of the play space available to study crowding. Below we see transcriptions of the 30-second narrative records for four observations of "Henry" as spoken into the tape recorder by an observer.

Henry (1)

Sitting on a chair at the table with Lego . . . he looks at Michael . . . at the moment not doing anything . . . he glances at Michael, Michael talks to him, he simply smiles and talks to Michael, picks up a plastic spanner and holds it . . . watches other children, rubs his eye.

Henry was parallel with Michael, Steven, and Andrew; no activity.

Henry (2)

Standing on his own . . . shuffles, watching other children, hand fumbles . . . he stares at Steven . . . walks along by himself . . . standing.

Henry was alone; no activity.

Henry (3)
Sitting on a chair at table, with plastic pin board, Helen talks to him, he talks to Helen . . . picks up, puts down, and manipulates pieces on the plastic pin board . . . talking to Helen contacts Helen.
    Henry was group with Helen; table play.

Henry (4)
Standing, holding some plasic Meccano, he looks at Mrs. Z, shuffles, manipulating the plastic meccano now . . . crouches down on the ground, manipulating the meccano by himself . . . stands up again and walks along.
    Henry was alone; miscellaneous play (pp. 344–5)

Table 4.1 is an example of their standard score sheet as prepared from these four transcriptions.

TABLE 4.1   Standard-Score Sheet Coded for Observation of Children

	Sample 1		Sample 2		Sample 3		Sample 4	
Henry: large group, large space								
Companions . . .	Group	Parallel Michael Steven Andrew	Group Alone	Parallel	Group Helen	Parallel	Group Alone	Parallel
Behaviours								
⋮	⋮		⋮					
Look CAO	Michael							Mrs. Z
Stare CAO		Steven						
Look around/distance								
Watch CAG	C	C						
Talk from CA	Michael				Helen			
Talk SPCAO	Michael				Helen			
Scream/cry								
Stand			x				x	
Walk/shuffle			Walk,shuffle				Walk/shuffle	
Run								
⋮	⋮							
Give/receive object								
Pick up object	x				x			
Hold/carry object	hold						hold	
Put down object					x			
Manipulate object					x			
Wear clothes							x	
Contact apparatus	x				x			
Automanipulate	rub eye		hand					
⋮	⋮							

A, adult   C, child   G, group   O, observer   P, parallel   S, solitary
SOURCE: Smith, P. K., & Connolly, K. J. (1980). *The ecology of preschool behaviour.* Cambridge: Cambridge University Press, pp. 346–347. Reprinted by permission.

For economy's sake, I have eliminated almost half their behavior categories and reduced the table by half. The data are then extracted from these score sheets and analyzed by computer. Table 4.2 shows a representative set of results. Again I have drastically condensed their original table.

Apparent differences in behavior frequencies, as a function of density, are evaluated via statistical analyses. In addition to observing behavior, "Spatial plots were made on standard record-sheets, showing the positions of children in the room, at regular intervals throughout a morning session. This enabled us to calculate the utilization of space and the distribution of children in the different conditions" (p. 32).

Figure 4.1 shows "sociometric relationships" for a small group—single-lines indicate these two children played together 15–20 percent of the time, double-lines, 40 percent or more. Less than 15 percent of the children were not connected. Boys are squares, girls are circles. When two groups were combined, increasing group size from 20 to 32 in the same amount of space, one large cluster broke up into four smaller clusters. This finding was quite consistent over time as Smith and Connolly (1980) repeatedly combined and broke apart classes. Interestingly, ". . . *fantasy play* was always seen more often in the smaller groups . . ." (p. 85). They attribute this to the fact that fantasy play requires a degree of trust and intimacy that was not as evident in larger groups.

TABLE 4.2 Frequency of Behaviors in Three Density Conditions

	Space		
Behaviours	1	2	3
Simple smile	142	158	170
Pucker	30	27	22
Cry/scream	29	22	24
:	:	:	:
Stare at child	228	231	255
Stare at adult	62	66	60
Stare at observer	41	38	64
Hold hands with child	12	18	21
:	:	:	:
Show object	32	41	36
Hold out object	25	22	24
Give object	111	76	95
Receive object	82	75	73
Pick up object	733	735	782
:	:	:	:
Dispute object	24	20	22
Fail take object	18	17	16
Submit	53	33	45
:	:	:	:

SOURCE: Smith, P. K., & Connolly, K. J. (1980). *The ecology of preschool behaviour.* Cambridge: Cambridge University Press, pp. 352–357. Reprinted by permission.

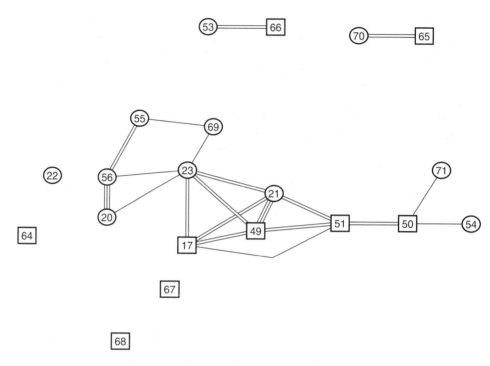

FIGURE 4.1 Sociometric relationships in nursery school group

SOURCE: Smith, P. K., & Connolly, K. J. (1980). *The ecology of preschool behaviour.* Cambridge: Cambridge University Press, p. 71. Reprinted by permission.

Figure 4.2 shows the "spatial plot" prepared from scanning data in the smallest play area. Comparative analysis shows, for example: ". . . the *climbing-frame* was used more in the smaller space conditions, and this was a substantial result,

FIGURE 4.2 Spatial plot of the one space condition (T = table, W = Wendy house, S = sand bath, B = book rack, E = easel, CS = climbing frame/slide)

SOURCE: Smith, P. K., & Connolly, K. J. (1980). *The ecology of preschool behaviour.* Cambridge: Cambridge University Press, p. 109. Reprinted by permission.

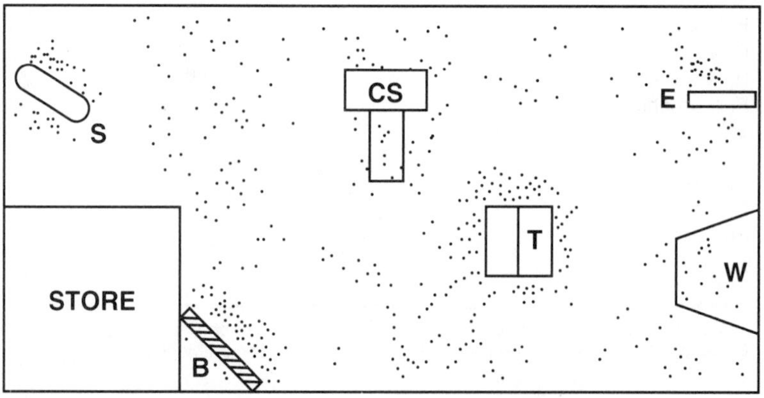

highly significant for both groups. There was less *rough-and-tumble play* in the one-space than in the two- or three-space conditions, and there were also less unusual *uses of apparatus* in the one-space condition" (p. 118). They also varied the amount of play equipment available and

> . . . the greater crowding of children relative to the equipment available did lead to greater levels of social discord and stress. For instance, the frequency of aggressive encounters can be considered. There was a significant increase in physical aggression—fighting, hitting, and pushing—and similar trends for most of the categories of object conflict. The overall category of agonistic behavior showed appreciable and significant increases for both groups of children. There was also rather more crying and screaming in these conditions. Most of the fights were over possessions, and these findings are probably due to increased competition over the relatively fewer items of equipment available (p. 130).

DENSITY STUDIES IN ECOLOGICAL PSYCHOLOGY

The remaining studies of group size and density all fall within the tradition of ecological psychology, and such closely related traditions as environmental psychology (Proshansky, Ittelson, and Rivlin 1970) and human ecology (Bronfenbrenner 1979). Hutt and Hutt (1970) identify several differences between ethological and ecological research (pp. 22–3). Ethologists study behaviors at a more atomic level—facial expressions and gestures as against "instruction," "helping," ete. But ecologists do strive for precision in defining their categories and use multiple observers. Ethologists tend to study what often appear to be goalless or purposeless behaviors, like play and the dominance hierarchy. Ecologists study goal-directed behavior and they tend to make inferences about people's motives, attitudes, and intentions. Also, ethologists are more united in their concern with ". . . four interlocking biological problems: those of causation, function, evolution, and ontogeny" (p. 24), whereas, the ecologist, like the anthropologist, is more likely to let the situation dictate the problem.[7]

Roger Barker (1967) initiated the tradition of ecological psychology, and he and his colleagues carried out numerous investigations within this tradition, primarily in the 1950s and 1960s. This tradition grew up, at least partly, as a reaction against quantitative methods in psychology.

> . . . when a research psychologist does not intrude himself, his software, or his hardware into the data-generating circuits of his investigation, i.e., when he is not a source of inputs to, or of constraints upon, the arrangements which produce the data—in short, when he becomes a naturalist—he frees himself to study new phenomena, to gain new understanding of old problems, and to make new integrations between research and practice. (p. 223)

Barker describes a naturalistic study of children, in which a huge data archive was assembled based on a meticulously detailed record of a day in the life of a small town boy. These data have been used by literally dozens of different investigators. As he says, "Naturalistic data have significance *per se*" (p. 226). He worked out of something called the Midwest Psychological Field Station in Oskaloosa, Kansas, which he likens to a Woods Hole or Mount Wilson, locales for marine and astronomical observatories, respectively.

In *Big School, Small School,* Barker and Gump (1964) were interested in the way size affected the life of a high school. They conducted intensive observation in over 50 high schools throughout Kansas in 1957–1959. Enrollment in these schools ranged from 35 to 2,300. One of their observational categories is the *setting.* These are emically derived and include such things as *chemistry, football,* and *medical services.* One of their more interesting findings was that the number of settings varied much less as a function of size than one might expect. Consequently, students (and one presumes faculty, as well) played many more roles in the small school in order to sustain this great variety of activities.

In these and other studies (Gump [1974] compares two open plan and two traditional plan schools—see Chapter 5). Barker and Gump (1964) aim to show that enduring aspects of the school, physical as well as institutional, govern what goes on there, as much or more so than the desires of the participants, social processes, etc. They see most typical scenes in the school as having prearranged scripts, unlike ethnomethodologists who see these same scenes as socially constructed. Here is a sampling of their arguments.

> One of the sticking points of social and educational psychology is how to account for the consensus, the norms, and the uniformities associated with school classes, business offices . . . and at the same time account for the individuality of the members. . . . A boundary surrounds a school class . . . [which] . . . is self-generated; it changes as the class changes in size and in the nature of its activity. . . . The class is objective in the sense that it exists independent of anyone's perception of it, *qua* class; it is a preperceptual ecological entity. . . . The behavior and physical objects that constitute the unit school class are internally organized and arranged to form a pattern that is by no means random. . . . The people who inhabit a class are to a considerable degree interchangeable and replaceable. Pupils come and go: even the teacher may be replaced. But the same entity continues as serenely as an old car with new rings and the right front wheel now carried as the spare. (pp. 16–17)

One of the more unusual works within this tradition is Berk and Berson's (1975) study of behavior on a school bus. A total of 19 six- to nine-year-olds rode the bus from 20–50 minutes each way. Their unit of analysis is the *episode* which " . . . is a goal directed action on the part of an observed child which is within his own normal sphere of awareness" (p. 3). And in a little over 15 hours of observation, a total of 896 episodes occurred (p. 7). The authors analyze these episodes in various ways. They also compare the children's behaviors with and without a teacher as an additional passenger, but they find that density does seem to affect social interaction. Specifically, that in the afternoon, when the bus starts out full, there is less social interaction than in the morning. Unfortunately, others have apparently not seen fit to study the ecology of school bus behavior and this study stands alone.

The final study we will consider in this section also makes use of a natural experiment to probe the relationship between density in student housing and helping behavior. "Although there has been an enormous amount of money invested in building high-rise dormitories, in spite of some student dissatisfaction, little research has been devoted to investigating the effect these buildings may have on their residents. Architects and planners have appeared to be mostly concerned with the aesthetics and economics of their designs" (Bickman et al. 1973,466). The investigators compared female dorms at the University of Massachusetts at Amherst and "houses" at Smith College. The 22-story-high dorms were taken as dense living conditions with 500 students per building, while the houses at Smith College were two stories high with less than 60 students. Stamped, addressed envelopes were dropped in residence hallways when students were in class. The number of them that were subsequently picked up and mailed was taken as a low-inference, unobtrusive measure of social cohesion. In the high density housing, 63 percent of the letters, and in the low density 100 percent, were returned.

The study was replicated at Penn.

> Much attention was given to claims by some students at Pennsylvania that the high-rises (25 stories) are emotionally depressing and socially suffocating places in which to live. Adjectives such as "cold" and "impersonal" have been used to describe them, and possibly the most common criticism is the extremely limited social interaction within them. Indeed, the whole complex has been somewhat pejoratively nicknamed "superblock." It was in this urban locale that the second study took place. (p. 479)

The results were similar, 91 percent returned in the low density housing, 64 percent in high density housing.

APPLYING ETHOLOGICAL/ECOLOGICAL METHODS

In recent years interest among education researchers in both human ethology and ecological psychology seems to have waned. However, many of the methods and constructs developed by these pioneering scholars have been adapted by researchers working within more quantitative and applied frameworks. Much of the current research on children's play, for example, is more concerned with its contribution to their intellectual and social growth (Bloch and Pellegrini 1989; Lancy 1984, 1987a), and explicitly or implicitly embraces the notion that play should, in many respects, be managed by adults. A typical example is Moore's (1989) ethological study of children's behavior before and after the redesign and reconstruction of a playground.

Gump (1974,1978) applied the Kansas school's methodology to an analysis of new schools with open-plan architecture (see also discussion of Kensington School in the next chapter, page 137). One of the constructs he uses is the *segment* and he discusses the problems with its use:

The lines between segments are defined by instructions ("take out your spelling books"), by location and facilities, by published schedules, by modeling behavior of some student for other students, and so on. The problem in unitization is the span or inclusiveness of a segment. If the teacher has students read aloud in turn, then starts a discussion of this reading, is this two segments or one? (p. 584)

Six dimensions of a segment are identified, such as duration, where it takes place, what its concern or instructional focus is, the nature of pupils' physical activity during the segment, and so on. Gump also identifies "non-substance time" or time spent waiting, getting organized, moving from place to place.

In the open-plan schools, the pilot children had far more non-substance time than pilot children in traditional schools. This was due to the fact that in self-contained classes, teachers could start a new segment with some students, while other students were finishing the last segment. In the open-plan schools, a change in segment usually meant moving to another area, so the move couldn't be made until all had finished, materials had been put away, etc. On the other hand, and contrary to expectations, small-group (as contrasted with whole-class) segments were no more common in open-plan than traditional schools. Gump makes clear that schools were open by design but not by program. However, pupils were more active in open-plan schools.

A much more recent example of research, which employs many of these methods, is Stodolsky's (1988) comparative study of classroom activity in both math and social studies classes.[8] She also uses the segment or activity segment as her unit of analysis.

> . . . activity segments are the major division of lessons. . . . In essence, an activity segment is a part of a lesson that has a focus or concern and starts and stops. . . . We need to know how each activity is structured, who is present, the activity's duration, its instructional purpose and format, and the materials in use. . . . A primary conceptual appeal of activity segments is their salience and their congruity with the way teachers think about conducting lessons. (pp. 11–12)

She discusses, at some length, the selection of her large, representative sample of classes. In keeping with the ecological psychology tradition, Stodolsky is seeking to discover enduring, firmly institutionalized features of math and social studies classes which are unaffected by the particular teacher and students in the classroom. Among segments which observers were trained to identify and check off were: seatwork, groupwork, cognitive level, and use of film. Here is a typical summary statement of her findings.

> In math one sees . . . checking work, recitations, and seatwork. . . . Only an occasional contest, game, or test broke the predictable work regimen . . . social studies lessons were not as predictable . . . [there was] more diversity in a given social studies class from day to day and more variety in instructional approach from class to class. (p. 35)

Stodolsky (1988), while seeking commonalities across classes in the same subject area, is not blind to variation. One school among the 13 visited ". . . adhered to a progressive philosophy that had been present in the district since WWII. The social studies curriculum was organized around cooperative work groups and used MACOS. Math classes . . . included ways to individualize instruction" (p. 106). She does not tell us whether this school served an upper-middle class community, but we can certainly speculate that it did.

One of the reasons for the relative paucity of research within the biological traditions is that, in my view, the cost-benefit ratio is very low. I have glossed over the magnitude of these studies from a logistical point of view, but consider: the typical study utilizes multiple observers (who have to be carefully trained) to observe upwards of 100 sudents for as many as 100 hours, all the while dictating into a tape recorder or noting behaviors on a complex coding form (Hutt & Hutt 1970, figure 19). In the studies which used tape, the observer's comments are transcribed then transferred onto coding forms which are, in turn, quantified and recoded into a computer file which can then be analyzed. The number of variables this yields, well over 100 in some cases, can lead to an orgy of computer runs to cross-classify the variables in every conceivable configuration in the lengthy search for meaningful patterns (Hartwig and Dearing 1979).

But a hallmark of homo sapiens is our extreme environmental adaptability, as well as the ability to camouflage our biological core under a veneer of culture. Hence, relatively few patterns emerge with great clarity and regularity from the data. And, when they do, as with studies of biology and gender, they may promote great controversy. Hence, the search moves towards discovering the patterned behaviors engendered by custom, tradition, social structure, in short, the perspective shifts to that of the anthropologist or the historian. As we have seen, however, scholars working within the human ethology and ecological psychology traditions have left us a method and some powerful research techniques such as the natural experiment, behavior sampling procedures, and procedures to monitor interobserver variability. These are being utilized by researchers concerned with the impact of, for example, curriculum changes on the life of the classroom, such as Jeanne Hoover's (1985) study of the impact of the introduction of microcomputers on the distribution of children's participation in other "centers" in a preschool.

CHOREOGRAPHING THE BEE'S DANCE

We now explore the boundary between two traditions, human ethology and sociology. Hatch's (1987) study of "Status and power in a kindergarten peer group" lies along this boundary. His review of literature draws on classic works in both fields (e.g., Freedman 1977; Goffman 1959), and he records both non-verbal as well as verbal behavior. Hatch . . . "took a passive role . . . making every effort to avoid interaction with children and to blend into the fabric of school life" (p. 81). Unlike the anthropologist, who must develop rapport with informants, ethologists must take great pains not to disrupt the "natural" stream of behavior. He recorded children's conversations in shorthand.

He made 26 visits and observed for 80 hours altogether, capturing 2,302 child-to-child interactions. Part of his report resembles much we've seen before in this chapter: "Boys averaged 8.8 dominance attempts, while girls averaged 7.6 attempts per child" (p. 89). However, Hatch more closely resembles an ethnomethodologist when he describes several reoccurring strategies that children use to enhance rank, including "self-promotion" and the "put-down."

> Children identify characteristics or possessions of family members or others with whom the children were closely associated that cast a favorable light on the speaker. . . .
>
> EDDY: My Uncle J. L. lives in California.
> BENJAMIN: You know what? My cousins live in California. I'm gonna go see 'em.
> EDDY: I'm gonna go see my Uncle J. L. [*pause*] When I go, I'm gonna stay overnight.
>
> When Benjamin does not respond, Eddy continues: "When I come back from California, I'm going to New York. [*pause*] Tomorrow I'm going to New York." (p. 183)

The most common kind of put-downs occurred when children pointed out the mistakes, weaknesses, or inadequacies of others. . . . Put-downs were seldom communicated in private conversations, but almost always undertaken with a wider audience in mind. . . .

> The teacher has instructed children to take three strips of paper from the box being passed through the class. Eddy sees Philip take only two strips, says:
>
> "You're spoze to have three of 'em."
> PHILLIP: Two.
> EDDY: You don't know what you're talkin' 'bout.
> HOLLY: Tell this dumbhead, he's spoze to have three. (p. 85)

Hence, we can see convergence in two very different traditions, studies of the dominance hierarchy from a biological perspective and studies of the social construction of stratification from a sociological perspective. Research in ethology suggests the inevitability of the dominance hierarchy, and this tradition provides a variety of techniques to document specific instances of the hierarchy and establish each member's rank.

K. von Frisch's (1954) study of the language of bees served as the one of the foundation stones of this tradition and can serve us, metaphorically, in trying to grasp the essence of the human ethologists' and ecologists' enterprise. When foraging honey bees return to the hive they do a waggle dance in a series of figure-8 rotations—however, to the uninitiated it appears as if the bees are just "milling around." By dint of prolonged and very precise observation, von Frisch determined that: a) the bee's dance was patterned; b) these patterns were interpretable by other bees; c) the patterns signaled the location of a food source that the returning bee had located; and d) bees that had attended the dance were indeed able to locate the food source on leaving the hive.

The ethologists have the hardest job of all, in many respects, as they attempt to document patterns and behavior that actors themselves are largely unaware of, and which are not generally discernable to the participant observer. Hence, the necessity for thorough, meticulous, and extensive sampling of discreet behaviors, in order to provide a massive data archive that can be systematically searched for these illusive patterns.

These patterns are not human inventions, ethologists do not study the impact of new rules or the presence of a supervisor on the behavior of children in the playground. They study the way the playground equipment itself, its design and layout, structure the children's behavior. Or, they compare the behavior of girls versus boys in the same playground, or six year olds versus four year olds.

Having documented a particular pattern that has been shaped by the animal's genes and the environment in which it resides, the ethologist must speculate on the adaptive value of the pattern. Because nature is conservative, it is a safe bet that what at first appears as damaging or threatening to the organism—r/t play, the dominance hierarchy—turns out, upon close examination, to serve some very useful purposes. Just as the bees seemingly random movements turn out to be a code that communicates vital information to the hive, the dominance hierarchy may serve to distribute scarce and/or desirable goods within the group with a minimum of discord and stress.

NOTES

1. Athough I cannot cite a study in which this has been done, the technology is now available that would permit the elimination ot most of these steps. An ethologist could use the same hand-held calculator-like devices that inventory takers use in stores and supermarkets, noting the various behaviors and their duration. Periodically this recording instrument would be interfaced (either physically or via radio transmission) with a large memory computer, and the data "downloaded" into prepared data files for virtually instant analysis via internal statistics programs.
2. Interestingly, ethologists (Hutt and Hutt 1970; Tinbergen and Tinbergen 1972) have also been drawn to the study of autistics because, since autistics are non-verbal, conventional means of testing or studying them (Lancy and Goldstein 1982) yield meaningless results. For example, Hutt and Ounsted (1966) noted that when autistic children became distressed they would rush to an adult to be comforted, but would avert their gaze so as not to have to interact with him/her—a finding consistent with the arousal homeostat theory (Goldstein and Lancy 1985) of autism.
3. Peter Smith (personal communication) would add *fighting* to this list.
4. McGrew (1977) later conducted research with young chimps at Jane Goodale's field station in Tanzania. He reports a vivid episode where 24-month-old FD "plays at" leaf-sponging, a procedure his mother uses to sop up water in cavities in trees when other sources of drinking water are not available.

5. As we have seen in the previous chapter, attention structure has some applicability in the regular classroom context where studies have shown that "good" students are attended to by their classmates while "poor" students are not.

6. Comparative research has both extended and restricted the range of applicability of prominant theories of human behavior and development. For example, Parker (1977) has found that Piaget's model for sensorimotor development can be successfully extended to nonhuman primates such as the macaque, while Lancy (1983) using a method referred to as "experimental anthropology" (Cole et al. 1971) has shown that Piaget's model for development in later stages has a much narrower range of applicability than was first thought.

7. Pellegrini (1991) provides a more thorough discussion of these distinctions.

8. For a review and summary of this and similar studies, see Anderson and Burns (1989).

CHAPTER 5

The Case Study

With no formally agreed-on procedure whereby students were to be dismissed . . . attempts at coordination of bus times, with existing district schools resulted in uncertainties, long waits, growing parental disapproval. With 200 children in one room, this lack of uniformity increased faculty tensions. Coupled with this was the fact that once decisions were made, members failed to adhere to them, and in other instances all were not informed as to the action to take. . . .

Another factor that required adjustment on the part of both faculty and students was the noise level. It was high in all of the divisions, and the staff was unable to speak loudly enough to be heard by all of the children. Initially, in the Basic Skills Division, teachers had to do the reading instead of the students. This minimized opportunities for pupil oral reading. In the Transition Division three whistles were in evidence, and in the ISD Liz, among others, was losing her voice and she "couldn't hear herself." (p. 156)

This painful scene was recorded by Lou Smith and Pat Keith (1971) in their *Anatomy of an Educational Innovation.* Actually, "Kensington" School incorporated numerous innovations, but it was the " . . . new and uniquely designed elementary school building" (p. 6) that prompted the study.

In addition to the radically designed building, other innovative elements included the provision of three clusters, rather than the usual six grades; team teaching; the elimination of text books, (staff were to design, produce and market their own curricula); and the use of technology. The staff were not just new to the school, the majority were new to the district; many had been hired from outside the St. Louis area. The majority had MAs, three had nearly completed their doctorates, all were liberal Democrats and had strongly student-centered views of teaching. Seven of the twenty were in their first year of teaching, nine of the twenty were male. Is this a recipe for disaster or for progressive change?

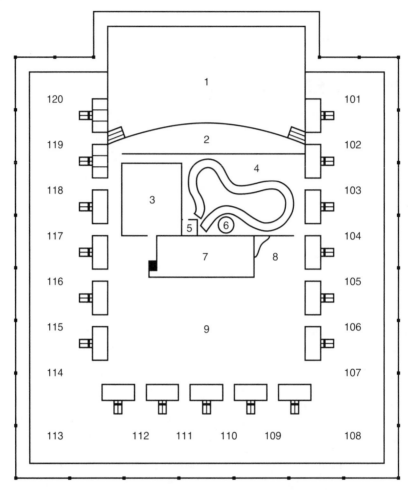

FIGURE 5.1 Floor plan for Kensington school. (1) Covered play shelter, (2) stage, (3) administrative suite, (4) children's theatre, (5) projection room, (6) acting tower, (7) curriculum center, (8) aquarium, (9) perception core, (101 to 120) laboratory suites.

SOURCE: Smith, L. & Keith, L. (1971). *Anatomy of an Educational Innovation*, NY: J. Wiley, p. 7. Reprinted by permission.

As Smith and his colleagues follow the fortunes of the school over a 15-year period (Smith et al. 1987), Kensington goes through several major changes. Its initial phase ends abruptly after two years, as the superintendent and principal, who had conceptualized and created the school, left the district, while 18 of the original teachers were gone within four years. But, during that brief period, the school enjoyed its "moment in the sun." Featured in a documentary on national television on innovations in education, it also played host to hundreds of visitors from around the world.

Anatomy is replete with vivid and dramatic vignettes, like the one above which convey, far better than tables full of test scores and attitude survey results, the essence of what was happening at Kensington. It is compiled from nearly daily participant observation during the 1965–66 school year; formal interviews with nearly every staff member; analysis of written records; and transcribed recordings of the very frequent staff meetings.

OUTLINE OF THE CHAPTER

The case study differs in significant ways from the ethnography or the field study which, in fact, resemble each other quite closely. Hence, I spend quite a bit of time giving an overview of the case study, using Linda McNeil's study of social studies instruction to illustrate these ideas. This section concludes with a very straightforward list of the main attributes of a case study. We then proceed to review a series of case studies of innovations in education, beginning with a second look at Kensington's open plan. I have broken these innovations down according to their underlying philosophies—progressive conservative, and mandated.

Among the progressive innovations, we will examine a "Lab" School in New York City, similar, in many respects, to Kensington. Then, we consider "Thinkabout"—designed to foster critical thinking skills. The case study of Thinkabout is part of a larger, essentially quantitative analysis of the program. A case study of the California Mathematics "Framework" is focused primarily on change among teachers, while "Pathways" focuses on parents. We review a couple more progressive programs—those that permit students and/or teachers greater autonomy and authority. We then turn to a comprehensive study of "SPECS," an extremely conservative effort to restrict student and teacher autonomy. This study was undertaken by noted anthropologist, Harry Wolcott, and flirts with the border between case study and anthropology. We then follow Huberman and Miles as they compare outcomes from several case study evaluations. They offer a number of methodological inventions, including the qualitative data display. As we move through the chapter, the case studies become more complex, more structured, and less "qualitative." This is particularly true in studies of two federally mandated programs for minority youth. Finally, we consider the trade-offs between an emphasis on formative evaluation—the case study author's sole purpose is to help developers improve the program—and generalization where the case study investigator seeks to generalize about some aspects of the phenomenon of interest. Along the way we garner ideas about why innovations succeed or fail, and about the way case studies are conducted and reported.

THE CASE STUDY METHOD

The studies reported in previous chapters have not had a primary concern with *policy*. The issues that were addressed were important to the investigator, to his/her discipline or tradition, but they were not the sorts of issues that immediately command the attention of teachers, administrators, school board members, and so on. It is the direct policy implications of their research that sets those who do case studies apart from other qualitative researchers. Smith and his colleagues do ask the kinds of questions that educational personnel, as opposed to academics, are interested in answers to.

In many respects, however, I must agree with Lincoln and Guba's (1985) assertion that ". . . while the literature is replete with references to case studies and with examples of case study reports, there seems to be little agreement about what a case study is" (p. 360). "Definitions of a case study vary widely . . ." (p. 214). These views are echoed by Merriam (1988) ". . . material on case study as a research strategy can be found everywhere and nowhere" (p. xi). ". . . There is little precision in the use of the term *case study* . . . [it] has become a catch-all category" (p. xii). "Case study," like ethnography, is used as a synonym for qualitative research, even by those who write about it as a method (e.g., Merriam 1988; Yin 1984). Nevertheless, Yin (1984) does give us a "handle" to begin to grasp the unique attributes of the case study. According to him, the case study has:

> . . . at least four different applications. The most important is to *explain* the causal links in real-life interventions that are too complex for the survey or experimental strategies. A second application is to *describe* the real-life context in which an intervention has occurred. Third, an evaluation can benefit, again in a descriptive mode, from an illustrative case study—even a journalistic account—of the intervention itself. Finally, the case study strategy may be used to *explore* those situations in which the intervention being evaluated has no clear, single set of outcomes. (p. 25)

The case study, used alone or as part of large-scale quantitative study, is the method of choice for studying interventions or innovations. And education is replete with these. One would be hard pressed to visit any school, at any point in time, that was not in the process of implementing and/or trying out new curricula, technology, staffing arrangements, student assessment procedures, etc.

Patton (1990) is critical of conventional, quantitative evaluation efforts. "Case studies are manageable, and it is more desirable to have a few carefully done case studies with results one can trust than to aim for large, probabilistic samples with results that are dubious because of the multitude of technical, logistic, and management problems . . ." (p. 100). He says that most program evaluation is based on the false premise that educational interventions are "true experiments," when in fact, uneven implementation of programs, self-interest of participants, and the difficulty of specifying, let alone measuring "outcomes" makes it too easy, and too likely to explain away or ignore negative results.

A personal experience that is consistent with Patton's skepticism concerning quantitative evaluation occurred at a recent conference where I heard a talk (Wolfe 1987) entitled "Effects of a Developmental Guidance Curriculum on the Interpersonal Cognitive Problem Solving Skills and Social Behavior of Elementary Pupils." The author presented an exhaustive catalog of results tables covering a plethora of outcomes and, without exception, statistical analyses yielded "no effects." Then, with no transition whatsoever, the presenter concluded by saying, in effect, "But, thank-goodness, our program was just re-funded for another three years." The point is, advocates and opponents of a particular innovation can be remarkably resistant to quantitative data and statistical analysis. But the narrative account of success or failure, liberally seasoned with spicy observations and quotations, is much harder to resist. Qualitative research, relatively open ended, concerned with "how" as well as "how well" can much more honestly depict these contextual factors. Stake (1983) refers to the "responsive" quality of the case study.

> An educational evaluation is responsive evaluation if it orients more directly to program activities than to program intents, if it responds to audience requirements for information, and if the different value perspectives of the people at hand are referred to in reporting the success and failure of the program. (p. 292)

The case study does not earn blanket approval, however, many see it as a costly alternative, further ". . . assuming that one does take the time to produce a worthy case sudy, the product may be deemed too lengthy, too detailed, or too involved for busy policy makers and educators to read and use" (Moore 1986,33).

This suggests that the case study is subject to an efficiency standard that is missing in much qualitative research, e.g.,

> Highly inductive and loosely designed studies make good sense when researchers have plenty of time and are exploring exotic cultures, understudied phenomena, or very complex social realities. But when one is interested in some better-understood social phenomena within a familiar culture or subculture, a loose, highly inductive design is a waste of time. Months of field work and voluminous case studies will yield a few banalities. (Miles and Huberman 1984b,27)

I do not want to imply that the case study is only used when one aims to evaluate a new program. It just so happens that innovation in education is fueled almost exclusively by grants, and granting agencies, not unreasonably, demand an accounting of what was done with these funds. Many Requests For Proposals (RFP) specifically require that project directors set aside at least 6 percent of the budget to hire an "outside" evaluator. Consequently, these mandated evaluations have been the stimulus for much research, including many single and multiple case study projects.

But one can do a case study which is not an evaluation of a specific innovation. One such project that may well have an impact on policy, is Linda McNeil's (1986) study of the teaching of social studies in four high schools. In effect, she chose to evaluate average or normal patterns of instruction. She found that:

> Defensive teaching was observed at each of these high schools . . . teachers . . . maintain discipline by the ways they present course content. They choose to simplify content and reduce demands on students in return for classroom order and minimal student compliance on assignments (p. 158). Defensive teaching consists of: *fragmentation*—the simplest . . . technique among social studies

teachers is the reduction of any topic to . . . disjointed pieces of information —lists (p. 167); *mystification*—Teachers often try to surround a controversial or complex topic with mystery in order to close off discussion of it . . . they make it appear very important but unknowable . . . Federal Reserve . . . International Monetary Fund . . . (p. 169); *omission*—variant points of view are glossed over, or a difficult topic is omitted altogether; and *defensive simplification*—teacher announces the topic of study, which may sound very complicated, then apologize for it and promises il will not demand much work. (p. 174)

McNeil probes further to discover the reason for this distressing state of affairs:

> The observations and interviews turned up several possible explanations behind this strategy of controlling students by simplifying the lessons. . . . Having reached middle-age, or seen their paychecks long ago outstripped by inflation, the teachers said that they no longer felt the energy and drive to do whatever was necessary to make students understand. They felt that neither the support nor the financial reward was commensurate with the out-of-class time needed to prepare learning activities adequately, or to read and comment on the student essay tests or written assignments that a real treatment of such topics would require. . . . A second factor was the minimal effort students seemed willing to put forth. In two of the four schools, over half the juniors and seniors interviewed worked more than twenty hours per week, in addition to going to school full-time. . . . Whatever school effort students were willing to spend, they saved for . . . math and science . . . courses, which they saw as more instrumental to job futures. . . . Tired, bored, and rushed to cover content, teachers and students met in a path of least resistance. Expected student resistance to taxing assignments was circumvented by making the assignments less taxing. (p. 176)

The spectre of defensive teaching will reappear when we shortly return to Kensington, but I would like here to summarize some of the general attributes of the case study.

1. Case study is a qualitative method and, although it " . . . does not claim any particular [techniques] for data collection or data analysis . . . " (Merriam 1988,10), the investigator is more likely to utilize the techniques associated with other qualitative methods such as ethnography, than with, say, the experimental or survey methods. Nevertheless, no less an authority than Mary Lee Smith (1986) strongly advocates combining qualitative and quantitative techniques.

2. However, case study does not adhere to the qualitative *paradigm*. Questions or issues are at least partly predetermined. What one studies is carefully delimited in advance. One adopts a realist rather than phenomenological stance, and one is not concerned particularly with *grounded theory*.

3. One's audience may include some subset of the academic community, but it must include some well-defined "client" group. This is not true, generally, for qualitative research. Furthermore, unlike "participatory

research" (see p. 00) which does address the needs of participants, the primary audience for the case study is more likely to be those in authority—government bodies, school boards, administrators—than teachers, parents, or students.

4. As a corollary, one may meet one's "professional responsibility" as a researcher without necessarily publishing the results of the case study. Indeed, some would argue (Patton 1990) that an oral report to one's clients may be a more effective way of presenting the results than a written report.

5. Case studies are often undertaken "under contract." Hence, the researcher's motives are primarily pecuniary rather than a quest for knowledge for its own sake. Thus, the "typical" case study tends to be rather narrowly focused, atheoretical, and will not be published. Therefore, the case studies reviewed in this chapter are admittedly atypical. But, they are well-written, they address important methodological concerns and, most importantly, they are accessible.

6. Although, as I have indicated, a case study is not always construed as an evaluation, the researcher will assume an evaluative stance. She will explicitly or implicitly compare what she observes with some standard (e.g., McNeil 1986). Walker (1975) in his case study of a two-year long project to develop an elementary school art curriculum,[1] continually contrasts what he observes with an implicit model of how curriculum development is "supposed to" occur: "If objectives were stated at all they came in the course of development work, not before it" (p. 99).

7. Likewise, the researcher is obligated to draw pointed conclusions from the case study, explicitly or implicitly making recommendations that will alter policy and/or practice. Walker's (1975) experience left him worried about the ". . . Kafkaesque image of thousands of teachers in schools . . . throughout the country . . . writing behavioral objectives . . . in response to demands from officials . . ." (p. 133).

KENSINGTON REVISITED

A number of policy issues were identified by Smith and his colleagues (Smith and Keith 1971; Smith et al. 1987) in their episodic, long-term study of Kensington. First, a new and dynamic superintendent was able to capitalize on an opportunity—the need to build a new school to meet increasing enrollment—to implement several radical ideas that were floating around. Indeed, we will soon review another case study of a school attempting many of the same innovations at about the same time (Gross, Giacquinta, and Bernstein 1971). However, his ideas were too advanced for what was, essentially, a lower-middle to working, class community, and soon ". . . school board members ran on a platform of firing the superintendent . . ." (Smith et al. 1987,44). While a new staff may have been an advantage in terms of their openness to innovation, their lack of experience was a hinderance, and too many strong egos (9 of 20 were male) made team-teaching and democratic decision making very difficult.

From 1966 to 1976 Kensington entered a kind of golden era. Many of the innovations were retained, while a more experienced and conservative principal and staff helped to achieve a welcome increase in structure and routine. Parents and school board were reassured. ". . . intellectuality was a highlight of the school . . . the place was alive with ideas" (Smith et al. 1987,172).

A major shift occurred in Kensington's climate from the mid-70s, precipitated by a change in the surrounding community from nearly 100 percent white suburbia to 60 percent black "urban fringe." When Smith and his colleagues visited in 1979, after a 15 year absence

> The unpleasant effect of barbed wire around the roof's periphery is punctuated by heavy metal grills, anti-vandal screens . . . broken glass, and other litter spread over the playground . . . graffito etched into . . . front door: "This school sucks!" . . . the office space, once open and airy, is now cluttered . . . the acting tower is stuffed with unused desks and chairs. The special screen displays only a ragged hole. The rear projector room is now a storage area for textbooks, clay molds, and a kiln (pp. 85–7) . . . conversion of open play shelter to lunchroom . . . removal of large aquarium . . . transformation of the audio-visual nerve center to a remedial reading classroom; and, of course, the erection of walls throughout much of the interior of the building (p. 175) . . . . The change in the physical appearance of Kensington was nothing compared to . . . the radical shifts in pedagogy and plant . . . [which] began with the fears of the staff, who suddenly faced a large number of students they didn't understand. Their urgent need to find mechanisms they could use to cope with the new student group, drove them back to what was most familiar, and what seemed to offer hope for the most control: self-contained classrooms, rigid curriculum, and tight—even coercive discipline . . . the issues of race, inner-city, and poverty, in the principal's eyes, are part of the influences that have taken the Kensington School from the most innovative school in the district to one of the most traditional in the district (Smith et al. 1987, 75–6). [Or, in the authors' view]: "From the culture of intellectual excitement to the culture of poverty."[2] (p. 168)

In the final analysis, Smith and his colleagues believe that ". . . social change overwhelms educational innovations" (p. 282). Kensington, despite formidable odds, had managed to incorporate a progressive, child-centered Deweyian vision of elementary schooling. This case study, based on two periods of intensive participant observation by students and faculty from Washington University, with gaps filled by lengthy interviews with key informants, including many no longer with the district, is unique in its broad scope.

PROGRESSIVE INITIATIVES: THE LAB SCHOOL

For convenience as much as anything else, I've grouped the case studies into three categories: studies of innovations that are essentially progressive in nature, that permit the teacher and/or students greater latitude and freedom; innovations that are conservative in nature, that restrict choice; and studies of mandated change. We begin with a study of a progressive innovation in a New York City school in 1966–67. "Cambire," while occupying a nearly 100-year-old building, was similar to Kensington in several respects. It was created as part of an administrator-launched reform effort, designated as a "Lab School," and incorporated what all acknowledged was a drastically different vision of the respective roles of teacher and pupil. The Lab School ". . . viewed the teacher as assisting children to learn according to *their* interests throughout the day . . . children are seen as different types of candles to be lit; the task of the teacher is to light each candle . . . . The pupil is given primary responsibility of directing his own education . . . [therefore the teacher's] primary function [is] as a guide" (Gross et al. 1971, 12–13). The researchers:

> . . . wanted to obtain a detailed description of the organizational dynamics that occurred after the introduction of a major innovation into an educational organization . . . and . . . the case study method was elected because it provided a . . . way to explore the complex . . . problem we proposed to study . . . [with] provision for the use of a variety of data-gathering methods . . . (pp. 42–3)

Nonparticipant observers used a small notebook to "jot down . . . key phrases . . . as the basis for . . . [later writing up] expanded notes" (p. 55). Archival material was gathered including school newsletters, teaching schedules, and reports prepared for the funding agency. Their initial impression was that teachers were favorable to innovation in general, but they ". . . did not have a clear understanding of the innovation [and] . . . appeared to be receiving little help . . . from their administrators who had asked them to change their role performance . . . " (p. 57).

The Lab School had a low pupil/teacher ratio; teachers were given a substantial salary boost to stay late two afternoons a week for staff meetings; they also developed new curricula during the summer; and per pupil expenditure was double that in surrounding schools. Staff were specially selected as being likely to succeed in a Lab School.

However, problems were apparent from the start and the authors make a point of stressing the thoroughness of their interviews. They interviewed all teachers, including student teachers for an average of four 45-minute sessions, although it was difficult pinning teachers down for these interview sessions.

> They responded to many "touchy" questions in a manner that indicated they were convinced of the confidentiality of the interview. There was little resistance to additional interview sessions. These experiences suggest that this aspect of the data collection was well received by the teachers. This conclusion is buttressed by the fact that a number of them voluntarily remarked that the interview served as a "soul searcher" or "a way of getting things off our chests. . . . " (p. 61)

From these interviews they constructed the following "data display" (see below p. 157).

They use the table not only to show what commonly occurred, but what was missing: "The key idea of the innovation . . . the teacher . . . as catalyst was only touched on . . . . Furthermore, these teachers could not, in spite of persistent probing, specify what it meant to be a 'guide' or 'supporting' " (p. 125).

TABLE 5.1   Types of Behavior that Teachers Reported They Would Need to Abandon or Adopt in Order to Conform to the New Role Model
(N = 10)

Types of Behavior	Teachers									
	1	2	3	4	5	6	7	8	9	10
Behavior to be abandoned:										
1. Teach formal lessons with group recitations			x			x	x	x	x	x
2. Serve as an authority figure	x						x		x	
New types of behavior:										
1. Give pupils feedom to choose activities	x	x	x	x	x	x	x		x	
2. Offer multiple activities, and individual attention		x	x		x	x		x		x
3. Saturate room with "self-instructional, high interest materials for pupils"		x	x	x			x	x		x
4. Tolerate noise	x		x		x		x			
5. Act as an advisor or offer support						x	x	x		x
6. Work with other teachers and subject specialists in the room		x	x			x	x			
7. Move about the room		x			x			x		

SOURCE: Gross, N., Giacquinta, J. B., & Bernstein, A. (1971). *Implementing organization innovations: a sociological analysis of planned educational change.* New York: Basic Books, p. 124. Reprinted by permission.

For a period of three weeks the investigators made random, unannounced visits to observe in the classrooms. Their focus was on the behavior of the teacher. Twelve criteria were used to determine the teacher's compliance with the new model, e.g., "permit students to choose their own activities, permit students to interact with each other. . . . These . . . criteria were selected on the basis of an analysis of documents describing the new role model . . ." (pp. 95–6). These criteria guided their observations and the analysis of their notes. They found that, overall, teachers had adopted the new model of instruction to only a very limited degree, using it from 0 percent to 20 percent of the time. The most notable alteration was the incorporation in many classes of "free-play" time (p. 119). From the authors' conclusions, it is clear that the administrators who developed the Cambire model were quite naive with respect to the difficulties teachers would encounter. The teachers got little advice in general and, in particular, found the child-centered philosophy to be incompatible with a constant stream of problems: "Pupil discipline . . . misuse of materials . . . lack of interest and motivation" (p. 133).

My own experience in a Lab School between 1984–1987 confirms the impression garnered from this work (Gross et al. 1971), that the very term Lab School is often an oxymoron. I was particularly interested in exploring the possible uses of microcomputers to create a new means of instruction. I found the regular school program to be, relatively, immutable; hence, I had to create a kind of "school within a school" (actually after school and summer school classes), to explore various models for computer use in schools (Lancy, 1987b).[3]

PROGRESSIVE INITIATIVES: CRITICAL THINKING

A decade or so before the microcomputer came on the scene, there was a great deal of interest in the instructional use of television. "Thinkabout," a series of sixty 15-minute programs, was developed for use in fifth and sixth grade classrooms to teach critical thinking skills, including: ". . . finding alternatives . . . using criteria . . . and collecting information" (Sanders and Sonnad 1982,1). It was evaluated by Jim Sanders and his associates using a hybrid quantitative/qualitative design.

Table 5.2 reflects what the authors consider to be the complementary strengths and weaknesses of the three major methods they employ (see also figure 1.3). Their goal was not to evaluate Thinkabout per se, but rather ". . . enlightenment, guidance in the use of Thinkabout, and planning for school television, in general . . . [their research was organized around a series of questions such as] . . . who made the decision to adopt [Thinkabout] into the curriculum? . . . How much change can be seen in students with respect to the series' basic goals?" (p. 3)

Testing was carried out in 241 classrooms, and 2,000 questionnaires were returned. While the survey results were highly positive, test results were mixed, and the case studies raised serious questions about some of the Thinkabout project's underlying premises. One such finding was that ". . . students perceived it as a break from work . . . [because there were] . . . few if any assignments, tests or projects—graded or ungraded—pertaining to it" (p. 10).

TABLE 5.2 Methods Used to Evaluate THINKABOUT

	Testing	Surveys	Case Studies
Strengths	—the participating classrooms were large in number and widespread geographically; they included both user and nonuser classrooms —multiple testing instruments were used; data on the classroom process were gathered —test data were collected three times during the year	—a large number of teachers and students responded —a large number of issues was addressed —surveys were conducted four times during the year	—holistic reports of experiences with the series in classrooms were generated —classrooms in different settings were examined —a wide range of issues and variables was addressed
Weaknesses	—only volunteer classrooms were used —no pilot testing in user classrooms was possible —the logistics of testing through the year were disruptive for the classrooms	—the sampling procedure limits generalizability —not all users could be identified for the mailing list —not all issues listed could be addressed by the surveys	—the number of sites and observers was limited —the only classrooms studied were those whose teachers were willing to open them up to outsiders —it is uncertain to what extent the findings will be applicable

SOURCE: Sanders, J., & Sonnad, S. (1982). *Research on the Introduction. Use and Impact of the Thinkabout Instructional Series.* Bloomington, IN: Agency for Instructional Television, pp 7–8. Reprinted by permission.

One of the in-depth case studies was conducted in 1979–80 by Sylvia Hart-Landsberg (1982) in a fifth grade class serving primarily white, middle-class children. As a trained anthropologist, Hart-Landsberg was obviously given considerable autonomy and this case study is unusually comprehensive, given its complementary nature vis-a-vis the quantitative components of the study. For example, to buttress her observations of Thinkabout in one class, she visited several other classes during Thinkabout broadcasts to gauge the degree of "typicality" of the case study teacher and her class. With respect to the former: ". . . she is more interested in social development (family influences, emotions, interpersonal relations) than cognitive development (particular skills acquired, levels of achievements, academic aspirations)" (p. 17). Hart-Landsberg also seeks out other instances of critical thinking instruction taking place in this particular class. Although there were several, she finds that the teacher and class handle most of these 'thought-provoking' opportunities in a shallow manner, using discussion exclusively. The issues are not used as a catalyst for further study and research.

The lack of correspondence between the published program schedule and the actual broadcast schedule thoroughly frustrated the teachers' limited attempts to foreshadow the programs and direct post-program discussions. Hence, ". . . The teacher and students did not appear to be self-consciously thinking about thinking. Rather, they seemed to try out a few isolated modes of thought without closely evaluating their effectiveness, associating them with the types of situations they fit, or comparing them" (p. 35).[4] And there was only one ". . . program which seems to have prodded the brightest minds in the class to probe deeply for ideas that were not immediately forthcoming" (p. 31).

Hence, while the quantitative data show positive attitudes toward Thinkabout, the case study material helps to illuminate why the test results were unspectacular. Everyone liked it but, in many cases, perhaps the majority, the program was used as a time-filler, a break from "work"—students were not given an opportunity to expand on their own knowledge base or improve their ability to process information. This teacher was unable to use the program to challenge students' preconceptions. On the contrary, as in the classes McNeil (1986) observed, there was an: "Avoidance of incendiary issues . . . religion, morality, power . . . money, sex, love" (p. 37).

Because of the thoroughness of Hart-Landsberg's study (it runs to 172 pages, at one point she uses three pages to present a verbatim transcription of one post-program discussion), any member of one of the several sponsoring agencies should have had no difficulty "experiencing" Thinkabout in a classroom setting—a distinct virtue of the well-done case study.

PROGRESSIVE INITIATIVES: THE CALIFORNIA MATHEMATICS FRAMEWORK

Hart-Landsberg's (1982) study, the Kensington study, and several more to be described below, approximate the wholistic thoroughness of an ethnography or field study, but what faith can we place in a research project where the non-participant observer spends only three class periods observing the phenomena of interest (Wilson, 1990)? That depends. A great deal, if the field of inquiry is carefully delimited, if the observation is supplemented by lengthy interviews with the teacher, if the study is one of a set of parallel case studies, and if the research team has carefully prepared their ground and drawn on published material and official documents to delineate the theoretical and political context for this particular innovation. Such is certainly true for a recently published study conducted by a team of faculty members from Michigan State University.

This group sought to study the impact of a new mathematics "Framework" adopted by the State of California in 1985. The Framework was intended to achieve profound change in the way math is taught in the schools. Textbook publishers were advised to adopt the Framework e.g., ". . . emphasize understanding rather than rules and to include novel topics [and] . . . if they did not make major changes, their book would be struck from . . . the adoption list" (p. 350). The Framework also precipitated change in the state's student achievement test. Twenty-three second and fifth grade teachers in three school districts varying in size, SES, and ethnicity were studied. Background or "policy context" was established by reviewing documents, and on-site and telephone interviews were conducted with key policy makers at state, district, and building levels.

Table 5.3 provides a very clear guide to the observer seeking to determine " . . . whether and how state-level mathematics curriculum policies have influenced classroom practice" (Cohen and Ball 1990,259). The study team visited the 23 teachers twice in December 1988 and once in March 1989, two years after the Framework had first been introduced. Observations of math lessons were supplemented by two hour-long interviews on: ". . . what the teacher was trying to teach, why the teacher was trying to teach it, how the teacher was trying to teach the material, and what the teacher thought the students got out of the lesson" (p. 260).

Let's consider the case of second grade teacher, Carol Turner (Ball 1990). " . . . her storehouse of devices includes . . . manipulatives . . . stories . . . metaphors, and gimmicks" (p. 265). She emphasizes "hands-on," active engagement, conveys enthusiasm for math, and devotes a long period each day to math instruction." While at first glance Carol appears to be in harmony with the Framework, a closer analysis reveals incongruities. For example, she does not subscribe to fundamental Framework premises like; ". . . mathematics . . . is something human beings have created and continue to construct . . . is inherently beautiful and fascinating . . . a domain of inquiry . . . as making and pursuing conjectures" (p. 272). She does not view mathematics the way mathematicians and others who use math creatively view it. She does not have a "whole language" view of mathematics (cf. Edelsky 1990). Ball's interpretation of the few lessons she observes as reflecting fundamental deviation from the Framework, is strengthened by the interviews with Carol, viz. "Carol has not actually spent any time studying the Framework or thinking about its implications for her practice . . . she stores it in a box . . ." (p. 270).

TABLE 5.3 Framework Versus Traditional Math Teaching Philosophies

Teaching for Understanding	Teaching Rules and Procedures
Emphasizes understanding	Emphasizes recall
Teaches a few generalizations	Teaches many rules
Develops conceptual schemes or interrelated concepts	Develops fixed or specific processes or skills
Identifies global relationships	Identifies sequential steps
Is adaptable to new tasks or situations (broad application)	Is used for specific tasks or situations (limited context)
Takes longer to learn but is retained more easily	Is learned more quickly but is quickly forgotten
Is difficult to teach	Is easy to teach
Is difficult to test	Is easy to test

SOURCE: Peterson, P. L. (1990). The California study of elementary mathematics. *Educational Evaluation and Policy Analysis,* 12(3), p. 258. Reprinted by permission.

Like Carol, Mark (Wilson 1990) is ". . . an energetic and enthusiastic teacher . . . [he] . . . has a reputation in the school for 'straightening out' troubled kids." "His students score very well in statewide achievement tests" (p. 309).

> Mark understood mathematics to be a set of procedures that students needed to master . . . while he was open to the possibility that there were alternative procedures that students could learn to solve those problems, he was aware of the limitations of his own knowledge . . . and concentrated on teaching students the methods he knew. He neither chose to help students generate their own algorithms nor explained how or why his procedures worked.
> Referring to a procedure in the new textbook . . . , he says: "I don't understand their procedure either. Let's do it my way for now. Boys and girls, if you look at the examples up there, they do it a completely different way in this book. I'm sorry, but I don't know that way, so if you don't know that way, do it as we've been doing it. Alright? I'm sorry, I don't know that way so we can only do it the way I know." (p. 312)

The other three case studies in this volume, and one presumes the 18 others that were not reported, all tell a similar tale. Namely that, even with very good teachers, even with those who are in synch with many aspects of the Framework, a drastic change in policy has had seemingly little impact on practice; a familiar theme in these studies of innovation (Cohen 1989).

PROGRESSIVE INITIATIVES: ENHANCING LITERACY EXPERIENCES AT HOME AND SCHOOL

A case study by the late David Logsdon and his colleagues (1988) suggests that parents are no quicker to change their "instructional" practices than are teachers. The study is interesting also because it reflects a refreshing degree of candor on the part of researchers who were also the program developers. "Pathways" was a ". . . new parent participation program [introduced] into a black, low income, urban school . . ." (p. 24). A great deal of data were collected during the very close monitoring of the project.

> . . . data were generated from interviews and observations that had their formal and informal sides. Throughout the project, . . . observations and interviews were conducted continuously by the project staff with teachers, parents, and the principal. This monitoring occurred on practically a daily basis, and the feedback was discussed by staff at biweekly meetings. Formal, open-ended, focused interviews were conducted by a graduate student with teachers, parents, and the school principal. These amounted to 39 phone interviews and indepth, face-to-face interviews with parents and their student-children. A midyear evaluation feedback meeting was held for staff, teachers, and the principal at the school. In addition, paper-and-pencil evaluative questionnaires were forwarded to parents for their ratings of the usefulness of the instructional materials. (Logsdon et al. 1988,24)

The focus of their research shifted from an evaluation of the Pathways activities to a consideration of the broader social and cultural issues that were implicated. "From our rather naive stance at the beginning, we have learned a great deal about teacher and parent involvement, parent/student activities . . . and the conduct of responsive evaluation . . . " (p. 36).

A lesson that seems to need to be learned anew by each potential innovator is reflected in this comment "It was never the teachers' project . . . they never embraced it with a level of enthusiasm that indicates commitment and ownership. Rather, the project belonged to and came from an external source: The university's faculty and staff . . . " (p. 35). Another lesson was that a majority of parents were not interested in "becoming involved," and the highest priority for those who were was "helping children with homework."

I will briefly report on two similar projects that I was involved in to further explicate some of these "lessons." From early 1990 until the end of the 1991 school year, I conducted a case study of "Running Start," a Chrysler Corporation funded effort to get parents to read more to their children and to encourage their children to read more books at home. Although I had no stake in the success of the project, I wanted the research effort to blend with and complement the program as much as possible. Every aspect of the case study was planned with the classroom teacher, Ann Zupsic. I have already mentioned (p. 18) "Ten Tips for Reading at Home With Your First Grader" that were sent home, and which I used as a basis for constructing my interview with each parent. In addition, I used Clay's (1979) *Concepts About Print* test in lieu of a "reading readiness test," because the CAP test is actually incorporated into a small picture book. Finally, our (Lancy and Zupsic, 1991) vehicle for determining whether children had indeed been read to at home was to have them retell the story into a tape recorder in school—a strategy that is advocated in some Family Literacy programs. Our findings are quite consistent with Logsdon and with much of the research reported in this chapter: Running Start may stimulate a preexisting storybook reading scheme in the home, but it did not create such a scheme where none existed before.

I was the developer for the "Parent-Assisted Early Reading Program," which contrasted with the two previously described parent-involvement projects along three dimensions. First, teachers were involved in planning the project—at least three months before the grant proposal was even submitted. Hence, they did have a genuine sense of ownership, subscribed to the goals of the project, and helped to define its methods. They continued to support the project after the grant ran out and the developer had left the scene, and have given workshops for other schools that want to adopt it. Along a second dimension, based on previous research, I (Lancy et al. 1989) knew that merely "inviting" parents to become involved in their children's emergent literacy would have little effect. Hence, this project was designed to bring volunteer parents into the classroom to "replicate" the storybook reading experience that is commonplace in upper-middle-class homes but, apparently, lacking in the homes of poor children (Teale 1986). Third, virtually all of the money from the small state grant that funded this project was spent on the innovation with little left to support the conduct of a careful case study (Lancy & Nattiv 1992). Hence, it is not clear whether education is better served by a relatively successful innovation that is inadequately documented, or by less successful innovations that are well-documented.

I would like to end this section on somewhat of an optimistic note by describing a case study of an innovation that seems to have "taken hold," at least in one classroom. Carole Edelsky and her students, Kelly Draper and Karen Smith (1983), report on the classroom dynamics during the first few weeks of the school year in the latter's sixth grade class. The innovation in question is the use of *whole language* philosophy (Edelsky et al. 1991) to guide the development of a language arts curriculum. Whole language, as contrasted with "bottom-up" or molecular approaches to teaching reading, emphasizes the importance of meaning construction, and the use of authentic texts, rather than dittoed "exercises." It is, in many ways, more complicated than other methods, and there should be striking differences in the way the classroom is organized. The authors used ". . . the teachers' goals, as revealed in interviews, as organizers of data" (Edelsky et al. 1983,263). They ended up with eight including "To get students to see opportunities everywhere for learning" (p. 263). Indeed, the qualities that Karen Smith seeks to infuse in her classroom bear more than a superficial resemblance to the qualities which one sees in the philosophies underlying Kensington, Cambire, and the California Framework.

Karen's class was selected because she was considered to be a model exponent of the whole language philosophy, and because her sixth graders, poor, Hispanic, and the recipients of at least five years of a "basic skills" approach to language instruction, might be expected to experience difficulty and display "resistance" when exposed to a radically different form of instruction (see also Meeks and Lancy, nd).

Edelsky and Draper conducted ". . . participant observation of teacher-student interaction all day, every day for the first two weeks of school and then three days per week for the next three weeks. Video and audio tape recordings made periodically, were used to confirm and modify the focus for further observation'' (p. 261).

From their notes they documented the myriad strategies Smith uses to give students "freedom without license," including "privatizing reprimands" and "minimal guidance," which was effective because " . . . when students carried out their own rather than the teacher's tasks, . . . they already knew what they would do" (p. 272). These terms, while not emic (e.g., not Karen Smith's) nevertheless are clearly grounded in the data; that is "privatizing reprimands" is a carefully phrased gloss to describe a pattern which was frequently found in the notes and video tapes.

Student interviews provide another "leg" of the triangulated inquiry, and one of the more revealing findings here was that " . . . despite conducting science experiments, participating in discussions, rehearsing reading performances they would later give for first graders, and so on, they thought that . . . so far they hadn't done any 'work' " (p. 262). Finally, quantitative data were used to show that the class was "successful" in more conventional terms as well—e.g., better attendance, higher levels of academic engagement, and higher standardized test scores.

CONSERVATIVE INITIATIVES: MANAGING AND TEACHING BY OBJECTIVES

Harry Wolcott's (1977) *Teachers vs Technocrats,* a " . . . case study in educational innovation . . ." (p. 1) makes for painful reading. Not because the innovation was not successful, but because, although obviously doomed from the start, it continued to consume tax dollars (1 million dollars +), and the time and energy of a group of fine "teachers and technocrats" for years! But it also makes fascinating reading because it reveals so clearly the often ambivalent role of the evaluator. In brief, Wolcott was hired to study the *process* whereby an innovative information management system was developed and trialed in the South Lane (Cottage Grove, OR) School District. He maintains his distance and neutrality in the face of teachers who are concerned that they are being (perhaps unfairly) evaluated; developers whose jobs and/or careers may be on the line; Wolcott's faculty colleagues at Oregon; gung ho administrators, and so on. After reading this, one is not surprised by Wolcott's confession that," Through my participation in this study I have also realized that I am far more favorably disposed towards basic research efforts that seek to learn about schools than towards developmental efforts that seek to manipulate educational processes" (p. 3).

Before proceeding to describe Wolcott's methods, an epistemological digression is in order. In the first chapter (p. 30), I discussed the problem of defining the researcher's perspective—should she maintain an independent, perhaps, even skeptical or antagonistic stance or should she totally adopt the perspective of the people whose work she is studying (William Foote Whyte [1984], a great advocate of this latter position, happily reports on two doctoral students doing dissertation research in the third world, one of whom joined an armed resistance movement and the second organized and led a postal workers' strike) or somewhere in between? This question takes on a special urgency when applied to the case study because the findings can inevitably be read as reflecting on how well someone is doing their job. Hemwall (1986) identifies the conflict between protecting informants whose jobs might be threatened vs ". . . the need for the forthright answers required in an honest evaluation . . ." (p. 149).

In the case studies reviewed to this point we've seen variations on this theme. Smith and his colleagues have nothing to do with the development of the Kensington School, but they are clearly excited by and sympathetic towards all these new ideas. Wolcott makes abundantly clear his lack of sympathy for the "SPECS" project, his *Introducion* is subtitled: *Bias at Work: Proceed with Caution.* Gross et al. (1971) seem to come closest to Patton's (1990) ideal "neutrality," one doesn't detect whether they were for or against the innovations at Cambire. Hart-Landsberg (1982) maintains a healthy skepticism, like these others, she's a hired outsider. Edelsky, Draper, and Smith (1983) have differentiated roles, and the systematic reporting of their data collection and analysis techniques inspires confidence. Also they stick to the "how" question, which is a lot less sticky than "how well?" Logsdon et al. (1988), on the other hand, and Lancy (Lancy, Forsyth, and Meeks 1987; Lancy and Hayes 1988) are developer/researchers and their reports reveal the inherent conflict that this dual role entails. Finally, we might cite Papert's (1980) "case study" of his own educational innovation, the LOGO programming language, which doesn't even leave open the possibility of failure.

SPECS was developed during an "accountability" movement that swept the schools in the early 1970s, and its essence is reflected in the following: ". . . School district personnel engage in a particular kind of rational, data-based planning of the district's operating programs . . . involving . . . development of an initial plan, implementation of that plan, collection of outcome information, analysis of expected and actual outcomes, generation of alternatives, selection of a new plan, implementation of it, and so forth . . . " (Wolcott 1977,24). With very little assistance, and with the program constantly undergoing revision, teachers were expected to implement the model at the classroom level by developing a set of objectives for each subject area, specifying what they would do to reach those objectives, and then carefully recording student progress towards meeting the objectives. Resistance from teachers was pronounced due to the loss of autonomy; their antipathy towards the superintendent and the developers, all of whom were seen as pursuing primarily their own career self-interests; and their belief that the *basic skills, mastery learning* philosophy imbedded in SPECS wasn't *needed* in their classrooms. Some representative comments:

> It was strictly a railroad job. . . . I should have a say in what is going on in my classroom . . . the developers are so far removed from those of us at the 'peon' level (p. 39). . . . I can't possibly do all the pretesting. Having all these goals, . . . this is all good, but if you've been teaching very long, you do these things anyway" (p. 40) . . . [this is] the sixth educational innovation I have worked with in the past 16 years. All but one was forced on the faculty by an eager ladder-climbing administrator . . . all ultimately failed—with much time,

energy, and money wasted . . . (p. 43). It has made glorified bookkeepers out of faculty instead of allowing them to teach. . . . The program insists that students learn *facts* rather than concepts . . . our educational system is already too fact-oriented. This program appears to set education back 70 years (p. 45) . . . teachers enjoyed toying with alternative labels that would accurately reflect their sentiment toward the program. One popular acronym . . . was CRAP—for Curriculum Recycling And Planning. (p. 82)

While Wolcott (1977), in one sense, passes immediate judgement on SPECS, in another sense, he is unable to reach any conclusion or lead the reader to any conclusion about the program's worth. This because it was never really *implemented* in any sense that the developers would acknowledge, ". . . the developers had never specified exactly what constituted SPECS . . ."(p. 87). This failure of developers to specify the nuts and bolts of their innovative visions, coupled with the teachers' "filter" makes a final determination (*summative evaluation*) of whether an innovation "works," nearly impossible. For example, Anderson (1977) sums up the massive, multi-million dollar evaluation of Project Follow Through, a comparison of 22 theoretically-inspired models to compensate for fall off in Head Start gains. There was no clear advantage for any program, rather: "*The effectiveness of each Follow Through model depended more on local circumstances than on the nature of the model*" (p. 13).

But Wolcott is not particularly concerned that he cannot evaluate SPECS, because he capitalizes on the opportunity given to him as the "staff ethnographer" to look at larger, more enduring issues. In particular, he uses most of the book to discuss the different world views held by teachers and technocrats. He, in fact, offers separate narrative accounts of the SPECS project from both perspectives and draws on constructs from anthropology to aid his analysis. Ultimately, ". . . SPECS . . . seemed simply to fade away without any dramatic final collapse" (p. 239); although, it is clear that it would have faded away years earlier had it not been for the steady infusion of federal funds. One staff member commented: "This is what happens when Universities go whoring after federal dollars" (p. 110).

AGGREGATING CASE STUDY DATA

Some sense of the enormous number of programmatic educational innovations, supported by various levels of government, can be gleaned from Huberman and Miles' (1984) comparative analysis. They conducted 12 in-depth case studies as part of a quantitative evaluation of 146 projects funded by the *National Diffusion Network* or *Title IV-C*.

> . . . each to be visited for a total of 8 to 12 days during the school year, along with intermittent phone contact . . . [we] . . . prespecified a general conceptual model . . . and derived from it a set of 34 systematic research questions that would guide our local inquiries, while still leaving us open to "what the site

had to tell us"...[using]...nonparticipant observation, informal and structured interviewing, and document review. (p. 5)

Sites were selected to reflect the inherent diversity in the larger sample, e.g., region of country, setting, program status (expanding, ongoing, dwindling), and program content (early childhood, reading/math, social studies), etc. However "... most of the programs we studied entailed few organizational changes; they were mostly modest, manageable, content-oriented efforts" (p. 6). During site visits the investigators used observations and interviews to ask fairly general questions like: "What was the school like before [the innovation] entered the picture? (p. 9)" Site visits were often timed to coincide with a "decisive event . . . a district office meeting, staff planning sessions . . . " (p. 8). They reviewed documents, but, in some cases ". . . the paper trail was almost nonexistent" (p. 9).

Data collection was done by hired assistants. Their observations were dictated after site visits. These were then typed and coded by the "principal investigators." They started with 34 research questions, as they worked through the data they identified 31 "core variables" (p. 13).

> *Descriptive* codes were used in the margin of field notes to characterize a "chunk" of the notes. For example, the code AP-MOT (adoption process—motives) was applied to this piece of the Tindale field notes: "I asked him what the need for the new program was, and he responded that the students coming into the ninth grade were two years below grade level, and that the old curriculum was ineffective. Through testing (the *Nelson Reading Test*) it was determined that students were growing academically only five to six months during the ten-month school year."
>
> The second kind of code—actually, a metacode—was *explanatory*. Such codes emerged from our experience with the sites and were usually *leitmotivs* (repeated themes) or causal explanations of outcomes that were offered by site people or that emerged from our own musings. For example, the explanatory code CL-EXPL (causal link—explanation) was applied to this segment of the Banestown field notes: "But he [Mr. Walt] says that he does not know that much about what is exactly involved in the catch-up program. He thinks that "it is a combination of a lot of things." The resource lab appears to be used in the morning for the FACILE program, which Mr. Walt knows a great deal more about. . . . In the afternoon, Mrs. Hampshire uses the lab for catch-up purposes. Mr. Walt says that this is a difrerent program, and therefore, it is a different use."
>
> This apparently innocuous statement, we learned very early in our Banestown contacts, reflected a long and acute power struggle between two factions in the central office, in one of which Mr. Walt was active. The CL-EXPL code was applied to other instances of this struggle (p. 14).

As new data came in, there was a need to revise the code, however, the "... coding system stabilized fairly [early] . . . so a minimum of back recoding was required" (p. 15).

All this discussion of codes, variables, the use of research assistants, structured interviews, 8–12 days observation, etc., should give us pause. Is this research qualitative? Indeed, Miles and Huberman (1988) quite recently have acknowledged that their work fails to adhere to most canons of the qualitative paradigm. However, the brief mention of a "power struggle" in the above excerpt suggests they were not blind to nuance. Furthermore, as we shall soon see, there is evidence that they derive their categories from the data. Regardless of where we place Miles and Huberman on the qualitative-quantitative continuum, we must acknowledge the enormous contribution they have made to the repertoire of tools for data reduction and display the qualitative researcher has access to. Annette Lareau's (1989) field study (see Chapter 3) is very evidently qualitative, but she freely acknowledges her debt to them.

Masepa School District was an example of a site where the innovation (ECRI: ". . . a highly regimented and task-oriented behavior modification teaching strategy" [Huberman and Miles, 1984,26]) did have a fairly large impact on practice. That is, many teachers adopted the ECRI model. Table 5.4 shows Miles and Huberman's (1984b) technique for analyzing qualitative data and creating a qualitative "data display." Some of their categories are externally imposed, such as "initial attitude toward program"; some derived from the data, "self-improvement," "social influence"; some are low inference, "early users," "administrators," and some high inference, "centrality." The data display provides a kind of middle ground between narrative description (Miles and Huberman are very critical of narrative description in evaluation reports) and frequency tables.[5]

Miles and Huberman (1984b) identify 12 techniques that they use to "make sense" of qualitative data, for example "When we identify a theme or pattern, we are isolating something (a) that happens a number of times and (b) that consistently happens in a specific way . . . [these] judgements are based on *counting*" (p. 215). They can then move towards quantification if this seems warranted. When they quantified their data regarding career moves, an unexpected and important theme, the analysis showed that while there were a large number of job moves attributed to the innovation process, ". . . only 35 percent of the job-related shifts were upward ones, contrary to our early impression" (Miles and Huberman 1984b,216). Note that they use quantitative data to check the credibility of their initial qualitative analysis of the data, in much the same way that others use qualitative data to check the validity of survey data. For example, Logsdon et al. (1988) discounted the high level of positive responses on their parent questionnaire because these were contradicted by more direct observation of the low parent participation in the Pathways project.

Table 5.5 shows Huberman and Miles at a later stage of analysis as they aggregate over all sites. They have extracted from their 31 core variables those that seemed likely predictors of "magnitude of change," which could be considered their *dependent variable.*

At the high-change sites, the projects began with a vengeance, induced pervasive changes (not only in daily routines but also in basic constructs), took a long settling-down time, consumed all available energy, caused negative changes (e.g., loss of variety and sacrifice of other, favorite activities), and did all this through administrative pressure. At the low-change sites, there was the inverse profile:

TABLE 5.4 Motives and Attitudes of Users, Nonusers, and Administrators at Masepa

	Motives	Career Relevance	Centrality	Initial Attitude toward Program
Early users: 1977–78				
R. Quint	*Self-improvement:* "To get better, I had to change. . . . Maybe I wasn't teaching the best ways." *Pressure:* "They wanted us to do it." *Social influence:* Everybody was saying what Gail's doing is great."	None—improvement of practice	*High:* "Biggest thing I've ever done that somebody else told me to do."	*Neutral:* "There wasn't any appeal. They said it worked so I was going to try it."
. . .		. . .	. . .	. . .
Recent users: 1979–80				
V. Sharpert	*Obligation:* Requirement to obtain teaching post: "I didn't have a choice." *Practice-improvement:* Complementing preservice training.	Ticket to teaching job in the district	*High:* "My first job."	*Neutral:* Apprehensive
. . .		. . .	. . .	. . .
Nonuser:				
C. Shinder	*Relative disadvantage: Poor fit with personal style:* "Too scholastic . . . too programmed."	None	Not applicable	*Unfavorable* "My program was *better.*"
. . .		. . .	. . .	. . .

TABLE 5.4 (continued)

	Motives	Career Relevance	Centrality	Initial Attitude toward Program
Administrators:				
K. Weeling Principal	*Met need:* "I was looking for a highly structured, skill-oriented reading program." *Novelty, promise of practical improvement:* Intrigued by reading about mastery learning; wanted to see it in operation.	None at first; later, appreciated	*High:* "Largest investment I've ever made."	*Neutral:* then favorable
J. Dahloff Curriculum Coordinator	*Relative advantage, face validity of program:* "Well organized," could be used for other subject matters. *Social influence:* "Impressed" that outstanding teachers favored the program. *Practice improvement:* beginning teachers ill-prepared in reading; "We didn't know what to do with them. . . . They just had to learn on the job."	Another in a series of implementations	*Moderate:* "It was one thing among a lot of things I was working on."	*Favorable*
	...	...	...	...

SOURCE: Huberman, A. M., & Miles, M. B. (1984). *Innovation up close: How school improvement works.* New York: Plenum, p.46. Reprinted by permission.

TABLE 5.5 Predictors of Magnitude of User Practice Change

Magnitude of change by sites	Early Impletation Requirements					Administrative Pressure	
	Required practice changes	Project size/scope	Classroom/ organizational fit	Index of early imple. req.	General attitude during implement	Direct: strong-arming	Indirect: exhorting reinforcing
High change							
Masepa (NDN)	Major	Large	Mod-good	14	Positive	High	High
Plummet (IV-C)	Mod-major	Large	Good-poor	12	Positive	Low	High
Moderate change							
Bannestown (NDN)	Major	Small-mod	Moderate	10	Positive	Mod	High
Tindale (IV-C)	Major	Large-mod	Moderate	12	Positive	High	High
Carson (IV-C)	Major	Large	Moderate	13	Positive	Low	High
Perry-Parkdale (NDN)	Mod-major	Mod	Moderate	10	Positive	Low	Low-mod
Moderate-low change							
Calston (NDN)	Moderate	Small	Poor	9	Positive	Mod	Mod
Lido (NDN)	Moderate	Small	Moderate	7	Positive	Low	Mod
Small-no change							
Burton (NDN)	Minor	Small	Good	3	Positive	Low	Mod
Dun Hollow (IV-C)	Minor	Small	Poor	7	Negative	Mod	Low
Proville (IV-C)	Minor	Moderate	Moderate	7	Negative	Mod	Mod
Astoria (NDN)	Minor	Small	Good	3	Positive	Low	Low

SOURCE: Huberman, A. M., & Miles, M. B. (1984). *Innovation up close: How school improvement works*. New York: Plenum, p. 162. Reprinted by permission.

timid beginnings, modest changes in daily routines, rapid practice mastery, minor energy expenditure, and little user sense of having been "stretched." (Huberman and Miles 1984,167)

The principal findings of this study are not aimed so much at determining which programs are good and which bad, but a better understanding of the process itself; viz: "As our analysis proceeded, we developed a more differentiated list of outcomes, as follows: . . . *stabilization of use* . . . [or] "settledness" of the new practice . . . *percentage of use* . . . *institutionalization,* the degree to which the innovation was . . . incorporated into the ordinary structures and procedures of the school . . ." (p. 188). There were some surprises as well ". . . at least half the projects we were studying did have decisive effects on job changes . . . an example of a frequent, but largely unremarked, outcome of school improvement projects" (p. 188).[6]

Our last study in this section is not, strictly speaking, a case study. Rather, it is a quantitative evaluation that also included some "unanticipated qualitative outcomes" (Robbins 1986). The project was a federally-funded ("Follow-Through") attempt to train teachers to enhance *academic learning time.* Quantitative results were generally positive, especially in years one and two, and compared to some of the other programs we've reviewed (e.g., SPECS, Cambire), teachers received extensive training and were given a great deal of "released time" for planning. The qualitative data consisted of ". . . notes submitted to the project director by teachers and principals throughout the four-year effort, and from participants' written reflections about their project experiences . . ." (p. 145).

The "outcomes" gleaned from this material included, among others, that teachers were given a great deal of autonomy and administrators responded to their complaints about problems with the program; there seemed to be much greater cooperation among teachers; and teachers developed a much richer "instructional strategies" schema. I include Robbins's study here, as much as anything, to show that even a very modest qualitative study can find its way into a respectable journal.

THE EVALUATION OF MANDATED INITIATIVES

As Huberman and Miles (1984) indicate, innovation may be enhanced by "external pressure." At the same time that various government entities promote various innovations on a voluntary basis, they also mandate change. And, not surprisingly, innovations that occur as a result of these mandates are often implemented more smoothly. There is much less "resistance" as educators "bow to the inevitable."

Chesterfield (1986) reports on a multiple case study of federally mandated bilingual Head Start programs. He does a very good job of characterizing this more ". . . 'formalized' qualitative research" (p. 147), viz.:

> . . . data collected . . . were sent weekly to the central office, where they were monitored by the supervisor/coordinator of field work. . . . To meet these

multiple goals, an evaluation approach that combined many techniques generally associated wih ethnographic research, such as relatively long-term immersion at a site, unstructured interviewing, and written narratives of observations, with psychometric testing and surveying of parents, was developed. In order to examine general trends, however, and to provide a framework for comparing the models, a number of the qualitative data collection and data reduction procedures were standardized . . . observers . . . job was not to define the nature of a particular social reality, but rather to focus on contextually relevant data that explained the presence or absence of outcomes or events expected by the model developers. (Chesterfield 1986,147–9)

Note the similarity in aim to the Thinkabout and Framework case studies reported above.

Although many of the large-scale studies reported in this chapter employed trained research assistants, this is one of the few reports that provides some information on how that was handled.

> . . . a number of procedures aimed at securing consistent data were also carried out. These included (1) an initial three-week training period in the techniques of naturalistic observation, including simulation of fieldwork in local preschool classrooms; (2) additional training sessions prior to each phase of fieldwork; (3) the use of standardized formats for data recording; (4) the development of a field manual to supplement training sessions by providing operational definitions of the phenomena under study, delineating role relationships, and specifying ethical and confidentiality considerations; and (5) the conducting of parallel observations by the coordinator of fieldworkers. . . . (p. 152)[7]

Observers were further "controlled" by the use of "implementation forms" and "time and event samples" (p. 148). Descriptions of each site were written which focused on the feasibility of exporting the particular model under investigation. These lengthy descriptions were then reviewed by ". . . senior staff [who] distilled them into . . . categories, each containing a list of specific factors which the individual researchers had identified as facilitating or impeding implementation . . ." (p. 153).

Chesterfield (1986) presents only a sampling of the findings, e.g., ". . . a single half-day session was the most effective type of daily schedule . . ." (p. 153). He also indicates some of the ways that observational data were used to aid in interpreting or qualifying the test results. For example, "Spanish preferred" children had a very different pattern of language development over the year, depending on whether they started the year "knowing some English."

Vanguard is the name given to the gifted and talented program in the Houston Public Schools. It became a critical agent in the federally mandated desegregation effort. In particular, specific schools were designated as Vanguard or "magnet" schools. Thus, racial segregation was replaced by segregation based on academic talent. Ferrell and Compton (1986) describe their case study of Vanguard during the 1981–82 school year. They made three site visits for observation and also conducted open-ended interviews with key personnel, including 23 teachers,

9 counselors, and 10 principals. Students were assessed in focus-group interviews. Parents were surveyed by mail.

One very interesting issue which they touch on is that: "Despite the fact that one of the purposes of magnet schools is to integrate the district at both student and staff levels, questions related to whether or not prejudicial attitudes existed and the extent to which integration was taking place were deleted by administration" (p. 175). Others report similar problems, suggesting the level of antipathy towards evaluative research that one should be prepared for. The Cambire observers found that occasionally their presence did make a difference, viz. ". . . during his visits . . . this teacher insisted on talking continuously to the field worker rather than interacting with pupils . . . another teacher . . . told . . . the children about his probable visits and asked them to be 'extra nice the next time he comes' " (Gross et al. 1971,94).

Overall their results reflected positively on the Vanguard program, academic achievement was high and, more important, there was little or no segregation or inter-racial conflict observed or mentioned in the interviews. "Vanguard students . . . stuck together. They were a very close multi-racial group" (p. 187). However, some problems were identified. Since the court order specified that any "magnet" program had to have a racial composition of 44 percent black, 30 percent Hispanic, 23 percent White, and 3 percent Asian, many white applicants were turned down with higher scores than Black and Hispanic students who were admitted. The quality of teachers was uneven and wealthier parents, in particular (see also Lareau 1989) were likely to be dissatisfied with the quality of teaching. Another problem was that the curriculum was not terribly distinctive, however, they did note a greater ". . . emphasis on the development of research skills by students" (p. 184). And Vanguard was mercifully free of the pervasive anti-intellectualism prevalent in student culture.

Finally, Ferrell and Compton (1986) make a number of recommendations, including: ". . . the development of a district wide job description for Vanguard teachers . . . [also to] . . . look for better ways to identify gifted minority children" (p. 190). These recommendations raise an important issue which we have just barely touched on (see general attribute #7, p. 143). Despite what I said about the problem-solving nature of the case-study in the introduction, one may not actually encounter any recommendations in the published report of the case study. First, the authors may be concerned primarily with process rather than outcome (e.g., Wolcott 1977). Second, recommendations may well have been included in the unpublished report to one's clients but in published work addressed to other academics, the emphasis may be on aspects of methodology, or grand theory (Smith and Keith 1971). Third, the report may indeed be aimed at a *summative* as against *formative* evaluation (Scriven 1967). The former assumes that the innovation is "finished," what we want to know is whether it worked (e.g., Robbins 1986) not how to improve it; while the latter assumes that there are still opportunities to modify the program, thereby rendering "recommendations" essential. The last case study to be reported on in this chapter was designed from the start to serve the purpose of formative evaluation.

Mainstreaming is one of the legacies of PL 94-142 described in Chapter 3. Hemwall (1984) conducted a study designed to provide ". . . an understanding of *every day* mainstreaming experiences" (p. 134, italics added) for a group of seven hearing-impaired students in a secondary school. Aside from the clear emphasis on formative evaluation, her report is unusual in the thoroughness of the historical context she creates. She reviews attempts as far back as the 1820s to integrate deaf students into regular classrooms.

The study was conducted during the 1979–1980 school year. It was the third year of the program and it was not running smoothly. This, despite the fact that it was only a "part-time placement . . . and . . . [provided a] full range of supportive services, including tutoring and sign interpreters in the classroom" (p. 136). The staff had mixed feelings about Hemwall, wanting her help but concerned that they would come out looking bad ". . . even though they had been assured that no direct evaluation of their teaching was being done" (p. 148). She played a participant-observer role (she was a tutor) which probably helped to ease these concerns.

Among the problems she was able to identify was that the hearing-impaired students made little attempt to "attend" to class proceedings, as they became dependent on their note-taker/tutor/interpreter to teach them after class whatever was covered during class. Teachers reinforced this tendency by addressing remarks to the interpreter rather than the students. The teacher also, unwittingly, gave them license to "tune out" by not holding them to the same discipline standards as the other students.

Hemwall (1984) made a number of formal recommendations e.g., the program should strive to promote independence on the part of students; and teachers require much more inservice training to assist them in working with the hearing-impaired. However, she claims that ". . . the nature of [qualitative] data is such that it allowed the staff . . . to be actively involved. . . . They awaited the latest . . . tidbits . . . with great anticipation . . ." (p. 150). This contrasts with the enormous frustration that teachers involved in the SPECS project felt at not getting feedback from the researchers, which moved Wolcott (1977) to write: "'When are the developers allowed to learn what the researchers find out?' To a developer, the satisfactory answer is, 'as soon as possible.' To a researcher, the satisfactory answer is, 'As soon as the project's completed and the information itself will no longer effect the course of events'" (p. 89). But note that in the SPECS case the researchers were charged with the task of summative evaluation, even though it is very clear that SPECS was not, by any means, a finished product.

Indeed, the "in process" nature ("expanding," "ongoing," "dwindling") of so many innovations, precludes summative evaluation in many cases. And, even when summative data are called for and are available, their implications may be ignored (e.g., Wolfe 1987). Alkin and his associates (1979) were interested in the question of just how evaluations (including both qualitative and quantitative studies) are used. They conducted case studies of five innovative projects in California that had a built-in evaluation component. In one case study the client felt hampered by the evaluation, the need to keep detailed records took time away from other things. Also, it was difficult to specify and measure "outcomes" as required by the terms of the grant. In this, and other projects, the teachers and administrators were unwilling to accept "standardized test scores" (which, presumably, didn't change) as evidence of the project's success or failure.[8] Another issue is that ". . . evaluators must be able to talk in the language of school people. Statistics frighten many people . . ." (p. 123). Indeed, many of the school personnel felt that the: ". . . evaluator should be totally involved in the full range of activities" (p. 105). Overall, they found that where evaluation results were formative in nature, couched in the form of useable recommendations, they had an impact. If they were presented primarily after the fact as summative judgements, they tended to have less impact.

WHAT IS THE CASE FOR GENERALIZATION?

As we have seen, the norm in qualitative research is long-term immersion in the field, which gives credence to the researcher's claim to speak for all similar groups or situations: "If the truth be known, ethnographers, like the rest of us, make whopping generalizations from rather modest observations of a few cases. Their forte lies in knowing those cases exceedingly well, and in recognizing a critical distinction between generalizing and overgeneralizing" (Wolcott 1987,50). But the examples presented in this chapter make clear that this criteria is rarely met in the case study. Instead Stake (1978) offers a different view of generalization as applied to the case study: ". . . case studies . . . may be . . . in harmony with the reader's experience and thus . . . a natural basis for generalization" (p. 5). Put differently ". . . generalizability is ultimately related to what the reader is trying to learn from the case study" (Kennedy 1979,672). This is comparable to the law where the applicability of a particular precedent case must be argued in each subsequent case. The reader must decide whether the findings apply or not.

I referred earlier to Linda McNeil's (1986) study of "defensive teaching." This is a 234-page book, and McNeil's entire "methods section" is reproduced below:

> The research reported herein included at least one full semester's classroom observation in selected teachers' social studies classes. Lectures were noted nearly verbatim; course materials were analyzed, as were classroom patterns of interaction. Teachers gave information through informal conversations over the course of one semester and in tape-recorded, semi-structural interviews. Administrators who had direct or indirect, formal or informal authority over subject fields, teachers' evaluation, or curriculum development were similarly interviewed. (p. 219n)

This statement alone hardly inspires confidence in McNeil's very broad generalization of her findings. However, I was prepared to treat them as credible because they so faithfully mirror my own observations. I am less willing to accept the wide applicability of Ferrell and Compton's (1986) principal finding because it contradicts my own, admittedly limited, observations.

What, then, can be said about innovation in education? I reproduce below two assessments written in 1971, the first in the U.S., the second in the UK. ". . . negligible educational effects resulting from the numerous innovations that have been introduced into . . . schools" (Gross et al. 1971,4).

> For nearly two decades now, we have seen large amounts of capital invested in the production of a variety of new curricula. Unfortunately, evidence is beginning to accumulate that much of this effort has had relatively little impact on the daily routine of the average classroom . . . [the writer goes on to identify the critical event in the process of extinition] . . . grant expires and . . . outside consultant or team leaves the scene. (Herron, cited in Stenhouse 1975,209)

One would be hard pressed to argue that things have changed a great deal in the last twenty years. For example, I have been a diligent observer of the impact of microcomputers on education, and aside from their contribution to fostering the learning of *writing as a process* (perhaps the lasting innovation of the last decade), I still see (Lancy 1987b; 1990) mostly "unrealized potential." Nevertheless, hope springs eternal and "programs" (as opposed to, say, just spending lots more money than we do presently on salaries, materials, and physical plant, or, say, drastically raising teaching certification standards), will continue to thrive. Which means that studies of some sort in the form of quantitative evaluation or more naturalistic case studies will be drawn along in their wake. I would hope, therefore, that we can continue to improve these studies and that we seek to find a larger audience for the final report, so that the public knowledge base (e.g., ERIC) will continue to grow. Because, to agree with Stake (1978), most project directors will make more reasoned decisions if they have access to a rich collection of reports bearing on similar situations.

NOTES

1. For a more recent analysis of elementary arts curricula based on the perspective referred to as "educational criticism" see Barone (1987) and the following critique of Barone's analysis by Rist (1987).
2. The original culture of poverty theory comes from Lewis (1961) and has been critiqued by Valentine (1968). Much the same concept is now referred to as "the permanent underclass."
3. We used "interactive fiction" to stimulate interest in reading (Lancy and Hayes 1988); simulation games to teach social studies (Forsyth and Lancy 1987, 1989; Lancy 1990); word processing in a composition class (Lancy, Forsyth, and Meeks 1987); and electronic construction sets" to teach reasoning (Lancy 1991).
4. As an aside, Thinkabout seems to add to rather than solve the "inert knowledge problem" that has become a major focus for curriculum developers (Cognition and Technology Group 1990).
5. A variety of computer programs which can be used to facilitate qualitative data analysis are described in Pfaffenberger (1988) and Tesch (1991), however " . . . such programs are substitutes for scissors, typewriters, folders, index cards, and so on. They do not analyze or interpret data" (Merriam 1988,158).

6. Stenhouse (1975) is critical of the involvement of teachers in curriculum development projects: "First, teachers working on projects give too much weight to their own past experiences which is not as generalizable as they often assume. Second, teachers commonly change radically and rapidly on taking up an appointment with a project; they become curriculum developers!" (p. 221)

7. But, no information on how they were selected and as Yin (1984) notes: "The problem is that we have little way of screening or testing for an investigator's ability to do good case studies" (p. 22).

8. From my experience, the problem is not test scores per se, but that inappropriate comparative data are provided. I believe "building level" personnel don't find "national norms" an appropriate reference point. Rather, comparison with the students' own previous score (e.g., "gain score") would be helpful as would comparison data drawn from a similar population. That is, if you are teaching a second grade class that is predominantly black and on ADC, you want to see reading scores for other students who fit this same background profile.

CHAPTER **6**

Personal Accounts

with Joyce Kinkead

> ### *Diary*
>
> I decided to teach school and help with the family finance, but it was in the days before free public schools and I had no building in which to work. Brother Charles A. Terry loaned several planks and blocks with which to improvise seats. Sister Whitmore loaned me an old kitchen table of small size for a desk. I mustered up another degree of courage to ask the loan of a blackboard. . . . Their refusal abashed me and I felt belittled for having been turned down. Auntie came to my relief. She took the large bread board and painted it. This great board, four feet by two and one-half, I carried to Brother Kelsey that very night under cover of darkness, and for five cents, he gave me a good coating of blacking. A piece of white chalk from my husband's tool box, and I was equipped. Now for my trial class.

This excerpt[1] from the unpublished reminiscences of Martha Cragan Cox describes her initial attempts to establish a school in the frontier town of St. George, Utah, in 1869. Written when Martha was 77, these reminiscences were meant for the edification and enjoyment of her many progeny. They reflect the enormous hardships faced by early public school teachers who were "pioneers" in every sense of the word.

Cox's autobiography is part of a collection of autobiographical writings (including diaries, confessionals, and cradle-to-grave like histories), assembled by Joyce Kinkead (in preparation). Kinkead had two broad aims in this task: To bring this obscure material to light and thereby illuminate important chapters in the history of teaching and the history of the Western U.S.; and to redress a limited and one-sided view of the early Western "schoolmarm." Mainly that,

---

unlike on most of the Western frontier where schoolteachers were unmarried, in Mormon Utah, they not only married, many were, like Martha, the second, third, or even fourth wives in a polygamous arrangement. Martha's account is filled with her struggles to support her own eight children, as well as those of her co-wives, with little help from her mostly absentee husband.

Kinkead provides the reader with lightly edited autobiographies so that the unique, idiographic aspects of these women's lives comes through, but she also, by aggregating across 24 such personal accounts, and by drawing on already published material, is able to search for and find nomothetic, or general patterns, that hold true for the group as a whole.

WHAT ARE PERSONAL ACCOUNTS?

This chapter differs from the others in one important respect. In those I started with fairly well established traditions, and could write a largely descriptive account of what a researcher finds when sampling the literature in a particular tradition. But, Personal Accounts do not yet constitute a tradition. Hence, I have had to pull together and analyze a great variety of material, which I see as naturally coalescing into a coherent body of scholarship, in order to "invent" a Personal Accounts tradition.[2] In general, I see this area as growing in importance as we find that humans use story or narrative to organize their understanding and memory of events (Bruner, 1986; Polkinghorne, 1988). I also see that our best access to teachers'[3] and students' understandings of the meaning of classroom experience may be through life history narratives, rather than through structured classroom observations and interviews (Connelly and Clandinin, 1990).

Personal Accounts, as the name suggests, are different from other kinds of reports in the social science literature because they focus on whole lives, or people in the round. The person is examined not just as a convenient exemplar of a category we are interested in (e.g. secondary social studies teacher), but to get at his/her very personal life story, views, and accomplishments. However, the way in which these personal accounts are gathered, presented, and analyzed varies enormously (Denzin, 1989), and Table 6.1 charts some of the more evident dimensions.

Initially we will look at autobiography and biography, focusing, in particular, on women teachers who were "pioneers." Then, we consider a unique collection of personal chronicles of men who taught in elementary schools serving poor black children. A theme that runs through much of this literature is culture shock.

The next several sections review case studies; first we look at beginning teachers; and then consider the lives of more experienced teachers. We contrast single, multiple, and collective case study research. Also, we take up the issue of teacher-researcher collaboration.

Our final major category is the self-generated case-study, specifically the Teacher - as - Researcher. This sub-genre of the Personal Accounts literature, like several others, is in a state of flux. In the concluding section of the chapter, I critically analyze this literature, suggesting some parameters we can apply in future research, using this method in order to enhance its value in education.

TABLE 6.1   Personal Accounts

	Life History	**Case Study**
Self-Generated	Autobiography: memoir, chronicle, diary, reminiscence (Robinson 1978)	Teacher as researcher (Ray 1987)
Generated by anthropologists, historians, psychologists, journalists	Compiled autobiography (Reilly, 1990) Collection of autobiographies (Kinkead, in prep)	Teacher-researcher collaboration (Clandinin 1986)
	Biography (Strane, 1990) Multiple biography (Clifford, 1989) Collective biography (Tyack and Hansot 1982)	Case study (Wolcott 1973) Multiple case study (Spencer 1986) Collective case study, Hargreaves 1984)

Before discussing the Table 6.1, I want to stress again that there is much ambivalence about where in the overall scheme of things Personal Accounts belong. Madeleine Grumet, who has drawn on life histories in her feminist analysis of teaching (1988), says ". . . before I began to think of narratives as forms for educational research and criticism, I thought of them as literature" (p. 67). However, how can we treat life history material as research data when ". . . every telling is a potential prevarication . . . our stories are the masks through which we can be seen . . ." (p. 69). In short, I have done my best to present a tidy picture, but you should be aware that the road ahead is a rough one.

(AUTO)BIOGRAPHY

As you can see in the table, certain dimensions are clear-cut, as denoted by the straight lines, while others areas are fuzzy. Personal Accounts can be self-generated or they can be solicited by a scholar, a "professional stranger." Clearly the purpose will differ. The autobiographer is not bound by the canons of scholarship to address a larger issue or question, for example. The Cox autobiography that opened the chapter actually lies in a fuzzy area between the two. While the original material was self-generated, it is now in the hands of a scholar whose methods and purposes are quite different from Martha Cragan Cox and her fellow Mormon schoolteachers.

The autobiography itself can take on a variety of forms: diary, memoir, confessional. There seems to be a noticeable split between works which describe the author's life during a highly circumscribed period (e.g., *Where's My Apple? Diary of a First Year Teacher,* Walter 1981) which I refer to as a chronicle, and works which cover the entire life span (e.g., *Sarah Jane Foster: Teacher of the Freedman, A diary and letters,* Reilly 1990). The autobiography is a venerable literary form, indeed what is considered the first "modern" autobiography was written in 1576 by a music tutor (Osborne 1961). And, for at least two hundred years, a hallmark of the educated person in Western society has been the keeping of a personal record, a journal, a diary and/or the crafting of a reflective account later in life.

That these materials exist is a boon to biographers and historians (Rury 1991). But what determines whether or not one's (auto)biography is published? It seems this occurs for one of three reasons. First, it helps to be famous. Jesse Stuart's (1970) *To Teach to Love* makes very good reading, but would it have been published if he hadn't gone on from teaching to become a best-selling novelist? Alas, there were few famous teachers. Second, the individual in question may have been caught up in an important historical event or movement, as were the pioneering teachers whose accounts are reviewed in the next section. But teachers are not generals or statesmen so, again, the published literature is not voluminous. Third, we often wish to "... record the direct testimony of those rare individuals who are able to provide us with a vivid picture of life in realms otherwise closed to us outsiders" (Langness and Frank 1981, 5).[4] Dianne Manning's (1990) oral history of teachers from rural Texas is an example from education.

I find that another important dimension is the number of accounts scholars are working with. Single accounts focus on the participant and his/her perspective (Table 6.1). Multiple accounts open up valuable opportunities for comparison and contrast and for addressing nomothetic problems. However, there is the danger that we will lose sight of the individual. The coherence of a single life is sacrificed for topical coherence. Indeed, this is the explicit methodology of the collective biography (e.g., Tyack and Hansot's [1982] history of the superintendency).

PIONEER TEACHERS: ARCHIVAL SOURCES

Letter

Arrived—went about gathering scholars; have forty. Did well enough till it rained; since then have walked three miles a day, ankle-deep in thick, black mud, that pulls off my shoes. Nothing to eat but strong pork and sour bread. Insulted for being a "nigger teacher." Can't buy anything on credit, and haven't a cent of money. The school shed has no floor, and the rains sweep clean across it, through the places where the windows should be. I have to huddle the children, first in one corner and then in another, to keep them from drowning or swamping. The Provost Marshal won't help me. Says "he don't believe in nigger teachers—didn't list to help them." The children come, rain, or shine, plunging through the mud—some of them as far as I do. Pretty pictures they are. What shall I do? If it will ever stop raining, I can get along. (Hoffman 1981, 112-3)

This anonymous letter home, from a Northern woman teaching newly freed slaves, is taken from an anthology of teachers' autobiographical material. It reflects the hardship and dedication such service demanded, as well as the burden of trying to live in a deeply racist and angry community. In the latter half of the 19th century, white, middleclass, unmarried women turned out in droves to teach in isolated rural areas, on the Western frontier, in schools for blacks in the reconstructed South, and on reservations. Hoffman draws on the personal accounts of these teachers to uncover a significant chapter in the history of women in the U.S. Indeed, it has been the rise of feminist scholarship (see also Acker 1989; Grumet 1988), as much or more than an interest in the history of teaching, that has provided the impetus for this new area of inquiry in education. Teaching was nearly the only way a woman could leave the confines of her own home. Once out in the world, these women wrote about their experiences, what they saw, and the people, especially students, who touched their lives. Sarah Jane Foster's autobiography, chronicling the experiences of another Northern woman who taught in a Southern freedom school, was constructed (Reilly 1990) from her voluminous writings, including two diaries, 23 letters, and assorted short stories, poems and essays.

Not to say that these materials are just there for the asking as Strane (1990) cautions us. "Researching a minor historical figure like Prudence Crandell requires a lot of detective work" (vii). Strane chose to study Crandell because, however minor, she was a woman who played a dramatic role in the abolitionist movement. She attended the Brown Seminary in Providence, where she came under the influence of its abolitionist director. Returning to her home in Canterbury, Connecticut, in 1831, she opened a female seminary. An ad was run to attract students and it had the desired effect.

> ### Advertisement
>
> . . . reading, writing, arithmetic, English grammar, geography, ancient and modern history "together with delineating maps," natural and moral philosophy, chemistry and astronomy would be taught. There would be no vacation during the year. Therefore, scholars could enter or leave anytime without interruption. Tuition was to be $3.00 per term, plus $1.50 per week for board, which would include laundry done "in the family of instructress." Every scholar was expected to attend public worship "somewhere" on the Sabbath. (p. 12)

However, a young woman of mixed race asked to be admitted to the seminary in order to get "a little more learning," so she could teach "colored children" (p. 25). Although, public elementary schools in Connecticut admitted blacks at that time, secondary schools—called seminaries, colleges—were segregated and private. Prudence, strongly influenced by the very active abolitionist press of the time period, agreed. She is supported by William Lloyd Garrison and other abolitionists, and her school becomes a cause celebré, prompting the enactment of racially motivated statutes in the Connecticut legislature. Finally, on Sept. 9, 1834, a band of men attacked the school and tore it to shreds, terrorizing the students in the process. Prudence was forced to close the school.

The term *pioneer* takes on a broad definition when applied to women in education. Marion Talbot was one of the earliest female faculty members at a major American university. Her biography (Fitzpatrick, 1989) appears as one of seven of early female academics in a collection titled *Lone Voyagers* (Clifford 1989; see also Gerlach and Monseau 1991). She studied at MIT and proposed legitimizing the study of the household and family as an academic discipline. Offered the position of assistant professor of Sanitary Science at the University of Chicago by the first president William Rainey Harper, her reply (dated August 11, 1892) shows just how much moxie these pioneers had, in stark contrast to the Victorian era stereotype of the genteel and modest "schoolmarm." Among several requests, few of which he acceded to, she proposes the creation of an entire department.

> ### Letter
>
> I would suggest the establishment of a "department of public health." . . . I realize that only the beginnings of such a department could be made at present, but it seems to me imperative that its cornerstone should be laid at once. Altho the general plan has been in my mind for some years, I have had but little time to consider its development with reference to the Univ. I can therefore present for your consideration only a brief outline.
>
> You must infer that I should feel much hampered if my work as a teacher were to be limited to 'lecturing.' Any success I have had as an instructor has depended on the use of other methods in addition, i.e. library, laboratory, written recitations, special investigations, theses. Books essential from the start should be ready in the library when work begins. It would be necessary to equip this small working laboratory . . . [it] would not involve at present a large outlay of money.
>
> In regard to your specific offer of position, may I suggest that the proposed work as a member of the faculty and as an adviser is a very responsible and difficult one and it could be carried on with more ease as well as dignity in the grade of associate rather than assistant professor.
>
> [And she is also concerned about the working climate, she questions whether:] . . . I should be in an atmosphere of intellectual integrity and cooperation. [She concludes:] I trust I have written in such a way that you can take formal and immediate action." (pp. 102–4)

Where might a researcher begin the detective work necessary to accumulating these personal accounts? Kinkead used church archives in compiling her material on schoolmarms, having used Bitton's *Guide to Mormon Diaries* to first identify promising accounts. The special collections or archives section of any university, local or regional library, will have such materials. At the 1990 AERA meetings, a special interest group (SIG) was established to foster archival and biographical research. By the 1992 conference, members were reporting on works underway including the *Encyclopedia of American Educational Biography,* and the journal *VITA* published by the International Society for Educational Biography. Among the dozens of archival collections identified by Society and SIG members, two major collections the novice scholar should be aware of are the Hanna Collection on the Role of Education in the 20th Century at Stanford, and the Museum of Education at the University of South Carolina.

PIONEER TEACHERS: ORAL HISTORIES

Another source for geographical material is the oral history. Manning (1990) uses this approach. She chose the Hill Country area of Texas, as it was one of the last areas to be electrified. In fact, one-room schools were the norm until the 1950s. She found her participants through the Hill Country Retired Teachers Association. Over 15 months, she interviewed 20 teachers at least twice for 3 hours or more. Manning finds some common themes—the prohibition against marriage and " . . . of equal importance was church life, and the young female teacher who failed to meet community religious standards lost her contract" (p. xvii). But, she finds that all of these teachers seemed to have " . . . the ability to extract positive elements from almost every situation, and emphasize them over negative aspects" (p. 81). However, the value of these accounts lies in their vivid idiosyncratic detail. Gladys Peterson Meyers started teaching at 17 in a one-teacher school in Knoxville, Kimble County, TX. " . . . Gladys knew as early as third grade that she wanted to be a teacher. She recalled loving the smell of crayolas and wanting to teach so that she could always be around them" (p. 65). Here is her recollection of her first job.

> ### Oral History Interview
>
> I met the school board president downtown, trying to look as dignified as I could. I wasn't but seventeen, and certificates weren't issued until you were eighteen . . . He said, 'Well, it doesn't pay very much. Seventy-five dollars a month for eight months. And I kinda wanted somebody with experience.' I said, 'Experience!' I stomped my foot and said, 'How will I get experience if somebody doesn't give me a start?'
>
> 'Well,' he said, 'at least you've got spunk. Let's give you a try.'
>
> That's how I got started. I boarded with him, his family. I rode a swayback mare to school. I wore a divided skirt over my dress because ladies didn't wear pants. And the little eight-year-old son rode on the rumble seat of the saddle while we went to school. We went about three miles to school.
>
> My students were ages eight to sixteen . . . I think the eighth grade just came to check me out. They didn't intend to spend the year . . . When I first saw them, my first day of school, I thought the school board was coming. There were these tall boys, taller than I was, and they said, 'Well, no, we are your pupils.' I couldn't believe it.
>
> Later on they threw a skunk in my well and stole my Bible, and a brass hand bell that I had planned to use for a keepsake all my life, and a dictionary. I said I hoped they would look up the word *thief* because that's what they were.
>
> The strange thing, shortly after that, I didn't have any big students. They had accomplished their purpose and decided that I was going to stay regardless of what happened." (pp. 77–8)

Manning (1990) sums up the stance taken by the biographer vis-a-vis her subjects: "Doing oral history is a lot of work, but the hard part is seeing to it that the trust these contributors have placed in me is not tarnished, even inadvertently" (p. xxi).

As difficult a time as Gladys Meyers had, Dorothy Redus Robinson's (1978) autobiography makes clear that a black teacher in rural Texas teaching at an all-black school had an even tougher time. Her account is a litany of privation brought on by penurious salary, non-existent supplies, budget and needy relatives. But, as her minister says in the forward, "She tells her story without bitterness, without blame. She simply tells it like it happened" (p. x).

Neither the Meyers nor the Robinson autobiographies follow what we would recognize as conventional chronology. In a single page, Meyers takes the reader from 1932 to the present, and then back to 1925. This is just one aspect of women's autobiographies which distinguish them from men's, according to Jelinek (1980) Male autobiographers focus on their achievements and their relationship to important events. The narrative is linear and focused—on a particular time period, a theme, or a personality characteristic. There are relatively few personal details. By contrast, female autobiographers are very personal and focus on family—children, spouses. They include the day-to-day details of domestic life, rather than affairs of state. The narrative is distinctive with flashbacks and digressions. It would seem that women are more likely to write "confessions," revelations of feelings, beliefs and spirituality, while men are more likely to write "memoirs"—straightforward chronologies of the main events in their lives (Cox 1971).

These differences in narrative style are just now beginning to attract scholarly attention and are, in any event, just one facet of life history that the biographer must attend to. Langness and Frank (1981) have prepared a good introduction to the methodology of biography from an anthropological point of view. Their work can be supplemented by Watson and Watson-Franke's (1985) more recent work, which incorporates a feminist perspective. Denzin's (1989) brief overview is particularly useful with respect to epistemological issues, especially the relationship between subject, biographer, and reader. "When a writer writes a biography, he or she writes him- or herself into the life of the subject written about . . . When the reader reads a biographical text, that text is read through the life of the reader" (p. 26). But the most practical and direct guide to doing biography was written by Lomask (1986), himself the author of numerous biographies. Among his pithy comments: " . . . the biographer . . . [while] gathering his material . . . uses the quasi-scientific methods of the historical researcher; writing his book, he uses the techniques of the fiction writer . . . A biography is not a compilation of facts. It is a portrait, in words, of a man or woman in conflict with himself or with the world around him, or with both (pp. 1–2). The most important step is " . . . to pick the subject that is right for you" (p. 5). His book is particularly helpful with the research and documentation (e.g., citations, notes) aspects of doing biography.

PROMINENT THEMES: CULTURE SHOCK

The modern equivalent of teachers being sent out to the frontier to teach school and save souls is the pilgrimage of white middle-class North American teachers into schools in the urban ghetto. For several years I taught a freshman orientation class in a Department of Elementary Education. My model student was 17, blonde and blue eyed, the third in a family of seven, had grown up on a dairy farm in Fernley, and had never been out of the state—Utah. Demographics dictated that she would be unlikely to find employment in any environment remotely approaching the one she went to school in, but would, in all likelihood, be recruited by any one of several large urban school districts in the West—Salt Lake City, Las Vegas, and Los Angeles among others. And, I knew from graduates who took my masters' level classes in the Salt Lake area, that they had felt utterly unprepared for the urban teaching experience (see pp. 184–5). So I began to gather a collection of chronicles, written by teachers in urban schools and other settings, dramatically different from rural Utah for them to read.

These works represent, in my view, an untapped resource for inquiry into the phenomenon of culture shock (among many other potential themes) in the lives of teachers.

Peter McLaren's (1980) *Cries from the Corridor* is, for me, the most compelling from a subgroup of this genre. These are works written by well-educated, middle-class white males who, fueled by what McLaren freely acknowledges as "sixties idealism" (p. xiii), decide to teach on the "Frontiers of Despair." Here is his description of his first classroom—his school was located in an ethnically mixed lower-class neighborhood of Toronto.

Journal Entries

The inside of the portable classroom was cold and lifeless and looked more like a funeral parlour than a classroom. An old-fashioned roller blind filtered the winter sun, shining a dead green light over the empty desk. There was only one picture on the wall: a washed-out, glue-streaked poster advertising dental hygiene. The girl on the poster had freckles and a pigtail, and the boy was wearing a brushcut. It could have sold as an antique in a flea market. In comparison with the furniture in the main building, the desks and chairs of my portable looked like they had been scrounged from some storage warehouse for junked school furniture of the 1940s. Desks were hacked and gouged, while the wobbly chairs were often equipped with only three legs. The green blackboard was in such poor condition that you almost had to chisel letters into it. (pp. xvi–xvii)

[He describes the dissonance between his idealism and the reality of school.]

I eagerly awaited the thrill of picking up my mail from my very own personal mailbox during my first trip to the office as an inner city teacher. Once inside the office, I saw a student lying on the bench. His knees were raised to his chest, arms holding them tight; he looked like a pale foetus. A second glance revealed a shiny piece of metal protruding from behind one of his ears. I looked closer. It was, in fact, a heavy steel dart lodged just above his ear. (p. 3)

[Another theme, common in teacher's narratives, is his inability to provoke "shop-talk" with other teachers.]

". . . what kind of techniques do *you* use with the kids? Maybe we can exchange ideas."

She cleared her throat, looking down at her lunch, smiling. "There *is* one thing that I find helps me make it through the day," she said softly.

"Yes?"

"I never talk about the kids during lunch. That's *my* secret for success!" (p. 27)

Like so many teachers, McLaren also suffers from the "discipline" crisis. "I found it hard to act 'the heavy.' The kids sensed my authoritarian image was merely a tactic, and called my bluff. When a class enjoys wearing down the patience of its teacher, all it needs is a hint the teacher is out of control. Then it moves in for the kill'' (p. 17). The reader notices the conspicuous absence of anything resembling "education" going on in the classroom, and McLaren lamely avers: "Although little learning, in the strict academic sense, seemed to have taken place, the kids did pick up some skills" (p. 61). He becomes discouraged by the lack of parental support for the children's education, and he gradually becomes disillusioned: " . . . I started blaming the entire universe for the problems I was encountering at school: parents, the school system, the government, Western culture in general. I'm becoming quite a cynic . . . " (p. 46). At the end of his third year, he can't take it any more. "The thought of teaching for another year made me feel that I was trapped in a dungeon, losing all count of time. The warden might be a nice guy and the food not bad, but I was suffocating—I had to get out. I'd put in my time" (p. 181).

Pat Conroy (1972/1987), the noted novelist, fictionalized the year (1969–1970) he spent teaching a sixth/seventh grade class in the only school on an extremely isolated (no electricity, phones, running water) island in Tidewater, South Carolina. All of the students are black, and they present formidable obstacles to his zeal. Their reading and writing skills were at minimal levels—some didn't know the alphabet, some couldn't write their names. "Each question I asked opened a new lesion of ignorance or misinformation" (p. 33). The language problem was enormous. The kids spoke a distinct dialect which he couldn't understand, while they couldn't understand standard English. Nevertheless, like all of the teachers discussed in this section, Conroy set very high expectations for himself and his students: "When I brought Leonard Bernstein's Children's Concert to the school, Leonard, was a mild, if not overwhelming success" (p. 49). However, unlike McLaren, who has a sympathetic and dedicated principal, Mrs. Brown, herself black, terrorizes the children and undermines Conroy's attempts to make schooling interesting and meaningful. Nor are the white school district authorities any more supportive. Their racism appalled him, and after 18 months of running battles, he is fired. As an author, however, he can take some parting shots; he writes that his adversaries:

Fiction

. . . were not evil men. They were just predictably mediocre. Their dreams and aspirations had the grandeur, scope, and breadth of postage stamps. They had rule books and Bibles and golf clubs and nice homes on rivers . . . They quoted the Bible liberally and authoritatively, and felt the presence of the Savior in their lives. They did not feel the need for redemption, because they had already been redeemed. The only thing they could not control was their fear. (p. 255)

Conroy's book makes compelling reading (it was made into a motion picture and now Broadway play with the title "Conrack"); the tension between the author and the authorities steadily builds to a climax. But it is also, oddly, very personal. We learn a lot about his friends, his courtship, and his marriage. It is clearly more autobiography than novel.

Herb Kohl graduated from Harvard with a degree in philosophy and after a year's training at Teachers College in 1962, he took on a sixth grade class in Harlem. He opens with a confession, "It was a shock to see thirty-six black faces before me" (p. 13). The book, published 5 years later (1967), is written with a level of confidence that he couldn't have felt that first year. Pascal (1960) in *Design and Truth in Autobiography* says,

> Autobiographies are suspect to historians not so much because of particular incorrect facts as because of the perspective of the writer, who must see the past from his present standpoint, in the light of all his experiences and knowledge since the facts recorded took place. These later experiences will sift the past and determine what was important and worth talking about from what merely seemed important then, will therefore give the author his coherent theme (p. 69).

By the time Kohl writes *36 Children,* he is on his way to becoming one of the most influential educators in America.[5] He is already addressing future teachers.

Autobiography

While teaching about early man, I read history, anthropology, archeology, art criticism; brought in books and pictures and maps for the children, and in trying to answer their questions, found myself looking into things as diverse as the domestication of animals, cave painting, stone implements, and early technology. The children began to look too, wanted increasingly to answer questions for themselves. Some of them began discovering encyclopedias in the library—things they had been subjected to before that had previously made no sense to them. Because they saw me researching, they learned to do research. They wouldn't have learned had I merely told them to do it. (p. 57)

We learn relatively little about Kohl (although, like Conroy, we learn of his courtship and marriage), little about the school system. The focus is on the 36 children, and he even shares with us many of their stories and art work. It is a hopeful book. We marvel at what he accomplishes with these children, but, after two years he takes off for Europe.

Another Harvard graduate (and Rhodes scholar), Kohl's friend and contemporary, Jonathan Kozol's ghetto teaching career is even shorter. His audience and his message are subtly different from Kohl's. His message is not that ghetto children (in this case the Roxbury section of Boston) can be reached with the right approach, although he uses, by now familiar tactics. "We had been spending the month reading and talking about Paris and about France" (pp. 194–195). Rather, this book is an exposé in the veritable tradition of muck-raking journalism. He wants the public to know how bad the segregated schools of Boston (this was in 1964–65)) are and is not afraid to use hyperbole to make his point, starting with his title (1967/1985) *Death at an Early Age: The Destruction of the Hearts and Minds of Negro Children in the Boston Public Schools.* He provides both vivid description—focusing on Stephen, a particularly pathetic child in his class—and official statistics, to highlight the imbalance in school spending between black and white areas, the revolving door of substitute teachers in his school (permanent teachers appear to be ". . . senile, physically degenerate, mentally unstable . . ." [p. 155]), and the grim physical conditions. He, too, is fired for reading an unsanctioned work—Langston Hughes's "Ballad of the Landlord"—to his class. Nevertheless, *Death at an Early Age* no doubt sped the eventual integration of Boston schools. However, Kozol, writing the epilogue in the 1985 edition of his book, sees this as ". . . a pyrrhic victory . . . today . . . poor whites, poor blacks, and poor Hispanics now become illiterate together" (p. 234).

The culture shock phenomenon is by no means limited to white males teaching in the urban ghetto, indeed it is one of the most common themes in the personal accounts literature. . . . For example, Valerie, one of Spencer's (1986) participants, is herself black and grew up near the poor black neighborhood she found herself teaching in, but she, too, experiences extreme dissonance. "Despite Valerie's own poor background, she always blamed parents for children's problems and had little sympathy for the poor" (p. 136). She hates her job and describes the school grounds as ". . . looking like a war zone in World War II" (p. 136). Valerie wants so much to abandon her class origins. On the other hand, Ryan and Sackrey (1984) sum up their collection of 24 life histories of men and women from working class backgrounds, who have become academics and, thereby join the elite: "What is clear, though, is the sense of not belonging, and more often than not, feeling one degree or another of contempt for those who do 'belong'" (p. 312). However, they also caution that ". . . we make no pretense here that we have, in any scientific sense, a representative or random sample of academics, who hail from working-class backgrounds. Our respondents are predominantly social scientists, and a few are from the humanities" (p. 7). Although there is no longer a "frontier" in its traditional sense, many teachers still feel that they are pioneers in spirit.

One of the most poignant stories of conflict during the transition across class boundaries is Richard Rodriguez's (1982) account of his education. He strove to be successful in the middle-class anglo world of the public school and he was, spectacularly so, but he earned the derisive *¡pocho!* from his Mexican–American classmates for his pains. Finally, Mike Rose (1989) also describes the perspective of the student who is "not supposed to" succeed. His book is an interesting blend of his own and his students' stories, and includes a chronicle of his early teaching experience (he is now at UCLA) in a barrio elementary school in East Los Angeles.

PROMINENT THEMES: THE BEGINNING TEACHER

One of the very interesting paradoxes that the personal accounts scholars have uncovered is that there appear to be detectable "stages" in the teachers' narratives (Newman 1980; Sikes 1985). At the same time, "The teaching profession, as it is traditionally construed, is 'flat.' It deals inadequately with the developmental processes of adulthood, with aging, with the passage of time in a person's life. There is no sense of movement, no distinction between apprentice, journeyman, and master craftsman" (Raphael 1985, p. 97). Newman (1980) and Sikes (1985) sought evidence of stages in the 10 and 48 histories they collected from mid- to late-career teachers. Neither analysis is compelling with respect to the thesis that all teachers go through roughly the same stages. The earliest stages seem not clearly demarcated, perhaps because these older teachers may have had some trouble remembering the details.

Measor (1985) has had commendable success in understanding the transition in teacher's careers by having her participants organize their narratives around ". . . 'critical incidents' which are key events in the individual's life, and around which pivotal decisions revolve" (p. 61). This is one of the more vivid examples.

> The woman began her career in a tough elementary school in Glasgow in 1939. During her first year there she experienced considerable discipline difficulties, which culminated in one day's events. The teacher entered the classroom to find that each of her male pupils had displayed their genitals on the desk in front of them. She told the pupils to put them away, and then frog-marched one of the boys out of the classroom. Her classroom was on a [2nd] floor balcony and somehow the woman teacher pushed the boy in such a way that he fell over the balcony and on to the floor some distance below. A now carefully buttoned-up group of boys watched his fall in a hushed and respectful silence. The woman had no further discipline problems. (p. 63)

Evidently, the commonly observed theme that discipline is a problem during the initial phase of teaching is highlighted in these critical incidents. There is often an incident which leads to resolution—the individual either exits from teaching or no longer has serious problems.

Estelle Fuchs's (1969) study of first-year teachers in New York schools is focused on culture shock, and also provides a convenient transition as we move from life history to case study. From 1963 to 1967, she followed the initial careers of 14 beginning teachers, meeting with them on consecutive Saturdays for lengthy, taped interview sessions. It is somewhat difficult to decipher Fuchs's intent; indeed, it was in wrestling with this work that Table 6.1 was first sketched out. One's initial sense is that the work is biographical, that we will be treated to 14 portraits or character studies. Although Fuchs uses much verbatim material from her interviews, these are extracted in checkerboard fashion so that one never really gets to know any single one of them. Next, one is attentive to the possibility that Fuchs has undertaken a systematic study; as we are treated to several generalizations. For example, all experience an initial honeymoon or euphoria phase, which does not survive the first day, in most cases, as the next phase, "culture shock" reflecting their inability to cope leads to a ". . . state of near collapse" (p. 21). But, in other respects, Fuchs deviates so widely from established canons of science—the only sampling detail provided is the size— that this cannot be her motive. Let's look at one of Fuchs's teacher's narratives, and then her "analysis."

Oral Narrative

I went on a trip this week with my children. It was quite enjoyable. We went to the airport. . . . I think the thing that impressed my children most was the escalator.

None of them, or practically none of them, had ever seen an escalator before. I explained that it was moving stairs and one girl asked me if it would tickle her feet. Many of the children were frightened to get on the escalator. I think that this experience helped me to understand that these children are from a very deprived background . . . It helped me to realize that I was assuming too much about these children. (pp. 38–9)

Analysis

This teacher's misconception really is a very common one. It connotes the notion that if you do not share knowledge of "my culture," more, of specific *details* of "my culture," that you are devoid of culture—for the word 'deprived' has come to carry with it the belief that the "deprived" lack ability, and are crippled by deficits that have prevented them from learning or achieving. (p. 42)

It seems to me that Fuchs is using these narratives in a purely illustrative manner (as McLaren 1989 does with his journal; see also Britzman 1991; Bullough 1989; Connelly and Clandinin 1989). She wishes to show how concepts, borrowed from cultural anthropology, can be applied to the problems of preparing teachers for the inner city. She uses anecdotes as points of entry for a series of mini-lectures.

WHY STUDY PERSONAL ACCOUNTS?

Before turning to a consideration of the case study, I would like to pause to address two issues: Why would one want to review a set of personal accounts in the first place, and second, how should one go about conducting an analysis and synthesis? I have already suggested an answer to the first question; given demographic trends, future teachers will teach children whose family life is radically different from their own. The nature of the school and classroom environment they teach in will be quite different in important ways from what they experienced. We need all the data we can get on how beginning teachers react when they first cross these boundaries.[6] A new program which has received much attention, "Teach for America" gives added urgency to this quest. Five hundred bright, well-educated middle-class graduates with academic majors from elite colleges are being trained to teach during an eight week summer session, and placed in ghetto schools or those serving the rural poor. If this program is less successful than its organizers hope, one reason may be the failure to learn from the ample precedent available in these chronicles.

The second question is more difficult to answer. James Herndon's (1968) *The Way it Spozed to be,* is broadly parallel to the works we have just been reviewing but, unlike the others, he does indicate an intended audience.

In this book I'm trying to tell about my year teaching—learning to teach—in a public school, a year spent in a particular school, at a particular time, and with particular students. The particulars are my anecdote. It is certainly the anecdote that counts. Not the moral, the point, or the interpretation. If just the particulars can be kept clear, then there will be a kind of thing made, something to see . . . the interpretations may then be numerous as readers. (p. 6)

This suggests that there is no single interpretation. Each reader must *deconstruct* (Derrida 1981) the text for her/himself. The issue of interpretation—by whom, for what purpose—is clearly central in the literature of personal accounts. McLaren (1989), after leaving teaching and going through a doctoral program, had doubts about how his journal was being interpreted: "I ran the risk of allowing readers to reinforce their stereotypes of what schooling was like in the "blackboard jungle" (p. ix). Hence, he turns his (auto)biography into a case study by incorporating it into an overview of marxist/critical theory, as applied to North American education. So now, instead of the "interpretations being as numerous as readers," McLaren tells us how his journal *should* be interpreted.

As I have suggested, there are two further alternatives for analysing and interpreting these works. Operating as a qualitative researcher, one can conduct a content analysis (see page 212), searching for themes in these personal accounts. For example, it is easy to see a common tendency to want to throw out the existing, boring, plebeian curriculum and replace it with elements of high culture (Miro and Klee, Greek Mythology, Symphony). Another pervasive theme is the violence that pollutes the schools, the streets, the homes.

> ### *Journal*
> Georgette and Wendy picked up some dolls at the activity centre. Georgette chose G.I. Joe, and Wendy picked up a Farrah Fawcett doll.
> "Let's pretend we're married," Georgette said.
> "Okay," Wendy agreed, "Let's start!"
> Georgette took G.I. Joe and promptly slapped the Farrah doll across the face with it, shouting: "That's what you get for talkin to me like that!" (McLaren 1980, 173)

But these chronicles are first and foremost works of literature. They were not written to serve as data to advance the cause of science. Hence, one can quite appropriately draw on the field of literary criticism for inspiration in conducting one's analysis and interpretation. ("Students of biographical method must learn how to use the strategies and techniques of literary interpretation and criticism" [Denzin 1989, 25]) as I have done in noting differences in literary quality (McLaren: journal-confessional in tone; Kozol: exposé, persuasive in tone). Until personal accounts acquire the institutionalized trappings of a unique tradition (Kuhn 1970), we must perforce read them through the lenses of one or another of the more established traditions.

CASE STUDIES

Turning to the right side of Table 6.1, we encounter the case study. In the case study, the focus shifts more obviously from the individual (Ed Bell) to the role (Elementary School Principal), although life historical details continue to be crucial to analysis and explanation. While we expect the subject of (auto)biography to be proudly identified, the participant of a case study is inevitably anonymous. One of the reasons for this is that the case study is (as we saw in Chapter 5) directly linked to the improvement of practice. Hence, judgments will be drawn; subjects[7] will be identified as "typical" (Wolcott 1973) as "experienced" (Spencer 1986) as "failures" (Knowles and Hoefler 1989).

But the most evident difference between works I'd place in the case-study, as opposed to the life history column, is that the life history material constitutes only a portion of the data collected on the individual or individuals. Hence, there are opportunities to triangulate among the various strands of data, and to use insights gleamed from one's observations of the participant to guide one's elicitation of narrative material.

Finally, those who do use case studies can choose to study a single individual (Knowles 1990) or a number of individuals whose individuality is retained (Spencer 1986). One can do a collective case study in which the cases are blended together into a single composite portrait (Hargreaves 1984). But, enough of this, let's have some stories, let's get down to cases.

THE BEGINNING TEACHER: SEVERAL EXAMPLES

Bullough's (1989) case study of "Kerrie's" first year of teaching seems to serve two ends. It is, first, a straightforward attempt to understand the nature of the beginning stage of teaching, and, second, a research report. Kerrie, too, has trouble with "discipline." She wants a "fun, warm, snuggly" class, but feels she must be a "bitch . . . a policewoman" (p. 28). "Kerrie had very little time to pause to consider the implications of her actions. Instead she, perhaps like most beginning teachers, fell back on long established patterns of belief and action . . . " (p. 43). Bullough, however, follows her into her second year, where she seems to right herself and move out of the "survival" stage (Ryan 1986).

Bullough's *First Year Teacher* is also an attempt to convey to a beginning teacher what to expect. Much like Fuchs (1969), the case study is wrapped around with didactic material, including questions and activities at the end of each chapter, and an appendix entitled "Advice on Selecting a School and Surviving the Year." This work is also our first example of the Teacher-as-Researcher case study, in that Kerrie was Bullough's student; the product of a leading Holmes Group Teacher Education program. Hence, he reflects on the implications of the case study for his own professional practice: "I reconsidered much of what I did in the past and have made some changes in content among other things" (p. 146–7), and teacher education, in general. Finally, note that, while we certainly obtain a more rounded portrait of Kerrie than we do of Fuchs' beginning teachers, Bullough makes clear that he has been quite careful to select aspects of her narrative that he sees as being typical of the beginning teacher. We do not see the attributes that make her unique. She is " . . . an object rather than a subject of study . . ." (Hoffman 1981, xvi).

With Lisa, prepared in the same program as Kerrie, we are shown unique aspects of her personal history, and the researcher (Knowles 1990) relates this history to Lisa's initial experience as a teacher. Gary Knowles (see also Ball and

Goodson 1985; Beynon 1985; Goodson 1989; Pinar 1980) argues that we can only understand the beginning teacher's situation if we are in possession of his/her life history. Lisa carried ideals which were incompatible with what she actually found in the urban, lower-middle-class high school where she is first employed.

> ### Supervisor's Notes
>
> I was surprised when I walked into Lisa's classroom to find that she had completely rearranged the seating. No longer were the desks in a U-shape that was meant to induce discussion. Rather, the desks had been arranged in neat rows, typical of most classrooms. Lisa told me that she had "a difficult week . . . and . . . I just think the other arrangement was too cozy." . . . With the original seating arrangement there was considerable student interaction developing that she was not able to control . . . Her solution was to change the seating because, as she clarified: "I think that this arrangement lets them know again that they need to be doing their work." [Her attitude was also affected.] "I am feeling like there's no hope for the public school system. I don't feel like it's worth a teacher's time to get out day after day, and have to face students who don't want to be here, don't want to do the work [and] are not interested in what you are doing." (p. 706)

Lisa, the eldest of seven children, a youth group leader, and teacher for many years in her church, evidently expected her public school students to behave like her siblings and church-school students. When they don't she is bitter. Lisa had also been heavily influenced by her mother, an ex-second grade teacher, other family members, and church authorities. She believed:

> ### Supervisor's Notes
>
> The classroom would be a place of learning . . . of discussion, of critical analysis. A place where people could come and . . . express their ideas . . . and get exposed to some ideas, but that's an ideal for me right now that is far away. I get glimpses of it once in a while, but it's not particularly close to me . . .
>
> Lisa believes that "teachers are not considered professionals." She explained that teachers have "lost the status of being professional," in part by unionism. At the beginning of the school year, during a teacher orientation session, she was "bombarded by union members . . . and . . . felt like a factory worker." (p. 710)

Interestingly, unlike Kerrie, who does begin to feel success and maintains a good working relationship with the researcher until the end of the case study, Lisa does not and she gradually and painfully withdraws from the case study (Knowles, personal communication).

Another of Knowles' participants (Knowles and Hoeffler, 1984) is even less successful than Lisa. Angela encounters much the same problems as Lisa for much the same reasons. "Angela considered herself 'radical,' she had read the works of educational reformers such as Holt and Illich, and she disagreed with the general social organization of schools" (p. 16). She is unable to control the class and the breakdown in discipline is increasingly evident to everyone. She does not "survive" the survival stage and drops out after seven weeks. "I found out really quickly that teaching wasn't what I'd thought it would be. Instead of being able to enjoy presenting an interesting lesson, I was undermined by administrative details, disruptive students, and a general unwillingness on the part of students to take the class seriously." (p. 18). But, unlike Lisa, she continues her association with Knowles, and with her help (Knowles and Hoeffler 1989) he thus gains further insights into the role of life history factors in one's initial orientation to teaching.

These accounts of beginning teachers do make painful reading, but, one hopes we can learn from them enough to fuel and guide the reform of teacher education.[8] This is Britzman's (1991) avowed intention in conducting a pair of case studies of student teachers. However, like several other authors we have reviewed, she seems more intent on using her cases in an illustrative manner, in this case of her *critical theory* of education, than taking a *grounded theory* approach to follow the cases to what seem like the most evident conclusions. Jamie is a graduate in English, completing a fifth-year teacher-training program. A number of unexpected events occur, hence, ". . . Jamie's student teaching experience . . . was far from normal" (p. 63). Furthermore, Britzman is denied permission to observe while Jamie is teaching. Despite these problems, Britzman evidently believes the interview material is sufficient for her purpose. Jamie starts out by trying to conduct a class analogous to some of the "wonderful seminars" she took as a senior ("Culture Through Literature" and "Marxism, Feminism and Black Nationalism" [p. 71]), and her students respond with silence. When she tried having them role play, ". . . the role playing activity did not work; students became silly and giggled" (p. 78). She then swings to the opposite extreme with no more success:

Teacher's Log

We started to do notes and I found out they don't know how to take notes. They feel everything is important and I had to slow down everything. One person started to say to the class "Not everything's important." And they all told him to shut up, just because he knows how to take notes and they don't.

I felt at a loss as to how to deal with that. How to say, well, this is important and this isn't important. But important to whom? To me? To them? To the quiz? An important fact? A lot of it was just trivia. But when I started to speed up, it was like, "Wait! Wait! We got to get this all down." (p. 95)

My reaction to this case study is very visceral—her teacher preparation program has sent her down some class V rapids without a paddle. But, this is Britzman's analysis of the note-taking lesson:

Analysis

As Jamie attempted to transfer her authority onto the curriculum, and give the canon the floor, she still found herself in the uncomfortable position of justifying the curriculum's power and relevance. Her story's language speaks of disengagement: Jamie depicted herself as being trapped in a predetermined curriculum whose implementation, as she read the situation, obligated her to "police" student learning. As the press for social control became coupled with pedagogy, the curriculum became an oppressive effect of institutional authority. Even this force, however, could not silence collective doubt, anxiety, and frustration. (p. 95)

We also differed in our analysis of Jack, her second case, whom she observes and interviews during his student-teaching in secondary social studies classes. Jack's experience is similar to Jamie's; he, too, tries a seminar approach and then abandons it to teach note-taking and outlining—with predictable results. Despite the fact that Jack has left his teacher preparation program with few clear plans for organizing his classes, he refuses to place himself in a mentor relationship with the two cooperating teachers he is assigned. The one seems too conservative and traditional, the other, while ". . . she used games, projects, and styles of discussion that engaged her students" (p. 138), she did not address critical social and political issues in her classes. Jack's self-immolatory behavior is immediately clarified when we hear, via Britzman's interview, from "Joe Probe," his social studies methods instructor. Joe emphasizes the need for the pre-service teacher to develop critical attitudes; they should then develop their own pedagogy. He is opposed to teaching "methods" in the methods course. He tries ". . . to instill an impatience or adversarial attitude toward existing arrangements. . . . I'm not interested in training technicians or skilled transmitters, or masters of the latest technology in education. They'll adapt to that naturally" (p. 209). But then he also says: "But I would never teach in the public schools right now. I couldn't teach. I'd have a heart attack the second day, I think" (p. 209).

Although I came away from Britzman's case studies with very different conclusions than she did, I do not see this as problematic. Indeed, I think one of the things that makes Personal Accounts so central to the qualitative research enterprise is their susceptibility to reanalysis, by scholars with differing purposes, ideologies, theoretical constructs, or from different historical epochs.

We don't really have this opportunity with the last study to be described in this section, a report of fifty accounts, focused on the process of "becoming a coach." Sage (1989) makes clear that he has an enormous amount of interview and observational material on his teacher/coaches but, unlike Britzman (1991), who has the luxury of a 250 page book to report her two cases (reporting the case material, however, takes up less than 10 percent of the book), Sage must make do with eleven journal pages. Hence, he offers a collective portrait: like beginning teachers, aspirant coaches also suffer "reality shock," but its nature is different. "One of the most prevalent . . . reality shocks . . . for neophyte coaches is the extent to which an ethos of hard work and long hours underlie the culture of coaching" (p. 89). "There was the bookkeeping and the maintenance, getting the busses running, keeping discipline—things that I had never thought of before. . . . The amount of hours that we put into coaching [was] a surprise" (p. 89). Furthermore, unlike beginning teachers, apprenticeship seems to be far more central in the experience of beginning coaches. Many begin as "assistants" and

> observing the behavior of more experienced coaches during practice and games, and listening to the "war stories" veteran coaches tell when coaches are together during informal periods in the coaches' locker room, lunchroom, or coffee room about persons, past events, places, and relationships makes its mark on the young coaches, regardless of whether they began as assistant or head coaches. It is largely

through these types of experiences that collective understanding begins to develop, and the shared meanings about the occupational culture of coaching start to take shape for the new coach. Thus, much of the accumulated wisdom of what a new coach learns about how one is supposed to work, dress, think, and how one will be treated, is learned from ongoing interactions with veteran coaches, as well as through a variety of informal sources. (p. 88)

FURTHER THEMES: EXPERIENCED AND MID-CAREER TEACHERS

Some themes characteristic of the beginning stage—culture shock, discipline—wane, as teachers lose the sense they are pioneers. Others—the search for an effective pedagogy, and the isolation from peers—persist into later stages. We now consider some of these additional themes. Nias (1985) conducted a collective case study of 99 elementary school teachers that had done a graduate program with her. She began her research by observing in their classrooms.

> The purpose of the school visit was to provide a background against which I could interpret subsequent interview data, and not to undertake any formal observation. Afterwards, I conducted semi-structured interviews taking rapid notes in a personal shorthand. Respondents were encouraged to give long, and if necessary, discursive replies, and I often used supplementary questions. Thus, the shortest of the interviews took one and a half hours, the longest five hours. Most took about three hours. (p. 108)

In the interview, she directed the teacher's attention to the general area of "reference group;" that is, she wanted to know who they relied upon for feedback and support in their work. In addition to the transcribed interviews, she had 22 keep a diary for one term which she ". . . used to triangulate individual accounts of perspective and practice" (p. 109). She found that "The most frequently invoked reference group of these teachers was pupils" (p. 109). Many, specifically eschew other teachers as a reference group either for teaching or for personal interests.

Narrative

I'm intellectually lonely at school. I'm the only one who reads *The Guardian,* the only one interested in politics or literature, and there is only one other who's ready to talk about art and music (from a man teaching in an infant school). I love the children and the work, but I have no contact with any adults with whom I have any ideas in common. I feel intellectually starved. (p. 112)

Even when teachers identify with other teachers, this was not necessarily a positive outcome: "We make each other lazy. It's difficult to work hard if no one does. The norm here is about putting teacher's interests first" (p. 113).

A major mitigating factor against the creation of strong, professionally-committed, reference groups of teachers within schools (see also Little 1990) appears to be an aversion to "talking shop." "It's been hard to get teachers in this school to talk about their philosophy; I always wanted to talk and they wouldn't" (p. 115). What teachers do talk about in the "staffroom" (Hammersley 1984) does not reflect favorably on the profession.

HOME VERSUS SCHOOL

Another factor here may be that mid-career teachers' lives outside of work are often stressful and demanding. This is Dee Ann Spencer's thesis in a study that combines aspects of the multiple and collective case study. Spencer very carefully selected her sample of eight female teachers, in order to insure a reasonably representative group.

> The teachers were observed at school and in their homes, interviewed continually, and [paid $25/month] to write diaries. The study lasted two years, although contact with the teachers has continued for over four years. To the extent possible in a research relationship, the women shared their lives with me. We discussed and interacted with students, graded papers together, made bulletin boards, went to meetings, left school together, shopped for groceries, shared meals, and baby-sat. We went to family reunions, fished, traveled, attended the theatre, and played piano duets. (p. vii)

The core of the book consists of one chapter devoted to each of eight teachers, sectioned in (1) typical day, (2) personal history (growing up, education, work, personal relationships), (3) school life (cultural setting, school administration, school facility, teacher morale, students, classes, leaving school), and (4) home life (household duties, financial conditions, leisure activities, health). As these portraits show, teachers are unable to prevent the interpenetration of home and school. For example, Sylvia sometimes felt she was sacrificing her home life for her job.

> ### Diary
>
> September 17, 1980: I get jealous, envious, or frustrated when I compare myself with teachers who don't take schoolwork home. What do they do that I don't do? Are they superefficient, or do they not give as much work: Am I patting myself on the back because I do take work home? Am I deluding myself: I know that everybody is different and that I shouldn't compare myself to others, but how do I keep from doing it?
>
>   Maybe I'm defensive because there have been several teachers in this school who are adamant about not taking work home, and who look with disdain at those of us who do. (p. 80)

At the same time, according to Spencer, it was evident that one's personal problems could have a deleterious effect on classroom performance: "When personal problems were particularly stressful, Chris's enthusiasm in the classroom was low, and she lacked motivation to interact with students or help them learn. Her affect was flat and her facial expression and bodily posture exhibited exhaustion and depression" (p. 50).

Only one of the eight seems to enjoy a completely successful relationship with a significant other, and this seems to be a major factor accounting for their feelings toward their work. One surprising finding (for me) was the fact that all but one of the teachers had a very poor diet ". . . she ate no breakfast, ate either a school lunch or something from a fast-food restaurant, and overate in the evenings. She had a very small body frame and was about 15 pounds overweight. She worried about her weight, but exercised only occasionally when she had the time or motivation" (p. 142). This life-style probably also contributes to the high incidence of chronic illness recorded in the diaries.

In addition to the eight teachers studied in depth, Spencer conducted (1.5 to 5 hours in their home) interviews with 42 other teachers from 6 states and 4 regions of the country. This allows her to move from the idiographic details of her small sample to a more nomothetic characterization of "contemporary women teachers." We see, for example, one reason for the lack of collegiality among teachers. A teacher's working day can vary widely: ". . . of the 50 teachers in the study . . . 28.6 percent took no work home at all . . . 30.6 percent took work home periodically, 8.2 percent did less than one hour of work at home daily, 22.4 percent worked one to two hours, and 10.2 percent worked over two hours daily" (p. 173, 186). Other nearly universal stressors are persistent financial problems, autocratic administrators, and students who are rude and turned off. What Spencer is able to do is balance the data from her small, thoroughly studied sample and her much larger less-well studied sample. By giving free reign to their thoughts in the diaries, some of her eight teachers are likely to mention themes which the investigator might never have thought to touch on during the career history interviews. On the other hand, she can compare the characteristics for the eight with the "statistically averaged" 42, and better judge their typicality. Her very thorough treatment of methodology in the appendix also recommends Spencer's (1986) work as a model for anyone who contemplates using a Personal Accounts methodology.

THE STORIES OF SUCCESSFUL TEACHERS

By now some among you may be questioning whether my sampling is biased, since teaching appears, in these pages, to be such a negative experience. In fact, one of Spencer's subjects, Marie, led a happy, stress-free life: her husband had a good income and her home life was comfortable. She had entered a teaching career as an insurance policy against something happening to her husband, and because it fit best with having a family. Furthermore, "Marie's case shows the positive effects of a good teaching situation. The gifted children in her classes were highly motivated, her classes were quite small, she taught in a good facility, and she was freer from administrative control than other teachers" (p. 53).

But, to find numerous examples of teachers who feel good about their careers, we need to look back, briefly, at the Life History side of Table 6.1. Ken Macrorie's

(1974) autobiography is upbeat because he can share with the reader the aftermath of the ". . . day in 1964 . . . [he] turned [his] teaching around" (p. 5). As an English teacher, he decided to take risks, to expose his vulnerability to students, and to encourage them to do the same. Twenty years later, Macrorie (1984) published a collection of twenty first person accounts that he had collected over the years from "outstanding" teachers. Not surprisingly, these accounts all pivot on turning points (Denzin 1989), signaling a stage shift (Newman 1980; Sikes 1985) in the teacher's career. These turning points revolve around the teacher breaking free from conventional pedagogy. Raphael (1985) published a similar collection of 14 life histories. In these situations, we see teachers who learn from their colleagues, are nurtured by their principals, and are liked by their students. Herb Kohl's praise on the cover of Raphael's book expresses sentiments many of its readers will share: "The book lends dignity and depth to the lives of working teachers." However, a note of skepticism is in order. Neither Raphael nor Macrorie give any indication to suggest either the typicality of these teachers nor of their classroom situations. Unlike Leinhardt's research on expert teachers (Chapter VII), it is not clear that these individuals were carefully chosen to reflect the best of their profession, on the other hand, enough details are provided to suggest that they are probably not typical either. So, contrary to the editors' claims I don't think these books can serve to ". . . elucidate the common occupational hazards of the educational profession." (Raphael 1985, 14)

Of course, neither Macrorie or Raphael would claim to be researchers, these are not case studies. However, I find that the typicality-generalizability problem also extends to works prepared by the University scholars in the field of Education. For example, in one of the chapters in Witherell and Noddings (1991) recent collection, the author (Makler 1991) describes an interesting writing assignment she developed for her high school social studies classes which allowed students to ". . . seek meaning in the history we were studying . . ." (p. 30). They write a fictionalized autobiography consistent with the time period they are studying; she also has them do research on their family origins. "I was surprised by the power of this curriculum, by the level of interest it generated among students and their families, by the change it provoked in my classroom" (p. 31). This remark cannot be interpreted without the contextualizing details which indicate the nature of the students, her school and the community. These are not provided nor does the author nor the editors juxtapose this description with the normative and very different portrait offered by Linda McNeil (1986). In short, I am left with a nagging sense that the "uplifting stories" all come from elite schools and/or classrooms of gifted students.

This sense was exacerbated recently following my reading of Tracy Kidder's (1989) bestseller *Among School Children,* a year in the life of a fifth grade teacher in an ethnically mixed working class community. I found it to be interesting reading on at least two levels. I was struck by the similarities and differences between his method—investigative journalism—and the methods identified with qualitative research. The level of detail and spontaneity in the description; the provision of a rich contextual background to set Chris Zajac and her class within; the detached, neutral and non-judgmental stance of the observer, all suggest the work of a qualitative researcher. However, Kidder provides no details of how he came to select Zajac, there is no "methodology" whatsoever. His prose reflects artistic license ("Pedro just didn't know how hard his life was, but he'd be a teenager soon, and then he would, and the comfort dispensed by drug dealers would be waiting for him . . ." [p. 84]), not permitted to scholars (see also Freedman 1990; Sachar 1991 for similar, recent works).

But the work is more interesting for the absolutely schizophrenic reaction it provokes both in the media—laudatory (Theroux 1989) and scathing (Ohanian 1989) reviews—and from my colleagues. Chris Zajac struck me as a good teacher, dedicated to making the most of a difficult situation. Indeed, it is one of the few contemporary "uplifting" stories from a non-elite school. However, this pragmatic perspective is juxtaposed with an idealist, or romantic perspective that seems to say that any teacher is bad who is unable to reach and assist every single child in her classroom. This distinction is important to bear in mind as one reads the personal accounts literature. Indeed, I began to feel a little schizophrenic myself (see also Hargreaves 1984) by the thirtieth or fortieth account.

ACTION AND KNOWLEDGE IN EDUCATION

In the next chapter we will review research on the cognitive structure or the knowledge that teachers bring to their work. Here we will take up another common theme in the personal accounts literature, the origins of the teacher's (and principal's) knowledge. A quotation from one of Raphael's (1985) colleagues pretty well sums it up: "I started teaching not from something I had learned in a book; I started to develop my own style. I started looking inside *myself*" (p. 62). One's collection of classroom lore, consequently, is more critical in guiding teacher's action than previous education, in-service training, professional organization, or one's colleagues.

Hargreaves's (1984) collective case study is a thorough inquiry into this phenomenon, by documenting an event in the life of the teaching staff of Riverdale, a newly established middle school. He records twenty meetings held over the summer, in which the mostly young staff are to develop the curriculum for the school. In this they are encouraged by well-trained and democratically-leaning administrators. One to two hour interviews are also conducted with each member of staff, and Hargreaves finds some discrepancies between the private and public personae of his cases.

> At Riverdale meetings, when teachers accounted for their practice, they drew overwhelmingly not on the logic and principles of formal education theory, but on their own experience . . . of all the different kinds of experience that Riverdale teachers might have cited, it was their experience with pupils in the classroom that seemed to count most, and that provided their most common source of justifications. . . . The specific examples that teachers cited were often populated by some of the school's more popular characters, sometimes to provide support for a proposal (if pupil X can do this, then anyone can), and sometimes to pour cold water on it (you couldn't do it with pupils like X). But, in either case, they played a crucial role in staff discussion. (p. 246)

First-year teachers had less experience to refer to so they drew on, apologetically, according to Hargreaves, their college training. But even here, they cited more their practical experiences than formal classes.

Hargreaves finds that there are informal constraints operating to exclude virtually everything except prior school experience in these discussions. In interviews, teachers mentioned many sources of influence—Sociology of Education course at Open University, experience as a parent, experience in their own families, prior experience as a pupil. These influences are not used as points of departure in the group meeting. This exclusion of potentially helpful resources:

> . . . meant that the legitimate resources . . . became limited in the main to teachers' classroom experience and to their collectively uncontested assumptions about pupil learning . . . It is not surprising that the discussions often became inconclusive, speculative, and tangential. The data at hand were simply not suited to the kind of broad questions the teachers were addressing. At times, the teachers themselves seemed to be aware of the inconclusiveness, and passed comment on the circularity of the discussion even as it proceeded:
>
>   MR. POOL: I'm a bit confused.
>
>   MRS. FLETCHER: This is all very vague.
>
>   MISS GOUGH: How many times have we been round in a circle, John?
>   (p. 252)

Ultimately, the staff is unable to complete the curriculum development task. They don't seem to be making much progress, and the Fall term is upon them. The Head took the task on himself, thus leaving everyone demoralized. Hargreaves suggests finally that teacher's exclusive reliance on their past experience to mediate any change in their practice provides a powerful barrier to innovation. But, again this could be an indictment of the way teachers are trained.

It's not only teachers who rely on personal experience; so do their administrators. Harry Wolcott's (1973) meticulously researched principal, "Ed Bell" who did not feel ". . . that his formal course work is administration was . . . related to his actual work as a school principal" (p. 200). Upon reading a draft of the case study, Ed admitted distress because he felt that at times he personally, and the principalship in general appeared rather inept. He particularly pointed out that many of the things which principals do, such as chasing dogs off the school grounds, or tracing a missing sandwich, are done not because principals want to do them, but because other people expect it. The limitations of the principal's role is linked to the restraints imposed by constantly having to meet the expectation of a multitude of others. "The demands of a position in which 'every problem is important,' mitigate the opportunity for constructive accomplishment" (p. 318). Perhaps this is why there is little connection between Ed's formal training and his actual role?

Wolcott (1973) begins by stating his purpose " . . . to a literature that has dealt almost exclusively with the behavior of school administrators as it *ought to be* or as it is interpreted, and reported by the person performing it, the present study adds another dimension: What an administrator actually does as observed by someone else" (p. xii). Then he describes his methods, paying particular attention to the laborious process of selecting a principal for study.[9] For example, "I did not want a subject whose success as a degree candidate might in any way be complicated by our research relationship" (p. 2). Furthermore, "I decided against working with one administrator, in part because he wore white socks with a dark business suit; I imagined that in two years, style of dress—one I personally dislike—might come to be as distracting as his patronizing manner with his pupils" (p. 2). He raises the issue of the grass-roots vs. the top-down approach. He did not want central administration to "assign some fair-haired principal to be my cooperating subject . . ." (p. 3). On the other hand, he ran the risk of, after having laboriously searched for and found Ed Bell, being shot down by the central administration because he hadn't gone through proper channels.[10] Harry became to everyone, "the shadow." Data collection consisted of:

> . . . maintaining a constant written record of what I observed in behavior and conversation; attending formal and informal meetings and conferences; accompanying him on school business away from the building, as well as occasionally accompanying him in non-school settings; interviewing 'everybody'; and . . . sifting through notes, records, and files. (p. 3)

The amount of data which Wolcott amasses on Ed Bell and his principalship is awesome, and allows him to do several things which aren't always found in a typical case study. First, it allows him to spice his "scientific account," with authenticating life history details.

> A dark and gloomy Tuesday morning in January, 1967, became a bit darker and gloomier when Ed Bell's car wouldn't start. Ed wasn't really surprised—he'd been having trouble with the old '61 Ford Falcon lately. A few weeks before he was all set to trade it in on a new (1965, new to him, at least) Mercury. The car dealer had offered so little for his old car as a trade-in, that he decided to keep it for travelling to school each morning. Now, just when he was in a rush to get to school after lingering a bit too long over eggs and coffee, the car battery was dead. (p. 19)

Second, it allows him the luxury of viewing Ed's role from several different perspectives. For example, he examines the principalship as both an annual cycle of activity (Chapter 7) and as a daily cycle (Chapter 6) of activity.

> He chatted briefly with Kay Johnson, the 'beginning' fourth-grade teacher, while he inspected his pet project at school, a salt water aquarium he referred to as 'the farm.' . . . Ed stepped into another sixth-grade classroom just as the bell rang to start school. . . . The substitute teacher had not yet arrived, so Ed remained with the class. As he left, he picked up a chair with a splintered leg which had caught his eye as he entered the classroom. He said he would take the chair to the office and break the leg so that it would not be used again. On the way back to the office, Ed stopped by the resource teacher's room to see how he was feeling. The resource teacher had missed several days the previous

week because of flu. Ed also wanted to inform him that the teacher's aide would not be at school that day because she was helping in the compilation of a school district census being made at the central office. When Ed walked into the office for the second time that morning, the secretary was talking to a woman accompanied by a seven-year-old girl, 'Mr. Bell, we have a new girl this morning for the second grade,' the secretary informed him. Another round in the morning's routines had begun. (pp. 124–5)

Third, his notes are so complete that he can actually quantify certain recurrent patterns, in order to achieve a statistical profile (Chapter 5) of the principalship. For example, Ed had 7 to 10 phone calls and spent just over 10 percent of each day on the phone.

Throughout the study, Wolcott (1973) continues to check on the typicality of his case. For example, from his interviews with Ed's mother, he began to appreciate the importance of the church in Ed's life history:

> Ed was involved in the activities of the Central Baptist Church to such an extent, that I had assumed him to be atypical of schoolmen in this regard. Yet a comparison with a national survey of elementary principals . . . shows him to be among the substantial 87 percent who hold some degree of membership in a church or religious body . . . (p. 49)

Ed's embodiment of the protestant ethic is quite evident in his fulfillment of his role.[11] Wolcott also measures Ed's typicality by comparing him to the many other principals he meets and interviews, when he accompanies Ed to principals' meetings and conferences. It is also possible, having read about many principals in the Personal Accounts literature,[12] for one to comment on Wolcott's selection. In my view, Ed is typical of those considered to be a "good" principal[13] as opposed to, say,

> Julie's first principal, who dressed in a leisure suit with a brass belt buckle that said 'Jesus Saves,' spent little time in the school because he planned early in the year to move on to another job. When in school, he avoided teachers, disciplined students, or lifted weights in his office. The second principal also lasted only a year and was seen as weak and ineffective by the teachers . . . . (Spencer 1986, 115)

RESEARCHER AND RESEARCHED

Finally, I want to draw on Wolcott to introduce an important methodological issue, namely his relationship with Ed.[14] Wolcott (1973) goes to considerable lengths to protect Ed's anonymity. He also seeks to shield Ed by not providing evaluative feedback.

> On several occasions I reviewed with Ed the fact that the project was not designed to be an evaluative one, and that he should not expect me to provide either a general review of how adequately I felt he fulfilled the role of principal, or specifically that he had handled some problem well or poorly. Ed was remarkable in his ability to accept this condition. (p. 6)

Another issue concerned friendship:

> I was conscious that "friendship" could present another nagging problem. . . .
> How does one develop a close working relationship with his subject, without
> the degree of involvement that has ultimately left some anthropologists unable
> to continue to write analytically about a people whom they have studied for years?
> My conscious goal was to establish a role as a warm, sympathetic observer without
> making all the commitments of a long-term friend." (p. 6)

Lastly, he had to be careful not to become so closely identified with the principal
that the staff would feel they could not speak to him without everything they
said finding its way straight back to Ed. However, he willingly shares his findings
with Ed and solicits his input.

> Ed thought the study fair and honest, although he felt that I had put undue
> emphasis on certain events and problems which made them appear out of
> proportion to the school year. . . . I now realize that Ed and I were at cross-
> purposes in that regard. His commitment was to resolve, and thus to eliminate
> problems and, when possible, to prevent them from ever happening; mine was
> to search them out, and keep them constantly in mind, in an effort to describe
> and understand how principals behave. (p. 317)

RESEARCHER-TEACHER COLLABORATION

Ed and Harry respect each other and are able to acknowledge that each will
have a slightly different perspective on the same events. While they may share
in an overall goal of improving education, their self-assigned roles in this enterprise
are quite different. I would like to review three more studies whose authors
seek to blur the distinction between teacher and researcher by conducting
collaborative research where ". . . the knowledge claims made depended
upon the shared meaning created by researcher and teacher participants"
(Clandinin 1986, 13).

One of the first such projects was undertaken by Elbaz (1983) in 1976 as her
dissertation. The problem she wishes to address, again, is the teacher's apparent
aversion to the use of professional knowledge ". . . Teachers are not commonly
seen to possess a body of knowledge and expertise appropriate to their work,
and this tends to diminish their status in the eyes of laymen" (p. 11). "I can think
of no other field of endeavor in which there is a comparable gap between the
value and importance attached to the work, and the level of ability generally
attributed to those performing it" (p. 10). Elbaz obviously is very critical of the
existing research literature on teaching practice and argues that, in lieu of
professional knowledge, teachers develop and use "practical knowledge" (what
Schubert [1991] refers to as "lore"), that functions like the professional knowledge
of doctors and lawyers.

Contrast Elbaz's selection strategy with Wolcott's. She chose Sarah because
she ". . . was a friend whose work I found interesting, and this made it probable

that we would establish a rapport easily and early on in the interviews" (p. 24).[15] Over 18 months she conducted five informal interviews with Sarah, each about two hours long, and two periods of classroom observation, then analyzed her material and ". . . when the analytic portion of the study was complete, I gave it to Sarah and we held a final talk which was taped but not transcribed" (p. 24). She doesn't really reveal what Sarah's reaction was, however, she suggests that it wasn't entirely positive ". . . I undertook to disclose my purposes and interpretations to the teacher, and to solicit her own purposes and interpretations. This proved to be much more difficult that I had anticipated . . ." (p. 25). At the end of the book, Elbaz makes a brave confession.

> When I set out to study Sarah's practical knowledge, I formulated a series of high-sounding statements about research as a shared endeavor, in which the interests and purposes of both teacher and researcher were to find a place. I proposed to invite the teacher's participation in every phase, from the formulation of precise questions to the final analyses of the data. I found that it is extremely difficult for two persons to simply come together, to talk, to explore ideas, much less to analyze data and interpret findings jointly. Inevitably, the social frameworks out of which they operate, will condition their discussion . . . I will be more cautious in the future in speaking about shared research efforts. To begin with, the research activity is embedded with a particular milieu; it is the business of the researcher to formulate researchable problems, to obtain funding for their investigation, and to publish findings. In doing so, he or she must be responsive to the ethos of the academic community, not the needs of the teachers. Teachers can play little or no role in these very crucial aspects of the work. Second, the researcher inevitably brings his own perspective to bear on his work, as does the teacher; the development of a common perspective takes much time and shared experience, while the option of taking up the teacher's perspective exclusively is largely impossible. Third, the interest and responsibilities of teachers will not always warrant their extensive involvement in research. (pp. 168–9)

I think that the major reason for her discouragement is that Sarah was, in a sense, uncooperative. Given Elbaz's preamble, we expect to see a "Super Teacher," someone who can handle any classroom contingency. On the contrary, Sarah does not appear to be an effective teacher, and it is not hard to account for this, ironically, by her evident lack of professional knowledge.

During the 18 month study, Sarah passes through three phases. After 10 years experience, Sarah finds herself teaching predominantly "academically oriented" high school students in a suburban, middle-class neighborhood. Despite getting this very desirable class, she seems unable to find ways to help students relate to English literature ". . . a student might . . . write an essay on *Hamlet*: 'I try to work with them, but I feel a sense of futility. If the purpose is to learn to write an essay, they could be doing it on a topic they choose, and if the purpose is to appreciate literature, then don't ask them to write a literary essay' " (p. 74).[16] Also,

> Sarah held some notion of the value of alternative interpretations of literature; at any rate, she seemed to view literature as an investigative discipline. But she

also had a sense of the value of the literary text as an object . . . she mentioned *Othello* taken as a point of departure for talking about jealousy or women's liberation: "That's quite exciting for the kids, but it's not studying *Othello*." (p. 56)

Not surprisingly,

> Sarah had begun to feel that students were not particularly interested in literature; many of them did not read for pleasure, and were not enthusiastic about the materials she presented in class, despite her efforts to make the work relevant to their concerns. Furthermore, she felt increasingly that students were not adequately equipped with the reading and writing skills needed to do the work she required of them in the upper grades. As a result, she was forced to lower her expectations, and often felt that her talent and energies were being wasted in the classroom; it seemed to her that classes were controlling her, with their limited abilities and lukewarm responses. (p. 34)

We are, therefore, also not surprised to learn ". . . she had done no in-service work in English literature, partly because she had felt no need for it, and partly because the trend . . . had been to focus on broad professional development concerns such as personal growth, values clarification, and group dynamics, rather than on specific content areas" (p. 34). And ". . . she had never taken a regular teacher training program, she had been allowed . . . to obtain certification through a series of summer courses" (p. 26).

Sarah, in a second phase, then becomes involved with faculty colleagues in the development of an "information-getting skills" (note-taking, outlining, paragraph structure) course. This is a "thoroughly negative" experience. Already somewhat isolated from her colleagues, she felt there was a lack of communication within the group. She felt the new course had been thrown together, and she was upset that there had been no provision for evaluating it.

As an outgrowth of this new class, however, the school establishes a Reading Center. Sarah, now enamored of "skills" (although "She appeared to have taken note of my suggestion that different subject matters require different skills . . ." [p. 61]), happily relinquishes the classroom for this sanctuary. Now, in phase three, her ". . . work . . . was largely ad hoc: rather than planning, researching, writing and preparing materials, Sarah had more confidence, she concluded, in a process where she met with students, heard their concerns, and then drew upon her *existing resources* to meet those concerns. This type of work emphasized responsiveness to students and improvisation, . . ." (p. 148, italics added).

Dorothy Clandinin (1986) draws heavily on Elbaz's approach in her pair of case studies of Aileen and Stephanie, and suffers comparable problems, in my view. Clandinin becomes very involved with her participants, and she reproduces letters she writes to them where she reflects on her ongoing analysis. She also shares with the reader excerpts from her journal and, indeed, the book is so self-absorbed, I considered reviewing it as an example of introspection in the Cognitive Studies chapter.

Researcher's Reflection

Now I had to see if I could use Elbaz's categories to make sense of the transcript. The following section represents my efforts to do just that. I feel great dissatisfaction with it. For while I have been able to fill in the categories, I have lost sight of Aileen as a whole person . . . of a sense of her aliveness, of her enthusiasm, and her love of children. Equally, I feel dissatisfaction because I have not put myself into the description. There is not a sense of my efforts to try and capture an understanding of Aileen's knowledge, and still make use of Elbaz's categories. . . . However, despite my dissatisfaction, I do feel that I am able to work with the categories. (p. 45)

Aileen and Stephanie[17] are primary teachers, their selection, like Sarah had been dictated by convenience and access, rather than typicality. We are left to wonder also about the typicality of their teaching situation. Clandinin tells us almost nothing about the students, the schools, the community. We are forced to play detective, and infer from statements like the following that Aileen, at least, is teaching in a middle to upper-middle class kindergarten. ". . . she asked the children to name their favorite nutritious snack, and then to classify the snack as fruit or vegetable" (p. 61). We learn a great deal about these teachers' beliefs and philosophy, but we rarely see it implemented (compare Grossman 1991). Equally distressing, we learn almost nothing about their backgrounds and their life outside of school; especially considering the following indictment from Clandinin of other's work " . . . research studies may assume that teachers' thoughts and ideas have a history, but the studies do not take that history into account" (Connelly and Clandinin 1988, 19) and also considering the fact that " . . . the relationship theme . . . [is] significant in Aileen's school life . . ." (p. 68) and to Stephanie " . . . a classroom to me is running a house, so I say, . . . 'we have to keep the house tidy for tomorrow . . .'" (p. 87).

Although Clandinin does not attempt to claim that these teachers are typical, the personal glimpses one gets of them (Aileen sees herself as a "little island." [p. 58]), suggest that they are not particularly unique either. The following implies that Clandinin (1986), like Elbaz (1983), is trying to attack a straw man: "In this account of Aileen, what may, at one level, be seen as disjointed practices can, at another, be seen to have a unity and commonality as expressions of the relationship theme" (p. 72). I don't think that those who "find" that teachers fail to use professional knowledge (Hargreaves 1984) are claiming that teachers have no knowledge, no plans, no ideas.

But, perhaps my greatest disappointment with this and similar reports is the failure to present the teachers' perspective[18] on the research enterprise. This would constitute a methodological breakthrough. That is, Clandinin regularly solicits feedback from the teachers to her preliminary analyses and theoretical constructs. But, she never shares with her readers what these reactions are. We never hear what they have to say. So, although I placed teacher-researcher collaboration in a fuzzy area of Table 6.1, between "self" and "other," it does not really seem to belong there at all.[19] Nowhere in these two books do I hear Sarah, Aileen, or Stephanie addressing me. They address only the researcher.

Consider, by way of contrast, the narratives in the Raphael (1985) collection Frances Marinera is not addressing Raphael here, she's addressing the world: "What I see happening in education is that these outside expectations are getting to be more numerous. I see teachers doing these bureaucratic chores, and they hate it" (p. 66).

The final note of caution regarding teacher-researcher collaboration is provided by a soul-searching paper (Munro 1991) delivered recently at an American Education Research Association meeting. Describing her doctoral research, Munro, notes that her ". . . first attempt at establishing a collaborative relationship was flatly rejected" (p. 7). Eventually, she secures the cooperation of two teachers, one of whom is retired; both, however, refuse to keep a journal or write about how they experience the research process. While Munro saw the meetings and interview sessions as "enjoyable talk," they saw it as work. They were willing to tell their stories, to facilitate interviews with principals and other teachers, to provide personal memorabilia, to let her poke and probe, but they resisted collaboration. "In establishing a collaborative relationship, I believed I should also share my story. I engaged in life history because of its reciprocal nature concerning mutual storytelling" (p. 8). However, her informants were ". . . not interested in hearing the researcher's story" (p. 8). Munro is also concerned about the following paradox: If "new" narrative inquiry requires mutual openness and revelation, won't the researcher's openness about her values and expectations, "bias" the responses of her informants? In this case, Munro is an avowed feminist. She isn't sure she should reveal this to her teacher informants, or as she calls them, "life historians." Another problem emerges. She picks up a theme *she* is interested in, a teacher's "allies," and deflects her informant from another theme, her "travels," that she is not interested in, but which the informant clearly is interested in telling about. "I questioned whether it was truly the life historian's understanding of her experience I was seeking, or if I was structuring the interview so that the subject told the story that conformed to my outlook" (p. 12).

I am far from believing that teacher-researcher collaboration is not a good thing, or is even that difficult to pull off. One the contrary, one of my most satisfying pieces of research has been a case study of Running Start, undertaken with first grade teacher Ann Zupsic (Lancy and Zupsic 1991). Zupsic had complete co-ownership of the study from start to finish. But, the study was focused on a specific project, and did not in any way serve to probe into Ann's beliefs, practices, or knowledge. Although primarily a parent-involvement program, there was a classroom component, but this, too, was our joint responsibility. That is, whatever success or failure that can be attributed to that part of the program which we designed, both of us must share the credit or blame. Clearly, this is not the case in the teacher-researcher projects reviewed here. As soon as the possibility exists that the research can be construed as an evaluation of the teacher, "collaboration" and "joint construction of meaning" becomes, I would argue, a virtual impossibility (Knowles and Hoefler 1989), the one glaring and uncanny exception.

THE TEACHER-AS-RESEARCHER

What happens when teachers do their own research? Here we have, usually, case studies that are self-directed. However, as we will see, only occasionally do the teachers writing in this area reveal enough of themselves to qualify their works as personal accounts. Indeed, some of this literature is indistinguishable from any other research literature in education; the fact that the "study" was done by a teacher is almost incidental.

Several recent collections of teacher-as-researcher material (Daiker and Morenberg 1990; Goswami & Stillman 1987; Bissex and Bullock 1987) are somewhat disappointing. They tend to focus more on exhortations to teachers to do research than actual reports by teachers of their research. Enough examples exist however, to show some of the primary traits of the is emerging sub-genre of the Personal Accounts literature.

First we take up a study of children's writing choices (Alofs and McKennis 1990), the equal of any study done by an academic. What is missing is a distinct teacher flavor to this report. Cornell's (1987) work is immediately distinguishable from other Personal Account by its curricular focus, in this case on poetry in a first grade classroom. Although she offers some conclusions ". . . poetry writing occurs after a considerable amount of exposure to poetry in the classroom, and also in direct proportion to that exposure" (p. 115). She bases this on having "witnessed the same happening with both first and second-grade children over the past eight years" (p. 115). In other words, there is very little sense of inquiry, of systematically varying the curriculum to observe the effects, or of long term observation, and she makes no attempt to relate her "finding" to the existing (and fairly large) literature on the role of rhyme in early literacy. But we do see evidence of considerable practical knowledge in Elbaz's (1983) terms.

Atwell (1987) provides another trait that is integral to this type of project. She indicates a moment of personal discovery and change (see also Pinnell and Matlin 1989). ". . . I saw through my defenses to the truth: I didn't know how to share responsibility with my students, and I wasn't sure I wanted to. I liked the vantage of my big desk; I liked setting topic and pace and establishing criteria. I liked being in charge . . ." (p. 179).

Two examples that seem to contain all of the critical traits of this approach were both done by teachers with the surname Ray. Lucinda Ray (1987) first provides a personal rationale for becoming a teacher/researcher:

Reflection

1. I was frustrated and dissatisfied with the lack of success I had in talking with my students about their writing.
2. I wanted to apply what I was learning about the writing process in summer courses, workshops, and reading.
3. I was tired of September enthusiasm fading by December. I thought an ongoing project might help keep me mentally alive and consistent.
4. A professor and several fellow teachers encouraged me to try it. (p. 219)

She carefully describes the setting and sample, remedial English class, with around 9–12 students in a rural high school in western Massachusetts. Her goal is to study the distribution of talk in teacher-student writing conferences, and the effect this has on students' essays. Initially she finds that the teacher (herself) dominated about 75 percent of the time. She changes her tactics.

> ### Reflection
>
> As this transcript shows, I am learning to let the student identify what part of the piece he/she will talk about. I try to reflect on the effect his/her changes (opening, paragraphing) have on me. I emphasize the parts I think are good. Perhaps this seems obvious. However, when working with a class such as this one, with so many possible writing errors and problems that I *might* focus on, it has taken me a long time to learn to praise. I have a hunch that I'm not much different from many other English teachers. (p. 228)

She is pleased with the outcome, and she notes personal changes: "I have new expectations and understandings of the function of the writing conference. I have a different definition of what revision means for these student writers" (p. 240). "I learned to focus much more on the content of their writing. Frankly, I became interested in their stories" (p. 241). Yet, she is not a Pollyanna either.

> ### Reflection
>
> . . . the conferences about more traditional expository writing are much less satisfactory that the ones I've transcribed and categorized about expressive writing. I have much more difficulty keeping quiet, because I have 'ownership' of the knowledge: the content of *The Crucible* or *Ethan Frome, the techniques of writing about books, the organizational strategies* of expository writing. And it must be admitted that these are students who feel no guilt at refusing to do a distasteful assignment. (p. 242)

She confesses, "My research may not break new ground . . ." (p. 224). The prime reason that her research does not break new ground is that she fails to adequately ascertain just where the old ground has already been broken. That is, she does not place her work at the leading edge of the extant research on teacher-student talk in the writing conference. Indeed, none of the teacher/researchers do this, and texts written to guide them, (Mohr & MacLean 1987; McClelland & Donovan 1985; Myers 1985) make short shrift of the "review of literature" (but see Kinkead & Lancy 1990). This may not be a bad thing if the vision is merely to encourage the development of reflective practitioners (Schön 1991). However, unless the teacher-as-researcher project is extended to include making an original contribution to knowledge in the discipline as a whole, as well as to that of the teacher-researcher, the audience for this work will evaporate.

The last example by Ruth Ray (1990) does make such an original contribution, which plays a vital role in the discussion of cognitive processes during composing in the next chapter. Ray (1990) identifies a downside to what is otherwise a model study, and, as it applies to all teacher/researchers I present it here.

Reflection

The case also demonstrates a crucial conflict I felt between my role as teacher and my role as researcher. As Fida's teacher, I felt responsible for her learning. As a researcher, I did not feel that same responsibility. In fact, I believed I had to maintain some sort of distanced, observer status, even after I had identified the strategies Fida used that hindered her growth as a writer. I was uncomfortable with my findings and unwilling to confront Fida with what I saw as one source of her failure—a dependency on teachers that I, as one of her teachers, had helped create. (p. 335)

Ray's frustration at having to sit back and describe a phenomenon is evident. It would seem that it is difficult for the teacher to study an essentially static problem, in this case one student's inability to grow as a writer.

PROMISES AND LIMITATIONS

I see the study of Personal Accounts as having enormous potential. Rather cursorily, I have reviewed several works (e.g., Conroy and others) which can be profitably studied as a group. Their collective wisdom about cross-cultural teaching, the role of values, institutionalized racism, and so on, being much greater than the sum of the individual chronicles. Almost any area of education can be illuminated by synthesizing material from the extant autobiographical record of teachers, principals, school board members, and so on. A literary critic studying genre or voice, a clinician looking for signs of stress, an historian searching for evidence of a transition from teaching as a calling to teaching as a job, will all find grist for their respective mills. While local archives can be searched for unpublished material, the inter-library loan system will prove invaluable for tracking down published works that are no longer in print. Of course, a researcher can also collect life history material from the living. One of the most direct sources is from our own students. Recent changes in the nature of public school curriculum have provided impetus for student autobiography. Teachers, in turn, and with proper safeguards, can analyze these materials for themes, so that we may gain a better understanding of, for example, how academic "careers" (see Chapter 3) are constructed.

The in-depth study of a single life in the conduct of biography can also be rewarding. Two issues need to be addressed by the aspiring biographer. Does this person's story illuminate issues that have contemporary significance? And, is this someone that you can treat sympathetically, but dispassionately? An area of biography that has an almost urgent appeal are the lives and stories of teachers who have had successful teaching careers in the inner-city (e.g., Edwards, 1989). Almost everyone has had, or heard, about these legendary figures, but we know almost nothing about what they have in common, what techniques they use in teaching, their philosophy, or their strategies for self-preservation and renewal.

With respect to the collection and analysis of multiple-life histories, there are numerous topics waiting to be addressed. For example, innovation in education has been looked at from a number of perspectives (Chapter 5), but no one, to my knowledge, has collected oral histories in which the participants were asked to reflect on their encounters with "new ideas." Where did these come from? How were they initially received? Was there a change in the classroom, school, or school district? What does the wisdom of hindsight suggest to the teacher?

As we have seen, the case study demands that the researcher acquire multiple sources on the participants—observation, collection of written material, and perhaps, interviews with their colleagues, employers, and family members. The researcher now has the opportunity to construct a universal or etic characterization to set alongside the emic perspective provided in the interview and diary material. Here the field is truly wide open, so to speak. I have earlier mentioned the need for a case study or studies of female principals. But imagine how our personnel preparation courses would be enhanced if we had vivid and thorough case studies of gym teachers, guidance counselors, speech pathologists, secretaries, and assistant principals to draw on? Would we need to revise the text material used in training these individuals for their roles, as real-world accounts became available?

Multiple case studies shorten the perspective. That is we invest less in any single individual, we learn less about them, in order to obtain comparative data on several individuals. "Unpackaging" the teacher's or administrator's instructional tool kit is amenable to study using several case studies. When a teacher says ". . . the 'Quality Circle' is particularly important for me now. It's an opportunity for me to grow" (Marinera in Raphael 1985, 77), what does that mean?

In order to realize this promise, some limitations in the present Personal Accounts literature must be addressed. There is a tendency to locate at one or another end of the idiographic-nomothetic continuum, rather than attempting to strike a balance as Spencer (1986) does. I think we are rapidly reaching the saturation point with respect to single-case or collections of teacher's stories that do not address a problem. On the other hand, some problem focused studies use such large samples that all sense of individual identity is lost.

The selection of participants has been treated in a rather off-hand fashion in too much of the Personal Accounts literature. Considering the enormous investment one makes over the course of the project, it is not sensible to select a participant who is unrepresentative of the class one wants to refer to (e.g., a 45-year old "beginning teacher"), or someone who does not possess the qualities or attributes one is interested in studying (e.g., selecting an administrator who turns out to be widely regarded as incompetent for a study of leadership style). It is clearly unwise to study one's friends, whether or not they are treated as "collaborators."

We need a truth in advertising policy. Far too often, when I expected to read a report of research, I was treated to a lecture, in which the life history material was not analyzed, but selectively drawn on to illustrate the lecture. Fortunately, in some of these works, sufficient material is presented so that one could use it to compare with other similar cases in the literature—this was particularly true of the works on beginning teachers. I am, obviously, an advocate of using life history material for instructional purposes, and see its usefulness in illustrating a novel thesis about the larger social forces that have an impact on teaching. But, one should be very careful to (e.g., "I am not sure that I want to call what I do research." Grumet 1991, 71) avoid claiming that one is reporting qualitative research findings.

Too many reports leave out what would seem to be essential pieces of the puzzle. Many scholars fail to gather and/or fail to report life history details that might have a bearing one one's character in school. Critical contextual detail should include: the subject's family life, including the subject's role as parent; personal school history, especially details of the professional training; significant others, parents and favorite teachers; some sense of the individual's daily routines and life-style; the nature of the school and classroom environments; students' characteristics and background, especially regarding class and ethnicity; some sense of school climate and the prevailing teaching ethos; and classroom routines, including the use of prepared curricula, grouping arrangements, management strategies, predominant instructional mode, etc. Again, I would cite Spencer (1986) as representing the ideal, although I missed any discussion of the teacher's pedagogical philosophy, another critical detail.

Let me now turn to two of the newer paradigms in the Personal Accounts tradition. The jointly constructed research project between a practitioner in the field and a researcher needs careful exploration. It certainly makes sense to suggest that in pursuing a study where an individuals' life history is a primary data source, that that individual should have considerable say in the conduct, outcome, and reporting of the research. However, in the published literature to date, the teachers seem not to have claimed ownership of the project. Largely, this seems to be due to selecting collaborators who are accessible, rather than seeking out teachers with a genuine interest in and understanding of research. When I contemplate this type of study, I think of a teacher of my acquaintance who did a superb job on her master's thesis; is widely recognized for her innovative teaching; and, is called upon frequently to provide leadership in her school, as well as in the district and state. She knows she is at the peak of her profession and would, I'm sure, be quite comfortable working with a researcher to pick apart some aspect of her pedagogical model (e.g., Gudmundsdottir 1990) or her practice.

The teacher-as-researcher[20] paradigm is a very welcome recent development, but it is too early to see just what further developments to expect. There are several possibilities. Recently, I met with a group of primary teachers to discuss an aspect of a multifaceted project they have been funded to carry out, a primary feature of which was teacher autonomy. It was interesting that, despite teachers' (perhaps legitimate) complaint of being bogged down with official record-keeping, these teachers did not immediately see the need to document, via narrative description as well as using quantitative indicators where available (e.g., "number of parents attending an open house"), their actions and the outcomes thereof. Too often teachers are charged with designing and carrying out new programs, while some district or building-level administrator is charged with "evaluation" and "reporting." Thus, the teacher-as-researcher movement may facilitate a development whereby teachers take greater responsibility for documenting and reporting the course of projects they are involved in.

Another possible development is that teachers will begin to incorporate the methods and techniques of researchers into their instruction (e.g., Cangelosi 1990). That is, they will "study" aspects of their own practice in order to make more systematic improvements. Teachers might go one step further and conduct these studies in such a way that permits the findings to be disseminated to wider and wider circles of colleagues. And, finally, all three of these developments may merge, and this would be the ideal. For this to happen, however, teachers must meet the same obligations for rigor as any academic scholar. For a start, they must locate their study at the edge of our present knowledge, and to do this they must first conduct a thorough and critical review of the literature, a step not advocated in the how-to literature for teacher/researchers, unfortunately.

In the culminating activity for the master's degree, we have an untapped resource of incalculable magnitude for producing teacher/researchers. Thousands of educators earn a masters degree every year and, as their final responsibility, submit a project or a piece of writing. Most of these are make-work undertakings, in my experience, of no value except to fulfill degree requirements. There is absolutely no reason in principle why the legion of masters degree candidates in education should not be required to conduct a publishable piece of research (as their counterparts are required to do in other disciplines). The major impediment for years was that teachers simply didn't have the resources to do "good" research meaning: access to large, randomly assigned samples of student "subjects"; who could be given elaborate treatments; the results of which could then be analyzed by sophisticated statistical techniques. This book should make abundantly clear that there are other avenues to good research which are accessible to teachers (and administrators as well).

Let me conclude by leading you back to an earlier chapter. There are many interesting themes which arise in the Personal Accounts literature which can be better pursued in another tradition. One of these is the issue of "shop talk" or discussion among educators of student and instructional issues. There is the suggestion in much of this literature that it occurs rarely, and when it does it may take on a very negative tone (Hammersley 1984). And then one comes across something like the following in, an interview with Tracy Kidder (Daniels 1989):

> Mr. Kidder's interest . . . was piqued by listening to conversations of several friends who teach elementary school. "I had thought teachers wouldn't talk about their work outside of a school setting. . . . But whenever they'd get together, that's exactly what they did. They seemed so animated, so invested in their students, I was intrigued." (p. 46)

Now it would be very hard to get at shop talk using the framework advanced in this chapter. It occupies too small a time and space in the life history of the individual. However, it is perfectly suited to an ethnomethodological approach (Chapter 3), where the social-interactional setting is the usual unit of analysis. In the next chapter, we again have the opportunity to observe the way in which a specialized methodology has evolved to tackle a particular set of issues in education.

NOTES

1. Kinkead suggested that, as there is such a great variety of genre expressions in this chapter, that those that differed markedly from earlier quotations should be "framed."
2. The contradiction is intended.
3. The personal accounts that are reviewed in this chapter are predominantly those of teachers, that's the nature of the literature. However, I have strived to find accounts of other actors on the education stage to provide some variety.
4. Many of the portraits of Indian Americans were published for this reason (e.g., "Ishi"- Kroeber 1961) as were oral histories or urban types (e.g., Stanley the "Jackroller"- Shaw [1930] 1966) collected by the Chicago School of Sociology.
5. In the course mentioned above, I used his (1984) *Growing Minds: On Becoming a Teacher* as the text.
6. With McLaren, Kozol, Kohl, and Conroy, I have certainly not exhausted the store of autobiographical material focused on teaching impoverished elementary school children. Furthermore, there is a parallel library of works on the challenges facing secondary school teachers (e.g., Best 1983; Channon 1970; Cherry 1978; James 1969; Kaufman 1964; Natkins 1986; Williams 1987; Welsh 1986) that I can't even touch on here.
7. In the older literature, pre-1985, those whose lives are studied or chronicled are referred to as subjects. This term, associated as it is with experimental psychology and conveying an air of manipulation and uneven status, has now fallen out of favor in the Personal Accounts literature. No widely agreed-upon substitute exists. I have used "cases" or "participants" where it seemed appropriate.
8. I lasted only one quarter as a supervisor of student teachers because I ran into two intractable cases (out of six supervisees!). In one, I had to conclude that the individual would need far more than one quarter of student teaching before she would be considered competent, and yet she had earned all A's and B's in her teacher education classes, and her "failure" in student teaching was unacceptable to my department head. In the second, the practicing teacher used an approach out of the dark ages, yet she was only aping her supervising teacher and following directions.
9. Wolcott (1983) himself describes a dramatically contrasting example which illustrates the difference between life history and case study. Here he discovers 19-year-old "Brad," squatting in a shack he has made for himself on a corner of Wolcott's wooded property. for two years, Wolcott gathers Brad's life history. A "stonie" and eventual dropout, Brad has gotten little from his schooling. He uses Brad's story to make the point that while school can teach you things, it can't give you reason for wanting to become educated, only your parents can do this. And Brad's parents have failed him. But what is interesting is that Wolcott treats Brad's case quite differently than Ed's, as he says, "There should be a high ratio of information to explanation in a life-story . . . ." (p. 8), and that's exactly what he does, his analysis is minor, instead he helps Brad tell his story.
10. Districts vary a great deal in how concerned they are about "managing" research contact with schools. The best approach is a modified grass-roots approach where you search for the teacher/school/students that are right for your study, while keeping contact with a "guardian angel" in central administration—someone who is sympathetic toward your project and can go to bat for you if someone in authority is upset that you didn't follow correct protocol. Of course, after getting informal agreement from teachers, principal, etc., you need to seek formal permission through the district office.

11. In the retrospective evaluation of Kensington School reviewed in the previous chapter, the researchers track down the principal actors 15 years later to conduct life history interviews (Smith, Klein, Dwyer, Prunty 1985). They were not surprised to find that the crusading innovators who established this "open" school, all revealed a history of deep involvement with organized religion. The authors refer to educational innovation as "secular religion."

12. One of these is Phil Bingham (Clandinin and Connely 1991), the very effective principal of an inner-city school in Toronto. Actually he sounds like McLaren's (1980) principal. Phil related a story about his being teased when he was sent to school in short pants to explain his empathy for minority students.

13. When the prospectus for this book was reviewed, one of the reviewers complained that my references all seemed quite dated. I took this concern into account in preparing this book. However, I would argue that neither the march of progress in educational administration, nor in educational research methodology are likely to have invalidated Wolcott's (1973) 20 year old study, except in one regard. Now I would have to say that Ed was typical of good, male principals. The time is right for a replication of Wolcott's original study with a female principal.

14. See also Bullough's (1990, 137–9) discussion of his relationship with Kerrie.

15. Studying a friend is not a good idea. Even in a project that attempts to be collaborative, it is extremely difficult to keep a hierarchical relationship at bay. And, in the analysis, more may be revealed than is comfortable for either researcher or subject.

16. Sarah seems muddled about pedagogy for teaching English, and unaware of the exciting developments taking place at the time, such as the National Writing Project, reader-response theory, and the integrated language arts curriculum.

17. Aileen and Stephanie make guest appearances in a recent textbook (Connelly and Clandinin 1988) for teachers. Their narratives are used illustratively as in Bullough (1989) and Fuchs (1969).

18. I was, for example, distressed that, given the pervasive emphasis on the cooperative nature of this work, the teachers, who should have been given co-authorship of the book, aren't even identified by their real names (see also Shulman 1990)!

19. An important work in progress, Adra Cole and Gary Knowles (1991) are starting to systematize the whole area of what they refer to as "partnership." Their work should provide an invaluable guide to the varied roles taken in, and purposes of (university) researcher—(school) teacher relationships.

20. There is an interesting parallel body of work that might be referred to as "counselor-as-researcher." Clark Moutsakis (1990) has written a useful guide for clinicians and counselors who would adopt a research perspective based on Personal Accounts.

CHAPTER 7

Cognitive Studies

INVESTIGATOR: If you had a chance to think about the assignment theme for today, could you tell me a bit about what kind of contemplation you had on the topic?

LYNN: Well I have, it's interesting I've been . . ., thinking about it, . . . This morning I had an idea to write about this thing we got from my sister, who is on vacation with our cousins. She sent us from, it might have been Disneyland, a two-foot-high cut-out of Snoopy, the Peanuts dog, dancing, and my mother set it up in the middle of the living room so you see it when you walk in the front door. And I thought it might be interesting to write about people's reactions to it, there have been quite a few. . . . Now the problem is how to start it. I could say that I walked into the house one evening after work, and there it was sitting in the middle of the living room. Or else, I could say something like, it's going to sound like a third grade introduction, but something about, "Can you imagine our surprise when we received a three-foot by three-foot cardboard packing thing in the mail?" That's also not too good a start. I have to think of how to begin the thing. You could say that it's not the ordinary thing to have in your living room, and people don't expect to see it. Uh, you could say something about "one of the last things that people would expect to find in our," yeah, I could say, "people in a," no, "in a living room such as ours with the oak," what is it, I think it's walnut-paneled "walnut paneled entranceway and shelves and book" yeah, "and book shelves lining the walls, almost the last thing one would expect to find would be a two-foot-high cardboard cut-out of Snoopy, the Peanuts dog. However, in the A____'s house just about anything is possible." (laughing) I think I can start like that.

Let's see, does this pen write, yeah (4 sec. pause). *One of the last things* (16 sec. pause [writing]) *someone would expect to find in a* now wait, to say, to get "in our living room," I'm now describing the living room. I either put "a," I could say, "our living room with its walnut-paneled entranceway and book-lined walls," but that's kind of a, I don't like the construction. I use it too much, I think. Then to put the height, some sort of hyphenated adjectives in front of "living room," that might be too awkward. *One of the last things one would expect to find in our,* (4 sec. pause). (Emig 1971, 129–31)

The preceding quotation is taken from a monograph by Janet Emig (1971) that has been described as ". . . the single most influential piece of . . . inquiry . . . in composition's short history" (North, 1987, 197). In this study, Emig had high school students (in this case, Lynn) share their thoughts as they composed several essays. Emig was the first scholar to apply Piaget's (she cites Piaget 1955) clinical method to the study of writing as a cognitive process. As the excerpt clearly shows, Lynn treats composing as a problem-solving activity, not unlike the student-subjects struggling to solve Piaget's (Inhelder and Piaget 1958) four chemicals problem.

In the late 1960s and early 1970s many scholars saw an opportunity in Piagetian methods and theory to reexamine underlying assumptions about how students acquired the cognitive strategies needed to solve academic or school-like problems. For example, Jack Easley (1974, 1980, 1982) has written extensively on the value of qualitative research in mathematics education. Although he sees the open-ended exploratory study of cognitive processes as a ". . . natural history phase in which one learns about the underlying structure of the phenomena . . . then . . . one can proceed to a more quantitative type of methodology" (1982, 193). His students (e.g., Erlwanger 1973) and others (Barody 1984; Confrey 1980) have dramatically demonstrated the fundamentally constructive nature of children's learning in arithmetic. Students are not just applying (or failing to apply) correct algorithms or rules. Similar findings have emerged in the study of reading (Afflerbach and Johnston 1984), in science (Simon and Simon 1978), and as we've seen, in composition.

OUTLINE OF THE CHAPTER

The chapter has two broad themes, cognitive processes implicated in writing and in teaching. We first consider evidence of differential thinking activity by elementary children just learning to compose. Then we review a series of studies that contrast the composing processes of experienced/inexperienced and expert/non-expert writers, illustrating a series of complex research techniques along the way.

We then meet several expert elementary school math teachers studied by Gaea Leinhardt and her colleagues. This allows us to again review a number of novel and challenging research techniques. Finally, we consider some of the limitations of the cognitive method.

BEGINNING TO COMPOSE

In this section I will review a series of studies on what young children do when faced with a writing "assignment." Several authors (e.g., Lamme and Childers 1983) have noted that, prior to ages five and six, children do not distinguish between drawing and writing. Their "stories" are as likely to be pictures, perhaps with a letter or two added. By first grade children are engaged in recognizable writing, but there are subtle differences among them that reveal the developmental process. Ann Haas Dyson (1985) has done extensive work with young writers, in particular, Dexter, Caillie and Anne ". . . who had contrasting ways of approaching literacy tasks and who were perceived by the teacher as being both at different levels of literacy skills, and also 'typical' of the young students with whom she worked" (p. 499).

Figure 7.1 is a sample of Dexter's free writing. In the upper right corner are his teacher, Mrs. Lin's notes, taken as Dexter read to her. Dyson recorded this reading as well as the comments he made to her as he wrote.

FIGURE 7.1 Dexter's free writing

SOURCE: Dyson, A. H. (1985). Three emergent writers and the school curriculum. Copying and other myths. *The Elementary School Journal, 85*(4), p. 505. Reprinted by permission.

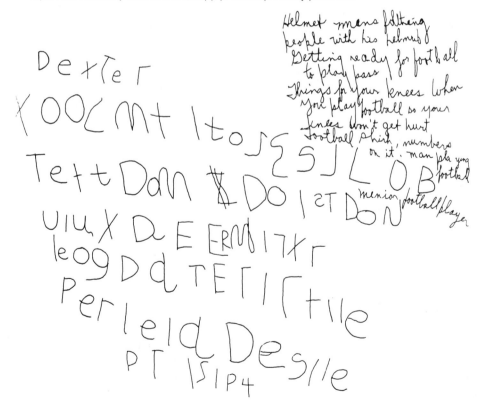

LINE 1 A: I'm writing about football.
Football helmet.
I'm writing things that are real. I'm writing helmet.

B: The man's hitting people with his helmet.

LINE 2 A: Now I'm going to write pass.

B: Getting ready for football to play pass.

LINE 3 A: Know those things that go on your knees? [In response to my question about what he was going to write now.]

B: Things for your knees when you play football so your knees won't get hurt.

LINE 4 A: I'm gonna write football shirt. I forgot to make number [and Dexter adds more letters].

B: Football shirt, numbers on it.

LINE 5 A: I'm writing man.

B: Man playing football.

LINE 6 A: [Dexter continued from line 5 to line 6 with no comment.]

B: Man is a football player. (p. 504)

She comments:

. . . Dexter seemed aware that written and read messages were related in a global way, but he could not effect this relationship in a precise manner. He appeared, in free writing, to put down letters to represent things ("I forgot to make numbers" on the football shirt), . . . [and] Dexter read his text as a particular object or as a sentence. (p. 504)

Anne, by contrast, has a more sophisticated understanding of the symbol system and the ways that oral and printed texts are related, and she could make use of this relationship in her writing. Figure 7.2 illustrates Anne's response to a free-writing assignment and shows (at the bottom) Mrs. Lin's notes made as she read.

Qualitative research with elementary age children consistently shows that, regardless of the subject area, they do not simply parrot back rules they have been taught, but actively invent or construct their own rules. They develop an internally consistent schema about how to operate in particular task environments. Another example is drawn from Carole Edelsky's (1983, 1986) in-depth study of writing in a bilingual education program in Arizona. As studies of composing go, she had a relatively large sample of 9 children in each of the first, second, and third grades. She collected all of the writing done in class during four week-long periods spread over the year, yielding a total of 424 pieces of writing. She searched for patterns in these writings. She also observed these classes and interviewed teachers and aides.

Edelsky's approach to the analysis of students' writing is referred to as content analysis,[1] a general description of which is provided by Lauer and Asher (1988).

The most crucial task . . . is the identification of important variables in the data. Sometimes this task is called *coding*—the setting up and labeling of categories,

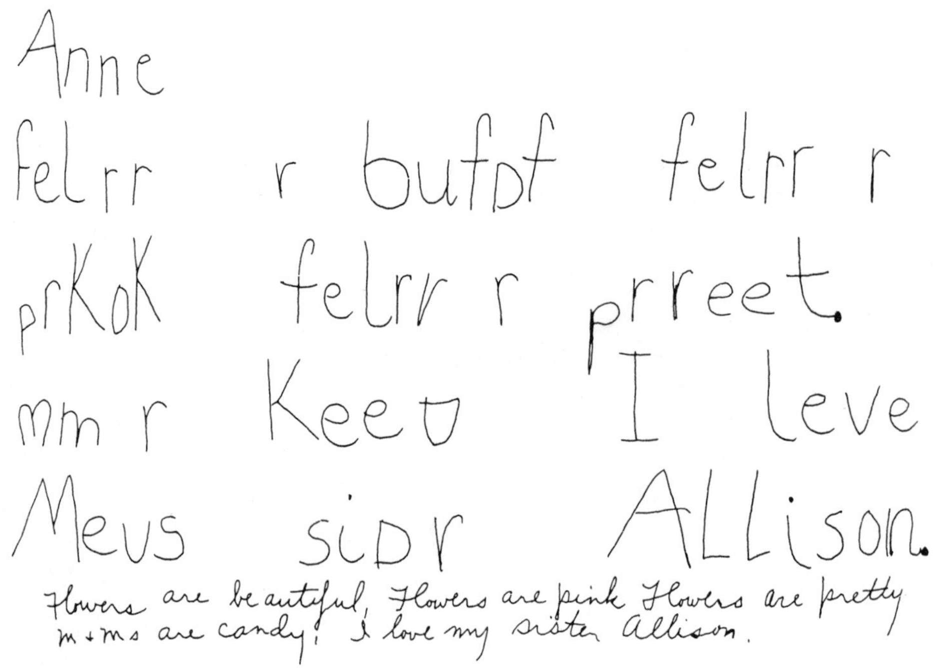

Anne
felrr   r bufof   felrr r
prKoK   felrr r prreet.
mm r Keeʊ   I leve
Meʊs   siɒr   ALLison.

Flowers are beautiful, Flowers are pink Flowers are pretty
m + ms are candy! I love my sister Allison.

FIGURE 7.2 Anne's free writing

source: Dyson, A. H. (1985). Three emergent writers and the school curriculum: Copying and other myths. *The Elementary School Journal, 85*(4), p. 508. Reprinted by permission.

which then become the *variables* of the study . . . . The broader term for this effort is *content analysis,* which is a major measurement procedure, allowing researchers to claim that materials and observations are ultimately quantifiable. The method is designed for use with communication data of all kinds: essays, television shows, presidential speeches, letters, and so forth. Researchers analyze the communication data, notice patterns, identify and operationally define variables, and relate them to one another. Once researchers have identified the categories or variables, they must test them for reliability . . . by developing instructions that will enable independent judges to conduct content analyses on representative data. (pp. 26–7)

Among the many aspects of composition that Edelsky (1983) analyzed was "invented punctuation." She knew that the punctuation patterns she was observing had been invented, because her observations and interviews showed that children were not taught punctuation nor drilled with punctuation exercises. Among the most common inventions were placing a period at the end of each line, and hyphens separating syllables or words. There were also developmental changes.

. . . early punctuation patterns were focused on local segments such as lines, and their function was separation. Thus, use of patterns such as a period after certain words and a period at the end of each line dropped off sharply or disappeared after early first grade, as did other patterns related to lines and pages. . . . Patterns that concerned 'textness' (such as a capital to start and a period to end the text) came into use later and increased in use over time. Later 'embellishments' were more controlled and content-related than were such features in the writing of the youngest children. For instance, third graders underlined titles and used iconic lettering. . . . (p. 150)

Donald Graves (1975) studied 14 (8 M, 6 F) seven-year-old student writers over a total of 53 writing episodes in a regular classroom. His approach was rather unusual in that he relied primarily on observation—his methods, in fact, resemble those of the human ethologist (see Chapter 4).

Whenever the researcher noted that a child was structuring materials for a writing episode, he moved close to the child and usually seated himself directly in front of his desk or table. Although the researcher was reviewing the child's work in the upside-down position, it was the best location to record behaviors accompanying the writing episode. In this way the child's body posture, use of overt language, and rereading could be better observed. (p. 231)

Occasionally also, he would question the child, "Tell me what you are going to write about when you finish your drawing" (p. 233). Like Dyson, Graves found interesting variation within this narrow age range. Some students seemed to be able to plan, mentally, what they were going to write, and acted as if they were writing for an audience. Others, less advanced, seemed to need to compose word-by-word and were much less concerned with an overall reading or review of what they had written. Echoes of this distinction will be heard shortly as we review studies of college-level writers.

WRITING AS A PROCESS

In order to understand where those who laboriously document the thought processes of students as they compose, or read, or solve math problems are coming from, it is necessary to understand some of their assumptions. First, they reject the overly mechanistic view of human learning characteristic of the "behavioral" school, and instead see human learners as actively constructing knowledge. The only limitations to this construction process are biological and functional. That is, one can only learn about five new things at a time (Miller 1956). So most of what we understand as cognition is actually the human mind trying to figure out ways around this bottleneck: by relating new information to old, so it won't appear as new; or by interrelating or clustering several new pieces of information into a compact package of five or fewer new items. The functional limitations are very straightforward, we only actively process the information[2] we have to or want to (Lancy 1990), that is, the normal human response to new information is to ignore it.

A second assumption is that it is possible to access one's cognitive processes directly through writing or speaking. This assumption reflects a second point of contrast with earlier views (e.g., "Since the triumph of behaviorism over 'introspectively' oriented competing viewpoints, verbal reports have been suspect as data'' (Ericsson and Simon 1984, 2). While interviewing is taken for granted as an essential technique in sociology and anthropology, for decades it was frowned upon in psychology, as being hopelessly biased and unscientific, only behavior was worthy of study. Ericsson and Simon (1984) have gone to great lengths to verify the validity and reliability of the research method described in this chapter, and have argued forcibly for the scientific value of a qualitative approach: ''Theory should not preclude the scientist from searching for new phenomena or from paying serious attention to phenomena he hits on adventitiously'' (p. 275). ''. . . data may exist that exhibit clear regularities without any current theory to describe or explain them . . .'' (p. 280).

A third assumption is that our pedagogy should reflect these first two assumptions. For example, the writing as a ''. . . process movement . . . had a profound effect on composition, shifting the emphasis of pedagogy from surface features of the text to the writing process . . . [which was] . . . founded on information processing theory . . .'' (Carter 1990, 276). This ''movement'' Carter (1990) refers to is most closely identified with the Bay Area (and later National) Writing Project (Early 1991). NWP has trained thousands of teachers around the country to abandon the teaching of writing as a series of recipe-like directives (e.g., the five paragraph essay), designed to lead to an easily graded ''product,'' and instead, to lead students to an understanding of writing as a process. Interestingly, while research on how people compose has obviously been translated into improved pedagogy (Beach and Bridwell 1984), prescriptions for changed practice are, at this stage, mostly unsupported empirically. That is, like most innovations in education, teachers' beliefs as to whether something will work seem more important in determining acceptance than the availability of evidence regarding efficacy.[3]

To sum up, those who conduct cognitive studies share the view that the acquisition of academic knowledge and skill, such as writing, is best characterized as the development of the student's information processing ability. They believe that learning environments can be structured in ways that enhance (or retard) these information processing abilities. And, they believe this development can be studied: by comparing the students' written work over an extended period (Emig 1971); by closely observing students as they write (Graves 1975); asking them to reflect, retrospectively on their past work (Odell, Goswami, and Harrington 1983); and by having them think aloud as they write (Perl 1979).

COGNITIVE PROCESSES DURING COMPOSING

Collaborators Linda Flower and Dick Hayes can be credited with the most significant long-term program of research on composition. They have contributed to a growing body of specific findings regarding the composing process, to a general theory of composing and to research methodology. Their (Hayes and Flower 1983) term for the set of research techniques mentioned in the previous paragraph is ''process tracing,'' under which they include for example:

1. In *behavior protocols,* we record what subjects *do* while they perform a task, but we do not ask them to report their thought processes verbally.
2. In *retrospective reports,* we ask subjects to tell us how they performed a task after the task has been completed. . . .
4. In *thinking-aloud protocols,* we instruct subjects to report on anything they are thinking while performing the task. (pp. 211–12)

They also provide a general rationale for these techniques.

> Because the data they yield are rich, . . . [there are] . . . valuable opportunities for scientific exploration. For example, the thinking-aloud protocol of a writer at work may yield fifteen pages of comment for every page of written text. Reading through the protocol is an occasion for discovering many things about the writing process that we did not suspect beforehand.
>
> There are some aspects of process that are difficult to observe without process-tracing. . . . For example, . . . that the order in which writers generate the ideas for writing a paper is quite different from the order in which these ideas are presented in the finished paper. If we look only at the finished paper, that is, the output, it may be difficult or impossible to study the order of idea generation. (p. 212)

Of the several techniques they review, in their own work they rely primarily on thinking-aloud and, elsewhere, (Swarts, Flower, and Hayes 1984) have been quite critical of the retrospective technique, which is, in any event, rarely used.

> While this method doesn't interfere with the process itself, the information obtained has some important limitations. Most obviously, much of it may have already been lost from short-term memory. Also, subjects are often unaware of the subtle processes that lead to judgments. When asked about their decisions, they may provide causal explanations that are logical, but are not always reports of the event as it actually occurred. . . . Subjects may also remember their processes selectively and give a distorted account of them, perhaps trying to say what they think the researcher wants to hear. (p. 55)

Here follows their (Swarts, Flower, and Hayes 1984) description of a general set of procedures which they follow.

> In a thinking-aloud writing protocol, the subject works in an experimental room with a desk, writing materials, and a cassette tape recorder and a tape. . . . The experimenter gives the subject general instructions and the time limit (usually about an hour). The subject is given a rough idea of the task, such as writing a magazine article, and is told '*The most important thing about this experiment is that we want you to say everything out loud as you are thinking and writing your essay. Even if it has nothing to do with the task—stray remarks and irrelevant comments are fine. We realize it's impossible to say everything you're thinking while you're writing, so just try to say as much as you can'* . . . the

writing task, the essay, and all written notes are numbered in order, and the tape recording of the subject's thinking aloud is transcribed (a process that takes a typist several hours with a transcribing machine). The transcript, which is usually 10–15 pages long, is the version of the writing protocol with which the researcher will probably spend the most time. This doublespaced, typed transcript of the writer's verbalized thought provides a unique window on the composing process. It allows the writing researcher to observe not only cognitive processes and their organization in the act of composing, but the development of the writer's ideas. (p. 54, italics added)

Figure 7.3 shows a typical protocol from a college English teacher who is in the process of describing her job in an essay for **Seventeen** magazine. As these

FIGURE 7.3 Experienced writer's protocol

SOURCE: Swarts, H., Flower, L. S., & Hayes, J. R. (1984). Designing protocol studies of the writing process: An introduction. In Beach, R., & Bridwell, L. S. *New Directions in Composition Research.* New York: Guilford, p. 59. Reprinted by permission.

what I [49] did as a) (—What I'm thinking of course is that [50] this is becoming ambiguous) —
(whereas—whereas I'm [51] trying to compose a troche) — (I may be [52] making something
that is impenetrably vague) — (for pay and when I [53] do — In a way I am able to continue
doing as an adult. . .what I did as a teenager) — (why don't [54] just leave it) — (take
out [55] for pay) — (that I did as an adult [56] what I did as a teenager for pleasure) —
(only now my reading and writing [57] and talking — and even talking — are part of —
of. . .an endeavor I share with others and for which the state — [Why [58] not. . .
make a joke] — and for which I am [59] paid. . .not grandly — though not grandly) . . . /
(It's my [60] sense that when we are thirteen or fourteen we [61] have — [at least I know —
we have — at least I known I did.] . . -a- a- a sense — [I don't know] it's my sense
that when we are thirteen or fourteen we have — at least I know I did — at
lease I know I did — we have certain leanings or tendencies or we have certain
inclinications or have certain — certain) -a- (I [62] don't know) — (I [63] don't want to say) —
(I want to say something that would [64] suggest the kind of -a- -a- inchoate -a-
direction) — (I mean a direction [65] which is not chaotic except it's moving in a very
purposeful way) — (In a sense we have — [66] at least I know I did — a kind of
individual purposiveness of -a- of individual — or say — personal personal
purposiveness which really — which — which — which emerges from who we are and
what's happened to us up to then. . .us — to then. . .) -a- / . . . (I notice as [67] I'm doing this
that when I'm — when I'm writing under normal circumstances my — I often, when I
go back to something that's not finished, I have a tendency to revise) -a- (I have
a tendency to start over and [68] over and over and over again) (and so [69] that my essays
often grow from the middle rather than in a kind of linear way.) (Here [70] I'm — I'm doing
this with sentences I think.) -a- (I think [71] if I were working on a typewriter I
would be doing much more revision) / (-a- kind [72] of purposiveness which emerges
from who we are and what's happening to us up to then.) (My — [73] What I'm thinking
of is. . .is that a person of that age — is that a person — of that — [74] age) — (It's
interesting.) (I just [75] realized that I — when I spoke that sentence before I — I
didn't know I hadn't written it down and I hadn't) (so I had to [76] go back and write

meta-comment

meta-comment

researchers point out—"A protocol offers a wealth of unsorted information" (p. 53) and

> The researcher who approaches a writing protocol with no idea of how to sort the data may well feel like someone who has never learned to float, and is poised for a dive into the Atlantic Ocean. . . . A protocol can be divided into various units, ranging from simple lines and clauses, to basic processes, such as planning and translating, to composing episodes that reflect a writer's unit of concentration and changing goals. We find it useful to parse a protocol on several levels, with the approach naturally depending on the purpose of the study. It should be emphasized that there is no single, correct way to analyze protocols: One's method is ultimately determined by the task, the subjects, and the research questions to be answered. (p. 56)

In this particular case, the protocol is marked in various ways.

> Lines are numbered at the left, clauses are enclosed in parentheses and numbered above, "writes" are underlined with a straight line, and "reads" with a wavy line. Episode boundaries (all major on this page) are marked with slashes; generally we use different colors for major and minor episodes. Meta-comments, or remarks, that do not relate to the assigned topic and often concerned with the situation or process itself, are here noted by braces in the margin . . . (p. 59)

As they say, how one analyzes the protocol depends on what one hopes to find. For example, in one study, they (Kaufer, Hayes, and Flower 1986) were interested in how writers compose sentences. Twelve writers, six described as experts, six as novices were asked to write on their jobs.

Protocol:

$\qquad$ 1 $\qquad$ 2

The best thing about it is that—what? Something about

$\qquad$ 3 $\qquad$ 4

using my mind—it allows me the opportunity to—uh—I

$\qquad$ 5

want to write something about my ideas—to put ideas

$\qquad$ 6 $\qquad$ 7 $\quad$ 8

into action or to—develop my ideas into—what?—into a

$\qquad$ 9 $\qquad$ 10 $\qquad$ 11

meaningful form? Oh, bleh!—um—say it allows me—to

12 13 14 $\quad$ 15 $\qquad$ 16

use—na—allows me—scratch that. The best thing about it is

$\qquad$ 17

that it allows me to use—my mind and my ideas in a

productive way.

Final Sentence: The best thing about it is that it allows me to use my mind

and my ideas in a productive way. (p. 125)

In the first part (the protocol) we see the writer's thoughts as she/he composed the final sentence. In their analysis of the 12 essays and thinking-aloud protocols, certain patterns held true for all writers. Referring to the fragment reproduced above:

> This segment shows all of the important features of sentence generation that we have observed in our sample of writers. First and most important, writers construct sentences by proposing and evaluating sentence parts. A sentence part was identified either by a pause of two or more seconds which separated it from adjacent parts in the verbal protocol, or by a grammatical discontinuity indicating that the current language represents a revision of earlier language (p. 126).

Certain aspects of the essays and protocols are quantifiable, and this permits a comparison of the groups of writers: "Experts wrote longer essays and . . . longer sentence parts . . . [and] experts . . . wrote essays which were ranked [1st–4th] by a panel of judges who evaluated all 12 essays for general merit" (p. 127).

Flower and Hayes are also interested in the more general issue of planning during composing, and extrapolate from the protocols to create a model (Figure 7.4) of planning underlying sentence composition. Models like this one are quite common in reports of cognitive studies and, not coincidentally, it resembles a flow-chart for a computer program. For some, the *sine qua non* of cognitive research is to learn enough to be able to program a computer to successfully mimic the cognitive processes humans display as they are solving problems (Ericsson & Simon 1984).

Planning is important because writing an essay is an "ill-defined" problem that calls forth, for its solution, a variety of heuristic procedures to make the task more manageable: "The problem we have set ourselves is to describe the heuristic procedures writers use during the act of composing. We will not, a priori, decide which procedures are most efficient, but rather attempt to describe the procedures writers actually use" (Flower and Hayes 1981a, 40–1). Some examples of these heuristics or planning devices include:

> . . . when a writer tells herself, "I'm just going to jot things down as they occur to me"; "I won't organize now"; "I'll worry about the spelling later"; or "I should make an outline," she is giving herself a set of procedural directions for how to go about the *process* of writing, regardless of what she has to say. . . . Another . . . generating plan which we identified in the protocols of our subjects is the *thinking by conflict* plan . . . the writer ask[s] himself to find a contradiction, to raise an objection, or to pose questions (p. 43) . . . [another] . . . group of plans for producing a paper is concerned with *organizing the writer's ideas* in terms of sequence of their significance. Here we found writers, apparently overwhelmed with the ideas they had produced, firmly instructing themselves to *find a focus,* or to *write a second draft from some angle.* (p. 47)

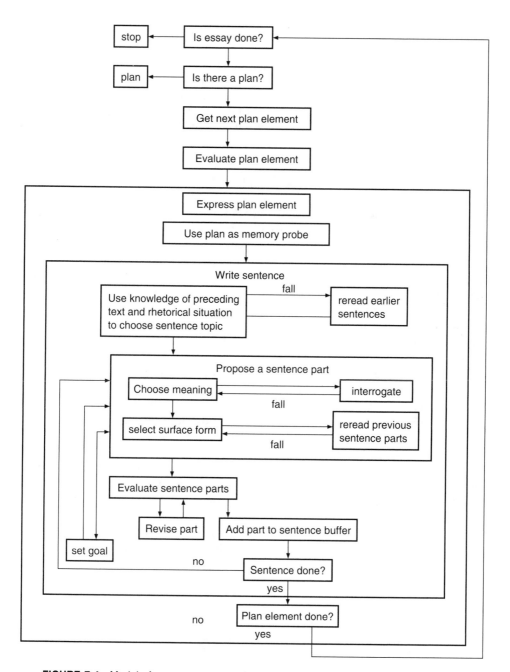

FIGURE 7.4 Model of sentence composition

SOURCE: Kaufer, D. S., Hayes, J. R., Flower, L. (1986). Composing written sentences. *Research in the Teaching of English, 20*(2), p. 139. Reprinted by permission.

They also found writers who failed to spontaneously generate plans.

> . . . some writers appeared to be making no self-conscious plans for their reader. This means that there were writers who not only neglected to mention or discuss their audience, but who also failed to think in terms of making a conclusion or a point, or to imagine the criticism, confusion, or argument they might stimulate by saying x, y, or z. These writers seemed to lack clear plans for communicating with or affecting a reader. (p. 57)

VARYING LEVELS OF SKILL IN COMPOSING

A general trend is detectable here (Flower & Hayes 1980). Less proficient writers seem to use most or all of their information processing capacity making decisions regarding word choice, spelling and punctuation. Whereas, better writers (or those who have been taught via process writing pedagogy) devote their information processing energy to thinking about the audience, theme, point-of-view, maintaining coherence—more global issues.[4] One way to tease out these differences is to study the naturally occurring boundaries in the composing process. "We initially noticed that writers appeared to work in units of concentration or periods of sustained focus, and, more importantly, found that the boundaries between these composing episodes could be agreed upon by independent readers" (Flowers and Hayes 1981b, 234). Another indication of boundaries are pauses: ". . . pauses at boundaries averaged a significant 2.43 seconds longer than other pauses—making them, on the average, almost, *twice* as long" (p. 239).

Matsuhashi (1981) carried out a major study of pauses during composing, a study which exhibits a varied and interesting set of research techniques. The subjects were four skilled writers from an upper-middle class high school. The writers could choose from among various topics, and could write from their own previous experience. Two video cameras ran as they wrote, one head-on, one overhead. Notes made from viewing the videotapes were used to conduct a stimulated recall interview. Matsuhashi explains her orienting focus: ". . . Because this exploratory study undertakes research in relatively uncharted territory—the temporal aspects of written language production—its approach represents an attempt at discovery procedures rather than the testing of hypotheses" (p. 115).

> To obtain a record of the length of each pause, the researcher played back the videotapes in slow motion (6 to 14 times slower than real time), and noted on typed transcripts each tenth of a second of transcribing time. The next step was to subtract the time the writer lifted the pen at the end of a word from the time the writer began the next word. . . . This information was marked on a worksheet . . . displaying the pause times between words. (p. 118)

Working with a total of 24 compositions from the four students, representing three distinct types of discourse—persuading, generalizing, and reporting—Matsuhashi had 4,146 pauses to work with in her analysis. She used what is often referred to as *exploratory data analysis* (Hartwig & Dearing 1979) for the qualitative analysis of quantitative data. Among her findings were that longer pauses tended to occur between fairly large thematic units (sentences, phrases) rather than words. Also, and not surprisingly, pauses were shorter when students were reporting, as opposed to persuading or generalizing.

Pianko (1979) and Perl (1979) studied a contrasting group of writers who evidence little of the care and planning shown by Matsuhashi's students or Flower and Hayes's expert writers. Pianko tracked 24 (a representative sample) community college freshmen through five writing assignments. During at least one session they were videotaped as they wrote, and they were interviewed following the completion of each assignment. The primary theme that emerges from Pianko's analysis is: "A piece of school sponsored writing is something to be written as quickly as possible, with as little effort as possible" (p. 10). The majority of the writing was in narrative, which, being most similar to speech, is easier to produce than, say, description, exposition, or argumentation. There was little evidence of global planning. Students spent an average of 1.26 minutes thinking before they began to write. And, "Considering that the students were given an entire afternoon to complete their writing, it was startling that such a brief span of time [average 40 minutes] was used to complete the assignment" (p. 9).

Perl (1979), in a closely parallel study, had five "unskilled" community college students think aloud during five essay writing sessions. While Pianko's more quantitative data on a relatively large sample of students gives a good sense of the general trends, Perl's more qualitative data from a much smaller sample yields far more detail and nuance, viz.:

> . . . all of the students studied displayed consistent composing processes; that is, . . . prewriting, writing, and editing appeared in sequential patterns that were recognizable across writing sessions and across students . . . [However] . . . their lack of proficiency may be attributable to the way in which premature and rigid attempts to edit their work truncate the flow of composing without substantially improving the form of what they have written (p. 328) . . . students wrote by shuttling from the sense of what they wanted to say, forward to the words on the page, and back from the words on the page to their intended meaning. This "back and forth" movement appeared to be a recursive feature: at one moment students were writing, moving their ideas, and their discourse forward; at the next they were backtracking, rereading, and digesting what had been written (p. 330). . . . Thus, editing occurs prematurely, before students have created enough discourse to approximate the ideas they have, and it often results in their losing track of their ideas . . . . Editing is primarily an exercise in error-hunting. The students are prematurely concerned with the "look of their writing"; thus, as soon as a few words are written on the paper, detection and correction of errors replaces writing and revising. Even when they begin writing with a tentative, flexible frame of mind, they soon become locked into whatever is on the page. (p. 333)

These remarks are based on several levels of analysis of the data. In her article Perl (1979) presents a lengthy picture of one of her five writers, but she also offers a detailed presentation of quantitative data obtained from coding the protocols. Her categories included:

Interpreting [I]—rephrasing the topic to get a "handle on it."

Assessing [A] (+); (−)—making a judgement about one's writing; may be positive or negative.

Questioning [Q]—asking a question.

Talking Leading to Writing [T>W]—voicing ideas on the topic, tentatively finding one's way, but not necessarily being committed to or using all one is saying. (p. 320)

WRITING AND BIOGRAPHY

In a study in which we repeatedly interviewed 12 ninth grade students in their first process writing class, Lynn Meeks and I (nd) found that some students actually preferred quick and dirty writing assignments, and actively resisted the open-ended creative assignments they were being given. After all, formulaic writing and the avoidance of error are what they had been rewarded for in their previous eight years of schooling. Students who claimed to enjoy writing in the new class, on the other hand, indicated that they had developed personal traditions of voluntary and creative writing outside of school. The point is, that much of the accumulated research on cognitive processes during composing tends to ignore the writer's personal history, and the nature of the writing environments that the schools have created for them. The next study (Ray 1990) to be reviewed, provides such background and also serves as a bridge to ideas introduced in the previous chapter.

Ray is a composition instructor at Wayne State University. She conducted what she calls a "long-term case study" of one student's meta-cognitive (see Figure 7.3) processes during writing.

Like the students Meeks and I studied, Fida, recently arrived from Iran, seemed to be resistant to process writing instruction, and Ray was intrigued. She followed Fida's "career" (see Chapter 3) through ". . . two terms of intensive English language instruction, a basic writing course, two composition courses, and a literature course" (p. 324). Fida's approach to writing challenged many of Ray's cherished assumptions.

> . . . my colleagues and I taught as if student writers developed in stages that directly correspond to the semester system: when students finished one English class they went on to the next class, performing at higher and higher levels of competence, until they reached the final stage—the ability to pass the English Proficiency Exam. The case of Fida challenges these assumptions about . . . students' progress . . . in four years of undergraduate study, Fida and her writing remained essentially unchanged. . . . (p. 323)

Fida's perspective on language and literacy is considerably different from her English teacher's perspective. She thinks of language solely in terms of correctness: if her language is grammatical and understandable, she is satisfied. She thinks of writing as a school requirement to be completed for teachers; it is something that she neither understands nor controls. In order to meet this requirement, she needs

a teacher to tell her exactly what to do and how to do it. This is the perspective
she has had on college writing since her first semester at the university. (p. 324)

In addition to collecting writing samples, several of which she reproduces
in the text, she repeatedly interviews Fida and she also draws on entries from
her own journal. Ray attributes Fida's perspective to her cultural background,
but also acknowledges that one of the reasons Fida's writing doesn't change
is that many of her teachers, in classes other than English, reinforce her view
of writing.

> Fida says her philosophy teacher helped teach her how to "think about the
> questions and the right way to answer the questions, to make a good sentence
> to let my professor understand what I mean."
> "HOW did philosophy teach you the right way to answer the question, how
> to think about a question?" I asked. From my teacher perspective, I anticipated
> a reference to the ways philosophy encourages inquiry into the relationships
> between language and thought.
> "OK. . . . First of all I answered the questions at home, and I went to her
> [the professor's] office. She read it, and if there were any mistakes she said, 'Here
> you have made a mistake' . . . like, 'this sentence, you can make it like this.'
> So I take it back home and I change it."
> From Fida's perspective the study of philosophy consisted of answering home-
> work questions according to teacher's specifications, and correcting whatever
> the teacher found wrong in her answers. (p. 326)

Fida demonstrates in her writing a preoccupation with correctness and a
great reliance on teachers to show her what they want. While maintaining a
high GPA throughout her studies, she failed the English Proficiency Exam
four times.

Ray's (1990) case study is included in a collection entitled *The Writing
Teacher as Researcher.* She would see herself primarily as a teacher, hence, this
work provided her with a very direct pay off: "In the process of collecting and
interpreting the data for this study, I was forced to question and ultimately
abandon the assumptions that had guided my teaching" (p. 333). As we have seen
in the last chapter, there is a burgeoning interest in promoting research by
teachers, and this is no more true than in the field of composition. In addition
to the Daiker & Morenberg (1990) collection, in which Ray's chapter appears, two
other collections of articles by composition teachers/researchers have appeared
recently (Bissex & Bullock 1987; Goswami & Stillman 1987).

Indeed, one instructor (Afflerbach et al. 1988) has pre-service teachers think
aloud as they write. The " . . . intent as teachers-as-researchers, was to capture
our own writing processes by thinking aloud while writing . . . we felt that
examination of our writing and conferencing processes might help us anticipate
instructional challenges in elementary writing programs" (p. 693). One of the
themes which emerged was that interest in a topic does not mean that the topic
is 'writable' " (p. 695).

COGNITIVE PROCESSES DURING TEACHING

Those who promote the idea of teachers doing research have a (not so) hidden agenda as it were. It is not the promise of an addition to our knowledge corpus about teaching and learning that motivates this movement. Rather, it is hoped that by taking a more analytical and reflective (as a researcher) stance towards his/her practice, the teacher/researcher will become a better teacher. There is, then, a growing interest in studying cognitive aspects of teaching.

Use of the clinical method, including protocol analysis, to study teaching has paralleled cognitive studies of problem-solving by students (Clark and Lampert 1986; Shavelson and Stern 1981). In an early study, McCutcheon (1980) interviewed twelve teachers from grades 1–6 ". . . about their planning processes and influences on their planning. Classroom observations were made to discern the nature of lessons, and to provide the basis for questions about planning" (p. 261). Overall, she found teachers did relatively little planning, because they tended to rely on published materials of various kinds which contained implicit plans. Also, these 12 teachers tended to reuse activities that had worked well in the past, obviating the need for elaborate plans. McCutcheon gives very little information about how these teachers were selected, so it is difficult to assess whether they were typical. But, the study does reinforce the call for teachers to become more "reflective practitioners" (Schön 1983).

Gaea Leinhardt has undertaken a prolonged program of research on the cognitive processes implicated in the teaching of math at the elementary level. Like Flower and Hayes, Leinhardt has found that, by comparing expert and novice teachers, cognitive processes are thrown into sharp relief. Her work (Leinhardt 1989) is distinguished by, among other things, a meticulously enacted operational definition of "expert teacher."

> The experts were initially identified by reviewing the achievement growth scores of students in the district, and selecting teachers at each grade whose students' *growth scores* were in the top 15 percent for at least 3-years in a 5-year period. From this select group, teachers with high-growth classrooms, in which the *final achievement* was in the top 20 percent, were ultimately chosen. All the teachers taught in self-contained classrooms, and two taught an additional mathematics section. The median class size was 28. The students in the classrooms came from families who ranged from lower to lower-middle class. Two classrooms were racially mixed: two were black. The student teachers [novices] were chosen from an available pool of 20, and were teaching fourth grade in two integrated middle-class schools. These student teachers were among the top four teachers in their cohort, as nominated by their supervisors. (p. 59)

As was the case with several of the studies of composing cited earlier, Leinhardt makes use of multiple data sources in her work with the four expert and two novice teachers. Teachers were observed and videotaped as they taught. The videotapes (up to 25 hours per teacher) were transcribed and analyzed for evidence of the teacher's explanation during the lesson. Also, all teachers were interviewed before and after each lesson. These protocols were analyzed for evidence of the teachers' agendas. There were also post-class interviews; stimulated-recall interviews, in which teachers were asked to comment on videotapes of their lessons; and interviews designed to reveal the teachers' understanding of the mathematics they were trying to teach. Despite the small sample size, Leinhardt clearly has an enormous volume of data to work with, and she and her graduate students have been engaged in the analysis and reporting of this material for several years.

One analysis (Leinhardt 1988) focused on the teacher's agenda . . . .

> . . . the expert teacher does carry a mental plan that we have been able to access by simply asking for it. We call this the teacher's agenda. An expert teacher's agenda is brief, but rich with information that she or he will use and modify while teaching. An agenda consists of goals and actions. It connects to the prior day's lesson by means of a goal structure. "We got this accomplished yesterday and now we need to do such and such." It contains a list of action segments appropriate for the stated topic of the lesson. The action segment statements refer to what the teacher will do, and to what students will be learning. In addition, an agenda includes tests that let the teacher know what she or he needs to look for in order to determine whether or not to continue. The agendas that experts construct also contain a logical flow that is dictated by the subject matter itself, the learning needs of the students, or the interest level of the students. (pp. 52–3)

The agendas of novice and expert teachers looked quite different. First, a protocol from a pre-lesson interview with a novice.

> Okay, today, I'm planning on going over the homework that I gave yesterday on fractions. I'm planning on going—on going over it on the board, okay? [*First instructional action*]
> It'd probably be good for this class, and I don't know how many I'm going to go over. There are 36 problems on the homework page, but I'm gonna see how it goes. If they're all getting them very quickly, then we'll move on. [*test*]
> [*Coding: 1 instructional move, 1 test, no student actions, no instructional logic*]. (p. 54)

Then an expert protocol.

> Okay, well, we're still working on fractions; looking at a complete set and reciting the fraction parts. Okay, tomorrow we'll be working on problem solving, word problems, have a pizza party. [*First instructional action*] And they have to identify what fraction has been taken out of the whole. [*Second instructional action*] We're still reinforcing the terms numerator, denominator. [*Third instructional action*] I have a muffin tin and I'll be putting, you know, like the muffin papers, something manipulative [*Fourth instructional action*]; like today we cut apart and matched fractions with the illustrations. And just anything manipulative, so tomorrow they'll be working with the muffin tins and writing fractions [*Student action*], using the sets and the regions, [*Fifth instructional action*] [*Instructional logic*], checking their homework [*Student action*] [*Sixth instructional action*] from today. [*Coding: 6 instructional actions, 1 instructional logic, 2 student actions*]. (p. 55)

Note Leinhardt's coding scheme (in italics) for these protocols which allows her to make quantitative comparisons. She finds remarkable:

> . . . the total absence of a usable plan in the statements of the novice. The novice had taught a lesson on reducing fractions which had failed, had retaught the same lesson, and had assigned homework. Her entire set of activities for this day was slated for going over the homework. Even though she stated she might "go on," she had no idea of what she would go on to. In contrast, the . . . expert not only had a rather complete action list, she also knew where she was within the broader topic of fractions . . . [also] The experts displayed a deeper understanding of fractions as a teachable topic. Although the experts would probably perform very similarly to the novice on a test of fractions as a topic, the accessible and useable knowledge about how fractions fit together, and which piece is needed for which other piece was much richer in experts' minds. (p. 56)

Another set of analyses (Leinhardt 1987) is concerned with explanation. In this report, one of the experts, "Mrs. Patrick," is observed as she conducted an 8-day-long unit on subtraction in her second grade class. Leinhardt uses what she refers to as a *semantic net* (for a more complete description of this procedure see Leinhardt & Smith 1985, 251–2) to represent the structure implicit in Patrick's explanation.

Figure 7.5 shows the semantic net for one lesson, and what follows are fragments of Leinhardt's narrative description of the same lesson:

> The first lesson can be described as setting up a series of linkages between already existing knowledge and new knowledge, attaching new knowledge to old. Ms. Patrick first reviewed adding tens to units (10 + 6 = 16). She reviewed the method for two-digit subtraction without regrouping, adding at the end of this segment two fooler problems (i.e., those which required regrouping because the number in the ones column of the subtrahend was larger than the number in the ones column of the minuend). . . . She repeated the review three times using different representations of tens and ones. Moving from the concrete to the abstract, she first demonstrated with banded and loose popsicle sticks, then with felt strips and squares, and finally with two-digit numbers that were renamed and partitioned (i.e., 27 = 2 tens and 7 ones, and 27 = 1 ten and 17 ones).
> During the lesson, Ms. Patrick cycled through several examples of subtraction using sticks, while simultaneously writing the problems on the blackboard in a tens chart . . . sticks were grouped into tens and ones, both of which were counted; amounts were "subtracted," "taken away," or "needed"; the partitioning operation resulted in a remaining set, which was the answer; . . . . The climax of this part of the lesson occurred at the end of this segment when Ms. Patrick gave the problem, 26 minus 8, and asked the students to solve it using their sticks. The first student was stumped, but another, Baron, "invented" the solution of unbinding the sticks, . . . the children remembered the significance of the event, and thereafter conceptually linked it to Baron. In this segment, the operational nature of subtraction emerged, practice was given, and concrete and written demonstrations were run in parallel. . . . This is shown in [the figure] by a convergence toward OPERATION. (pp. 233, 235)

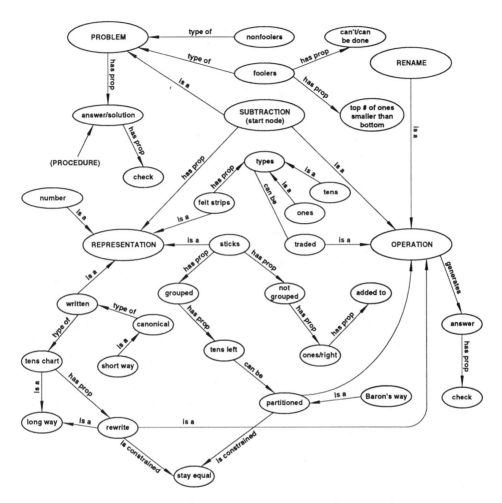

FIGURE 7.5 Semantic net of explanation

SOURCE: Leinhardt, G. (1989). Math lessons: A contrast of novice and expert competence. *Journal for Research in Mathematics Education,* p. 71. Reprinted by permission.

With this particular set of lessons, Leinhardt (1987) also interviewed a sample of eight students, once using the videotape of the lesson to stimulate recall, and once by having students think-aloud as they solved the problems Ms. Patrick gave them. She analyzes these protocols in much the same way as she had the teacher's protocols, including producing the students' semantic nets for the lesson. There was wide variation in the students' grasp of the lesson, from a near perfect match with Figure 7.5 to only a partial understanding: Terry's semantic nets had a "... disconnected quality ... [and] three days into the lesson sequence she showed none of the connections between PROBLEM, solution, checking, and operation that were present in the teacher's [explanation] and in [another student's] *first* lesson representation" (p. 250). Leinhardt does not dwell on the implications of Terry's (and others') failure to master the material for the designation of Ms. Patrick as an "expert." However, Ralph Putnam (1987), in his doctoral dissertation, found that six experienced (all ten years +) teachers he studied all failed to closely monitor their students' learning: ". . . the teacher's goal appeared to be teaching the correct fact, procedure, or concept—not determining more precisely the nature or source of the student's error" (p. 28).

Leinhardt (1987) then moves from the explanations in a single lesson to a very general model (compare to Figure 7.4) of an explanation. This model is based not only on an analysis of the lessons themselves, but includes material taken from stimulated recall interviews with Ms. Patrick. She doesn't tell us how she conducted this interview, but her questions probably didn't differ greatly from those used by Peterson and Clark (1978) in an earlier study.

1. What were you doing and why?
2. What were you noticing about the students? How were the students responding?
3. Were you thinking of any alternative actions or strategies at that time?
4. Did any student reactions cause you to act differently than you had planned?
    (p. 559)

In many ways, the model in Figure 7.6 can be seen as an (extremely complex) expansion of the IRE model (Figure 3.1) we have seen earlier. Many of the components of the model would appear to be broadly applicable to any teacher trying to teach subtraction. Some would only be seen in "experts," and still others ("ask for too many sticks") may be unique to Ms. Patrick. However, as complex as this model is, Leinhardt's work suggests that even experts' explanations are often inadequate. In an analysis of experts' fraction lessons, Leinhardt and Smith (1985) conclude:

> . . . textbooks and teachers often provide incomplete descriptions of the concepts and relationships in a domain. In general, the less complete the student's knowledge base, the greater the likelihood that the student will generate incorrect inferences, develop misconceptions, and produce inaccurate problem solutions.
> . . . For example, equivalence can be maintained by either reducing or raising a fraction. The text and the teachers, however, focused on the maintenance of equivalence by raising a fraction by multiplication, and failed to note the symmetry of multiplication and division. In no case was the interrelationship of these concepts made explicit. (p. 269)

There are, of course, major constraints on an elementary school teacher's ability to teach mathematics expertly. For one thing, she/he has to teach several other subjects. For another, as we have seen in the previous chapter, a teacher's personal history colors his/her classroom performance. (See also Nespor 1987; Peterson et al. 1989.) Leinhardt and Fienberg (1990) allude to this as a factor in the expert teachers they worked with.

> She had taught for approximately 20 years at the time of the study. During one period of time she had coordinated an individualized math program for kindergarten through 8th grade at one of the schools. She felt that her original

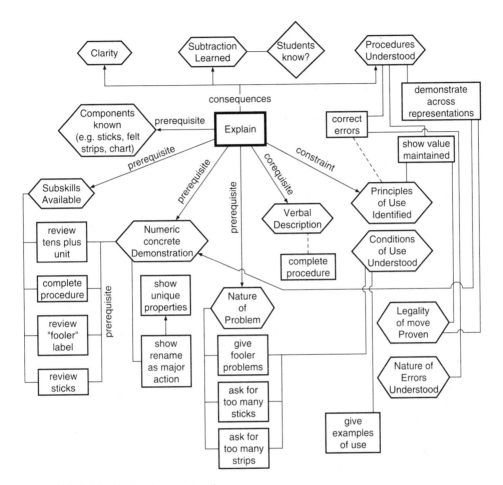

FIGURE 7.6 Model of an explanation

SOURCE: Leinhardt, G. (1987). Development of expert explanation: An analysis of a sequence of subtraction lessons. *Cognition and Instruction, 4*(4), p. 278. Reprinted by permission.

vision of sharing knowledge and growing with her students had gotten worn away by issues of discipline and burdens of paperwork . . . . [Another] . . . had taught in various parts of the country and believed strongly in the importance of expressing sympathy, love, and encouragement to students. She had felt most comfortable in Hispanic communities. At the time of the study, she was providing personal support for her students by sewing clothes and cooking weekend meals for at least five of them. (p. 19)

PROBLEMS WITH THE METHOD

In many personal accounts (see Chapter 6) the individual is central. Our concern is with the unique qualities of each person/situation—the goal idiographic description. In other traditions, the goal is to achieve a nomothetic portrait—a statement about the teacher, the student rather than a teacher or a student. Clearly, those who work in the cognitive studies tradition flirt with this dividing line.[6] Leinhardt is deeply committed to achieving a general model of expertise in teaching. Indeed, she serves as a consultant to the Carnegie Foundation on efforts to develop assessment procedures concommitant with a national teacher licensure exam (personal communication). However, the enormous volume of data she must work with constrains the scope of her generously funded research. She can only work with a small number of teachers, and her analysis veers between the twin perils of triviality—discovering something we already know about "good" teaching, and idiosyncracy—discovering some interesting things about Ms. Patrick. The key, it seems to me, of her success is the comparison of individuals whose performance we would expect to differ quite dramatically. If these differences don't emerge in open-ended analysis of videotapes and interview protocols, and do not cohere into recognizable patterns, then we are dealing with a phenomenon that eludes systematic study.[7] A second evident issue in cognitive studies methodology is the enormous amount of data one must deal with. I have spoken earlier about the perils of being buried under a mountain of video/audio tape transcriptions.

As we have seen, studies of composing and math teaching involve not only taped material, but multiple interviews with one's subjects, and the content analysis of written materials—essays, lesson plans, and so on. Siegler and Crowley (1991) comment on something they call a microgenetic experiment which closely resemble the clinical or process-tracing method: ". . . one might expect microgenetic experiments to be extremely prevalent. In fact, they are not. . . . The reason for the relative paucity of such experiments is not hard to grasp: they are difficult and time consuming to conduct" (p. 609).

Nearly all of the research reviewed in the section on cognitive processes during composing was based on doctoral dissertations (e.g., Emig, Graves, Matsuhashi, Perl, Pianko), suggesting an all-consuming experience lasting several years. Significantly, of this group, only Graves has continued with this line of research since earning the doctorate.

Their use of the term "experiment" tips us off to another pitfall—the accusation that one's methods of study are too intrusive, that one is no longer studying a naturally occurring phenomenon. North (1987) is particularly concerned about this issue. Not to brush this problem aside, I'm convinced by the arguments and evidence (e.g., Ericsson and Simon 1984) that one can carefully select subjects who are both "typical," and who do not find these methods overly intrusive. Flowers' and Hayes' writers and Leinhardt's teachers are very real to me, and they look like they're doing the sorts of things I observe when I observe writers and teachers.

North (1987) raises another issue which is, however, not so easily dealt with. Having praised Emig (see p. 209), he then proceeds to bury her because she is vague in the extreme about how she moved from her data to her conclusions. The same can be said about many of the works reviewed here, including the study of expert elementary math teachers. Nowhere does Leinhardt demonstrate the precise steps she has taken to boil down the many pages of tape and interview transcriptions to produce Figure 7.5. But if she did, her article might grow to the size of a book. Of course, this problem is not unique to this particular tradition; however, where Annette Lareau (1990) readily finds a publisher for her book-length treatment of her work on social class and schooling, it will be harder to find an audience for a book-length treatment on the teaching of fractions (but see Lawler 1985). In other words, while the constraints of journal article length exert a hardship for all qualitative researchers, this is a special challenge for those doing cognitive studies. Fortunately, at least one journal in the field, *Cognition and Instruction,* does publish extraordinarily long pieces when necessary.

In short, a persistent problem with the wider acceptance of this methodology will be the critical reader's unwillingness to take on faith the author's systematic application of a consistent set of analytical procedures in order to reduce large volumes of data to a relatively few meaningful conclusions. Also, as indicated earlier, these studies represent enormous undertakings. One "study" may pre-occupy the researcher for years, hence replications are almost nonexistent. For example, Leinhardt is now studying history teachers.

I believe the prospective researcher must select the problem to be studied, and the sample with great care to avoid these pitfalls. I've already mentioned the value of the expert-novice (or similar) contrast. In addition, one should select a problem for one's subjects to solve which is well-delimited (e.g., teaching or learning two-digit subtraction); which occurs with great frequency in education and, hence, lots of people will care about your research; and which is viewed as being problematic, that is some/many teachers/learners find this to be a difficult problem to teach/solve. Fortunately, (or unfortunately) the supply of such problems is almost inexhaustible.

NOTES

1. Just as the clinical interview used by Emig has been available as a research technique for a long time, so, too, content analysis has a venerable history (Altheide 1987) and, indeed, specialized computer programs to facilitate the content analysis of texts were first developed in the early 1960s (Stone 1966).
2. There are a number of discrete variations on information processing theory, the most influential for composition researchers is that of Newell and Simon (1972). Also note that information processing theory undergirds the work of those who do cognitive studies in much the way that natural selection theory undergirds human ethology (see Chapter 4).
3. A fourth assumption, not as widely shared as the preceding three, is that the study of what writers (thinkers) say as they compose (solve problems) reveals an underlying model which can be simulated on the computer. "Intensive analysis [is] made of a small number of verbal protocols for a task, sometimes a single protocol, to demonstrate that the information in the protocol could be regenerated, approximately by the [computer] simulation model operating on the same task" (Ericsson and Simon 1984, 262). An example of such a model is shown in Figure 7.4. While those who pursue cognitive studies have much in common, strictly speaking, those scholars working or trained at Carnegie Mellon University and the University of Pittsburgh's Learning Research and Development Center come closest to approximating the notion of a "tradition" as introduced in the first chapter.

4. It would be a mistake to condemn all writers who are preoccupied with "correctness." In a very important study, Odell, Goswami, and Harrington (1983) interviewed and observed case-workers and administrators who spend an inordinate amount of time reworking short memos and reports because they are concerned with: "How are my readers likely to react to what I am going to say? How can I create a persona that will cause as little undue stress as possible?" (p. 232)

5. There are discrepancies in Leinhardt's reports on her data base. Elsewhere (Leinhardt, Weidman, and Hammond 1987) for example, six expert teachers are mentioned.

6. A case in point. Those who do cognitive studies in the teaching and learning of mathematics invariably cite Maggie Lampert. Lampert is a faculty member at Michigan who has, for years, taught fourth grade math on a part-time basis. A 1986 article on teaching multiplication represents a typical report of her work: "In my fourth grade class, I have been doing several different sorts of lessons which are intended to help children make sense of the process of multiplication with numbers larger than 10, including telling and illustrating stories, working on problems whose solutions require different ways of grouping, and counting and solving problems drawn from 'real world' situations in which multiplication is a useful tool" (p. 245).

    Lampert proceeds to lengthy descriptions of lessons, showing classroom discourse, as well as what was placed on the board. However, she doesn't indicate any time span which these lessons cover. There is no sense of how many lessons these conclusions are based on, there is no sense of the frequency of different types of student responses. At best we get "On some occasions, I did not work with stories, but represented . . ." (p. 253). How should we treat this? As autobiography? But we learn almost nothing about Lampert as a person. As a case study of expert teaching? Perhaps, but she is utterly atypical of elementary school teachers, expert or otherwise. Ultimately, I see her work as having inspirational value, in much the same way Willie Mays might function as a "teacher" at a youth baseball camp. But, I can't see where we can take it in terms of understanding the nature of what goes on in elementary school math classrooms.

7. Indeed, this would seem to be Eliot Eisner's argument (1976, 1991) when he calls for an "aesthetic" approach to the study and evaluation of teachers. In 1976 he laid out the twin methods of "educational connoisseurship" and "educational criticism" as alternatives to prevailing research practice. However in a 1991 book, on qualitative inquiry, he devotes a chapter to each, and is, apparently, unable to cite a single published article in which either method had been used—despite the lapse of more than 15 years during which his proposals have received a great deal of attention.

CHAPTER **8**

Decisions, Decisions

As Dobbert (1982) rather pithily notes, "Just as a set of metric wrenches will not make a Volkswagen mechanic, neither will a set of research techniques make an ethnographer" (p. 86). Hence, I have taken an inductive and reflective approach throughout this book in order to show that, ultimately, qualitative research methods cannot be extracted from the traditions that spawned them, and must be viewed within the context of specific research questions and problems. Nevertheless, in this chapter I venture to offer pointed direction to the would-be qualitative researcher, and at the same time present highlights of what has gone before.

One way to characterize the conduct of qualitative research is as a decision structure, much like the flow-chart that precedes the composition of a computer program. If we start with a published study and retrace the investigator's steps backward, we find her hesitating at a number of decision points and then deciding to move in one direction and not another. Each qualitative research project is, for this reason, unique. It is not possible therefore to write a prescription or recipe which everyone can then follow to do a qualitative study. On the other hand, sending the novice out to grope around in the dark isn't very sensible either. Using our flow chart analogy, however, what we can do is call attention to these decision points, so you will know when these are coming up and what your options are.

THE IMPORTANCE OF SELF-ANALYSIS

Inevitably, I have students confess, during the first few weeks of class,[1] as they get into the material and agonize over the design for the mini-research project, that qualitative research makes them very uncomfortable. Shades of gray, ambiguity, and uncertainty may be fine for some aspects of their life—how they decorate their homes, perhaps—but when it comes to their classes, their careers, their dissertations, they want the certainty afforded by an algorithm or at least an iron-clad heuristic.[2] They want to be assured that if they invest time and energy in a project, that they won't get lost in the middle and will have a recognizable (acceptable to a graduate committee, publishable) product when they are finished. If you are like this, qualitative research is not for you. Indeed, if you are uncomfortable with any degree of uncertainty, clearly quantitative research is not for you either. Of course, it is not at all uncommon in Colleges of Education to find students and faculty whose primary raison d'etre is the promotion of a particular curriculum, teaching technique, or technological marvel, and they somehow see research as the means to this end. We do research when we are uncertain about what the state of the world is and are curious or concerned to reduce that uncertainty. If we are certain about the state of the world and what changes are needed, our means of attack will be political and/or rhetorical. We will be activists in trying to persuade others to adopt our cause.

Next, I would ask whether this research will be a once-in-a-life time effort, for example, that you will be doing a dissertation but, once finished, you will go into administration rather than academia. If so, consider doing a quantitative study. Your chances of achieving quick closure, and a publishable product are much greater. Many doctoral dissertations, that are qualitative in nature, stretch out indefinitely and are unpublishable. "Getting it right" as a qualitative researcher sometimes takes at least one major false start. Hence, it is best to see the qualitative dissertation project as a lengthy and difficult apprenticeship preparing for what will be a long and distinguished research career.

OK, so you've decided that there are some things in the world that you want to find out about, your degree of certainty is fairly low, you can maintain a "neutral" stance vis-a-vis this phenomenon, and you can live with the fluid and ad hoc nature of the qualitative study. How well do you write? Every aspect of one's work as a qualitative researcher demands more writing than would be the case for a quantitative scholar. Writing is to qualitative research what mathematics is to quantitative research. One's data base consists of written notes, one's report is in narrative form, and is inevitably longer than comparable reports of quantitative research. Can you write well in English? Academics, virtually anywhere in the world, are expected to publish in English language journals. "International" journals are inevitably published in English with, perhaps, abstracts of articles in 3 to 4 other languages.

Can you type and/or do you have funds to hire a typist? Qualitative research means hundreds of pages of text—field notes, interview transcripts, and the (inevitably lengthy) write-up; whether dissertation, article, book, or final report. And, if you plan to have others code your materials and/or plan to make use of qualitative data analysis programs, all this material must be typed by someone.

Typing no problem, then ask whether there is a qualitative research tradition (Table 1.2) to which you can attach yourself.[3] Do you have an undergraduate major in history? Are you a Native American and aware how much the literature on Native Americans has been done by anthropologists? One must first steep oneself in a particular tradition. For example, an undergraduate degree and/or graduate minor in sociology would seem to be a prerequisite to doing a field study.

Or, perhaps, you have an opportunity to work on a funded intervention project. You are a graduate assistant on a state-funded program to introduce "master" math teachers to new methods, and have them mentor and train "cross-over" teachers. Clearly a case study is suggested. But, will your case study focus on the intervention project, or will you do multiple case studies of a sample of the teacher pairs? To finesse one of these traditions altogether is unwise. As I write this, the analogy that comes to mind (from *All Creatures Great and Small*) is the orphan lamb, that, because it is not chemically recognizable to any of the ewes, will not be nursed by them, even those that have lost their offspring. Pursuing your research within one of the traditions makes it recognizable. You'll know what to call it and how to talk about it. You'll find faculty colleagues/supervisors who are familiar with the area; if not at your own institution then at conferences where members of particular traditions are wont to gather. Most importantly, when you write up your work, you'll know what journal/book series to submit it to. And, if you're mistaken, you will receive nasty reviews that chide you for selecting an inappropriate journal to submit your work to.

FINDING A PROBLEM IN THE SETTING

The study may begin with the desire to describe/analyze/explore a particularly interesting phenomenon/situation/classroom that is already known to the researcher (e.g., Lancy 1976a). One negotiates entry, and obtains tentative agreement from the parties involved to cooperate in the study. The nature of the phenomenon one has chosen to investigate should immediately suggest a broader topic or issue to guide the study. Peshkin's (1986) initial look at Bethany Baptist Academy led him to examine it as a "total institution" (cf. Goffman 1961). Smith (1978) refers to this process as ". . . locating the case as an instance of a more general class of events" (p. 356).

It is also, at this point, that some refinement takes place in the selection of your tradition. You may recognize in your study of staff interaction in a school, that not only are gender and power relations implicated—you had earlier decided to undertake a study of stratification from a sociological perspective—but that you will need to draw on the literature in discourse analysis because how people talk to each other seems very important.

Starting with a setting first is characteristic of anthropologists. We look for interesting and unusual settings or groups (e.g., MacLeod 1987), or those that have not been described often in the literature. The present ethnographic literature is very sparse with respect to Dance Academies, Montessori Pre-Schools, Yeshivas, Prep Schools, and education in corporate settings and in the military, among others. We need to understand the way unique cultural groups relate to public schooling such as people in Appalachia; Hmong immigrants; Paradise Valley, Arizona (a wealthy bedroom-community) residents; and migrant workers, to name but a few. Anthropology provides a theoretical framework and the research methodology to help us gain such understanding.

FINDING A SETTING FOR THE PROBLEM

Contrariwise, the researcher may be motivated to address a particular question, and this issue guides the selection of the research site(s). In my comparative study in Papua New Guinea (Lancy 1983), I was interested in discovering whether different cultural/ecological configurations influenced children's intellectual/ academic development. Therefore, research sites were chosen specifically with this aim in view. Here one has somewhat greater leeway; if one fails to gain entry to a particular site, one can search for a similar site as an alternative. Barring anthropology and the case study, where one begins with a site and searches for a problem, in other traditions the problem comes first. Defining a problem is no easy task as Meloy (1989) makes clear. One way to move toward a clearer definition is through the process of describing your problem to others. In the case of the study just mentioned, the problem was a residual from previous research. A piece of research (one's own or that of others as reported in the literature) usually leaves one's questions only partially answered, or opens up new questions not previously addressed. Just as often, the existing literature reveals two or more contradictory findings, or at least some tension between different points of view. Or, is there an area of relatively little controversy that has been investigated primarily by quantitative means, where a qualitative approach might yield fresh insights, such as student motivation?

THE REVIEW OF LITERATURE

The review of literature in a qualitative study describes both a piece of prose— a section of one's research proposal or chapter in the dissertation and an ongoing process. There will always be several relevant areas to consider in doing the review of literature. There will be a body of literature on the **topic**; student groups, parent-school relations, gender, and communication; or the particular **culture/ setting** one has chosen to work in; hearing impaired youth, Punjabi Sikhs, inner-city parochial schools. Finally, one will need to review appropriate literature relating to one's **research design,** content analysis, multiple case studies, and thinking aloud. All too often I have had students tell me that there is "no literature on my topic." My standard reply: "Well, that could mean one of two things, generations of scholars have either avoided the topic because they thought it wasn't worth investigating, or because they thought it was too difficult to study given the present level of research technology. Which is it in the case of your topic?" The point here is that failure to find a literature base to support one's study is usually a sign that we need to do some reconceptualizing. Unfortunately, there seems to be a lamentable tendency, in some of the recent qualitative literature, to only include in the review of literature other qualitative studies or, worse, only those studies which share a particular tradition or narrow theoretical/

ideological framework. Don't fall into this trap. Review all the available literature on your topic, carefully weighing its relevance to your study.

Save yourself many headaches later on by beginning an annotated bibliography as soon as you have even a hint of an idea for your setting/topic. Record all relevant citation information. It may be very difficult to relocate a reference to extract volume or page numbers three years after you've read it and are now ready to cite it in a publication. Extract other critical details: sample size, date study was conducted, class and ethnicity information, and so on. Store your annotated bibliography in *Pro-Cite,* or other similar program, that automatically converts your references from APA to MLA style, for example. You can also quickly build new reference lists from your annotated bibliography which has become, in effect, a data base. As you would with your field notes (see below), include reflective comments in your annotated bibliography touching on emerging themes, contradictions, and linkages between unrelated studies. It is not at all a bad idea to think of the literature review for a major qualitative research undertaking (such as a doctoral dissertation) as publishable in its own right. I have found that I generate about 100 typed pages of notes for every 20 pages of final text in doing a review article. Bear in mind, that a lengthy and thorough annotated bibliography can be drawn on, again and again, as you write additional articles/chapters.

As I have said, the literature review is an ongoing process. At some point, fairly early in this process, you will need to begin to project yourself into the studies you are reading as the "principal investigator." Like trying on clothing, some will clearly not look good on you, others will fit fairly well. Once you've found a study that you are comfortable with, you may need to learn more about the project than was reported in the publication(s). Seek out unpublished technical reports on the project in the ERIC microfiche section of the library. These usually provide critical methodological details. Additionally, write to the authors for information you are unable to find in these printed sources. Virtually all national scholarly organizations publish annual membership rosters including addresses, which you can use to track down peripatetic academics.

You may also decide, at this point, that you need further training in specific areas of methodology, and this is not available at your present institution. Most national organizations sponsor workshops in research methodology, usually accompanying the annual convention. Some universities are exceptionally strong in faculty who use qualitative methods and, consequently, offer a range of advanced courses. These include, but are not limited to: Colorado, UC San Diego, Stanford, Ohio State, Georgia, and Pennsylvania. These last two host annual conferences focused on qualitative research in education. Carnegie-Mellon and the University of Pittsburgh in the three-rivers city are centers for research in cognitive studies; Cornell is a center for research from a biological perspective.

THE PRELIMINARY PROPOSAL

One develops a two to three page "preliminary proposal" (see Locke et al. 1987, Chapter 4). This includes rationale (reason for doing the study) and problem statement; background (description of previous research, history or known aspects of research site/culture/group); and method and plan for data analysis/write-up/ dissemination. This mini-proposal can be used to give clients/informants/authority figures an idea of your plans, so that they can make an informed decision about whether to permit you to do the research. Many school districts require just such a proposal as part of the project approval process. It will be submitted with the "Human Subjects" paperwork to your "Institutional Review Board."[4] It can be circulated to members of one's committee in the case of thesis/dissertation research.[5] A number of funding sources encourage the submission of such preliminary proposals as a way of saving themselves and the principal investigator time wasted writing/reviewing an inappropriate proposal. The point to be stressed here is that the tentative nature of this mini-proposal encourages constructive input that could have a significant impact on the direction and success of the project.

Many, many decisions will get made in the process of preparing and revising the preliminary proposal. A tentative problem, site, and tradition will be identified. The scope of the project will be established. When will it start and end?[6] All other things being equal, if it is a study in a school, it better begin on the first day of school or earlier. What is the unit of analysis—is this a district level study; a study of primary grade teachers in a medium size elementary school; or a study of fourth-graders learning fractions? How many of these units will be studied and how will they be selected? For example, will the teachers be "typical" or "expert," "beginning" or "experienced?" What will be the role of the investigator (Table 1.4)? What will be the principal sources of data: field notes, interviews, artifacts, videotape recordings? Where will you get equipment—videocamera, still camera, computer, etc?[7] How will these sources be used? For example, will you use participant observation to identify general themes, and then videotape recordings to meticulously quantify the variables which your more informal analysis suggested should be there? How much data will you collect? How will you analyze them?

Can you cite a similar, already published study to provide at least a partial rationale for the answers you provide? For example, "Doe and Doe (1986), in their widely cited study, videotaped four half-hour lessons taught by their sample of six algebra teachers." Of course the tradition one chooses to work in will also dictate many methodological choices. I tend to believe that "ethnography" is so often the method of choice because there are so many works on the subject which provide good materials for the "methods" sections of the proposal. Other traditions have not been as well documented, methodologically speaking, although I hope this book will redress that imbalance. Of course the principal source of inspiration for making these decisions is the topic you have chosen to study. If you are interested in cognitive processes underlying the composition of poetry, the data base will be very different that if you're interested in the process whereby schools manage their relationship with an irate parent.

Doesn't all this discussion about specifying one's topic, data sources, and analytical procedures in advance contradict what I said about qualitative research being fluid and ad hoc? It does. Many of the decisions you make at this stage will be reversed once the study gets underway. But sooner or later, you will have to justify whatever decisions you have made. Simply making decisions "on the fly," based on what is most expedient or convenient won't do. By being very specific in your preliminary proposal, you demonstrate to those who will review it that you understand the interactive and reciprocal nature of these choices; that making some choices precludes others; and also that you can successfully justify your choices in terms of optimizing the credibility and usability of your research. At the same time, you must leave loopholes for yourself in the proposal, indicate that sorts of contingencies that may arise that could cause you to increase or decrease your sample, to rely less on video and more on audiotape, shift from second to third grade, and so forth.

For a thesis/dissertation, or if one is seeking outside funding for the project, a longer, more formal version of the proposal will be necessary. Typically in a dissertation proposal, the review of literature is quite long because it serves to provide a rationale for the study at hand, and to demonstrate that the student has mastered this particular topic. That he/she has read all the important and current pertinent works, but also that he/she can synthesize and weave them together into a coherent pattern. A very common and sometimes fatal flaw, that is revealed in the reviewers' comments on proposals, is the failure to cite some critical piece or pieces of literature.

ENTERING THE FIELD

By now the project has been approved in principle by committees, funding agencies, school authorities. The evolving proposal has been instrumental in this process, but it has also been helped along by frequent visits/phone calls by the Principal Investigator to chat informally with interested parties, and authority figures about the study. Ironically, it is not usually critical that the Principal Investigator demonstrate that the project provides a direct benefit/payoff to students, teachers, or administrators. Trying to argue that your research will provide direct benefits may promote skepticism; it may provoke anxiety that you will call attention to problems in your zeal to be helpful; it may raise false expectations. A far more credible approach is to argue that you will be the primary beneficiary, you will earn a degree, gather material for publication, fulfill the terms of your fellowship, or whatever. All educators have had to jump through these ''hoops'' at some point in their careers, and will empathize with your situation. Don't expect approval and support on that basis alone, your proposal must provide a convincing rationale that your work will contribute in important ways to helping us understand and, eventually, solve a particular problem. In this context, make sure your audience agrees that what you've chosen to call a problem is, in their view, a problem. For example, many people see youth unemployment as a problem, whereas most secondary school teachers see youth employment as the problem. Don't waste peoples' time on a fishing expedition, where you are not sure what you'll catch if anything, or by angling for the Loch Ness monster.

The point here is that you better get your story straight. Whereas your university colleagues might be comfortable with qualitative research, practitioners in the field will be much less so. They will want to know how, and in what ways your research will disrupt institutional routines; they will want to know the extent to which your work will highlight their assets and liabilities; they will want to know who will read your report, and whether that report will reflect positively or negatively on individuals and the institution as a whole. Clearly you must establish trust, and qualitative research design offers some rather paradoxical features in this endeavor. Its openness makes it impossible to specify probable outcomes in advance, and this makes people nervous. On the other hand, that same openness allows you to adjust the project more easily to people's needs and concerns.

Bear in mind that any research you contemplate with students under 18, even "just" observing, may require the informed consent of the parents. So you simply have to specify what your research will entail.

You can get permission to be an observer, but you must be invited to become a participant. If this is your goal, you should move fairly quickly to try and find a niche for yourself. You must be enough of a participant so that you can avoid being labelled a "spy"; but not so much of a participant that you lose your detachment, as well as foreclose on opportunities for research. If you become too much of an insider, some people will stop being candid with you because of who else in the institution is intimate and candid with you. It is not wise to do ethnographic, field study, or personal accounts research in a setting in which you are already identified as an insider. You will need to do a major piece of plastic surgery on the image you present to colleagues, and many of these may be so skeptical about your "neutrality" that they fail to accord you the level of trust and confidentiality that they would willingly afford an outsider. By the same token do not assume, for example, that as a Hispanic your entré into the Hispanic community will be eased. People expect researchers to be outsiders, as they expect politicians to lie.

DATA COLLECTION

Look for ways to gather data unobtrusively (Webb et al. 1966). If you are interested in how students learn to work with integers, offer to tutor them. Working one-on-one in a tutorial capacity is a well-established niche. Go bowling with the teachers after school, and conduct informal interviews in the car to and from the bowling alley. Volunteer to chaperone the Saturday night dances. Go along on the team bus to away games. Sign up to supervise student teachers.

Depending on the degree of trust you expect to establish, as well as the nature of your problem ("cheating" versus "school spirit"), you must choose between videotaping, audiotaping, openly taking notes, taking notes after the fact but within the setting, or writing up your notes away from the setting. Where your work falls on this continuum will depend, again, on your problem. If you will need to quantify variables eventually, or to study subtle aspects of discourse, audio and/or video recording are essential. However, if your subject demands discretion, you may want to just listen carefully. Obviously there are trade-offs, but consider that almost anything added to our knowledge base about those who vandalize schools would be welcome. However, if you are studying student activity in second grade reading groups, you better be gathering the kind of data that permits of very fine-grained analyses, or have discovered a kind of reading group arrangement/instructional strategy not, as yet, described in the literature.

Regularly returning to your problem statement and literature you've read will provide more focused questions for your observations and interviews. However, if you want to prime your pump, review Bogdan and Biklen's (1992) very helpful listing of "observational questions for educational settings" (pp. 232–43). Your observations should include, as your annotated bibliography, critical details of person, place, and activity, as well as date and time, class period, etc. Use abbreviations, nicknames, and other shorthand to get it down more efficiently. Break up your notes into more easily codable blocks. When done describing an activity, leave white space before describing the next, likewise with turn-taking in conversation. Draw diagrams, maps, and make sketches and/or take photos to provide a record of the physical setting, especially where this might change over time (bulletin boards, seating patterns).

You should have several different kinds of notes. One type of notation provides a general description, background. Another type is precise, detailed. Use a specifically designed form to more easily check off or note behaviors that are fleeting. This is tedious work, so you'll want to observe on a schedule, for 30 seconds every 5 minutes, for example. A form containing space for contextual notes, as well as boxes to check off specific behaviors of interest can be helpful. A third type of notation provides an "explanation" for what you are observing, or links the present scene to antecedents in your data base. Fourth, your notes should contain a running commentary where you reflect on what it all means, you search for themes, you identify questions or issues to follow up later— something you observed in class which you will ask the teacher/student about after class. Your observation can be conceived of as a kind of zoom lens (Everhart 1983). Even if your analysis demands a macro-focus most of the time, it is important to zoom out occasionally to make sure you haven't lost sight of the larger picture. Also, if your analysis is broader, and you observe mostly at the "normal" setting, it is important to zoom in for authenticating detail, critical incidents, juicy quotations that build the credibility of your report. Move the lens from normal to wide angle occasionally to take in a broader context. This helps to enhance the applicability of your research.

As a participant observer, even casual conversations can, when recorded, serve as "interview" data. Playing other roles (Figure 1.4) requires a more formally constructed interview arrangement. However, do make all of your informants aware that even casual conversations will provide grist for your mill. But these interviews can range all the way from "Say, can I talk to you guys in the teachers' lounge at break?" to "I'd like to set up an appointment to interview you." Generally speaking, unless you are conducting a case study using a personal accounts approach, you want to interview multiple informants—it is not good to rely too heavily on the views of only one or two informants in the setting. How long these interviews last, and how often they are done will depend on the evolving problem focus. But, one general rule is that you start with longer, more open-ended exploratory interviews, and as your thesis firms up, you shift to shorter, more focused confirmatory interviews.

Virtually any qualitative study will involve the collection of artifacts, primarily printed material of various sorts. Some of this material will come to you as a matter of course if you are a participant. Often public material, like newsletters, is there for the asking. Access to other material must be negotiated during the initial entry stage. If you are conducting a cognitive study, permission to copy and analyze individuals' written work will be negotiated, along with rights to interview and observe the problem-solvers at work. However, you must be careful to specify just exactly what will happen to this material—and the protection of people's identity should be a paramount concern. Minutes of meetings, interoffice memos, letters and material from student, and personnel records are even more delicate areas. Resist the temptation to access this material without specific consent to do so from all parties involved. The very trust that you are struggling to achieve can be your downfall, as administrators and helpful secretaries give you ready access to material they really should be guarding more carefully.

Even when test scores, performance appraisals, and psychologist's reports fall legitimately into your hands, remember the lessons from Chapter 3. All of these "objective" indicators have been socially constructed, and they cannot be treated as any more "real" or valid than your observations and conversations with the individual. Of course, the focus of your study may well be on unravelling how it is that these facts and decisions were arrived at, so official records may be the starting point for your study.

A final decision about data is to decide when you've got enough. If you are working within the biological tradition you will have created a fairly strict schedule for yourself in order to adequately capture variation in the phenomena of interest over its life span or cycle. Most projects in education suggest gathering data, at least, intermittently, over the course of the year, with heaviest observation at the beginning. Otherwise, you continue collecting data until no new patterns emerge, what you are observing/hearing you have heard before. Then you consider the possibility of triangulation. Would interviews with parents provide material which complements and supports what you have learned from the teachers? Would archived records indicate that what you have observed is a long-standing phenomenon, or suggest that this is an effect of change in leadership?

REFOCUSING THE STUDY

You are now in the field, your role established, and you have begun to collect data. There are yet further decisions to be made. It is virtually inevitable that as a qualitative researcher, you will reassess your focus, methods, purposes etc. based on "what turns up." At an extreme, the original site/topic is abandoned completely as being unworkable and the investigator must start over. For example, Meeks and I were hired to evaluate student attitudes towards the use of a new microcomputer lab incorporated into composition classes. Our initial interviews turned up almost uniformly positive attitudes towards the computer and word-processing, however, attitudes towards the instructional approach (writing as a process) were quite mixed, and this became the focus for our case study (Meeks and Lancy nd).

As you adjust your focus, it is critically important that you return to the library for additional material. Your annotated bibliography should continue to grow throughout the duration of the study.

At another intermediate stop in your ". . . voyage of discovery" (Peshkin 1986, 15), you begin to develop a "theory," "model," "story" that will encapsulate/explain/represent the bulk of your findings. It is important that this process begin early, so that you can start to test the model by looking for disconfirming evidence. For example, in my study (Lancy 1976a) of student culture in an elementary school, it seemed that the primary organizing framework for them was "activity" rather than, as the literature on older students (Cusick 1973; Palonsky 1975) indicated, "type of kids." So, in on-going interviews, I probed for these types (e.g., "jocks," "brains," "goody-goodies"), and didn't get any positive response thereby helping to confirm my initial impression. Hammersley and Atkinson (1983) refer to "progressive focusing" which may ". . . involve a gradual shift from concern with describing social events and processes to developing and testing explanations" (p. 175).

This grounded theory will dictate the foci of your data collection during the remainder of the study. You will need to seek patterns in your data, and begin some preliminary analysis.

DATA ANALYSIS

Once the data collection is complete (or you have run out of time/funds), you must review notes/tape-recordings/archival material, and firm up a scheme to analyze and reduce what has often been described as a "mountain" of material. There is such a thing as too much data. Many researchers founder at this point, the task seems so formidable. One is haunted by the specter of seriously distorting the phenomenon one has studied in the process that follows. Analysis schemes can be as simple as the investigator identifying a major "theme" from the material, and then proceeding to elucidate this theme illustrated by anecdotes, discourse transcripts, and snippets of "memos" (Ball 1981). On the other hand, one can develop an extremely complex "coding form," with dozens of categories for use in minutely analyzing the hours of videotape one has made of the phenomenon (e.g., Bergin and Lancy 1991). And, of course, there are innumerable points between these two extremes. You must wrestle with the decision as to how far to go in reducing the data. Again, your best guide is the published literature.

Just as you prepared a preliminary proposal, you should prepare a preliminary report. If this is a case study, write up or prepare an oral presentation for your clients, or the subjects of your study. Offer to make a presentation at a colloquium—most Schools of Education that grant the doctorate provide such a forum to showcase current student and faculty research, or wrangle yourself a slot on a local or regional conference. This presentation forces you to pull your material together and to try and make sense of it. Anticipating your public debut is a wonderful antidote to procrastination, collecting too much data, and failing to define the problem. You desperately need to get feedback on your thesis, does it hang together? Is it, perhaps, less novel than you assumed, e.g., have you missed a precedent in the literature? Is it contradicted by other extant research? Have you failed to consider an equally plausible alternative thesis that better explains your observations? Is your thesis perhaps more complex than it needs to be, or more complex than your slender data base (interviews with two teachers) will support? Your audience will help you see these pitfalls before you fold your tent and leave the field, or at least before you have invested a lot of time in what may be a fruitless analytical scheme.

Your colleagues in the field also deserve to be informed about your emerging thesis and findings. However, they can only tell you whether your arguments make sense from their (emic) perspective; they are not a good audience as far as feedback regarding the value of your work to scholars.

STRUCTURING THE REPORT

During data analysis, if not sooner, major themes/issues emerge, and these serve as natural divisions as the investigator wrestles with the problem of how to structure the report. Other natural divisions reflect different data bases (e.g., sections reporting "interview results," "classroom observations," "achievement records"). Unlike quantitative research, these divisions aren't always anticipated at the outset of qualitative research; thus the report (thesis/dissertation/article) may be structured quite differently from the original proposal. Return to the model study or studies which you felt best reflected the assumptions and methods you would use in your study. How are the reports structured? If this is a dissertation, look at other dissertations that employed similar methodology. If this is a report to an agency, ask to see earlier reports; if this is to be an article, study the format of articles that appear in your target journals, read the "advice to authors" section.

If quantitative analyses are to be undertaken on some part of your data base, arrange to have this done. Use multiple coders (fellow graduate students), and take full advantage of state of the art technology to simplify this process. A visit to consultants at the university's main computer facility is de rigueur. This analysis stage can be a welcome breather between being in the field and "writing it up." You are moving forward, but, for the time being, you don't have to face your notes. But don't let this stage become a dead end, don't keep looking for "significance" or patterns that may not be there. Get on with it. However, it is not necessarily the case that your report will be written from the beginning straight through to the end. One way to avoid "writer's block" is to start with a section or chapter that is relatively straightforward such as methods or review of literature.

A draft of the final report is prepared. This draft is shared with one's colleagues, professors, and key informants for feedback on clarity, cohesion, accuracy, creditability, and so on. Given the dearth of qualitative researchers, one often has to go far afield to seek informed scholarly feedback. A good strategy is to seek assistance from published scholars one has cited or relied upon heavily. However, don't be surprised if they fail to respond to your query.

Your key informants may be very disappointed, even upset by your report. If they claim that you have misrepresented them or their institution, this is a serious charge. You must either alter your text or, if you believe this is a genuine difference of opinion, provide them with some means of rebuttal, perhaps in an appendix (cf Grant 1977), or by yourself reporting the contradictory views. If your report is "accurate" but unflattering, you can go to greater lengths to protect the anonymity of your subjects. Remember they have come to trust you, they believe you have come to share their view of the world. If you don't, they shouldn't find this out for the first time when they read your report. On the other hand, don't be at all surprised if your colleagues in the field are indifferent to your report, or if they evince selective attention, reading, and perhaps enjoying, the descriptive material, but bypassing the analysis.

Colleagues in the university will also range in their level of interest, and in what aspects of your study they choose to focus on. Again the fluid nature of qualitative research can create problems for you at this juncture. There may be differences of opinion on what direction the thesis should take. One colleague wants you to focus on aspects of "gender relations," and foreground that issue; while another feels your best material relates to the issue of "stages in teaching." If you are doing this as a dissertation, you can find yourself in a tug-of-war, where you're the rope. This suggests the importance of selecting a dissertation chair with very high interest (ownership) in your problem, who you will work closely with throughout this process. He/She should then be ready and willing to referee any of these disagreements. A journal editor plays, or should play, a similar role when two or more outside reviewers of your work provide contradictory recommendations.

The final draft, while possibly acceptable for a thesis/dissertation committee or a funding agency or client (e.g., "Lincoln School District"), will not usually be suitable for publication. It will be too long, particularly the review of literature and methods sections. A truly unique work, one that has uncovered some previously unreported aspect of mainstream public education (Mehan, Hertwick, and Miehls 1986), or some exotic species of educational endeavor (Peshkin 1986) has a fair chance of being published as a book. It is useful to ask colleagues who read your work to comment on its "publishability."

On the other hand, many qualitative studies can be broken into pieces along the "natural divisions" mentioned above. This is, once again, the time to return to your annotated bibliography to find out where people whose work you've cited are publishing. Also, don't be bashful at conferences. Some very high proportion of qualitative research is now being published in edited collections, and these publishing opportunities arise almost entirely through personal contacts. If you want to get your qualitative research published, you must become a joiner. So, yet another decision relates to which organizations you should patronize. An excellent place to start is one or more of the American Educational Research Association's Special Interest Groups (SIG).

Well, I guess it's time for you to be getting started. I hope you've enjoyed this conversation. It really is a reasonable approximation of dozens I've had over the years. I hope **my** enjoyment of those conversations came through.

NOTES

1. On self-analysis: I am continually chagrined when I meet students who put off thinking about their dissertation topic until after they've (nearly) completed course work and comps. In my view, the student should start the program of study with a topic, or at least a general topic area, already in mind. That way one can use course assignments and comp exam preparation to advance one's reading and understanding of the topic and one can apply the substance of each course very directly towards building a stronger and stronger "specialization."

2. Actually, even when students are relatively open–minded about qualitative research, they bring such a strong quantitative mental set to the course that a primary task for me as instructor is to get them to externalize this mental set so they can set it aside long enough to explore qualitative approaches. In concrete terms, many students treat the call to "find a topic" or "state a problem" as inevitably involving the development of an "intervention" of some sort, which will be evaluated by comparing treated and untreated groups. Harry Wolcott's 1992 AERA address was replete with examples of students' prior misconceptions about qualitative research. I think it is critical for the instructor/mentor to be very sensitive and uncritical of these preconceptions and biases, because students have been enculturated throughout their schooling to think of research in terms of experiments and surveys, rather than as something more neutral like inquiry.

3. When I teach the qualitative research course, I first have students write a topic statement. This takes several iterations. As I've indicated, the first attempt is usually framed as a tightly constrained intervention. Next they prepare an annotated bibliography on the topic—which gets added to over the quarter. Then they begin a series of mini-proposals, short research proposals where they take their topic and apply one or another of the research traditions. For example, when James Mims took my course, his topic was "peer interaction in writing"; for his "ethnography" mini-proposal he outlined a study of "note-passing" among seventh graders. Applying each of these perspectives or traditions to a self-selected and personally interesting topic is an excellent way to consolidate one's understanding of qualitative research.

4. Murphy and Johnson (1990) suggest that Institutional Review Board (IRB) guidelines do not work very well with ethnographic research, created as they were primarily to deal with experimental research with a biomedical slant.

5. Or peer input for post-doctoral research, e.g., "When this study was no more than an idea, I wrote proposal drafts that benefitted from the criticism of Steve Asher, Eric Bredo . . ." (Peshkin 1986, p. x).

6. A nice range of examples from 2 hours to 2 years can be found in Dobbert (1982).

7. Do use professional standard equipment that is new and/or recently refurbished and avoid great tragedy. I have audio tapes made on outmoded equipment that are nearly indecipherable and videotapes with an audible hum—from fluorescent lighting—made with a "home" videocamera.

CHAPTER 9

Historical Inquiry

by John L. Rury

Historical research may be the oldest form of qualitative inquiry currently in use. Although historians presently employ a wide range of research strategies and different types of data, they have long relied upon a generally inductive approach to practicing their craft. Like qualitative researchers in other disciplines, historians typically employ methods of observation to construct interpretations of the problems they have selected to study. A critical difference, however, is that historians must use documents and other artifacts from the past to develop such explanations. This is what is especially challenging about historical research. To a very large extent, historians rely upon interpretation to generate coherent explanations of the past. And because interpretive frames of reference always change, this makes history both an exciting field in which to conduct research, and a difficult one to assess at any given time.

There is a popular misconception that historical research is largely a matter of simply chronicling what happened in the past. Another popular impression—and one which historians debate themselves—is that history is an "objective" social science, primarily concerned with verifying the conditions under which particular events occurred. But there is much more than simple chronology to historical inquiry (Berkhofer 1969). And there is a great deal of room in history for interpretation, perhaps more than in any other social science discipline, because historical investigation begins and ends with interpretation (Bloch 1953). Historians begin the research process with a question in mind, and an idea about its answer. But unlike, say, sociologists, historians cannot query informants to determine their point of view. Indeed, they usually are unable to determine whether their account even matches that of most people who witnessed the event directly. Thus, historians are required, as Robert Berkhofer (1969) has argued, to "fill in the gaps" by constructing a coherent explanation of their own. They must strive for a creative reconstruction of the past (Gottschalk, 1950).

CHILD REARING IN EIGHTEENTH-CENTURY NEW ENGLAND

Perhaps the best way to discuss methods in historical inquiry is to begin with a particular problem. How did parents teach their children three hundred years ago? Was it similar to the ways parents deal with kids today? More importantly, do contemporary theories of human development account for the development of adult-child relationships some two or three centuries ago? These are some of the questions addressed by historian N. Ray Hiner (1979) as he examined the life of Cotton Mather, the famous Puritan cleric and author, who lived between 1686 and 1728. In doing this, he was addressing a number of different purposes. One was to simply explore the dynamics of early eighteenth century child rearing practices, a critical and often overlooked aspect of educational history. Another was to see just how contemporary theories seem to explain behavior in the past. To address these issues Hiner had to examine letters, papers, books, articles, and other writings which have survived the two centuries since Mather's death. Fortunately, Mather produced a great volume of such material, and most of it has been preserved in special collections, which makes him an excellent subject for this sort of study. But even a historical figure such as Cotton Mather, who wrote literally hundreds of published and unpublished pages of commentary on family life, provides an incomplete picture of how eighteenth century child rearing practices may or may not have conformed to our twentieth century ideas about human development. Mather, after all, did not know of such ideas, and never directly addressed them. Consequently, it is the task of the historian to reconstruct the practices at the time with the evidence at hand. This is a major difference between historical research and other forms of qualitative inquiry.

Childhood was fraught with dangers in colonial society. Only two of Mather's sixteen children survived him, the vast majority dying while quite young. Referring to the great anguish and pain which Mather clearly suffered in the wake of his family's misfortune, Hiner argues that he identified very strongly with his children, and that he exhibited great empathy for them in their suffering, leading, Hinder believes, to a severe depression. This, he suggests, is evidence of a distinctly modern outlook on childhood and socialization, an attitude seemingly at variance with the emotional distance which parents in premodern families were supposed to have maintained from their children. Childhood socialization in New England during the 1700s, Hinder would have us believe, was similar—at least psychologically—in many ways to what it is today.

Hiner arrived at these conclusions, of course, without having ever directly observed an eighteenth century family, or even talking with anyone who had observed one (much less an actual family member). His account of the ways in which these family members thought about one another and interacted is based, rather, on his interpretation of artifacts from the past. A large element of conducting historical research, in that case, is deriving interpretations from incomplete evidence. This is one of the central challenges of the discipline.

EXPLANATIONS IN HISTORY

The centrality of one's interpretative framework in historical research has important implications for the historical profession, both for the ways in which historians conduct their research, and the ways they respond to one another's work. In the words of one recent analysis of historical inquiry (Coats 1989), historians seek "sufficient" explanations of events, unlike other social scientists who often use experimental methods to define causal models which can be replicated and verified. The work of historians normally cannot be subjected to these kinds of tests. It is possible, even probable, for two historians to come to completely different conclusions about the causes and consequences of a single event, simply because of their differing interpretive frameworks. For this reason, history is often an acrimonious field of study. Historical inquiry simply does not lend itself to an easy or straight-forward test of a particular explanation, especially if it is carefully reasoned and based on a wide range of evidence. Thus, historians are constantly debating the merits of one interpretation over another (Novick 1989).

Of course, there are standards for argumentation and the evaluation of evidence, which make it possible to weigh the value of one interpretation over another in explaining a particular event. A strong historical argument is one which takes into account all relevant evidence, and provides a coherent explanation of a particular problem in the past. In Hiner's research on Mather, he benefitted from the availability of a rich array of letters and other documents outlining Mather's thoughts about childhood and his own children. But even in cases where historians have looked at the same materials, there is still room for debate, for it is the task of the historian to offer an explanation which goes beyond the evidence at hand (more on this later). Some historians call for the use of "common sense" in the development of such explanations; while others write that a particular "intuition" is needed. More rationalistic historians, such as Berkhofer, call for the explicit use of theory drawn from other social sciences (Gottschalk 1950; Bloch 1953; Berkhofer 1969). In all cases, historical inquiry goes well beyond simple description, and there are few universally recognized rules in the construction of an interpretation. In some instances, consequently, the acceptance of a particular historian's point of view depends as much on the views of his/her audience, as it does on the quality of the evidence of arguments he/she can muster.

As suggested in earlier chapters, of course, other forms of qualitative research are also inductive in orientation, and pose many of the same interpretive challenges as history. How, then, is historical analysis different from, say, the qualitative inquiry of anthropologists or sociologists? For one thing, the focus is generally somewhat different. Historians are often concerned with explaining why and how certain events occurred, while other social scientists are trying to draw conclusions about cultural processes or the social structure. Consequently, non-historical social scientists are considerably more conscious of theory than most historians. According to a recent analysis of history and sociology, the latter has been viewed "as the more general and theoretical (nomothetic), and history as the more particular and descriptive (idiographic) of the two disciplines" (Kiser and Hechter 1991). With the development of qualitative studies in other social sciences, including sociology, and the growth of social scientific methods among historians, such distinctions may have become blurred in recent years. But history is still generally viewed as a fundamentally descriptive enterprise, as opposed to such theoretically inclined disciplines as psychology, sociology, or political science.

History is distinguished by more than a commitment to description, however. Even when historians and other social scientists are concerned with similar issues, there are perceptible differences in the way in which they approach research and analysis. Perhaps the most important concern is the historian's preoccupation with context. Historians explain events in terms of other events, and attempt to situate them in the general context of the period. Historian H. Stuart Hughes (1964) has written that historians identify meaning in the "connectedness of things." This, of course, is an important feature of most qualitative research, but historians are particularly concerned with the temporal dimensions of context. For many narrative historians, the ultimate objective is to contribute to an explanation of the period itself, to convey an idea of what it was like to live in a certain time, and ways in which that set of conditions contributed to the course of events (Barzun 1974). While the work of other social scientists may contribute to such an understanding, it is usually not their principal objective. For most historians, on the other hand, to explain how and why a certain series of events occurred in a particular period is an end in itself.

What does it mean, exactly, to explain an event? A large part of most explanations in history—as in other social sciences—concerns the idea of causation. But like other qualitative researchers, historians often treat the issue of causation implicitly in the course of their generally descriptive enterprise. In his discussion of Cotton Mather, for instance, Hiner argues that it was Mather's own developmental processes which shaped (or caused) his behavior as a parent, but his explanation of how this occurred is embedded in an account of Mather's life and parenting experiences. The reader is supposed to acquire an understanding of how it happened from reading the story. The explanations which historians offer for events, in that case, are not formal, and are not intended to be testable or subject to strict replication. Rather, they are often situational, as they describe how events grow out of certain contexts. Identifying causes in this way is somewhat indeterminate, as it is difficult—if not impossible—to clearly distinguish the effects of one causal factor from another. Consequently, historians often discuss causes in concert with one another. Some historians discuss "chains of causality" or "multiple causality" to capture the idea of many factors operating simultaneously to produce a given outcome (Barzun and Graff 1985). In the case of Cotton Mather, the parenting process was affected by contemporary social expectations, the vicissitudes of eighteenth century childhood (especially mortality), and the demands of Mather's public life—in addition to his own psychological development. These factors are not clearly delineated in Hiner's narrative, but they are all present. In describing the course of Mather's experience, Hiner demonstrates how they interacted to produce a given outcome. Explanation, in that case, is revealed in a descriptive account. In this respect, history is similar to many other qualitative fields of social research, but distinctive in its central concern with explaining and describing events.

There are important methodological differences between historians and other qualitative researchers, of course. Perhaps the most important has been alluded to above: The evidence historians rely upon is fragmentary and often difficult to interpret. Unlike other social scientists, historians cannot collect evidence until they feel they have a complete picture of what they are studying. While ethnographers can often return to the classroom (or other setting they are observing), and sociologists can go back to their subjects to ask follow-up questions, historians are limited to evidence of the past which has survived. As a consequence, they must collect as much of this evidence as possible, read what other scholars have concluded about the issue (and related issues), and then develop their own interpretation. Women's historian, Linda Gordon has written of the liberty to exercise their own judgement historians feel as a consequence of such arbitrary gaps in the evidence (Gordon 1991). Gordon also writes of allowing primary documents and other historical artifacts to "speak" to her, the historian thus becomes a "medium" through which the past is transmitted. Of course, the process of interpreting documents occurs inside the historian's head, and in this regard it is hardly a pure transmission of "the past." Indeed, the highly respected French historian Marc Bloch (1953), using a similar metaphor, wrote of forcing sources to speak, "even against their will" (p. 64), cross-examining them with evidence obtained elsewhere. The point is that historical research always involves a complex interplay between discovery and interpretation.

Does the foregoing mean that there is no objectivity in historical research? Of course not! Like other forms of scholarship, historical argumentation can be assessed for its use of evidence and internal consistency. Historians are always uncovering new evidence which challenges earlier interpretations. Due to limitations in the evidence, however, this research is less amenable to the kind of scientific verification of findings characteristic of the other social sciences. Because of this, history is probably the original qualitative discipline in social research.

THE ROLE OF INTERPRETATION

The role of interpretation has been especially important in the history of education. Because educational historians often deal with matters which have relevance to current policies or practices, contemporary debates over these issues sometimes find their way into the literature. Perhaps the best known case of this concerned the "revisionist" historians who wrote in the 1960s and 1970s. Inspired by radical critiques of schooling which grew out of the civil rights and alternative schools movements, these historians (e.g., Bowles and Gintis 1976) re-examined key periods in the history of American education, looking for evidence of inequality and discrimination. Informed by a different view of the role of education in society, they offered a different vision of educational history. Where previous generations of historians saw the development of state-sponsored and state-controlled education as a vehicle of opportunity, the revisionists identified patterns of elite domination, and the imposition of mainstream values on cultural minorities. Earlier historians (and many of their contemporaries) considered educational reformers as benevolent and sincere, while the revisionists often depicted them as self-serving or manipulative. Where other historians saw schooling as a force for social development, the revisionists, following the ideas of critical sociologists, felt it simply reproduced the social division of labor. By and large, the revisionists looked at history through a different lens, and arrived at an altogether different understanding of the past. This historian's interpretive starting point is often a critical factor in shaping her or his analysis of the evidence (Cohen 1976).

In part, controversies in the history of education reflect the fact that education itself has become a considerably more controversial issue in the past several decades. Other fields of historical research have exhibited the same tendency, reflecting what Peter Novick (1989) has described as a pattern of "polarization" in recent historical interpretation. Studies of slavery, for instance, changed dramatically with the development of the civil rights movement. Earlier studies had suggested that slavery was a benevolent institution which was necessary to the economic development of the South. Studies published in the 1950s, 1960s, and 1970s, on the other hand, revealed the cruel and inhumane dimensions of the slave system, and ways in which slaves developed a culture of resistance to it (Stamp 1956; Blassingame 1977). Likewise, critiques of American foreign policy in the same period led to radical re-examination of diplomatic history. Troubled by the interventionist policies of the cold war era, William Appleman Williams (1959) and his students depicted American foreign policy as motivated by domestic economic concerns or expansionist impulses. Both of these examples indicate ways in which historians are influenced by the times they live in. To a very large extent, in that case, historical writing often is shaped by the immediate concerns of historians. This is true to one extent or another of all social science disciplines, but it is especially so for history because of the large interpretive component in most historical research.

As suggested above, of course, historians must also marshall evidence to support their interpretations, and many of the academic controversies in the history of education—and other fields of history as well—revolve around the use of various types of evidence to support particular interpretations. But the sharpest debates, and those most difficult to resolve, have revolved around matters of interpretation. Because it has been affected by disputes of this kind, the history of education is an especially good field in which to consider problems in historical methodology.

HISTORICAL WRITING: ART AND SCIENCE

It is often observed that history is both an art and a science (Hughes 1964). But what exactly does this mean? Traditionally, the science of history refers to the matter of finding and critically analyzing sources to ascertain the truth about an event in the past. More recently, this has come to include many techniques of social scientific research, particularly the use of statistical data to test explicit hypotheses or identify general patterns of social development (Rury 1980). Both uses of the term, however, entail precision in the evaluation and use of evidence, and in constructing arguments to explain events in the past. The art of doing historical research, on the other hand, resides in the creative use of evidence to construct imaginative recreations of the past. Historians employ this set of skills in imagining how historical actors may have felt about various issues, or in constructing an argument about what motivated someone to behave in an observed manner, as well as in other situations. These questions often go beyond the immediate evidence, and call for a peculiar type of judgement grounded in a deep knowledge of the problem's historical context, somewhat like an anthropologist's intimate knowledge of a particular society. Here the historian relies on his or her experience to create an explanation which is probably not directly verifiable, but which is rooted in a wide assortment of ancillary evidence. The historian, in that case, is somewhat like an artist who relies upon various techniques and principles of science to pursue his or her craft; or, alternatively, a social scientist who employs an artistic sensibility to construct explanations for which direct evidence is sketchy or unavailable.

The art and science distinction in historical research extends to issues of presentation. In recent years there has been a debate in the field about different ways of writing history. One view hold that history should be presented in narrative form, that the elements of historical explanation should be woven into a story, and that arguments about causation should be implicit for the most part (Bailyn 1982). I will refer to this as the ''narrative tradition'' in historical writing. The opposite view is that historians should state their assumptions and methods of analysis explicitly, and clearly identify their causal arguments and the evidence they are using to test them (Berkhofer 1969; Aydolette 1966). This is sometimes referred to as ''social science history.'' (I will discuss social science history in greater detail in another section below.) Generally speaking, the first view holds that history is fundamentally artistic, and the second that it is basically a branch of social science, although, proponents of both schools would argue that both art and science enter into their understanding of the discipline. In practice, basic principles of historical research and writing incorporate both perspectives, but with different degrees of emphasis.

The narrative tradition has long been the dominant form of research and exposition for historians, and this is true of historians of education as well. Methodologically, narrative historians conduct research from a highly developed understanding of the period and problem they are writing about. This means reading what other historians have written about a particular period, and carefully examining all available and relevant documents (and often many irrelevant ones as well). ''It would be sheer fantasy to imagine that for each historical problem there is a unique type of document,'' Mark Bloch (1953) wrote. ''On the contrary, the deeper the research, the more the light of evidence must converge from sources of many different kinds'' (p. 67). It is only out of such immersion in the sources, both primary and secondary, that a historian can begin to develop an explanation of past events.

THE NARRATIVE TRADITION
IN EDUCATIONAL HISTORY

A much admired example of a historian examining and using the social context of education is Lawrence Cremin's three-volume study, *American Education.* Cremin is a masterful narrative historian, one especially sensitive to the importance of context in interpreting historical developments. His definition of education, furthermore, is unusually broad, encompassing a wide range of formal and informal learning experiences. In order to accomplish this, he had to master a wide diversity of sources, and to read a vast array of literature from many different fields. In *American Education: The Metropolitan Experience* (1988)—the third, and last published, of the American Education series—Cremin examines the development of education in the late nineteenth and twentieth centuries. To do this he writes about themes as diverse as theological currents in American Protestantism, immigrant community organization, corporate training ventures, and popular media. Of course he also says something about schools, children, and educators. Cremin is especially skilled at weaving brief biographical portraits together with efficient summaries of contextual material to make a coherent story about the whole of American education. The result is a narrative which informs the reader both about individual contributions to the development of education, while also providing a comprehensive interpretation of larger intellectual and social factors which affected educational policies. Like many historical narratives, it is intended to both entertain, or otherwise engage, the reader while informing him or her. Its pages are populated by real people, with diverse points of view and values, as well as such abstract social constructs as class and ethnicity. It is the challenge of the narrative historian to bring all of these elements together in a cohesive story with a distinctive point of view. The explanation of events in the past is situated in the narrative description.

Cremin's multi-volume history of American education is conceived on such a grand scale that it is probably rather daunting for most students of historical methodology. Yet it is a good example of taking context seriously. History, after all, is more than just the isolated story of a single institution, or even a series of events. It is also creating a synthesis of contextual factors which seem to have affected them. This is where reading the works of other historians and social scientists is especially critical. When evaluating one another's work, historians often comment on whether a particular historical account is based on a wide range of relevant sources. One of the highest compliments that historians can pay a colleague is to agree that his or her research is based on an exhaustive reading, of both secondary sources (works written by historians and other commentators) and primary sources (documents and other artifacts from the period being studied). Cremin clearly exhibited this quality in his work. His reading of pertinent secondary sources was sweeping in scope (the bibliographical essay—his discussion of published sources—for Volume Three alone is nearly seventy pages long), and his knowledge of educational history was built up over a career spanning four decades. This enabled him to accomplish one of the central goals of a historian: creating a synthesis of this knowledge to set events in a larger context of historical forces, whether events in the lives of an individual or in the development of a national system of education.

In the narrative tradition, a historian is supposed to construct an interpretation from the sources, developing an explanation of events which takes account of all the evidence he or she has examined. In this regard, the methodology of narrative historians is inductive and qualitative; it begins with careful and thorough observation, and proceeds to constructing explanations which are derived from the available evidence. And the explanation is usually implicit in the generally descriptive narrative account of events. Were he still alive, Lawrence Cremin would probably maintain that this was indeed his methodology in the American Education volumes, but these works also reflect Cremin's long experience as a working historian. Given their sweeping scope, they are perhaps better thought of as "meta-history," historical analysis derived from wide reading and broad familiarity with an unusually wide range of historical sources, rather than a single set of documents or other artifacts (Hughes 1964).

Most narrative historians, however, are concerned with particular issues and themes in the history of education, and do indeed seem to employ such a methodology (most historians are notoriously silent about their methods, so it is difficult to say exactly how they have arrived at an interpretation). In her highly acclaimed biography of influential nineteenth century educator and writer Catharine Beecher, for instance, Kathryn Kish Sklar (1974) examined a wide range of primary sources from the period of Beecher's life, including all of her surviving personal papers, materials from other members of her family, papers of Beecher's friends and colleagues, and other collections of pertinent documents which shed light on Beecher's views. It was only after studying these materials—and setting them in a context derived from a careful reading of the work of other historians— that Sklar was able to construct her own interpretation of Beecher's life, her attitudes and values, and the role she played in shaping women's education (although education is not the principal focus of this book). Of course, Sklar undoubtedly had developed views of certain aspects of Beecher's life as she conducted her research (which spanned a decade), but even these ideas were subject to modification after reviewing additional material. In the end, Sklar presents a complex portrait of a woman whose life was shaped by a confluence of family circumstances and ill fortune, who straddled two different eras, and whose views defy easy characterization. Yet it is a study which is rich in insight about the values and motives which moved nineteenth century reformers, male and female, largely because of Sklar's painstaking research and thoughtful interpretation. According to the conventions of narrative historical research, it is only after the entire historical record has been reviewed that a particular interpretation can be forged.

Sklar's work on Beecher represents the basic elements of narrative historical research. Because the evidence is often fragmentary, and subject to a variety of interpretations, narrative historians are usually somewhat circumspect in identifying their interpretive stance. Instead of openly declaring what they believe about an historical process, they generally construct a narrative account of events in the past, with implied causal links to other events, particular personalities, or larger social-historical forces. In short, they construct a story, based on the evidence they have accumulated, but going beyond it as well. The story is judged believable if it is based on sufficient evidence—the standards for which may shift over time—and a reasonable understanding of the larger scholarly and historical context within which it is set. According to H. Stuart Hughes (1964), historical arguments are plausible as long as they are not contradicted by the known body of available evidence. Moreover, it is also often judged believable if it conforms with popular expectations.

History has long held wide popular appeal, and many narrative historians believe that history ought to be written for the general public, or at the very least the educated general public, and hence must be free of the jargon and technical terms which often make other social science studies difficult to read. This makes matters of presentation of paramount concern. Cremin's work exhibits a special interest in making history of education accessible to the reading public, as does the work of a number of other historians. An example of history written for the general reading public, and particularly for professionals working in the schools, is David Tyack and Elisabeth Hansot's (1982) *Managers of Virtue.* Tyack and Hansot's book is primarily a history of the school superintendency, but embraces a wide range of issues in the history of school administration. More importantly, it is written in a way that makes it wonderfully accessible to readers without a background in educational history, or even the field of education itself. Like Cremin, Tyack and Hansot use biography as a vehicle through which to tell a story about the men who have administered America's schools over the past century. Their account is sprinkled with interesting sketches of key individuals. These vignettes, however, provide substance to Tyack and Hansot's larger purpose in this volume: Collective biography (see also Chapter 6). In identifying scores of nineteenth and twentieth century school leaders, they are able to identify common elements in their lives (small town or rural Protestant backgrounds, conservative disposition, and a commitment to orderly reform), which are illuminated in the individuals they highlight. They are able to generalize beyond the vignettes because of their assiduous research, and they set the whole discussion against a backdrop of larger patterns of social and cultural change in American life. The result is a highly textured account of changes in school leadership, a story which is rich in detail, broad in scope, and informative to readers with little or no background in history or education.

REVISIONIST HISTORY

As suggested earlier, Lawrence Cremin is a well known and highly regarded practitioner of narrative historical analysis. His book *Transformation of the School* (1961) is often identified as an exemplary study of education in a particular period. *Transformation* focuses on the progressive education movement, which flourished in the United States between 1890 and 1940. In this book, Cremin gives special attention to certain leading educational reformers of the day, and through pointed but effective biographical sketches, identifies what he believed were the humane and democratic impulses which motivated them. In addition to these accounts, Cremin also describes the progressive reforms which these men and women instituted themselves or which they inspired. Dealing with such prominent and influential reformers as John Dewey, Francis Parker, Jane Addams, Edward Thorndike, and George Counts (among many others), and extending its analysis to the mid 1950s, *Transformation* is sweeping in scope, and seemingly comprehensive in its coverage of progressive reform. The story Cremin tells is exciting, featuring humane and indefatigable reformers working to improve the schools and address the problems of children. In the second half of the book, he suggests that progressivism lost much of its initial vigor and originality when it became the "conventional wisdom" in many school districts across the country. But this only serves to underscore the dynamism of the earlier period. By Cremin's account, progressivism in education was the great American contribution to education, one which made schools happier and more effective institutions.

Cremin's study was awarded the Bancroft Prize, a high honor for books in American history, and was praised both by historians (and not just historians of education) and by professional educators. Cremin's research was prodigious, and he clearly had read the literature on his period. From his vantage point as a faculty member at Columbia University,[1] Cremin was perfectly situated to write the authoritative account of progressive education. In little more than a decade, however, his interpretation of progressivism was seriously challenged by other historians. The nature of the challenge did not directly impugn Cremin's scholarship—his use of historical evidence. Rather, it dealt with matters of interpretation, especially his characterization of progressivism as fundamentally humane and democratic. Using a different frame of reference, other historians were able to draw dramatically different conclusions from a body of evidence very similar to the material Cremin had examined himself.

In 1973 Clarence Karier, Paul Violas, and Joel Spring published a set of historical essays titled *Roots of Crisis.* This volume had grown out of a strain of interpretation in educational history which had developed over the previous decade. Although the focus of the essays in *Roots* varied substantially, they all shared a vision of progressive education which was dramatically different from Cremin's. In their introduction, Karier and his co-authors declared that their vision of the past was shaped in large part by their understanding of the present, particularly a critique of what they described as the "corporate liberal state." Rather than examining what Cremin had seen as democratic and humane aspects of progressivism; Karier, Violas, and Spring explored the ways in which educators designed schools to insure social stability, and hence to preserve inequality. In one essay, Karier (1973a) examined the role of such business values as efficiency and order in the development of the public schools. In another, Violas (1973) probed the thought of Jane Addams—a major figure in progressive reform at the turn of the century—to find the limits of her support for the dispossessed and disadvantaged. In yet another, Karier (1973b) outlined the history of standardized testing, a major preoccupation of educational reformers in the opening decades of the twentieth century. Throughout the book, a common theme is the role of schooling in meeting the social goals of elites, generally at the expense of the poor and dispossessed. Progressive educational reform, according to this account, simply served to more rationally reproduce the existing inequalities in American corporate capitalism. Needless to say, this interpretation posed a serious challenge to Cremin and other historians who had painted a rather different picture of progressive education.

Who is right? That is a difficult question. Both accounts have elements of the "truth." Cremin is undoubtedly right in characterizing many progressive educators as humane and compassionate reformers. On the other hand, Karier is probably correct in arguing that the effect of many policies they supported was to exacerbate existing inequalities, and preserve the advantages enjoyed by corporate elites then assuming control of American society. In other words, it is possible for both interpretations to be compatible, provided they do not directly contradict one another in interpreting a specific event or person's role in history. Remember that historical explanations need only be sufficient, not conclusive. Karier and Cremin each have constructed compelling narrative accounts of educational reform at the turn of the century, and therefore both yield important insights into the development of modern education.

In *The One Best System,* Tyack (1974) distinguishes between what he describes as "administrative progressives," the men and women Karier and other revisionists have focused on, who were principally concerned with using education to insure social stability or promote capitalist economic development; and "pedagogical progressives," who included many of the reformers Cremin wrote about, those concerned with making schools more responsive to the needs of children. Both groups contributed to educational reform at this time, making schools better places to learn, at the same time that education was adapted to the larger purposes of social integration. Tyack succeeded in using the disparate— even contradictory—findings of Cremin, Karier, and other historians to create what is described as a new synthesis, or an interpretation of the past which is constructed from the studies of other historians. Without the continuing application of new interpretive frameworks to historical problems, however, such developments would not be possible.

Of course there is often more to interpretive controversies in history than differing points of focus. Sometimes historians also disagree about interpreting particular events or individuals and their roles in history. Then evidence becomes critical to deciding which account is credible. There were a number of such disagreements with the development of a revisionist perspective in the history of education. Some historians, for instance, took exception to the way in which Karier and Violas characterized such leading progressive reformers as Jane Addams and John Dewey. They argued that Violas' argument about Addams did not present a complete picture of her views, and that he selected quotes which supported his viewpoint and ignored statements which did not (Ravitch 1977). The result, the critics maintained, was a seriously distorted picture of Addams' ideas on education and the future of the disadvantaged. Other scholars (Zerby 1975; Eisele 1975) criticized Karier for his treatment of Dewey in connection with the question of Polish-immigrant workers. Karier (1973b) used a number of quotes to suggest that Dewey regarded education as a mechanism to "Americanize" Polish workers, implying that their native culture was somehow deficient. Karier, of course, interpreted this as evidence that Dewey, like other educational reformers of his time, was concerned with using education to promote conformity to mainstream values, and thus to reinforce, by implication, existing inequalities. But other scholars objected, arguing that his evidence about Dewey's views was taken out of context, and that Karier had misrepresented his ideas on the social function of education. After a somewhat heated series of articles in the *History of Education Quarterly,* the matter was never quite resolved (Feinberg 1975; Karier 1975). But there continued to be challenges to the revisionists' use of evidence in constructing their interpretation, charges which damaged their credibility among historians (Ravitch 1977).

A clear and compelling interpretive framework with inadequate evidence is unlikely to be treated seriously by most historians. One example of this is Colin Greer's (1972) book, *The Great School Legend.* Writing in the revisionist tradition, Greer argued that schools discriminated against immigrant children in various ways at the turn of the century, leading them to fail in a manner similar to patterns of failure for inner city minority groups in the post-World War Two era. While there may be considerable truth in such an assertion, Greer failed to examine rigorously just how immigrants fared in schools at the start of the century. His argument is based on a rather cursory examination of certain school reports, which show that many immigrants dropped out of school, or exhibited high rates of failure (called "retardation" at the time). He failed to consider all the reasons why immigrants left the schools, and did not examine carefully enough differences in the way immigrants utilized the schools. Furthermore, he did not carefully identify the sources he used to make rather sweeping generalizations about the nature of public education in American history. Subsequent studies have suggested that the historical circumstances of urban schools, and immigrant students in particular, was considerably more complex than suggested by Greer. Hogan (1984), Perlmann (1989), and other historians have demonstrated that early school leaving—and labor force entry—was often a deliberate strategy of maximizing household economic resources to accomplish certain goals, such as buying a home. A number of other studies have demonstrated that some immigrants did quite well in the schools, and indeed that high schools in some areas were dominated—academically as well as numerically—by the children of immigrants (Fass 1989). While there are probably elements of truth in many of Greer's observations about the history of American education, he was not careful enough in compiling evidence to support his arguments to satisfy most professional historians. History, after all, is more than an elegant or compelling story. Historians, even those who write in a narrative tradition, must be especially attentive to matters of evidence.

Historical inquiry involves, therefore a constant interplay between evidence and interpretation. Most narrative historians carefully construct their interpretations after reviewing as much of the historical record as possible—documents and other artifacts, and the work of other historians. This is not to say that they do not have a point of view, even at the start of their studies. But historians are supposed to suspend judgement about the character of a particular event or personality until all the relevant evidence has been examined. This is the mistake that Greer and other revisionist historians have been accused of making: Constructing an argument without considering evidence which may contradict it, a problem identified earlier with respect to some scholars in anthropology and sociology (Chapters 2, 3). In the end, the history with the best evidence to support it is usually the one which is accepted, but revisionist visions of the past—with their own compelling messages—do become part of our collective understanding.

SCHOOL ATTENDANCE AND HISTORY AS SOCIAL SCIENCE

Not all historians write in a narrative tradition, of course. In the past several decades, a small but influential group of historians have employed a range of inquiry strategies taken from other disciplines to study historical problems. Most of these new methods have involved the use of quantitative data, and they generally have entailed a more direct approach to the testing of hypotheses than traditional narrative history. But even the "new" quantitative historians are required to set their findings in the context of a general interpretive framework. Again, this is due to the fragmentary nature of the evidence, a characteristic of historical inquiry which even affects quantitative research. Consequently, social science historians are often not able to perform the same kinds of tests that scientists who can conduct experiments might demand. Rather than providing a rigorous test of competing hypotheses, quantitative analysis in history has generally been used to buttress a more generalized interpretation of a wide range of historical sources. In the end, even quantitative history is fundamentally qualitative. Rather than revolutionizing history, as some of its early proponents had claimed it would, so called social science history has simply provided historians with a wider array of tools with which to study the past (Sharpless and Warner 1977).

Beginning in the late 1960s, quantitative data have been employed in a wide range of studies in the history of American education. The overwhelming majority of these studies have focused on school attendance. This, of course, may sound like a fairly trivial aspect of educational history, but the matter of determining who did and did not attend school can be linked to a wide range of issues. The simple observation, for instance, that the children of Italian immigrants enrolled in school at much lower rates that those from non–immigrant background raises a host of interesting questions. Did the schools in some way discriminate against Italian children, keeping them out or otherwise creating an inhospitable atmosphere for them? Or did the families of these children simply value education less than families in other groups, preferring instead to send their children to work or to shelter them at home? Katz (1972) has suggested that the matter of "who went to school" may be among the most fundamental questions in educational history, because it deals directly with issues of access to education as a resource, and provides critical evidence on the demographic composition of school populations.

As suggested earlier, even quantitative data cannot settle matters of interpretation conclusively. Because of the fragmentary and inert quality of historical evidence, it is quite possible to have alternative interpretations of similar sets of quantitative data. A good example of this is the debate over determinants of school attendance which occurred in the late seventies and early eighties among a small group of historians. One group, led by Michael Katz (Katz and Davey 1978), held that income and occupational background differences—both elements of social class—were the most important determinants of school enrollment among children in Canada (Toronto and Hamilton) during the nineteenth century. Katz and his associates argued that children from working class families were forced to leave school early—or were otherwise excluded—and hence the schools served a clientele comprised principally of the middle and upper classes, despite their rhetorical commitment to democracy and universal education.

Other quantitative historians examined similar data sets and came to somewhat different conclusions. Examining nineteenth century school enrollment data from Massachusetts, Kaestle and Vinovskis (1979) concluded that while social class background factors (principally occupational) were important, ethnic differences seemed to account for a larger share of the variation in enrollment rates across groups, suggesting that a set of cultural preferences (see pp. 70–72) or nativistic discrimination patterns (or both, of course) may have contributed to lower school enrollment rates among immigrant children. While there was little direct engagement and testing of arguments by historians on either side of this issue, it soon became clear that the matter of whether class or ethnicity was the primary determinant of school participation was not going to be definitively settled simply by comparing regression coefficients.

The principal problem, as most historians recognized, was that the data employed in these analyses—usually census manuscripts and school reports— was too fragmentary to allow a rigorous test of either point of view. The items recorded by nineteenth century census takers—father's occupation and place of birth—were only loose approximations of the concepts of class and ethnicity. And they usually were interrelated themselves. Most immigrants from Southern and Eastern Europe, after all, worked in low skill manual jobs. In reality, both social class and ethnicity—characteristics which were largely inseparable in the lives of most poor immigrant families—probably accounted for their attitudes and behavior towards the schools, even if one or the other was more important in a particular context.

For historical inquiry, there are limits to the explanatory power of quantitative data. Among the best examples of recent educational history written from the new social science perspective is Joel Perlmann's (1988) study of the outcomes of education for different ethnic groups in Providence, Rhode Island. Taking the years between 1880 and 1935, Perlmann painstakingly tracked a large sample of the city's 1880 and 1900 population (taken from census manuscripts and school reports) into future records (census manuscripts, tax records, and city directories) to determine how individuals from these groups fared in achieving status and social mobility. Perlmann was especially interested in studying which groups invested a great deal in education, and which ones accorded it less importance, and how education appears to have contributed to each group's success. Using a variety of sophisticated statistical techniques, he calculated the probability of individuals from these groups achieving different levels of schooling and occupational status. The result was the most thorough and careful analysis of the effect of education in history yet conducted. Perlmann was able to identify—in rather precise terms—clear differences in the educational experiences of individuals from various ethnic groups, and point to ways in which it appeared to be related to group differences in occupational and social status (compare Ogbu 1978). In many respects it was a classic community-based study of inter-group differences in social mobility, in the tradition of such influential sociologists as Hollingshead and others (Hollingshead [1949] 1975; Warner 1949; Lynd and Lynd 1939).

Like other quantitative studies in educational history, Perlmann's book occupies something of a middle ground between history and sociology. By and large, unlike the narrative historians, he does not attempt to construct a story about his subject. Rather, he builds a formal explanation, drawing on a wide range of evidence. His method is somewhat less inductive than that employed by most other historians, as the major categories of analysis—schooling, ethnic group identity, and occupational outcomes—have been specified in advance. To a very large extent, Perlmann is testing a number of explicit hypotheses about the relationship of education to social mobility and success in urban America at the turn of the century. Because of this, and to the extent that he subjects these hypotheses to rigorous statistical analysis, his study represents the extension of deductive (quantitative, positivist) social science methodology to an historical problem.

The problem that Perlmann encountered, however, was that his quantitative evidence did not adequately "explain" the occupational outcomes he was able to identify for the groups in question. The schooling differences between groups were significant, but not fully explainable in terms of quantifiable background factors Perlmann was able to identify. Likewise, occupational outcomes were also different, but not totally—or even principally—attributable to differences in education. As a consequence, Perlmann was left with a very large element of "unexplained variance" to account for in his explanation of ethnic differences in schooling and occupational status. To provide an explanation of the events he was describing, in that case, he was compelled to rely on a number of more conventional historical sources. And it was at this juncture that the historical elements in Perlmann's study came to the fore.

Despite his considerable precision and sophistication in statistical analysis, Perlmann's study yields precious few rigorous tests of theory. Rather, like previous qualitative studies (Covello 1967), it shows that different ethnic groups used the schools for their own purposes. He found, for instance, that Jewish students, most of whom were from Russia, did better than their counterparts from Italian and Irish backgrounds, even when differences in occupational background, wealth, and length of time in the U.S. were controlled. Perlmann also found that black Americans, despite their comparatively high levels of schooling, did not enjoy the same degree of occupational mobility as the other groups, even though they had been a part of the community for a longer time than most immigrant groups.

In both cases, he was required to interpret these findings in much the same way that most historians do: construct an explanation based on all the evidence, including non-quanitative materials, he could pull together on these questions. As a consequence, Perlmann's argument is a sufficient one, not a necessary or definitive explanation. No matter how scientifically the evidence is collected and analyzed, historians must still practice the art of interpreting the past, based on observation and knowledge of disparate sources.

USING PERSONAL ACCOUNTS IN THE ANALYSIS OF SCHOOL ATTENDANCE

Perlmann's study is an example of how even the best quantitative data need to be augmented with other data and interpreted by historians. In many cases, however, the quality of quantitative evidence is much lower, and the importance of relevant documentary evidence and interpretation becomes correspondingly more critical. An example of such limitations in social science history is represented in my own work (Rury 1991) on the history of women's education. In trying to explain why teenage women attended high school in comparatively large numbers in the late nineteenth century, I employed a wide range of quantitative data to test the hypothesis that they enrolled because of interest in employment. Looking at state-level indices of female labor force participation in a variety of fields, including such then-growing occupations as teaching and clerical work, I used a number of statistical tests to determine whether patterns of female employment were associated with high levels of school enrollment. However, I was forced to accept the null hypothesis. No matter which dimension of female schooling I used—enrollment or graduation rates—I could not establish a clear statistical link with employment trends across states. A statistical association did exist between male graduation rates and employment in white collar jobs, a finding which made the absence of a similar link between women's schooling and work even more striking. Put simply, women attended high school in relatively high numbers in areas where female employment rates were low, as well as in areas where large numbers of women worked. Even though I was able to find some statistical relationships between patterns of female labor force participation and schooling, the association of these aspects of women's lives seemed to be quite weak in this period.[2] Consequently, I was unable to account for the development of women's education using the quantitative data at hand.

My response to this dilemma was to consult an altogether different body of evidence. Unable to infer women's reasons for attending school from their behavior (as reflected in the statistical data available), I decided to look for it in their own personal documents. Using special libraries in Massachusetts and Michigan, and drawing material from other sources, I examined the diaries and other personal papers of some two dozen women attending high school in the late nineteenth century. I read these documents with attention to what they did and did not say. None of the women whose papers I read ever explicitly discussed their reasons for attending school. No one even mentioned anything about working after school, or about the value which school represented in the labor market. Rather, they wrote about all the good and bad times they were having, about their friends and families, and about their hopes and fears. Not unlike teenage women today, perhaps, they were interested in the social world the high school represented, their immediate circle of friends, and of course the young men in their classes. And they were interested in learning, and the excitement of accomplishment which the high school represented for them. They identified with their women teachers (even though they did not write about teaching themselves), and took their schoolwork seriously. Only after spending some time reading through all these papers, including letters from home, school papers, correspondence from friends, and other documents, did I begin to get a picture of what their lives were like. It was from the process of systematic and thorough observation of the evidence at hand, that I began to develop a new explanation of women's behavior in school: they went to school because they enjoyed it.

Saying that young women attended school in the late nineteenth century because it was fun may not sound like much of an insight, but it was far removed from the conceptual framework I had started my study with. Moreover, it was an explanation which drew from observing a body of evidence which was fragmentary and incomplete, and it was arrived at inductively. I read widely in women's history, and found that other historians had discovered similar patterns of behavior in nineteenth century women, particularly in schools. And this led me to still further collateral reading, for example, in adolescent psychology, to understand the motives which may have moved these teenage women. All of these elements were combined in an explanation which took account of the difficult transition to adulthood, which these women were beginning, and considering how the schools may have mediated that process.

I concluded that (Rury 1991) young women attended high school in the late nineteenth century to begin developing their own personal identities in a setting outside of their immediate families, but in a context which met with considerable social approval. They enjoyed the growing peer culture of the high school, and welcomed their studies as a chance to prove themselves in an esteemed field. By and large, they were not interested in breaking social conventions—which aspiring to work careers may have done—but they were interested in beginning the process of separating themselves from their families.

Social science methods, particularly statistical analysis of quantitative evidence, do not fundamentally alter the nature of historical research. They provide the historian with a variety of additional tools with which to make inferences about the past, allowing some limited testing of hypotheses, but without diminishing the need for interpretation. The reason for this is that virtually all historical evidence is in some way incomplete. Consequently, historians will never be able to construct a data set to thoroughly or scientifically test a hypothesis. Even Joel Perlmann, who systematically compiled one of the most complete quantitative bodies of historical evidence in the field, was only able to test a limited range of propositions, and was ultimately compelled to rely on many of the same materials as other historians, to forge his own interpretation. Likewise, in my own research, the limitations of available quantitative data made it necessary to examine a wide range of additional material in order to construct an explanation of female school participation in the latter nineteenth century. This does not mean, of course, that quantitative data are useless or irrelevant to historical research. Indeed, they add a great deal of power and precision to historical interpretation, enabling historians to provide more complete and sophisticated reconstructions of the past. They expand the scientific component of history (methods of data collection and analysis), but do not diminish the art of historical analysis and interpretation. In the end, it is the historian's judgement which must be called upon to interpret the past. For this reason, the development of social science history has not altered the essentially qualitative nature of historical inquiry.

STEPS IN THE PROCESS OF HISTORICAL INQUIRY

As suggested earlier, there is no single approach to doing historical research. There are a number of important steps to be taken, however, for most historical research projects to meet professional standards. Of course it is possible to write histories which do not meet these standards, but most such works have rather limited appeal, and generally are not considered serious scholarship by other historians. Basically, good historical research takes the work of other historians as a starting point—and additional, relevant, secondary works—and continues with new research in primary sources to forge a novel interpretation of developments in the past (I will define "secondary" and "primary" sources in greater detail below). Historians must choose whether to frame their presentation in terms of traditional narrative, or such explicitly argumentative forms as social science history. Finally, historians should always aim to have a clear point of view, an internally consistent interpretive outlook, which is supported by the best available evidence.

In history, as in other areas of inquiry, the first step is having a clear idea of what one is studying. This is not as simple as it may sound. Historical problems are framed in many different ways, depending on how the question is initially posed. Some, for instance, are derived from present-day issues, such as Diane Ravitch's (1984) examination of American education since World War Two, *The Troubled Crusade,* (one should also consult Katz's (1985) review for a critique of her approach). Others are taken from reading history, and are derived from being curious about events, institutions, or people in the past. This is probably the largest category, and includes most studies undertaken by professional historians of education. Yet others pose a direct challenge to the interpretations of other historians, and marshall new evidence to present an alternative point of view.

Each of these ways of thinking about an historical problem suggests a somewhat different strategy of inquiry, with different approaches to data collection, and the task of constructing an historical interpretation. Investigating a particular policy or problem often entails less background reading, and may entail methodologies such as oral history, while a challenge to a particular interpretation may hinge on a special body of new evidence. It is important, in that case, to be clear about just what is being investigated at the outset of the process.

Historians usually do not have formal hypotheses, of course, but they should have a hunch about the causes or circumstances of a particular event in the past.

This is not always possible at the outset of a research project, but it is necessary to acknowledge one's opinions (or hunches), in order to adequately test them (recognizing that they may change too). History, as we have seen, is a fundamentally interpretive enterprise, and the hunches an historian begins the research process with will usually have an impact on the interpretive position he or she finally takes. Good history is written with a distinct point of view, and being aware of one's opinions is an important part of developing a clear perspective in one's research and writing.

Another important step is determining what other scholars have had to say about the issue. This is work in secondary sources (or synthetic and interpretive works), those written by persons who did not participate, or otherwise directly observe, the events being analyzed. It corresponds to the literature review described in Chapter 8, but most historians do not include formal literature reviews in their written work. Rather, historians and other scholars who have addressed pertinent issues are cited as they are relevant to the story being told, or to the historical analysis being performed. There are exceptions to this, of course, especially among historians whose work is influenced by the social sciences (see, for instance, Vinovskis 1985). But for most historians, particularly those working in the narrative tradition, a free-standing discussion of the literature is considered cumbersome and obtrusive. The objective of history, in their view, is to tell a story with as little explicit reference to other works as possible. In the narrative tradition, the historical account should ideally be a virtually seamless description and analysis of events, personalities, and other forces at work in connection with a particular problem, and it should be accessible to non-specialists.

This does not mean, however, that historians do not value the work of other scholars. On the contrary, as I have suggested earlier, having a firm grasp of the literature on a given problem is highly prized among historians. In terms of writing history to meet professional standards, it is virtually indispensable. There are a number of reasons for this. The first is context. As noted earlier, an axiom of historical inquiry is that it is impossible to understand an event without knowing its context. And the best way to study context is to read the work of other historians who have written about the same period or problem. The better an historian's understanding of contextual issues—the range of factors which may have affected the events in question—the more compelling his or her explanation is likely to be. Put yet another way, overlooking the work of a particular historian could lead to serious oversights in the development of one's own analysis.

Historians have come to employ a wide range of data collection and analysis techniques in their work. Reading widely can be a great stimulant to one's thinking about methodology. Of course, such reading should not be limited to history alone. One reason why history has undergone such great change in recent years is because historians have read widely in other fields. Consulting the work of other scholars on methodological questions can broaden one's view of a topic, and provide new tools with which to collect and analyze historical data.

Yet another reason for collateral reading is getting information about sources. At the heart of historical research is the process of identifying, locating, and interpreting primary source materials, which shed light on the events or problems in question. Even though the task of locating documents and other materials has been made immeasurably easier in recent decades by the development of specialized research libraries, with carefully indexed collections, other historians can call attention to certain classes of sources one might overlook, and identify where they are located, and which are likely to be relevant. Secondary sources can provide a guide to the range of sources which have been used, and help to identify especially critical, or otherwise indispensable documents for one's research. In reading the work of other scholars, therefore the footnotes may, occasionally, be more important than the text!

The most critical step in historical research, of course, is identifying and analyzing primary source materials. Usually this is undertaken after an historian has a good understanding of the period or problem being studied, although there is a constant interplay between primary and secondary sources in historical research, just as in other forms of qualitative inquiry. Primary sources are those which directly reflect the views or the behavior of individuals or groups the historian is attempting to explain, and not the interpretation of some intervening observer, whether a contemporary or not. These are often difficult to find, and it is important for historians to be sure that a large enough body of relevant primary sources exists for the problems they plan to address. There are many issues in history, after all, which are likely to remain mysterious because there is little documentation for historians to work with, such as Horace Mann's views of immigrant workers—an issue of potential interest to historians of early school reform. Indeed, many studies have started with the intrepid historian finding a cache of such material, which had not been utilized by other scholars (see, for instance, Rury and Harper 1986). Having a good collection of primary source materials to begin one's research with is an important element in conducting historical research. The quality of the documentation, after all, will determine, to a certain extent, the value of the insights one can achieve.

Locating relevant sources is only the beginning state of working with primary documents, however. The difficult part is making sense of them. As noted earlier, Gordon (1991) has described historical research as letting the documents "speak," but one has to know what to listen for. This is where having a clear idea of what one is studying—and a clearly formulated set of expectations (or "hunches")—can be very valuable. Of course, one must also be willing to "hear" the unexpected, and to discover the unanticipated, so it is not advisable to look only for what one wants or expects to find. Rather, expectations can serve as a kind of foil against which to read the sources, to evaluate their relevance and utility for the study at hand. Here too, one's knowledge of other historical studies—contextual issues—can be critical as well, for identifying points of relevance in primary sources which might not be directly linked to the issue at hand, but which may ultimately prove important. For this reason, and for purposes of clarifying one's expectations, it is advisable to do a good deal of secondary reading before beginning work in primary sources for historical research.

What kinds of primary materials do historians of education generally work with? Documents from schools and other agencies are often useful for institutional perspectives. Letters, diaries, and other personal papers tell us much about the views and values of individuals, and quantitative data, collected by government agencies or even individual researchers in the past, are an indispensable source of information about the social structure. Historians have even used artifacts, such as household implements, to draw inferences about such issues as the differentiation of family roles and the socialization of children (Demos 1971). In a recent study of coeducation, David Tyack and Elizabeth Hansot (1990) used photographs of classrooms taken during the twentieth century to draw inferences about the ways gender operated in the daily lives of students. There is, therefore, a wide variety of evidence that historians can utilize to analyze events in the past.

Every scholar has a personal style of taking notes, whether it is field notes during ethnographic research, or notes from reading of historical documents. There are certain conventions, however, associated with the various disciplines. For historians, the preferred method is the use of index cards, with one card for each idea or fact recorded. Thus, a particular document may require many cards, many different notations. The value of this method is that it allows the greatest flexibility in using notes to construct an historical narrative or explanation. Having a single bibliographical card for each source saves the trouble of repeating this information on each card. A good review of steps to follow in taking notes for historical research can be found in Barzun and Graff (1985).

The final step, of course, is actually constructing an historical narrative, or an analysis of historical data, with a distinctive interpretation. There are many intervening steps, for one rarely goes directly from collecting notes on primary sources to writing a narrative. There is the tricky business of analyzing the information taken from sources, including performing any quantitative analysis necessary. And, inevitably, there is a constant movement back and forth between primary and secondary sources to determine the meaning of one's findings. But once one has a definite interpretive direction, and the bulk of evidence has been gathered, it is time to set about writing.

Do not be surprised to find that impressions formed early in the research will change as more evidence is discovered, or while one is writing. As is commonly observed, writing is a form of thinking, and new insights are bound to occur when evidence is finally put together in a coherent narrative or explanation. It is even possible for new questions to arise during the writing process, as unanticipated gaps in the sources become evident, or new dimensions of the issue being explored come into view. I have found this to be true a number of times in my own work, and have heard literally dozens of other historians describe the same experience. Like other forms of qualitative research, historical inquiry and writing do not follow easily prescribed or linear paths of development. Often it is necessary to simply keep pounding away at it, and finding new evidence to address questions which come up, until one arrives at an interpretive stance, and a degree of description, which seems to be adequate. It is only at this point that the investigation abates.

As in other forms of qualitative inquiry, there is no "cookbook" approach to doing historical research. While it is true that researchers in history (as in most other fields) ought to have a clear idea of what they are pursuing, and be self conscious about their "hunches" as they proceed, the steps I have described above need not be followed in any particular order. Most historians are trained with wide reading in a particular field or period preceding any foray into primary sources, but as noted earlier, many research projects begin with the discovery of a previously unknown hoard of documents or artifacts. It often matters little whether secondary reading is done before or after primary research, or even if the two alternate—or proceed simultaneously—as often seems to be the case in reality. At times it may even seem as though all the steps described above are commingled, as "hunches" change in the midst of writing, new evidence is found, and additional secondary sources come to light. The point is not the particular order of these steps, but the necessity of performing all of them. Good, professional-quality historical research generally requires that each of these steps be taken, whatever the sequence. What matters, after all, is not the particular process of inquiry, but the historical narrative that is ultimately constructed.

NOTES

1. Columbia has been a focal point of progressive thought, and hence a depository for much of the material Cremin had to review, and a major center of historical research at the time he was writing. He had such famous American historians as Richard Hofstadter and Allen Nevins as colleagues.
2. This may still be the case today, see Mickelson (1989).

Bibliography

Abramovitch, R. "The Relation of Attention and Proximity to Rank in Preschool Children." In *The Social Structure of Attention,* edited by M. R. A. Chance and R. R. Larsen, 154–176. London: Academic Press, 1976.

Acker, S., ed. *Teachers, Gender, and Careers.* London: Falmer Press, 1989.

Afflerbach, P., Bass, L., Hoo, D., Smith, S., Weiss, S., & Williams, L. "Preservice Teachers Use Think-Aloud Protocols to Study Writing." *Language Arts 65*(7) (1988): 693–701.

Afflerbach, P., & Johnston, P. "On the Use of Verbal Reports in Reading Research." *Journal of Reading Behavior 16* (1984): 307–322.

Agar, M. H. *Speaking of ethnography.* Newbury Park, CA: Sage, 1986.

Agar, M. H., & Hobbs, J. R. "Interpreting Discourse: Coherence and the Analysis of Ethnographic Interview." *Discourse Processes 5* (1981): 1–32.

Aldis, O. *Play Fighting.* New York: Academic Press, 1975.

Alkin, M., Daillak, R., & White, P. *Using Evaluations: Does Evaluation Make a Difference?* Newbury Park, CA: Sage, 1979.

Alofs, J. E., & Gray-McKennis, J. "Children's Choices: The Topics of Young Writers." In *The Writing Teacher as Researcher,* edited by D. A. Daiker and M. Morenbeurg, 94–112. Portsmouth, NH: Boynton Cook, 1990.

Altheide, D. L. "Ethnographic Content Analysis." *Qualitative Sociology, 10*(1) (1987): 65–77.

Altman, J. "Observational Study of Behavior: Sampling Methods." *Behaviour 49* (1974): 227–265.

Anderson, G. L. "Critical Ethnography in Education: Origins, Current Status and New Directions." *Review of Educational Research, 59*(3) (1989): 249–270.

Anderson, L. W. & Burns, R. B. *Research in Classrooms.* New York: Pergamon Press, 1990.

Anderson, R. B. "The Effectiveness of Follow Through: What Have We Learned?" Paper presented at the annual meeting of the American Educational Research Association, New York, April, 1977.

Anyon, J. "Social Class and the Hidden Curriculum of Work." *Journal of Education 162* (1980): 67–92.

Ashton-Warner, S. *Teacher.* New York: Simon & Schuster, 1963.

Atwell, N. "Everyone Sits at a Big Desk: Discovering Topics for Writing." In *Reclaiming the Classroom: Teacher Research as an Agency for Change,* edited by D. Goswami and P. R. Stillman, 178–187. Portsmouth, NH: Heinemann, 1987.

Au, K. "Participation Structures in a Reading Lesson with Hawaiian Children." *Anthropology and Education Quarterly 11* (1980): 91–115.

Aydolette, William O. "Quantification in History." *American Historical Review 71*(3) (1966): 803–825.

Bailyn, B. "The Challenge of Modern Historiography." *American Historical Review 87*(2): 1–24 (1982).

Baker, C. *Ernest Hemingway: A Life Story.* New York: Scribners, 1969.

Baker, D. & Stevenson, D. "Mothers' Strategies for School Achievement: Managing the Transition to High School." *Sociology of Education 59* (1986): 156–167.

Ball, D. L. Reflections and Deflections of Policy: The Case of Carol Turner. *Educational Evaluation and Policy Analysis 12*(3) (1990): 263–275.

Ball, S. J. *Beachside Comprehensive: A Case Study of Secondary Schooling.* Cambridge: Cambridge University Press, 1981.

Ball, S. J. "Beachside Revisited." In *Field Research: A Sourcebook and Field Manual,* edited by R. G. Burgess, 69–96. London: Allen and Unwin, 1984.

Ball, S. J., & Goodson, I. F. "Understanding Teachers: Concepts and Contexts." In *Teachers' Lives and Careers,* edited by S. J. Ball and I. F. Goodson, 1–26. London: Falmer, 1985.

Barker, R. G., & Gump, P. B. *Big School, Small School: High School Size and Student Behavior.* Stanford: Stanford University Press, 1964.

Barker, R. G. "Naturalistic Methods in Psychological Research." *Human Development 10* (1976): 223–229.

Barone, T. E. "On Equality, Visibility, and the Fine Arts Program in a Black Elementary School: An Example of Educational Criticism." *Curriculum Inquiry. 17*(4) (1987): 421–446.

Baroody, A. J. "The Case of Felicia: A Young Child's Strategies for Reducing Memory Demands During Mental Addition." *Cognition and Instruction 1*(1) (1984): 109–116.

Barr, R., & Dreeben, R. *How Schools Work.* Chicago: University of Chicago Press, 1983.

Bar-Tal, D. "Attributional Analysis of Achievement-related Behavior." *Review of Educational Research 48*(2) (1978): 259–271.

Barzun, J. *Clio and the Doctors: Psycho-history, Quanto-history and History.* Chicago: University of Chicago Press, 1974.

Barzun, J., and Graff, H. *The Modern Researcher* (Fourth Edition). New York: Harcourt, Brace, Jovanovich, 1985.

Beach, M. "History of Education." *Review of Education Research 39* (1969): 561–576.

Beach, R., & Bridwell, L. S. *New Directions in Composition Research.* New York: Guilford, 1984.

Becker, H. S. "Role and Career Problems of the Chicago Public School Teacher." Ph.D. diss. University of Chicago, 1951.

Becker, H. S. *Sociological Work: Method and Substance.* Chicago: Aldine, 1970.

Becker, H. S., Geer, B., Hughes, E. C., & Strauss, L. A. *Boys in White: Student Culture in Medical School.* Chicago: University of Chicago Press, 1961.

Bengston, J. K. "What Makes a Study Qualitative? A Critique of Gershman's Surviving Through Time." *Qualitative Studies in Education 1*(4) (1988): 343–346.

Bennett, K. P. & LeCompte, M. D. *How Schools Work: A Sociological Analysis of Education.* White Plains, NY: Longman, 1990.

Bergin, C., & Lancy, D. F. "The Role of Parents in Supporting Beginning Reading." Paper presented at conference on New Directions in Child & Family Research, June. Washington, D.C., 1991.

Bergin, C. & Lancy, D. F. "The Relationship Between Reading Affect and Parent-Child Interaction in Beginning Readers." Paper presented at the annual conference, American Educational Research Association, April, San Francisco, 1992.

Berk, L. E., & Berson, M. P. "The School Bus as a Developmental Experience for Young Children." *Illinois School Research 11*(3) (1975): 1–14.

Berkhofer, R. *A Behavioral Approach to Historical Analysis.* New York: The Free Press, 1969.

Bernstein, S. "Getting It Done—Notes on Student Fritters." In *Interaction in Everyday Life,* edited by J. Lofland. Beverly Hills: Sage, 1978.

Best, R. *We've All Got Scars.* Bloomington, IN: University of Indiana Press, 1983.

Beynon, J. "Ways in and Staying in: Field Work as Problem Solving." In *The Ethnography of Schooling: Methodological Issues,* edited by M. Hammersley. Duffield: Natterton, 1983.

Beynon, J. "Institutional Change and Career Histories in a Comprehensive School." In *Teachers' Lives and Careers* edited by S. J. Ball and I. F. Goodson, 158–179. London: Falmer, 1985.

Bickman, L., Tegar, A., Gabriele, T., McLaughlin, C., Berger, M., & Sunaday, E. "Dormitory Density and Helping Behavior." *Environment and Behavior* 5(4) (1973): 465–490.

Bissex, G. L., & Bullock, R. H., eds. *Seeing for Ourselves: Case Study Research by Teachers of Writing.* Portsmouth, NH: Heinemann, 1987.

Bitton, D. *Guide to Mormon Diaries and Autobiographies.* Provo, UT: BYU Press, 1977.

Blassingame, J. W. *The Slave Community: Plantation Life in the Ante Bellum South.* New York: Oxford University Press, 1977.

Bloch, M. N. & Pellegrini, A. D., eds. *The Ecological Context of Children's Play.* Norwood, NJ: Ablex, 1989.

Bloch, M. *The Historian's Craft.* New York: Alfred Knopf, 1953.

Bloome, D. "Anthropology and Research on Teaching the English Language Arts." In *Handbook of Research on Teaching the English Language Arts,* edited by J. Flood, J. M. Jensen, D. Lapp, and J. R. Squire, 46–56. New York: Macmillan, 1991.

Blumer, H. *Symbolic Interaction.* Englewood Cliffs, NJ: Prentice-Hall, 1969.

Blurton-Jones, N. G. "An Ethological Study of Some Aspects of Social Behavior of Children in Nursery School." In *Primate Ethology,* edited by D. Morris, 347–367. London: Weidenfield and Nicolson, 1967.

Blurton-Jones, N. G. "Observations and Experiment on the Causation of Threat Displays of the Great Tit *Parus Major.*" *Animal Behavior Monographs 1* (1968): 75–158.

Boas, F. "Recent Anthropology." *Science 98* (1943): 311–314.

Bogdan, R. "Interviewing People Labeled Retarded." In *Fieldwork Experience: Qualitative Approaches to Social Research,* edited by W. B. Shaffer, R. A. Stebbins, and A. Turowetz, 235–243. New York: St. Martins, 1980.

Bogdan, R. C., & Biklen, S. K. *Qualitative Research for Education: An Introduction to Theory and Methods.* Boston: Allyn & Bacon, 1982.

Bogdan, R. C., & Biklen, S. K. *Qualitative Research for Education: An Introduction to Theory and Methods,* 2nd ed. Boston: Allyn & Bacon, 1992.

Borg, W. R., & Gall, M. D. *Educational Research: An Introduction,* 4th ed. White Plains, NY: Longman, 1983.

Borg, W. R., & Gall, M. D. *Educational Research: An Introduction,* 5th ed. White Plains, NY: Longman, 1989.

Borko, H., & Eisenhart, M. "Students' Conceptions of Reading and their Reading Experiences in School." *The Elementary School Journal 86*(5) (1986): 589–611.

Bossert, S. T. *Tasks and Social Relationships in the Classroom.* Cambridge: Cambridge University Press, 1979.

Boulton, M., & Smith, P. K. "Issues in the Study of Children's Rough and Tumble Play." In *The Ecological Context of Children's Play* edited by M. N. Bloch and A. D. Pellegrini, 57–83. Norwood, NJ: Ablex, 1989.

Bourdieu, P. "Cultural Reproduction and Social Reproduction." In *Power and Ideology in Education,* edited by J. Karabel and A. H. Halsey, 487–511. New York: Oxford, 1977.

Bourdieu, P., & Passeron, J. C. *Reproduction in Education, Society and Culture.* Newbury Park, CA: Sage, 1977.

Bowles, S., & Gintis, H. *Schooling in Capitalist America.* New York: Basic Books, 1976.

Britain, G. M. *Bureaucracy and Innovation: Anthropology of Policy Changes.* Newbury Park, CA: Sage, 1981.

Britzman, D. P. *Practice Makes Practice: A Critical Study of Learning to Teach.* Albany: SUNY Press, 1991.

Bronfenbrenner, U. *The Ecology of Human Development.* Cambridge, MA: Harvard University Press, 1979.

Brown, L. D. "People-centered Development and Participatory Research." *Harvard Education Review, 55*(1) (1985): 69–75.

Brumberg, S. *Going to America, Going to School.* Wesport, CT: Praeger Publishers, 1986.

Bruner, J. *Actual lives: Possible worlds.* Cambridge, MA: Harvard University Press, 1986.

Bruner, J. "Life as Narrative." *Language Arts 65*(6) (1988): 574–583.

Bullough, Jr., R. V. *First-year Teacher: A Case Study.* New York: Teachers College Press, 1989.

Burgess, R. G. *Experiencing Comprehensive Education: A Study of Bishop McGregor School.* London: Methuen, 1983.

Burgess, R. G., ed. *Field Methods in the Study of Education.* London: Falmer, 1985.

Burnett, J. H. "Ceremony, Rites and Economy in the Student System of an American High School." *Human Organization 28*(1) (1969): 1–10.

Calhoun, J. B. "Population Density and Social Pathology." *Scientific American 206*(2) (1962): 138–148.

Cangelosi, J. S. *Designing Tests for Evaluating Student Achievement.* White Plains, NY: Longman, 1990.

Caplan, N., Choy, M. H. Whitmore, J. K. "Indochinese Refugee Families and Academic Achievement." *Scientific American 236*(2) (1992): 36–42.

Carrier, J. "School and Community on Ponam." In *The Community School,* special issue of the *Papua New Guinea Journal of Education 15,* edited by D. F. Lancy, (1979): 66–77.

Carter, M. "The Idea of Expertise: An Exploration of Cognitive and Social Dimensions of Writing." *College Composition and Communication 41* (1990): 265–286.

Cazden, C. B. (1979). Forward to Hugh Mehan's *Learning Lessons,* vii–xi. Cambridge, MA: Harvard University Press, 1979.

Cazden, C. B. *Classroom Discourse: The Language of Teaching and Learning.* Portsmouth, NH: Heinemann, 1988.

Champaign, A. B., & Klopfer, L. E. "An Individualized Elementary School Science Program." *Theory Into Practice 13* (1974): 136–148.

Chance, M. R. A., & Jolly, C. J. *Social Groups of Monkeys, Apes, and Men.* New York: Dutton, 1970.

Channon, G. *Homework.* New York: Quaterbridge and Dienstfrey, 1970.

Charlesworth, W. R., & Dzur, C. "Gender Comparison of Preschoolers' Behavior and Resource Utilization in Group Problem Solving." *Child Development 58* (1987): 191–200.

Cheetham, B. "School and Community in the Huli Area of the Southern Highlands Province." In *The Community School,* special issue of the *Papua New Guinea Journal of Education 15,* edited by D. F. Lancy, (1979): 78–96.

Cherry, M. *Train Whistle Blues.* Garden City, NY: Doubleday, 1978.

Chesterfield, R. A. "Qualitative Methodology in the Evaluation of Early Childhood Bilingual Curriculum Models." In *Educational Evaluation: Ethnography in Theory, Practice and Politics,* edited by D. M. Fetterman & M. A. Pitman, 145–168. Newbury Park, CA: Sage, 1986.

Chilcott, J. H. "Enculturation in a Mexican Rancheria." *Journal of Educational Sociology 36*(1) (1962): 42–47.

Churchill, L. *Questioning Strategies in Sociolinguistics.* Rowley, MA: Newbury House, 1978.

Cicourel, A. V. *The Social Organization of Juvenile Justice.* New York: Wiley, 1968.

Cicourel, A. V. *Cognitive Sociology.* New York: Free Press, 1974.

Cicourel, A. V., Jennings, K. H., Jennings, S. H. M., Leiter, K. C. W., MacKay, R. W., Mehan, H., & Roth, D. R. *Language Use and School Performance.* New York: Academic, 1974.

Cicourel, A. V. & Kitsuse, J. A. *The Educational Decision Makers.* Indianapolis, IN: Bobbs-Merrill, 1963.

Cicourel, A. V. & Mehan, H. "Universal Development, Stratifying Practices, and Status Attainment." *Research in Social Stratification and Mobility 4* (1983): 3–27.

Clandinin, D. J. *Classroom Practice: Teacher Images in Action.* London: Falmer, 1986.

Clandinin, D. J., & Connelly, F. M. (1991). Narrative and Story in Practice and Research. In *The Reflective Eye: Case Studies in and on Educational Practice,* edited by D. A. Schön, 258–281. New York: Teachers College, 1991.

Clark, C. M. "What you can learn from Applesauce: A Case of Qualitative Inquiry in Use." In *Qualitative Inquiry in Education: The Continuing Debate,* edited by E. W. Eisner & A. Peshkin, 325–328. New York: Columbia Teachers College Press, 1990.

Clark, C. M., & Peterson, P. L. "Teachers' Thought Processes." In *Handbook of Research on Teaching,* 3rd ed., edited by M. C. Wittrock, 255–296. New York: MacMillan, 1983.

Clark, C. M., & Lampert, M. "The Study of Teacher Thinking: Implications for Teacher Education." *Journal of Teacher Education 37*(5) (1986): 27–31.

Clay, M. *The Early Detection of Reading Difficulties,* 3rd ed. Auckland: Heinemann, 1979.

Clifford, G. J. "Introduction." In *Lone Voyagers: Academic Women in Coeducational Universities 1870–1937,* edited by G. J. Clifford. New York: Feminist Press of CUNY, 1989.

Clifford, G. J., ed. *Lone Voyagers: Academic Women in Coeducational Universities 1870–1937,* New York: Feminist Press of CUNY, 1989.

Coats, A. W. "Explanations in History and Economics." *Social Research 56*(2): 331–60 (1989).

Cohen, D. K. "Teaching Practice: Plus ça change . . ." In *Contributing to Educational Change: Perspectives on Research and Practice,* edited by P. W. Jackson, 27–84. Berkeley, CA: McCutchan, 1989.

Cohen, D. K., & Ball, D. L. "Policy and Practice: An Overview." *Educational Evaluation and Policy Analysis 12*(3) (1990): 347–353.

Cohen, S. "History of the History of American Education, 1900–1976: The Uses of the Past." *Harvard Educational Review 36*(2) (1976): 298–330.

Cohen, Y. "The Shaping of Men's Minds: Adaptations to Imperatives of Culture." In *Anthropological Perspectives on Education,* edited by M. L. Wax, S. Diamond, and F. O. Gearing, 19–50. New York: Basic Books, 1971.

Cole, A. L. & Knowles, J. G. 1991. "Teacher Development Partnership Research: A Focus on Methods and Issues." Paper presented at the Continuity and Change in Teacher Education Conference, November. London, Ontario.

Cole, M., & Cole, S. *The Development of Children.* New York, Scientific American, 1989.

Cole, M. et al, *The Cultural Context of Learning & Thinking*. New York: Basic Books, 1971.

Collier, J. "Survival at Rough Rock: An Historical Overview of Rough Rock Demonstration School." *Anthropology and Education Quarterly 19*(3) (1988): 253–269.

Collins, J. "Language and Class in Minority Education." *Anthropology and Education Quarterly 17* (1988): 299–323.

Collins, T., & Noblit, G. W. "Stratification and Desegregation: The Case of Crossover High School." Final Report of NIE Contract #400-76-009, 1978.

Confrey, J. "Clinical Interviewing: Its Potential to Reveal Insights in Mathematics Education." In *Proceedings of the 4th International Conference for the Psychology of Mathematics Education,* edited by R. Karplus, 400–408. Berkeley, CA: University of California, 1980.

Connelly, F. M., & Clandinin, D. J. "Stories of Experience and Narrative Inquiry." *Educational Researcher 19*(5) (1990): 2–14.

Connelly, F. M., & Clandinin, D. J. *Teachers as Curriculum Planners: Narratives of Experience.* New York: Teachers College Press, 1988.

Conroy, P. *The Water is Wide.* New York: Bantam, [1972] 1987.

Cornell, E. "The Effect of Poetry in a First Grade Classroom." In *Seeing for Ourselves: Case Study Research by Teachers of Writing,* edited by G. L. Bissex, and G. L. and R. M. Bullock, 103–126. Portsmouth, NH: Heinemann, 1987.

Corsaro, W. A. *Friendship and Peer Culture in the Early Years.* Norwood, NJ: Ablex, 1985.

Corsaro, W. A. "Routines in the Peer Culture of American and Italian Nursery School Children." *Sociology of Education 61* (1988): 1–14.

Corsaro, W. A. "Peer Culture in the Preschool." *Theory into Practice 27*(1) (1988b): 19–24.

Corsaro, W. A., & Rizzo, T. A. "Discussions and Friendship: Socialization Processes in the Peer Culture of Italian Nursery School Children." *American Sociological Review 53* (1988): 879–894.

Covello, L. *The Social Background of the Italo-American School Child.* Leiden, Mouton, 1967.

Cox, J. M. "Autobiography and America." In *Aspects of Narrative,* edited by J. H. Miller, 252–277. New York: Columbia University Press, 1971.

Craig, E. *P. S. You're Not Listening.* New York: Baron, 1972.

Cremin, L., *Transformation of the School.* New York: Alfred Knopf, 1961.

Cremin, L. *American Education: The Metropolitan Experience,* 1876–1980: New York: Harper & Row, 1988.

Cronbach, L. & Associates. *Toward Reform of Program Evaluation.* San Francisco: Jossey Bass, 1980.

Csikszentmihalyi, M., & Larson, R. *Being Adolescent: Conflict and Growth in the Teenage Years.* New York: Basic Books, 1984.

Cusick, P. A. *Inside High School: The Student's World.* New York: Holt, Rinehart, and Winston, 1973.

Daiker, D. A., & Morenberg, M. *The Writing Teacher as Researcher.* Portsmouth, NH: Heinemann, 1990.

Daniels, L. A. "Little Things Add Up to Life." *New York Times Review of Books 94*(1): 46 (1989).

Davies, L. "Ethnography and Status: Focusing on Gender in Educational Research." In *Field Methods in the Study of Education,* edited by R. G. Burgess, 79–96. London: Falmer, 1985.

Davis, J. "Teachers, Kids and Conflict: Ethnography of a Junior High School." In *The Cultural Experience: Ethnography in Complex Society,* edited by J. P. Spradley and D. W. McCurdy, 103–119. Chicago: SRA, 1972.

Delamont, S. "The Old Girl Network: Reflections on Fieldwork at St. Luke's." In *The*

Research Process in Educational Settings: Ten Case Studies, edited by R. G. Burgess, 15–38. London: Methuen, 1984a.

Delamont, S. "Debs, Dollies, Swots and Weeds: Classroom Styles at St. Luke's." In *British Public Schools: Policy and Practice,* edited by G. Walford, 65–86. Lewes: Falmer Press, 1984b.

Delamont, S. *Fieldwork in Educational Settings: Method, Pitfalls, Perspectives.* London: Falmer, 1992.

Demos, J. *A Little Commonwealth: Family Life in Plymouth Colony.* New York: Oxford University Press, 1971.

Dennis, W. "The Hopi Child." In *Child Behavior and Development,* edited by R. G. Barnes, J. S. Kounin & H. F. Wright, 621–636. New York: McGraw Hill, 1943.

Denzin, N. K. *The Research Act: A Theoretical Introduction to Sociological Methods.* Chicago, Aldine, 1970.

Denzin, N. K. *The Research Act* (2nd ed.). New York: McGraw-Hill, 1978.

Denzin, N. K. *Interpretive Biography.* Newbury Park, CA: Sage, 1989.

Derrida, J. *Positions.* Chicago: University of Chicago Press, 1981.

DeWalt, M. K., & Troxell, B. K. "Old Order Mennonite One Room School." *Anthropology and Education Quarterly 20*(4) (1989): 308–325.

Deyhle, D. "Break Dancing and Breaking Out: Anglos, Utes and Navajos in a Border Reservation High School." *Anthropology and Education Quarterly 17*(2) (1986): 111–127.

Diesing, P. *Patterns of Discovery in the Social Sciences.* Chicago: Aldine, 1971.

Dobbert, M. L. "Another Route to a General Theory of Cultural Transmission: A Systems Model." *Anthropology and Education Quarterly 6*(2) (1975), 22–26.

Dobbert, M. L. *Ethnographic Research: Theory and Application for Modern Societies and Schools.* New York: Praeger, 1982.

Douglas, J. D. *Investigative Social Research.* Newbury Park, CA: Sage, 1976.

Douglas, J. D. *Creative Interviewing.* Newbury Park, CA: Sage, 1985.

Dubois, C. *The People of Alor.* Minneapolis: University of Minnesota Press, 1944.

Dyson, A. H. "Three Emergent Writers and the School Curriculum: Copying and other Myths." *The Elementary School Journal 85*(4) (1985): 497–512.

Early, M. "Major Research Programs." In *Handbook of Research on Teaching the English Language Arts,* edited by J. Flood, J. M. Jensen, D. Lapp, and J. R. Squire, 143–158. New York: Macmillan, 1991.

Easley, J. A., Jr. The Structual Paradigm in Protocol Analysis. *Journal for Research on Science Teaching 11*(3) (1974): 281–290.

Easley, J. A., Jr. Naturalistic Case Studies Exploring Social-Cognitive Mechanisms, and some Methodological Issues in Research on Problems of Teachers. *Journal for Research on Science Teaching 19* (1982): 191–203.

Easley, J. A., Jr. Alterative Research Metaphors and the Social Context of Mathematics Teaching and Learning. *For the Learning of Mathematics 1*(1) (1980): 32–40.

Eckert, P. *Jocks and Burnouts: Social Categories and Identity in the High School.* New York: Teachers College Press, 1989.

Eddy, E. *Becoming a Teacher.* New York: Teachers College Press, 1969.

Edelsky, C. Who's Got the Floor? *Language in Society 10* (1981): 383–421.

Edelsky, C. "Segmentation and Punctuation: Developmental Data from Young Writers in a Bilingual Program." *Research and the Teaching of English 17*(2) (1983): 135–156.

Edelsky, C. "Whose Agenda is this Anyway?" A response to McKenna, Robinson & Miller. *Educational Researcher 20*(8) (1990): 7–11.

Edelsky, C., Altwerger, B. & Flores, B. *Whole Language: What's the Difference?* Portsmouth, NH: Heinemann, 1991.

Edelsky, C., & Draper, K. "Reading/Reading, Writing/Writing, Text/Text." *Reading-Canada-Lecture 7* (1989): 201–16.

Edelsky, C., Draper, K., & Smith, K. "Hookin' 'em in at the Start of School in a 'Whole Language' Classroom." *Anthropology and Education Quarterly 14*(4) (1983): 257–281.

Eder, D. (1982). "Differences in Communicative Styles across Ability Groups." In *Communication in the Classroom,* edited by L. C. Wilkinson, 245–264. New York: Academic Press, 1982.

Edwards, N. *Stand and Deliver.* New York: Scholastic, 1989.

Eibl-Eibesfeldt, I. Patterns of Parent-Child Interaction in a Cross-Cultural Perspective. In *The Behavior of Human Infants,* edited by A. Oliverio and M. Cappella, 177–217. New York: Plenum, 1983.

Eisele, C. "John Dewey and the Immigrants." *History of Education Quarterly 15*(1) (1975): 67–86.

Eisenhart, M. A. "Women Choose their Careers: A Study of Natural Decision Making." *The Review of Higher Education 8*(3) (1985): 247–270.

Eisner, E. W. "Educational Connoisseurship and Educational Criticism: Their Forms and Functions in Educational Evaluation." *Journal of Aesthetic Education 10*(3–4) (1976): 135–150.

Eisner, E. W. "On the Differences between Scientific and Artistic Approaches to Qualitative Research." *Educational Researcher 10* (1981): 5–9.

Eisner, E. W. "Anastasia Might Still be Alive but the Monarchy is Dead." *Educational Researcher 12*(5) (1983): 13–14, 23–24.

Eisner, E. W. *The Enlightened Eye: Qualitative Inquiry and the Enhancement of Educational Practice.* New York: Macmillan, 1991.

Eisner, E. W., & Peshkin, A. eds. *Qualitative Inquiry in Education: The Continuing Debate.* New York: Columbia Teachers College Press, 1990.

Elbaz, F. *Teacher Thinking: A Study of Practical Knowledge.* London: Croom Helm, 1983.

Ellis, J. J., & Moore, R. *School for Soldiers: West Point and the Profession of Arms.* New York: Oxford University Press, 1974.

Emig, J. *The Composing Processes of Twelfth Graders.* Urbana, IL: NCTE, 1971.

Erickson, F. "What Makes School Ethnography Ethnographic?" Revised version. *Anthropology and Education Quarterly 15*(1) ([1973] 1984): 51–66.

Erickson, F. "Classroom Discourse as Improvisation: Relationships between Academic Task Structure and Social Participation Structure in Lessons." In *Communication in the Classroom,* edited by L. C. Wilkinson, 153–182. New York: Academic Press, 1982a.

Erickson, F. "Taught Cognitive Learning in its Immediate Environments—A Neglected Topic in the Anthropology of Education." *Anthropology of Education Quarterly 15* (1982b): 148–80.

Erickson, F. "What Critical and Feminist Theory have done for Qualitative Methods." Paper presented at the annual meeting of the American Educational Research Association. April. San Francisco, 1992.

Erickson, F. & Schultz, J. *The Counselor as Gatekeeper: Social Interaction in Interviews.* New York: Academic Press, 1982.

Ericsson, K. A., & Simon, H. A. *Protocol Analysis.* Cambridge, MA: MIT Press, 1984.

Erlwanger, S. H. "Benny's Conceptions of Rules and Answers in IPI Mathematics." *Journal of Children's Mathematical Behavior 1*(2) (1973): 7–26.

Everhart, R. B. "Cognitive Mapping in the Study of the Social and Formal Organization of the School." Paper presented to the meeting of the American Anthropological Association, December. San Francisco, 1975.

Everhart, R. B. *Reading, Writing, and Resistance: Adolescence and Labor in a Junior High School.* Boston: Routledge, Kegan, and Paul, 1983.

Fantino, E., Weigele, S., & Lancy, D. F. "Aggressive Display in the Siamese Fighting Fish (Betta Splenden)." *Learning and Motivation 3* (1972): 457–468.

Fass, P. *Outside in: Minorities and American Education in the Twentieth Century.* New York: Oxford University Press, 1988.

Feinburg, W. On Reading Dewey. *History of Education Quarterly 15*(3) (1975): 395–415.

Ferrell, B. G., & Compton, D. W. "Use of Ethnographic Techniques for Evaluation in a Large School District: The Vanguard Case." In *Educational Evaluation: Ethnography in Theory, Practice and Politics,* edited by D. M. Fetterman & M. A. Pitman, 171–191. Newbury Park, CA: Sage, 1986.

Fetterman, D. M., ed. *Qualitative Approaches to Evaluation in Education.* New York: Praeger, 1988.

Fetterman, D. M. *Ethnography: Step by Step.* Newbury Park, CA: Sage, 1989.

Fetterman, D. M., & Pitman, M. A., eds. *Educational Evaluation: Ethnography in Theory, Practice and Politics.* Newbury Park, CA: Sage, 1986.

Fine, G. A. *Shared Fantasy.* Chicago: University of Chicago Press, 1983.

Firestone, W. A. "Meaning in Method: The Rhetoric of Quantitative and Qualitative Research." *Educational Researcher 16*(7) (1987): 16–21.

Fitzpatrick, E. (1989). "For the Women of the University: Marion Talbot 1858–1948." In *Lone Voyagers: Academic Women in Coeducational Universities 1870–1937,* edited by G. J. Clifford, 87–124. New York: Feminist Press of CUNY, 1989.

Florio-Ruane, S. "Conversation and Narrative in Collaborative Research." In *Stories Lives Tell: Narrative and Dialogue in Education,* edited by C. Witherell and N. Noddings, 234–256. New York: Teachers College Press, 1991.

Flower, L. S., & Hayes, J. R. "The Dynamics of Composing: Making Plans and Juggling Constraints." In *Cognitive Processes in Writing,* edited by L. W. Gregg and E. R. Steinberg, 31–50. Hillsdale, NJ: Erlbaum, 1980.

Flower, L. S., Hayes, J. R. "Plans that Guide the Composing Process." In *Writing: The Nature, Development, and Teaching of Written Communication,* edited by C. H. Frederiksen and J. F. Dominic, 39–66. Hillsdale, NJ: Erlbaum, 1981a.

Flower, L. S., & Hayes, J. R. "The Pregnant Pause: An Inquiry into the Nature of Planning." *Research and the Teaching of English 15*(3) (1981b): 229–243.

Fordham, S., & Obgu, J. U. "Black Students' School Success: Coping with the Burden of 'Acting White.' " *The Urban Review 18*(3) (1986): 176–206.

Forsyth, A. S., & Lancy, D. F. "Simulated Travel and Place Location Learning in a Computer Adventure Game." *Journal of Educational Computing Research 3* (1987): 377–394.

Forsyth, A. S., & Lancy, D. F. Girls and Microcomputers: A Hopeful Finding Regarding Software. *Computers in the Schools 6*(3/4) (1989): 51–59.

Frake, C. O. The Ethnographic Study of Cognitive Systems. In *Cognitive Anthropology,* edited by S. A. Tyler, 28–41. New York: Holt, Rinehart, and Winston, 1969.

Frazer, J. G. (1900/1922). *The Golden Bough.* Macmillan, 1922.

Freedman, D. G. "The Development of Social Hierarchies." In *Contemporary Readings in Child Psychology,* edited by E. M. Hetherington and R. C. Parke, 372–379. New York: McGraw-Hill, 1977.

Freedman, D. G., & Omark, D. R. "Ethology, Genetics, and Education." In *Cultural Relevance and Educational Issues,* edited by F. A. J. Ianni & E. Storey, 250–283. Boston: Little, Brown, 1973.

Freedman, S. G. *Small Victories: The Real World of a Teacher, Her Students and their High School.* New York: Harper & Row, 1990.

Freeman, D. *Margaret Mead and Samoa: The Making and Unmaking of an Anthropological Myth.* Cambridge, MA: Harvard University Press, 1983.

Fuchs, E. *Teacher's Talk: Views from Inside City Schools.* Garden City, NY: Doubleday, 1969.

Gage, N. L. "The Paradigm Wars and their Aftermath." *Educational Researcher 18*(7) (1989): 4–10.

Gallimore, R. J., Boggs, J. W., & Jordan, C. *Culture, Behavior, and Education: A Study of Hawaiian Americans.* Beverly Hills, CA: Sage, 1974.

Gamoran, A., & Berends, M. "The Effects of Stratification in Secondary Schools: Synthesis of Survey and Ethnographic Research." *Review of Educational Research 57*(4) (1987): 415–435.

Garfinkel, H. *Studies in Ethnomethodology.* Englewood Cliffs, NJ: Prentice Hall, 1967.

Garfinkel, H. (1974). "The Origins of the term 'Ethnomethodology'." In *Ethnomethodology,* edited by R. Turner, 15–18. Baltimore, MD: Penguin, 1974.

Garling, T., & Valsiner, J., eds. *Children within Environments: Toward a Psychology of Accident Prevention.* New York: Plenum Press, 1985.

Gearing, F. O., & Epstein, P. "Learning to Wait: An Ethnographic Probe into the Operations of an Item of Hidden Curriculum." In *Doing the Ethnography of Schooling: Educational Anthropology in Action,* edited by G. D. Spindler, 240–267. New York: Holt, Rinehart, & Winston, 1982.

Geertz, C. *The Interpretation of Cultures.* New York: Basic Books, 1973.

Geertz, C. "From the Native's Point of View." *Bulletin of the American Academy of Arts and Sciences 28* (1974): 27–45.

Gerlach, J. M., & Monseau, V. R. *Missing Chapters: Ten Pioneering Women in NCTE and English Education.* Urbana, IL: National Council of Teachers of English, 1992.

Gershman, K. "Surviving through Time: A Life History of a High School Drama Production." *International Journal of Qualitative Studies in Education 1*(3) (1988): 239–262.

Gibson, M. A. "Reputation and Respectability: How Competing Cultural Systems Affect Students' Performance in School." *Anthropology and Education Quarterly 13*(1) (1982): 3–27.

Gibson, M. A. "Home-School-Community Linkages: A Study of Education Opportunity for Punjabi Youth." Final report to the National Institute of Education, Washington, DC: 1983.

Gibson, M. A. "Collaborative Educational Ethnography: Problems and Profits." Anthropology and Education Quarterly *16* (1985): 124–148.

Gibson, M. A. (1987). "Punjabi Immigrants in an American High School." In *Interpretive Ethnography of Education,* edited by G. D. Spindler & L. Spindler, 281–310. Hillsdale, NJ: Erlbaum, 1987.

Gibson, M. A. (1988). *Accommodation without Assimilation: Sikh Immigrants in an American High School.* Ithaca, New York: Cornell University Press, 1988.

Glaser, B. G., & Strauss, A. L. *The Discovery of Grounded Theory: Strategies for Qualitative Research.* Chicago: Aldine, 1967.

Glaser, R. *Adaptive Education: Individual Diversity and Learning.* New York: Holt, Rinehart, and Winston, 1976.

Gleason, J. J. *Special Education in Context.* New York: Cambridge University Press, 1989.

Goetz, J. P. "Behavioral Configurations in the Classroom: A Case Study." *Journal of Research and Development in Education 9*(4) (1976): 36–49.

Goetz, J. P., & LeCompte, M. D. *Ethnography and Qualitative Design in Educational Research.* New York: Academic Press, 1984.

Goffman, E. *The Presentation of Self in Everyday Life.* Garden City, NY: Doubleday, Anchor, 1959.

Goffman, E. *Asylums.* Garden City, NY: Anchor, 1961.

Goffman, E. *Behavior in Public Places.* Glencoe, IL: Free Press, 1963.

Goldstein, G., & Lancy D. F. "Cognitive Development in Autistic Children." In *Cognitive*

Development in Atypical Children, edited by F. J. Morrison and L. S. Siegel, 83–112. New York: Springer, 1985.

Goodenough, W. M. *Culture, Language, and Society.* Reading, MA: Addison-Wesley, 1971.

Goodlad, J. I. *A Place Called School.* New York: McGraw-Hill, 1984.

Goodnow, J. J., Cashmore, J., Cotton, S., & Knight, R. "Mother's Developmental Timetables in Two Cultural Groups." *International Journal of Psychology 19* (1984): 193–205.

Goodson, I. F. "Teachers' Lives." In *Qualitative Research in Education: Teaching and Learning Qualitative Traditions,* edited by J. B. Allen and J. P. Goetz, 150–159. Athens: University of Georgia, 1989.

Goodson, I. F. "Teachers' Lives and Educational Research." In *Biography, Identity and Schooling: Episodes in Educational Research,* edited by I. F. Goodson and R. Walker, 137–149. London: Falmer, 1991.

Gorden, R. L. *Interviewing: Strategy, Techniques & Tactics* (rev. ed.). Homewood, IL: Dorsey, 1980.

Gordon, L. "Comments on 'That Noble Dream.'" *American Historical Review 3:96,* 683–687 (1991).

Goswami, D., & Stillman, P. R., eds. *Reclaiming the Classroom: Teacher Research as an Agency for Change.* Portsmouth, NH: Boynton/Cook, 1987.

Gottshalk, L. *Understanding History: A Primer of Historical Method.* New York: Alfred Knopf, 1950.

Gould, S. J. *The Mismeasure of Man.* New York: Norton, 1981.

Grant, G. *The Perpetual Dream: Reform and Experiment in American Education.* Chicago: University of Chicago Press, 1977.

Graves, D. H. "An Examination of the Writing Processes of Seven-Year-Old Children." *Research and the Teaching of English 9* (1975): 227–241.

Green, J. L. "Pedagogical Style Differences as Related to Comprehension Performance: Grades One through Three." Ph.D. diss., University of California, Berkeley, 1977.

Green, J. L., & Harker, J. O. "Gaining Access to Learning: Conversational, Social and Cognitive Demands of Group Participation." In *Communication in the Classroom,* edited by L. C. Wilkinson, 183–222. New York: Academic Press, 1982.

Green, J. L., & Harker, J. O., & Golden, J. M. In *Schooling in Social Context,* edited by G. W. Noblit and W. T. Pink, 46–77. Norwood, NJ: Ablex, 1987.

Greer, C. *The Great School Legend: A Revisionist Interpretation of American Public Education.* New York: Viking Press, 1972.

Grieve, R. "Decentralization and the Community School in Northern Province." In *The community school,* special issue of the *Papua New Guinea Journal of Education 15,* edited by D. F. Lancy, (1979): 97–102.

Grindal, B. *Growing Up in Two Worlds: Education and Transition Among the Sisala of Northern Ghana.* New York: Holt, Rinehart, and Winston, 1972.

Gross, N., Giacquinta, J. B., & Bernstein, A. *Implementing Organization Innovations: A Sociological Analysis of Planned Educational Change.* New York: Basic Books, 1971.

Grossman, P. L. "What are We Talking about Anyway? Subject-Matter Knowledge of Secondary English Teachers." *Advances in Research on Teaching 2* (1991): 245–262.

Grumet, M. R. *Bitter Milk: Women and Teaching.* Amherst, MA: University of Massachusetts Press, 1988.

Grumet, M. R. "The Politics of Personal Knowledge." In *Stories Lives Tell: Narrative and Dialogue in Education,* edited by C. C. Witherell and N. Noddings, 67–77. New York: Teachers College Press, 1991.

Guba, E. G., & Lincoln, Y. S. *Effective Evaluation: Improving the Usefulness of Evaluation Results through Responsive and Naturalistic Approaches.* San Francisco: Jossey Bass, 1981.

Gudmundsdottir, S. "Values in Pedagogical Content Knowledge." *Journal of Teacher Education. 41*(3) (1990): 44–52.

Gump, P. V. "Operating Environments in Schools of Open and Traditional Design." *School Review 84*(4) (1974): 575–593.

Gump, P. V. "School Environment." In *Children and the Environment,* edited by I. Altman and J. F. Wohlwill, 33–51. New York: Plenum, 1978.

Gumperz, J. "Conversational Inference and Classroom Learning." In *Ethnography and Language in Educational Settings,* edited by J. Green and C. Wallat, 3–24. Norwood, NJ: Ablex, 1981.

Hallpike, C. R. *Bloodshed and Vengeance in the Papuan Mountains.* Oxford: Oxford University Press, 1977.

Hamilton, D. *In Search of Structure. Essays from an Open Plan School.* Edinburgh, Scottish Council for Research in Education, 1976.

Hammersley, M. *The Ethnography of Schooling: Methodological Issues.* Duffield: Natterton, 1983.

Hammersley, M. "Staffroom News." In *Classrooms and Staffrooms,* edited by A. Hargreaves and P. Woods, 203–214. London: Open University Press, 1984.

Hammersley, M., & Atkinson P. *Ethnography: Principles in Practice.* London: Tavistock, 1983.

Hanks, L. M. "Indifference to Modern Education in a Thai Farming Community." In *Cultural Relevance and Educational Issues,* edited by F. A. J. Ianni and E. Storey, 357–371. Boston: Little, Brown, 1973.

Hanna, J. L. *Disruptive School Behavior: Class, Race, and Culture.* New York: Holmes & Meier, 1988.

Hareven, T. K. *Transitions: The Family and the Life Course in Historical Perspective.* New York: Academic Press, 1978.

Hargreaves, A. "Experience Counts, Theory Doesn't: Teachers Talk about Their Work." *Sociology of Education 57*: 244–254 (1984).

Hargreaves, D. H. *The Challenge for the Comprehensive School.* London: Routledge, 1982.

Harris, M. *The Rise of Anthropological Theory.* New York: Crowell, 1968.

Hart-Landsberg, S. *Toward a Clear Picture of Thinkabout: An Account of Classroom Use.* Bloomington, IN: Agency for Instructional Television, 1982.

Hartwig, F., & Dearing, B. E. *Exploratory Data Analysis.* Newbury Park, CA: Sage, 1979.,

Hatch, J. A. "Status and Power in a Kindergarten Peer Group." *The Elementary School Journal 88*(1): 79–92 (1987).

Hayes, J. R., & Flower, L. S. "Uncovering Cognitive Processes in Writing: An Introduction to Protocol Analysis." In *Research on Writing,* edited by Mosenthal, P., Tamor, L., & Walmsely, S. A., 207–220. New York: Longman, 1983.

Hayes, J. R., & Flower, L. S. "Identifying the Organization of Writing Processes." In *Cognitive Processes in Writing,* edited by L. W. Gregg and E. R. Steinberg, 3–30. Hillsdale, NJ: Erlbaum, 1980.

Heath, S. B. "What No Bedtime Story Means." *Language in Society 11*(1): 49–76 (1982).

Heath, S. B. *Ways with Words.* New York: Cambridge University Press, 1983.

Hemwall, M. K. (1984). "Hearing Impaired Students in the Mainstream." In *Ethnography in Educational Evaluation,* edited by D. M. Fetterman, 133–152. Newbury Park, CA: Sage, 1984.

Herndon, J. *The Way it Spozed to be.* New York: Simon & Schuster, 1968.

Hiner, N. R. "Cotton Mather and His Children: The Evaluation of a Parent Educator, 1686–1728." In *Regulated Children/Liberated Children: Education in Psychohistorical Perspectives,* edited by B. Finkelstein, 24–43. New York: Psychohistory Press, 1979.

Hirsch, E. D. *Cultural Literacy.* Boston: Houghton-Mifflin, 1987.

Hitchcock, G., & Hughes, D. *Research and the Teacher.* London: Routledge, 1989.

Hoffer, T., Greely, A. M., & Coleman, J. S. "Achievement Growth in Public and Catholic Schools." *Sociology of Education 58*: 74–97 (1985).

Hoffman, N. *Woman's "True" Profession: Voices from the History of Teaching.* Old Westbury, NY: Feminist, 1981.

Hogan, D. J. *Class and Reform: School and Society in Chicago, 1880–1930.* Philadelphia: University of Pennsylvania Press, 1985.

Hold, B. C. L. "Attention Structure and Rank Specific Behavior in Preschool Children." In *The Social Structure of Attention,* edited by M. R. A. Chance and R. R. Larsen. London: Academic Press, 1976.

Hollingshead, A. B. *Elmtown's Youth and Elmtown Revisited.* New York: Wiley, [1949] 1975.

Hoover, J. H. "A Comparison of Traditional Pre-School and Companion Play from a Social/Cognitive Perspective." Master's thesis, Utah State University, 1985.

Horowitz, R. *Honor and the American Dream.* Brunswick, NJ: Rutgers University Press, 1983.

Hostetler, J. A., & Huntington, G. E. *Children in Amish Society.* New York: Holt, Rinehart, and Winston, 1971.

Hostetler, J. H. "Education in Communitarian Societies—The Old Order Amish and Hutterite Brethren." In *Education and Cultural Process,* edited by G. D. Spindler, 119–138. New York: Holt, Rinehart, and Winston, 1974.

Howard, A. *Learning to be Rotuman.* New York: Teachers College Press, 1970.

Howe, K. R. "Two Dogmas of Educational Research." *Educational Researcher 44*(8) (1985): 10–18.

Howe, K. R., & Eisenhart, M. "Standards for Qualitative (and Quantitative) Research: A Prolegomenon." *Educational Researcher, 19*(4) (1990): 2–9.

Huberman, A. M., & Miles, M. B. *Innovation up Close: How School Improvement Works.* New York: Plenum, 1984.

Hughes, H. S. *History as Art and as Science: Twin Vistas on the Past.* New York: Harper & Row, 1964.

Humphreys, A. P., & Smith, P. K. "Rough and Tumble, Friendship, and Dominance in School Children: Evidence for Continuity and Change with Age." *Child Development 58* (1987): 201–212.

Husserl, E. *Ideas: General Introduction to Pure Phenomenology.* New York: Macmillan, [1913] 1962.

Hutt, C. Exploration and Play in Children. In *Child's Play,* edited by R. E. Heron and B. Sutton-Smith, 231–251. New York: Wiley, 1971.

Hutt, S., & Hutt, C. *Direct Observation and Measurement of Behavior.* Springfield, IL: Thomas, 1970.

Hymes, D. H. "What is Ethnography?" Philadelphia, PA: University of Pennsylvania, ED 159–234, 1977.

Ianni, F. A. J., & Storey, E., eds. *Cultural Relevance and Educational Issues.* Boston: Little, Brown, 1973.

Inhelder, B., & Piaget, J. *The Growth of Logical Thinking from Children to Adolescence: An Essay on the Construction of Formal Operational Structures.* Translated by A. Parsons & S. Milgram. (pp. 107–122) New York: Basic Books, 1958.

Jackson, P. W. *Life in Classrooms.* New York: Holt, Rinehart, and Winston, 1968.

Jacob, E. "Qualitative Research Traditions: A Review." *Review of Educational Research, 57* (1987): 1–50.

James, D. *The Taming: A Teacher Speaks.* New York: McGraw Hill, 1969.

Jelinek, E. C. *Women's Autobiography: Essays in Criticism.* Bloomington, IN: Indiana University Press, 1980.

Jenkins, R. *Lads, Citizens and Ordinary Kids: Working Class Life Styles in Belfast.* London: Routledge, 1983.

Jocano, F. L. *Growing up in a Philippine Barrio.* New York, Holt, Rinehart and Winston, 1969.

Johnson, N. B. "The Material Culture of Public School Classrooms: The Symbolic Integration of Local Schools and National Culture." *Anthropology and Education Quarterly 9*(3) (1980): 173–190.

Kaestle, C., & Vinovskis, M. *Education and Social Change in Nineteenth Century Massachusetts.* New York: Cambridge University Press, 1979.

Karier, C. "Business Values and the Educational State." In *Roots of Crisis,* edited by C. Karier, P. Violas, & J. Spring, 6–29. Chicago: Rand McNally, 1973a.

Karier, C. "Liberal Ideology and Orderly Change. In *Roots of Crisis,* edited by C. Karier, P. Violas, & J. Spring, 84–107. Chicago: Rand McNally, 1973b.

Karier, C. "John Dewey and the New Liberalism: Some Reflections and Responses." *History of Education Quarterly 15*(3) (1975): 417–44.

Karier, C., Violas, P., & Spring, J., eds. *Roots of Crisis: American Education in the Twentieth Century.* Chicago: Rand McNally, 1973.

Katz, M. *The Irony of Early School Reform: Educational Innovation in Mid-Nineteenth Century Massachusetts.* Cambridge: Harvard University Press, 1968.

Katz, M. "Who Went to School?" *History of Education Quarterly 12*(4) (1972): 432–454.

Katz, M. "Not the whole story." *History of Education Quarterly 25* (1/2): 175–179 (1985).

Katz, M., and Davey, I. "School Attendance and Early Industrialization in a Canadian City: A Multivariate Analysis." *History of Education Quarterly 18*(2) (1978): 271–293.

Kaufer, D. S., Hayes, J. R., & Flower, L. S. "Composing Written Sentences." *Research and the Teaching of English 20*(2) (1986): 121–140.

Kennedy, M. M. "Generalizing from Single Case Studies." *Evaluation Quarterly 3*(4) (1979): 661–679.

Kidder, T. *Soul of a New Machine.* Boston: Little, Brown, 1981.

Kidder, T. *Among Schoolchildren.* Boston: Houghton Mifflin, 1989.

King, A. R. *The School at Mopass.* New York: Holt, Rinehart and Winston, 1967.

King, R. A. *All Things Bright and Beautiful: A Sociological Study of Infants' Classrooms.* Chichester, UK: Wiley, 1978.

Kinkead, J. A. (in preparation). *Uncommon Women: Personal Narratives of 19th Century Utah Schoolmarms.*

Kinkead, J. A., & Lancy, D. F. "Looking for Yourself: The Classroom Teacher as Researcher." *Utah English Journal 18*(1) (1990): 2–13.

Kirk, J., & Miller, M. L. *Reliability and Validity in Qualitative Research.* Beverly Hills, CA: Sage, 1986.

Kiser, E., and Hechter, M. "The Role of General Theory in Comparative-Historical Sociology." *American Journal of Sociology 97*(1) (1991): 1–30.

Kleinfeld, J. "First Do No Harm: A Reply to Courtney Cazden." *Anthropology and Education Quarterly, 14*(4) (1983): 282–287.

Knowles, J. G. "A Beginning Teacher's Experience: Reflections on Becoming a Teacher." *Language Arts 65*(7) (1990): 702–712.

Knowles, J. G., & Hoefler, V. B. "The Student Teacher Who Couldn't Go Away: Learning from Failure." *Journal of Experiential Education 12*(2) (1989): 14–21.

Kohl, H. *36 Children.* New York, NY: New American Library, 1967.

Kohl, H. *Growing Minds: On Becoming a Teacher.* New York: Harper & Row, 1984.

Kounin, J. *Discipline and Group Management in Classrooms.* New York: Holt, Rinehart, and Winston, 1970.

Kounin, J. S., & Gump, P. V. "Signal Systems of Lesson Settings and the Task-Related Behavior of Preschool Children." *Journal of Educational Psychology 66* (1974): 554–562.

Kozol, J. *Death at an Early Age: The Destruction of the Hearts and Minds of Negro Children in the Boston Public Schools,* 2nd ed. New York: New American Library, [1967] 1985.

Kroeber, T. *Ishi in Two Worlds: A Biography of the Last Wild Indian in North America.* Berkeley: University of California Press, 1961.

Kuhn, T. *The Structure of Scientific Revolutions.* Chicago: University of Chicago Press, 1970.

Lacey, C. *Hightown Grammar: The School in a Social System.* Manchester: Manchester University Press, 1970.

Lacey, C. "Intragroup Competitive Pressures and the Selection of Social Strategies: Neglected Paradigms in the Study of Adolescent Socialization." In *The Anthropological Study of Education,* edited by C. J. Calhoun and F. A. J. Ianni, 190–216. The Hague: Mouton, 1976.

LaFreniere, P. J., & Charlesworth, W. F. "Effects of Friendship and Dominance Status on Pupil's Resource Utilization in Cooperative/Competitive Situations." *International Journal of Behavior Development 10*(3) (1987): 345–358.

Lamme, L. L., & Childers, N. M. "The Composing Processes of Three Young Children." *Research and the Teaching of English 17*(1) (1983): 31–50.

Lampert, M. "Teaching Multiplication." *Journal of Mathematical Behavior 5* (1986): 241–280.

Lancy, D. F. "The Social Organization of Learning: Initiation Rituals and Public Schools." *Human Organization 34* (1975): 371–380.

Lancy, D. F. "The Beliefs and Behaviors of Pupils in an Experimental School: Introduction and Overview." *Learning Research and Development Center Publication Series 3*: ED 127301 (1976a).

Lancy, D. F. "The Beliefs and Behaviors of Pupils in an Experimental School: The Science Lab." *Learning Research and Development Center Publication Series 6*: ED 127300 (1976b).

Lancy, D. F. "The Beliefs and Behaviors of Pupils in an Experimental School: School Settings" *Learning Research and Development Center Publication Series 21*: ED 134573 (1976c).

Lancy, D. F. "The Impact of the Modern World on Village Life: Gbarngasuakwelle." *Papua New Guinea Journal of Education 13*(1) (1977a): 36–44.

Lancy, D. F. "Studies of Memory in Culture." *Annals of the New York Academy of Sciences 285* (1977b): 297–307.

Lancy, D. F. "The Classroom as Phenomenon." In *The Contribution of Social Psychology to Education,* edited by D. Bar-Tal and L. Saxe, 111–132. New York: Wiley, 1978.

Lancy, D. F. , ed. "The Community School." *Papua New Guinea Journal of Education,* special issue, 15, 1979.

Lancy, D. F. "Becoming a Blacksmith in Gbarngasuakwelle." *Anthropology and Education Quarterly 11* (1980a): 266–274.

Lancy, D. F. "Play in Species Adaptation." *Annual Review of Anthropology 9* (1980b): 471–495.

Lancy, D. F. "Socio-dramatic Play and the Acquisition of Occupational Roles." *Review Journal of Philosophy and Social Science 7* (1982): 285–295.

Lancy, D. F. *Cross-Cultural Studies in Cognition and Mathematics.* New York: Academic Press, 1983.

Lancy, D. F. "Play in Anthropological Perspective." In *Play in Animals and Humans,* edited by P. K. Smith, 295–303. Oxford: Basil Blackwell, 1984.

Lancy, D. F. "Will Video Games Alter the Relationship between Play and Development?" In *Meaningful Play, Playful Meanings,* edited by G. A. Fine, 219–230. Champaign, IL: Human Kinetics, 1987a.

Lancy, D. F. "The Message is the Medium: Studies of Computer Applications in Schools." In *The Study of Learning Environments 2,* edited by B. J. Fraser, 64–71. Perth: Curtin University Press, 1987b.

Lancy, D. F. "An Information Processing Framework for the Study of Culture and Thought." In *Thinking Across Cultures,* edited by D. Topping, V. Kobayashi and D. Crowell, 13–26. Hillsdale, NJ: Erlbaum, 1989.

Lancy, D. F. "The Microcomputer and Social Studies. *OCCS Review 26*(1) (1990): 30–38.

Lancy, D. F. "The Autotelic Learning Environment Revisited: An Exploratory Study." *Play and Culture 4* (1991): 124–128.

Lancy, D. F. *Playing on the Motherground: Cultural Routines for Childrens' Development.* New York: Guilford, forthcoming.

Lancy, D. F., Cohen, H., Evans, B., Levine, N., & Nevin, M. L. "Using the Joystick as a Tool to Promote Intellectual Growth and Social Interaction." *Laboratory for the Comparative Study of Human Cognition Newsletter 7* (1985): 110–185.

Lancy, D. F, Draper, K., & Boyce, G. "Parental Influence on Children's Acquisition of Reading." *Contemporary Issues in Reading 4*(1) (1989): 83–93.

Lancy, D. F., Forsyth, A. S., Jr., & Meeks, L. L. "An After-School Program Utilizing Computers." *National Association of Laboratory Schools Journal 11*(2) (1987): 1–9.

Lancy, D. F., & Goldstein, G. "Using Nonverbal Piagetian Tasks to Assess the Cognitive Development of Autistic Children." *Child Development 53* (1982): 1233–1244.

Lancy, D. F., & Hayes, B. L. "Interactive Fiction and the Reluctant Reader." *English Journal* 77(6) (1988): 42–46.

Lancy, D. F., & Madsen, M. C. "Cultural Patterns and the Social Behavior of Children: Two Studies from Papua New Guinea." *Ethos 9* (1981): 201–216.

Lancy, D. F., & Nattiv, A. "Parents as Volunteer Story-Book Readers/Listeners: The Sunrise Project." *Childhood Education 68*(4) 208–212, 1992.

Lancy, D. F., Souviney, R. J., & Kada, V. "Intracultural Variation in Cognitive Development: Conservation of Length among the Imbonggu." *International Journal of Behavioral Development 4* (1981): 455–468.

Lancy, D. F., & Stranthern, A. J. "Making-Twos: Pairing as an Alternative to the Taxonomic Mode of Representation." *American Anthropologist 81* (1981): 777–795.

Lancy, D. F., & Tindall, B. D., eds. *The Anthropological Study of Play: Problems and Prospects.* West Point, NY: Leisure Press, [1976] 1979.

Lancy, D. F., & Zupsic, A. B. "A Case Study of Running Start." Paper presented at a conference on Family and School Support for Early Literacy, Toledo, May, 1991.

Langer, J. A. "Musings . . . Red Herrings in Language Research: Qualitative vs Quantitative Methods Endorsement of Traditions." *Research in the Teaching of English 21*(2) (1987): 117–119.

Langness, L. L., & Frank, G. *Lives: An Anthropological Approach to Biography.* Novato, CA: Chandler and Sharp, 1981.

Lareau, A. "Family-School Relationships: A View from the Classroom." *Educational Policy 3*(3) (1989a): 245–259.

Lareau, A. *Home Advantage: Social Class and Parental Intervention in Elementary Education.* New York: Falmer, 1989b.

Lather, P. "Research as Praxis." *Harvard Educational Review 56*(3) (1986): 257–277.

Lauer, J. M., & Asher, J. W. *Composition Research: Empirical Designs.* New York: Oxford University Press, 1988.

Lawler, R. W. *Computer Experience and Cognitive Development: A Child's Learning in a Computer Culture.* New York: Wiley, 1985.

Leacock, E. B. *Teaching and Learning in City Schools.* New York: Basic, 1969.

Leean, C. "Illustrative Examples of Case Studies." In *Case Study Methodology in Educational Evaluation,* edited by W. W. Welch, 15–29. Minneapolis: University of Minnesota, 1981.

Leinhardt, G. "Development of an Expert Explanation: An Analysis of a Sequence of Subtraction Lessons." *Cognition and Instruction* 4(4) (1987): 225–282.

Leinhardt, G. "Expertise in Instructional Lessons: An Example from Fractions." In *Prospectives on Research on Effective Mathematics Teaching,* edited by D. A. Grouws and T. J. Cooney, 48–64. Hillsdale, NJ: Erlbaum, 1988.

Leinhardt, G. "Math Lessons: A Contrast of Novice and Expert Competence." *Journal of Research in Mathematics Education* 20(1) (1989): 52–75.

Leinhardt, G., & Fienberg, J. "Integration of Lesson Structure and Teachers' Subject Matter Knowledge." University of Pittsburgh Learning Research and Development Center, 1990.

Leinhardt, G., & Smith, D. A. "Expertise in Mathematics Instruction: Subject Matter Knowledge." *Journal of Educational Psychology* 77(3) (1985): 247–271.

Leinhardt, G., Weidman, C., & Hammond, K. M. "Introduction and Integration of Classroom Routines by Expert Teachers." *Curriculum Inquiry* 17(2) (1987): 135–176.

Leis, P. E. *Enculturation and Socialization in Ijaw Village.* New York: Holt, Rinehart and Winston, 1972.

Leiter, K. C. W. "Teachers' Use of Background Knowledge to Interpret Test Scores." *Sociology of Education* 49 (1976): 59–65.

Leiter, K. C. W. *A Primer on Ethnomethodology.* New York: Oxford University Press, 1980.

Lewis, O. *La Vida.* New York: Random House, 1966.

Lightfoot, S. L. *Worlds Apart: Relationships Between Families and Schools.* New York: Basic Books, 1978.

Lincoln, Y. S., & Guba, E. G. *Naturalistic Inquiry.* Newbury Park, CA: Sage, 1985.

Little, J. W. "The Persistence of Privacy: Autonomy and Initiative in Teachers' Professional Relations." *Teachers College Record* 91(4) (1990): 509–536.

Locke, L. F., Spirduso, W. W., & Silverman, S. J. *Proposals that Work.* Newbury Park, CA: Sage, 1987.

Lofland, J. "Styles of Reporting Qualitative Field Research." *American Sociologist* 9 (1974): 101–111.

Logsdon, D. M., Taylor, N., & Bloom, I. H. "It Was a Good Learning Experience: The Problems and Trials of Implementing and Evaluating a Parent Participation Program." In *Qualitative Approaches to Evaluation in Education,* edited by D. M. Fetterman, 23–41. New York: Praeger, 1988.

Lomask, M. *The Biographer's Craft.* New York: Harper & Row, 1986.

Lopate, P. *Being with Children.* New York: Bantam, 1975.

Louis, M. R. "Surprise and Sense Making: What Newcomers Experience on Entering Unfamiliar Organizational Settings." *Administrative Science Quarterly* 25 (1980): 226–250.

Lubeck, S. "Kinship and Classrooms: An Ethnographic Perspective on Education as Cultural Transmission." *Sociology of Education* 57 (1984): 219–232.

Lynd, R. S., and Lynd, H. M. *Middletown: A Study in Modern American Culture.* New York: Harcourt, Brace and World, 1929.

MacLeod, J. *Ain't No Makin' It.* Boulder, CO: Westview, 1987.

Macrorie, K. *A Vulnerable Teacher.* Rochelle Park, NJ: Hayden, 1974.

Macrorie, K. *20 Teachers.* New York: Oxford University Press, 1984.

Maddaus, J. "Parental Choice of School: What Parents Think and Do." In *Review of Research in Education,* edited by C. B. Cazden, 267–295. Washington, DC: American Educational Research Association, 1970.

Madsen, M. C., & Lancy, D. F. "Cooperative and Competitive Behavior: Experiments Related to Ethnic Identity and Urbanization in Papua New Guinea." *Journal of Cross-cultural Psychology 12* (1981): 389–408.

Makler, A. "Imagining History: A Good Story and a Well-Formed Argument." In *Stories Lives Tell: Narrative and Dialogue in Education,* edited by C. Witherell, and N. Noddings., 29–47. New York: Teachers College Press, 1991.

Malinowski, B. *Argonauts in the Western Pacific.* London: Routledge, 1922.

Malinowski, B. *A Diary in the Strict Sense of the Term.* Translated by N. Guterman. New York: Harcourt Brace Jovanovich, 1967.

Manning, D. *Hill Country Teacher: Oral Histories from the One-Room School and Beyond.* Boston: Twayne, 1990.

Marshall, C., & Rossman, G. *Designing Qualitative Research.* Newbury Park, CA: Sage, 1989.

Martin, F. "Phenomenography: Exploring Different Conceptions of Reality." In *Qualitative Approaches to Evaluation in Education,* edited by D. Fetterman, 210–235. New York: Praeger, 1988.

Matsuhashi, A. "Pausing and Planning: The Tempo of Written Discourse Production." *Research and the Teaching of English 15* (1981): 113–134.

McClelland, B. W., & Donovan, T. R. *Perspectives on Research and Scholarship in Composition.* New York: MLA, 1985.

McCracken, G. *The Long Interview.* Newbury Park, CA: Sage, 1988.

McCutcheon, G. "How Do Elementary School Teachers Plan? The Nature of Planning and Influences on It." *Elementary School Journal 8*(1) (1980): 260–279.

McCutcheon, G. On the Interpretation of Classroom Observations. *Educational Researcher* (May 1981): 5–10.

McDermott, R. "Kids Make Sense." Ph.D. diss. Stanford University, 1976.

McDermott, R., & Hood, L. (1982). "Institutionalized Psychology and the Ethnography of Schooling." In *Children In and Out of School,* edited by P. Gilmore and A. A. Glatthorn, 232–249. Washington, DC: Center for Applied Linguistics, 1982.

McGrew, W. C. *An Ethological Study of Children's Behavior.* New York: Academic Press, 1972a.

McGrew, W. C. "Aspects of Social Development in Nursery School Children with Emphasis on Introduction to the Group." In *Ethological Studies of Child Behavior,* edited by N. Burton Jones, 129–156. Cambridge: Cambridge University Press, 1972b.

McLaren, P. *Cries from the Corridor.* Toronto: Methuen, 1980.

McLaren, P. *Life in Schools: An Introduction to Critical Pedagogy in the Foundations of Education.* White Plains, NY: Longman, 1989.

McNeil, L. M. *Contradictions of Control: School Structure and School Knowledge.* New York: Routledge & Kegan Paul, 1986.

McNeil, L. M. "Contradictions of Control: Part III-Contradictions of Reform." *Phi Delta Kappan 69*(7) (1988): 478–785.

McPherson, G. H. *Small Town Teacher.* Cambridge: Harvard University Press, 1972.

Mead, M. *Coming of Age in Samoa.* New York: Morrow, 1928.

Mead, M. *Growing up in New Guinea.* New York: Morrow, 1930.

Mead, M. "Our Educational Emphasis in Primitive Perspective." In *From Child to Adult: Studies in the Anthropology of Education,* edited by J. Middleton, 1–13. Garden City, NY: Natural History Press, 1970.

Measor, L. "Critical Incidents in the Classroom: Identities, Choices, and Careers." In *Teachers' Lives and Careers,* edited by S. J. Ball and I. F. Goodson, 61–77. London: Falmer, 1985.

Meeks, L. L., & Lancy, D. F. "Varying Student Conceptions of Writing: Implications for Teaching Composition with the Aid of Computers." Unpublished manuscript. Utah State University.

Mehan, H. "Structuring School Structure." *Harvard Education Review 48*(1) (1978): 32–64.

Mehan, H. *Learning Lessons: Social Organization in the Classroom.* Cambridge, MA: Harvard University Press, 1979.

Mehan, H., Hertweck, A., Combs, S. E., & Flynn, P. J. "Teachers' Interpretations of Students' Behavior." In L. C. Wilkinson, *Communicating in the Classroom,* 297–321. New York: Academic Press, 1982.

Mehan, H., Hertweck, A., & Meihls, J. L. *Handicapping the Handicapped.* Stanford: Stanford University Press, 1986.

Mehan, H., & Wood, H. *The Reality of Ethnomethodology.* New York: Wiley, 1975.

Meloy, J. "Got a Problem?" In *Qualitative Research in Education: Teaching and Learning Qualitative Traditions,* edited by J. B. Allen & J. P. Goetz, 29–35. Athens, GA: University of Georgia College of Education, 1989.

Melson, G. F., & Dyar, D. "Dominance and Visual Attention Rank Orders in Preschool Groups." *Perceptual and Motor Skills 65* (1987): 570.

Merriam, S. B. *Case Study Research in Education.* San Francisco: Jossey Bass, 1988.

Metz, M. H. *Classrooms and Corridors.* Los Angeles: University of California Press, 1978.

Metz, M. H. *Different by Design: The Context and Character of Three Magnet Schools.* New York: Routledge, 1991.

Mickelson, R. A. "Why Does Jane Read and Write So Well? The Anomaly of Women's Achievement." *Sociology of Education 62* (1989): 47–63.

Middleton, J., ed. *From Child to Adult.* Garden City, NY: Natural History Press, 1970.

Miles, M. B., & Huberman, A. M. "Drawing Valid Meaning from Qualitative Data: Toward a Shared Craft." *Educational Researcher 13* (1984a): 12–20.

Miles, M. B., & Huberman, A. M. *Qualitative Data Analysis: A Source Book of New Methods.* Newbury Park, CA: Sage, 1984.

Miles, M. B., & Huberman, A. M. "Drawing Valid Meaning from Qualitative Data: Toward a Shared Craft." In *Qualitative Approaches to Evaluation in Education,* edited by D. Fetterman, 222–244. New York: Praeger, 1988.

Miller, G. A. "The Magical Number Seven, Plus or Minus Two: Some Limits on our Capacity for Processing Information." *Psychological Review 63* (1956): 81–97.

Miller, S. E., Leinhardt. G., & Zigmond. N. "Influencing Engagement through Accommo-dation: An Ethnographic Study of At-Risk Students." *American Educational Research Journal 25*(4) (1988): 465–487.

Mischler, E. G. "Meaning in Context: Is There Any Other Kind?" *Harvard Educational Review 49*(1) (1979): 1–19.

Modiano, N. *Indian Education in the Chiapas Highlands.* New York: Holt, Rinehart and Winston, 1973.

Moffatt, M. *Coming of Age in New Jersey: College and American Culture.* New Brunswick: Rutgers University Press, 1989.

Mohr, M. M., & MacLean, M. S. *Working Together: A Guide for Teacher-Researchers.* Urbana, IL: National Council of Teachers of English, 1987.

Moore, D. T. "Learning at Work: Case Studies in Nonschool Education." *Anthropology and Education Quarterly 17*(3) (1986): 166–184.

Moore, R. C. "Before and After Asphalt: Diversity as an Ecological Measure of Quality in Children's Outdoor Environments." In *The Ecological Context of Children's Play,* edited by M. N. Bloch and A. D. Pellegrini, 191–213. Norwood, NJ: Ablex, 1989.

Morine-Dershimer, G. "Instructional Strategy and the 'Creation' of Classroom Status." *American Educational Research Journal 20*(4) (1983): 645–661.

Morine-Dershimer, G. *Talking, Listening and Learning in Elementary Classrooms.* White Plains, NY: Longman, 1985.

Moutsakis, C. *Heurstic Research: Design, Methodology and Applications.* Newbury Park, CA: Sage, 1990.

Munro, P. "Multiple 'Is': Dilemmas of Life History Research." Paper presented at the annual meeting of the American Educational Research Association. Chicago, April, 1991.

Murdock, G. P. *Ethnographic Atlas.* Pittsburgh: University of Pittsburgh Press, 1967.

Murphy, M. D., & Johannsen, A. "Ethical Obligations and Federal Regulations in Ethnographic Research and Anthropological Education." *Human Organization 49*(2) (1990): 127–154.

Myers, M. *The Teacher-Researcher: How to Study Writing in the Classroom.* Urbana, IL: National Council of Teachers of English, 1985.

Natkins, L. G. *Our Last Term: A Teacher's Diary.* Lanham, MD: University Press of America, 1986.

Nespor, J. "The Role of Beliefs in the Practice of Teaching." *Journal of Curriculum Studies 19*(4) (1987): 317–328.

Newell, A., & Simon, H. A. *Human Problem Solving.* Englewood Cliffs, NJ: Prentice-Hall, 1972.

Newman, K. K. "Stages in an Unstaged Occupation." *Educational Leadership 37* (1980): 514–516.

Nias, J. (1985). "Reference Groups in Primary Teaching: Talking, Listening, and Identity." In *Teachers' Lives and Careers,* edited by S. J. Ball and I. F. Goodson, 105–119. London: Falmer, 1985.

Ninio, A. "The Naive Theory of the Infant and Other Maternal Attitudes in Two Subgroups in Israel." *Child Development 50* (1979): 976–980.

Noblit, G. W., & Pink, W. T., eds. *Schooling in Social Context.* Norwood, NJ: Ablex, 1987.

Noblit, G. W., & Hare, R. D. *Meta-ethnography: Synthesizing Qualitative Studies.* Newbury Park, CA: Sage, 1988.

North, S. M. *The Making of Knowledge in Composition.* Upper Montclair, NJ: Boynton/ Cook, 1987.

Novick, P. *That Noble Dream: The Objectivity Question in American History.* New York: Cambridge University Press, 1989.

Oakes, J. *Keeping Track: How Schools Structure Inequality.* New Haven: Yale University Press, 1985.

Oakes, J. "Tracking, Inequality, and the Rhetoric of Reform: Why Schools Don't Change." *Journal of Education 168*(1) (1986): 60–80.

Odell, L., Goswami, D., & Harrington, A. (1983). "The Discourse Based Interview: A Procedure for Exploring the Tacit Knowledge of Writers in Nonacademic Settings." In *Research on Writing,* edited by P. Mosenthal, L. Tamor, and S. A. Walmsley, 221–236. New York: Longman, 1983.

Ogbu, J. *The Next Generation: An Ethnography of Education in an Urban Community,* New York: Academic Press, 1974.

Ogbu, J. U. *Minority Education and Caste: The American System in Cross-Cultural Perspective.* New York: Academic, 1978.

Ogbu, J. U. "Cultural Discontinuities and Schooling." *Anthropology and Education Quarterly 13*(4) (1982): 290–307.

Ogbu, J. U. "Variability in Minority School Performance: A Problem in Search of an Explanation." *Anthropology and Education Quarterly 18*(4) (1987): 312–334.

Ohanian, S. "Searching for the 'Soul' of a Classroom Review of *Among Schoolchildren.*" *Education Week* (September 6, 1989): 35–36.

Omark, D. R., & Edelman, M. S. "The Development of Attention Structures in Young Children." In *The Social Structure of Attention,* edited by M. R. A. Chance and R. R. Larsen, 120–151. London: Academic Press, 1976.

Osborne, J. M. *The Autobiography of Thomas Whythorne.* Oxford: The Clarendon Press, 1961.

Palincsar, A. M. "Review of Hugh Mehan, Alma Hertweck, J. Lee Meihls *Handicapping the Handicapped, Anthropology and Education Quarterly, 17*(3) 190–192, 1986.

Palonsky, S. B. "Hempies and Squeaks, Truckers, and Cruisers: A Participant Observer Study in a City High School." *Educational Administration Quarterly 11*(2) (1975): 86–103.

Papert, S. *Mindstorms.* New York: Basic Books, 1980.

Pascal, R. *Design and Truth in Autobiography.* Cambridge, MA: Harvard University Press, 1960.

Patton, M. Q. *Qualitative Evaluation and Research Methods,* 2nd ed. Newbury Park, CA: Sage, 1990.

Payne, G. C. F. "Dealing with the Late-Comer." In *Doing Teaching,* edited by G. C. F. Payne and E. C. Cuff, 90–103. London: Batsford, 1982.

Pellegrini, A. D. "Elementary School Children's Rough and Tumble Play and Social Competence." *Developmental Psychology 24*(6) (1988): 802–806.

Pellegrini, A. D. "Elementary School Children's Rough and Tumble Play." *Early Childhood Research Quarterly 4* (1989): 245–260.

Pellegrini, A. D. *Applied Child Study,* 2nd ed. Hillsdale, NJ: Erlbaum, 1991.

Pelto, P. J., & Pelto, G. H. *Anthropological Research,* 2nd ed. Cambridge: Cambridge University Press, 1978.

Perl, S. "The Composing Processes of Unskilled College Writers." *Research and the Teaching of English 13*(4) (1979): 317–336.

Perlmann, J. *Ethnic Differences: Schooling and the Social Structure among the Irish, Italians, Jews and Blacks in an American City, 1880–1935.* New York: Cambridge University Press, 1988.

Peshkin, A. *Kanuri Schoolchildren.* New York: Holt, Rinehart and Winston, 1972.

Peshkin, A. *God's Choice: The Total World of a Fundamentalist Christian School.* Chicago: University of Chicago Press, 1986.

Peterson, P. L. "The California Study of Elementary Mathematics." *Educational Evaluation & Policy Analysis 12*(3) (1990): 257–261.

Peterson, P. L., & Clark, C. M. "Teachers' Reports of their Cognitive Processes during Teaching." *American Educational Research Journal 15*(4) (1978): 555–565.

Peterson, P. L., Fennema, E., Carpenter, T. P., & Loef, M. "Teachers' Pedagogical Content Beliefs in Mathematics." *Cognition and Instruction 6*(1) (1989): 1–40.

Pfaffenberger, B. *Microcomputer Applications in Qualitative Research.* Newbury Park, CA: Sage, 1988.

Phillips, D. C. "After the Wake: Post Positivist Educational Thought." *Educational Researcher 12*(5) (1983): 4–12.

Phillips, S. U. "Participant Structures and Communicative Competence: Warm Springs Children in Community and Classroom." In *Functions of Language in the Classroom,* edited by C. B. Cazden, V. P. John, & D. Hymes, 370–394. New York: Teachers College Press, 1972.

Pianko, S. "A Description of the Composing Processes of College Freshman Writers." *Research and the Teaching of English 13* (1979): 5–22.

Piestrup, A. *Black Dialect Interference and Accommodation in First Grade.* [Monograph No. 4]. Berkeley, CA: Language Behavior Research Laboratory, 1973.

Pike, K. *Language in Relation to a Unified Theory of the Structure of Human Behavior.* Orange, CA: Summer Institute of Linguistics, 1954.

Pinar, W. F. "Life History and Educational Experience." *Journal of Curriculum Theorizing* 2(2) (1980): 159–212.

Pinnell, G. S., & Matlin, M. L., Eds. *Teachers and Research: Language Learning in the Classroom.* Newark, DE:IRA, 1989.

Poirer, F. E. *Primate Socialization.* New York: Random House, 1972.

Polkinghorne, D. F. *Narrative Psychology.* Albany, NY: SUNY Press, 1988.

Pomponio, A., & Lancy, D. F. "A Pen or a Bush Knife: School, Work and Personal Investment in Papua New Guinea." *Anthropology and Education Quarterly 17* (1986): 40–61.

Proshansky, H. M., Ittelson, W. H., Rivlin, L. G. eds. *Environmental Psychology.* New York: Holt, Rinehart, and Winston, 1970.

Punch, M. *The Politics and Ethics of Fieldwork, Muddy Boots, and Grubby Hands.* Beverly Hills, CA: Sage, 1985.

Putnam, R. T. "Structuring and Adjusting Content for Students: A Study of Live and Simulated Tutoring of Addition." *American Educational Research Journal 24*(1) (1987): 13–48.

Raitt, M., & Lancy, D. F. "Rhinestone Cowgirl: The Education of a Rodeo Queen." *Play and Culture 1*(4) (1988): 267–281.

Raphael, R. *The Teacher's Voice: A Sense of Who We Are.* Portsmouth, NH: Heinemann, 1985.

Ravitch, D. *The Revisionists Revised.* New York: Basic Books, 1977.

Ravitch, D. *The Troubled Crusade: American Education Since 1945.* New York: Basic Books, 1984.

Ray, L. C. "Reflections on Classroom Research." In *Reclaiming the Classroom: Teacher Research as an Agency for Change,* edited by D. Goswami and P. R. Stillman, 219–242. Portsmouth, NH: Heinemann, 1987.

Ray, R. "Language and Literacy from the Student's Perspective: What We Can Learn from the Long-Term Case Study." In *The Writing Teacher as Researcher,* edited by D. A. Daiker & M. Morenberg, 321–335. Portsmouth, NH: Heinemann, 1990.

Read, M. H. *Children of Their Fathers: Growing Up Among the Ngoni of Nyasaland.* New York: Holt, Rinehart and Winston, [1960] 1968.

Reilly, W. E., ed. *Sarah Jane Foster: Teacher of the Freedman. A Diary and Letters.* Charlottesville: University of Virginia Press, 1990.

Richardson-Koehler, V. Editorial. *American Educational Research Journal 24*(2): 171 (1987).

Riseborough, G. F. "Pupils, Teachers' Careers and Schooling: An Empirical Study." In *Teachers' Lives and Careers,* edited by S. J. Ball and I. F. Goodson, 202–265. London: Falmer, 1985.

Rist, R. C. *The Invisible Children: School Integration in American Society.* Cambridge, MA: Harvard University Press, 1978.

Rist, R. C., ed. *Desegregated Schools: Appraisals of an American Experiment.* New York: Academic Press, 1979.

Rist, R. C. "Blitzkrieg Ethnography: On the Transformation of a Method into a Movement." *Educational Researcher 9*(2) (1980): 8–10.

Rist, R. C. "Research in the Shadows: A Critique." *Curriculum Inquiry 17*(4) (1987): 447–451.

Robbins, P. "The Napa Vacaville Follow-through Project: Qualitative Outcomes, Related Procedures, and Implications for Practice." *Elementary School Journal 87*(2) (1986): 139–157.

Roberts, J. M. (1951). "Three Navajo Households: A Comparative Study in Small Group Culture." *Peabody Museum of Harvard University papers, 40, No. 3,* 1951.

Roberts, J. M., Arth, M. J., Bush, R. R. "Games in Culture." *American Anthropologist 61* (1959): 597–605.

Roberts, R. *Learning Environments of Young Children at Home and at School: The Hawaiian Experience.* Norwood, NJ: Ablex, in press.

Robinson, D. R. *The Bell Rings at Four: A Black Teacher's Chronicle of Change.* Austin: Madrona, 1978.

Rodriguez, R. *Hunger of Memory: The Education of Richard Rodriguez.* New York: David R. Godine, 1982.

Rogoff, B. *Apprenticeship in Thinking: Cognitive Development in Social Context.* New York: Oxford University Press.

Rogoff, B., & Gardner, W. "Adult Guidance of Cognitive Development." In *Everyday Cognition: Its Development in Social Context,* edited by B. Rogoff and J. Lave, 95–116. Cambridge, MA: Harvard University Press, 1984.

Rose, M. *Lives on the Boundary.* New York: Free Press, 1989.

Roth, D. R. "Intelligence Testing as a Social Activity." In *Language Use and School Performance,* edited by A. V. Cicourel et al., 143–217. New York: Academic Press, 1973.

Rumberger, R. W., Ghatak, R., Poulos, G., Ritter, P. L., & Dornbusch, S. M. "Family Influences on Dropout Behaviors in One California High School." *Sociology of Education 63* (1990): 283–299.

Rury, J. I. "Elements of a 'New' Comparative History of Education." *Comparative Education Review 22*(2) (1980): 342–351.

Rury, J. L. *Education and Womens' Work: Female Schooling and the Division of Labor in Urban American 1870–1930.* Albany, NY: SUNY Press, 1991.

Rury, J., and Harper, G. "The Trouble with Coeducation: Mann and Women at Antioch, 1953–1959." *History of Education Quarterly, 26*(4) (1986) 481–502.

Ryan, J., & Sackrey, C. *Strangers in Paradise: Academics from the Working Class.* Boston: South End, 1984.

Ryan, K. *The Induction of New Teachers.* Bloomington, IN: Phi Delta Kappa Education Foundation, 1986.

Sachar, E. *Shut Up and Let the Lady Teach.* New York: Poseidon Press, 1991.

Sackett, G. P. *Observing Behavior: Data Collection and Analysis Method.* Baltimore, MD: University Park Press, 1987.

Sage, G. H. "Becoming a High School Coach: From Playing Sports to Coaching." *Research Quarterly of Exercise and Sports 60*(1) (1989): 81–92.

Sanders, J. R., & Sonnad, S. R. *Research on the Introduction, Use and Impact of the Thinkabout Instructional Series.* Bloomington, IN: Agency for Instructional Television, 1982.

Savin-Williams, R. C. "Dominance Hierarchies in Groups of Early Adolescents." *Child Development 50* (1979): 923–935.

Savin-Williams, R. C. "A Field Study of Adolescent Social Interactions: Development and Contextual Influences." *The Journal of Social Psychology 117* (1982): 203–209.

Savin-Williams, R. C. *Adolescence: An Ethological Perspective.* New York: Springer-Verlag, 1987.

Schjeldesup-Ebbe, T. Beitrage Zur Sozial Psychologie des Haushuhns. *Zeitschrift für Tierpsychologie 88* (1922): 225–252.

Schneider, B., & Lee, Y. "A Model for Academic Success: The School and Home Environment of East Asian Students." *Anthropology and Education Quarterly 12*(4) (1990): 358–377.

Schofield, J. W. *Black and White in School.* New York: Teacher College Press, 1989.

Schofield, J. W. "Increasing the Generalizability of Qualitative Research." In *Qualitative Inquiry in Education: The Continuing Debate,* edited by E. W. Eisner and A. Peshkin, 201–232. New York: Columbia Teachers College Press, 1990.

Schön, D. A. *The Reflective Practitioner: How Professionals Think in Action.* New York: Basic Books, 1983.

Schubert, W. H. "Teacher Lore: A Basis for Understanding Praxis." In *Stories Lives Tell: Narrative and Dialogue in Education,* edited by C. Witherell and N. Noddings, 207–33. New York: Teachers College Press, 1991.

Schwartz, F. "Supporting or Subverting Learning: Peer Group Patterns in Four Tracked Schools." *Anthropology and Education Quarterly 12* (1981): 99–121.

Scott, S. Working Through the Contradictions of Researching Post-Graduate Education. In *Field Methods in the Study of Education,* edited by R. G. Burgess, 115–130. London: Falmer, 1985.

Scriven, M. "The Methodology of Evaluation." In *Perspectives of Curriculum Evaluation,* edited by R. E. Stake, 39–89. Chicago: Rand McNally, 1967.

Seginer, R. "Parent's Educational Expectations and Children's Academic Achievements: A Literature Review." *Merril Palmer Quarterly 29* (1983): 1–23.

Selfe, C. "The Predrafting Processes of Four High and Low Apprehensive Writers." *Research and the Teaching of English 18* (1984): 45–64.

Sevigny, M. J. "Triangulated Inquiry: A Methodology for the Analysis of Classroom Interaction." In *Ethnography and Language in Educational Settings,* edited by J. L Green & C. Wallat, 65–86. Norwood, NJ: Ablex, 1981.

Sharpless, J. B., & Warner, S. B. "Urban History." *American Behavioral Scientist 21* (1977): 221–44.

Shavelson, R., & Stern, P. "Research on Teachers' Pedagogical Thoughts, Judgements, Decisions, and Behavior." *Review of Educational Research 51*(4) (1981): 455–498.

Shaw, C. *The Jack-Roller.* Chicago: University of Chicago Press, [1930] 1966.

Shulman, J. M. "Now You See Them, Now You Don't: Anonymity Versus Visibility in Case Studies of Teachers." *Educational Researcher 19*(5) (1990): 11–15.

Shultz, J., & Florio, S. "Stop and Freeze: The Negotiation of Social and Physical Space in a Kindergarten/First Grade Classroom." *Anthropology and Education Quarterly 10* (1979): 166–181.

Siegler, R. S., & Crowley, K. "The Microgenetic Method: A Direct Means of Studying Cognitive Development." *American Psychologist 46*(6) (1991): 606–620.

Sikes, P. J. (1985). "The Life Cycle of the Teacher." In *Teachers' Lives and Careers,* edited by S. J. Ball and I. F. Goodson, 27–60. London: Falmer, 1985.

Silverman, D. *Qualitative Methodology and Sociology.* Aldershot, UK: Gower, 1985.

Silvers, R. J. "Appearances: A Videographic Study of Children's Culture." In *School Experience,* edited by P. Woods and M. Hammersley, 129–161. London: Croom Helm, 1977.

Simmons, L. W., ed. *Sun Chief: The Autobiography of a Hopi Indian.* New Haven: Yale University Press, 1942.

Simon, D. P., & Simon, H. A. Individual Differences in Solving Physics Word Problems. In *Children's Thinking: What Develops?* edited by R. S. Siegler, 325–348. Hillsdale, NJ: Earlbaum, 1978.

Singleton, J. *Nichu: A Japanese School.* NY: Holt, Rinehart, and Winston, 1967.

Singleton, J. "Origins of the AEQ: Methods, Myths, and Cultural Transmission." *Anthropology and Education Quarterly 15*(1) (1984): 11–16.

Sklar, K. K. *Catharine Beecher: A Study in American Domesticity.* New York: Norton, 1974.

Sleeter, C. S. M., & Grant, C. A. "Race, Class, and Gender in an Urban School: A Case Study." *Urban Education 10*(1) (1985): 31–60.

Smith, J. K. "Quantitative vs. Qualitative Research: An Attempt to Clarify the Issue." *Educational Researcher 12* (1983): 6–13.

Smith, J. K., & Heshusius, L. "Closing Down the Conversation: The End of the Quantitative-Qualitative Debate among Educational Inquirers." *Educational Researcher 15* (1986): 4–12.

Smith, L. M. "An Evolving Logic of Participant Observation, Educational Ethnography, and other Case Studies." In *Review of Research in Education,* edited by L. S. Shulman, 316–377. Itasca, IL: Peacock, 1978.

Smith, L. M., & Geoffrey, W. *The Complexities of an Urban Classroom.* NY: Holt, Rinehart, and Winston, 1968.

Smith, L. M., & Keith, P. M. *Anatomy of Educational Innovation: An Organizational Analysis of an Elementary School.* New York: Wiley, 1971.

Smith, L. M., Klein, P. F., Dwyer, D. C., & Prunty, J. J. "Pupils, Teachers' Careers and Schooling: An Empirical Study." In *Teachers' Lives and Careers,* edited by S. J. Ball and I. F. Goodson, 27–60. London: Falmer, 1985.

Smith, L. M., Prunty, J. P., Dwyer, D. C., & Kleine, P. F. The *Fate of an Innovative School.* Philadelphia: Falmer, 1987.

Smith, M. L. *How Educators Decide Who is Learning Disabled.* Springfield, IL: Thomas, 1982.

Smith, M. L. "The Whole is Greater: Combining Qualitative and Quantitative Approaches in Evaluation Studies." In *Naturalistic Evaluation,* edited by D. D. Williams, 37–54. San Francisco: Jossey Bass, 1986.

Smith, M. L., & Glass, G. V. *Research and Evaluation in Education and the Social Sciences.* Englewood Cliffs, NJ: Prentice-hall, 1987.

Smith, P. K. "Ethological Methods." In *New Perspective in Child Development,* edited by B. Foss, 85–137. Hammondsworth: Penguin, 1974.

Smith, P. K. "Does Play Matter? Functional and Evolutionary Aspects of Animal and Human Play." *The Behavioral and Brain Sciences 5* (1982): 139–184.

Smith, P. K., & Lewis, K. "Rough & Tumble Play, Fighting, and Chasing in Nursery School Children." *Ethology & Sociobiology 6* (1985): 175–181.

Smith, P. K. "Ethology, Sociobiology and Development Psychology: In Memory of Niki Tinbergen and Konrad Lorenz." *British Journal of Development Psychology 8* (1990): 187–200.

Smith, P. K., & Connolly, K. J. *The Ecology of Preschool Behaviour.* Cambridge: Cambridge University Press, 1980.

Smith, P. L. "On the Distinction between Quantitative and Qualitative Research." *CEDR Quarterly 13*(3) (1980): 3–6.

Soltis, J. F. "The Ethics of Qualitative Research." *Qualitative Studies in Education 2*(2) (1989): 123–130.

Speier, M. *How to Observe Face-to-Face Communication: A Sociological Introduction.* Pacific Palisades, CA: Goodyear, 1973.

Spencer, D. A. *Contemporary Women Teachers: Balancing School and Home.* New York: Longman, 1986.

Spindler, G. D. "Review of R. T. Sieber and A. J. Gordon." Eds. *Children and their Organizations. Anthropology and Education Quarterly 14*(1) (1983): 70–72.

Spindler, G. D. ed. *Education and Anthropology.* Palo Alto: Stanford University Press, 1955.

Spradley, J. P. *You Owe Yourself a Drunk: An Ethnography of Urban Nomads.* Boston: Little, Brown, 1970.

Spradley, J. P. *The Ethnographic Interview.* NY: Holt, Rinehart, and Winston, 1979.

Spradley, J. P. *Participant Observation.* NY: Holt, Rinehart, and Winston, 1980.

Spradley, J. P., & McCurdy, D. W. *The Cultural Experience: Ethnography in Complex Society.* Chicago: SRA, 1972.

Stake, R. E. "Case Study Methodology: An Epistemological Advocacy." In *Case Study Methodology in Educational Evaluation,* edited by W. W. Welsh, 31–40. Minneapolis, MN: Minnesota Research and Evaluation Center, 1981.

Stake, R. E. "Program Evaluation, particularly Responsive Evaluation." In *Evaluation Models,* edited by G. F. Madaus, M. S. Scriven, and D. K. Stufflebeam, 287–310. Boston, MA: Kluwer-Nijhoff, 1983.

Stake, R. E. "The Case Study Method in Social Inquiry." *Educational Researcher* 7 (1978): 5–8.

Stake, R. E., & Easley, J. eds. *Case Studies in Science Education.* Urbana, IL: Center for Instructional Research and Evaluation, 1978.

Stallings, J. A. *Learning to Look: A Handbook on Classroom Observation and Teaching Models.* Belmont, CA: Wadsworth, 1977.

Stamp, K. *The Peculiar Institution: Slavery in the Ante Bellum South.* New York: Alfred A. Knopf, 1956.

Stenhouse, L. *An Introduction to Curriculum Research and Development.* London: Heinemann, 1975.

Stenhouse, L. "A Note on Case Study and Educational Practice." In *Field Methods in the Study of Education,* edited by R. G. Burgess, 263–271. London: Falmer, 1985.

Stodolsky, S. S. *The Subject Matters: Classroom Activity in Math and Social Studies.* Chicago: University of Chicago Press, 1988.

Stone, P. J. *The General Inquirer: A Computer Approach to Content Analysis.* Cambridge, MA: MIT Press, 1966.

Strane, S. *A Whole-Souled Woman: Prudence Crandall and the Education of Black Women.* New York: Norton, 1990.

Strayer, F. F., & Strayer, J. "An Ethological Analysis of Social Agonism and Dominance Relations among Preschool Children." *Child Development* 47 (1976): 980–989.

Stuart, J. *To Teach, To Love.* New York: World, 1970.

Sturtevant, W. G. "Studies in Ethnoscience." *American Anthropologist* 66(1) (1964): 99–131.

Suransky, V. P. *The Erosion of Childhood.* Chicago: University of Chicago Press, 1982.

Swarts, H., Flower, L. S., & Hayes, J. R. "Designing Protocol Studies of the Writing Process: An Introduction." In *New Directions in Composition Research,* edited by R. Beach, and L. S. Bridwell. New York: Guilford, 1984.

Szanton, P. *Not Well Advised.* New York: Russell Sage, 1981.

Talbot, M. *More than Lore: Reminiscences of Marion Talbot, Dean of Women, the University of Chicago 1892–1925.* Chicago: University of Chicago Press, 1936.

Tammivaara, J., & Enright, D. S. "On Eliciting Information: Dialogues with Child Informants." *Anthropology and Education Quarterly* 17(4) (1986): 218–238.

Teale, W. H. "Home Background Influences on Young Children's Literacy Development." In *Emergent Literacy: Reading and Writing,* edited by W. H. Teale and E. Sultzby, 173–206. Norwood, NJ: Ablex, 1986.

Templin, T. J., & Griffey, D. C. "Editorial." *Journal of Teaching in Physical Education* 7(1) (1987): 11–14.

Tesch, R. *Qualitative Research.* Philadelphia: Falmer, 1990.

Theroux, P. "One Woman Against the Odds: Review of *Among Schoolchildren.*" *New York Times Review of Books* 94(1) (1989): 1, 46.

Thrasher, F. *The Gang.* Chicago: University of Chicago Press, 1927.

Tinbergen, E. A., & Tinbergen, N. "Early Childhood Autism: An Ethological Approach." *Zeitschrift Für Tierpsychologie,* Supplement 10 (1972): 1–53.

Tinbergen, N. *The Study of Instinct.* Oxford: Clarendon Press, 1951.

Treisman, P. U. 1983. "Improving the Performance of Minority Students in College-Level Mathematics." MS, ED 234874.

Trueba, H. T. "Culturally Based Explanations of Minority Students' Academic Achievement." *Anthropology and Education Quarterly 19*(3) (1988): 270–287.

Turkle, S. *The Second Self: The Computer and the Human Spirit.* New York: Simon & Schuster, 1984.

Tyack, D. *The One Best System.* Cambridge, MA: Harvard University Press, 1974.

Tyack, D. B., & Hansot, E. *Managers of Virtue: Public School Leadership in America 1820–1980.* New York: Basic Books, 1982.

Tyack, D. B., and Hansot, E. "Silence and Policy Talk: Historical Puzzles about Gender and Education." *Educational Research 17*(1) (1988): 33–41.

Tyack, D. B., and Hansot, E. *Learning Together: A History of Coeducation in American Public Schools.* New Haven: Yale University Press, 1990.

Tyler, W. *The Sociology of Educational Inequality.* London: Methuen, 1977.

Valentine, C. A. *Culture and Poverty.* Chicago: University of Chicago Press, 1968.

Van Galen, J. "Maintaining Control: The Structuring of Parent Involvement." In *Schooling in Social Context: Qualitative Studies,* edited by G. W. Noblitt & W. T. Pink, 78–90. Norwood, N.J.: Ablex, 1987.

Van Maanen, J. *Tales of the Field: On Writing Ethnography.* Chicago: University of Chicago, Press, 1988.

Van Manen, M. *Researching Lived Experience: Human Science for Action Sensitive Pedagogy.* Albany, NY: SUNY Press, 1990.

Varenne, H. "American Culture in the School: A Case Study." In *The Anthropological Study of Education,* edited by C. J. Calhoun & F. A. J. Ianni, 227–239. The Hague: Mouton, 1976.

Varenne, H. "Jocks and Freaks." In *Doing the Ethnography of Schooling,* edited by G. D. Spindler. New York: Holt, Rinehart and Winston, 1982.

Vinovskis, M. *The Origins of Public High Schools: A Reexamination of the Beverly High School Controversy.* Madison: The University of Wisconsin Press, 1985.

Violas, P. "Jane Addams and the New Liberalism." In *Roots of Crisis,* edited by C. Karier, P. Violas, & J. Spring, 66–83. Chicago: Rand McNally, 1973.

von Frisch, K. *The Dancing Bees: An Account of the Life and Senses of the Honeybee.* (D. L. Ilse, trans.). London: Methuen, 1954.

Vygotsky, L. *Mind in Society.* Cambridge, MA: Harvard University Press, 1978.

Walford, G. *Life in Public Schools.* London: Methuen, 1986.

Walker, D. F. "Curriculum Development in an Art Project." In *Case Studies in Curriculum change: Great Britain and the United States,* edited by W. A. Reid and D. F. Walker, 91–135. London: Routledge, Kegan & Paul, 1975.

Waller, W. *Sociology of Teaching.* New York: Wiley, 1932.

Walter, G. *So Where's my Apple? Diary of a First-Year Teacher.* Prospect Heights, IL: Waveland, 1981.

Watson, L. C., & Watson-Franke, M. B. *Interpreting Life Histories: An Anthropological Inquiry.* New Brunswick, NJ: Rutgers, 1985.

Wax, R. *Doing Fieldwork: Warning and Advice.* Chicago: University of Chicago Press, 1971.

Webb, E. J., Campbell, D. T., Schwartz, R. D., Sechrest, L. *Unobtrusive Measures.* Chicago: Rand McNally, 1966.

Weber, J. G. *My Country School Diary.* NY: Dell, [1946] 1970.

Weiner, A. *Women of Value, Men of Renown.* Austin, TX: University of Texas Press, 1976.

Weis, L. *Between Two Worlds: Black Students in an Urban Community College.* Boston: Routledge, Kegan Paul, 1985.

Weisfeld, G. E., & Weisfeld, C. C. "An Observational Study of Social Evaluation: An Application of the Dominance Hierarchy Model." *Journal of Genetic Psychology 145* (1984): 89–99.

Weisner, T. S., Gallimore, R., & Jordan, C. "Unpackaging Cultural Effects on Classroom Learning: Native Hawaiian Peer Assistance and Child-Generated Activity." *Anthropology and Education Quarterly 19*(4) (1988): 327–353.

Welch, W. W., ed. *Case Study Methodology in Educational Evaluation.* Minneapolis, MN: Minneapolis Research and Evaluation Center, 1981.

Welsh, P. *Tales Out of School: A Teacher's Candid Account from the Front Lines of the American High School Today.* New York: Viking Penguin, 1986.

Wertsch, J. *Vygotsky and the Social Formation of Mind.* Cambridge, MA: Harvard University Press, 1985.

Whitford, B. L. "Effects of Organizational Context on Program Implementation." In *Schooling in Social Context: Qualitative Studies,* edited by G. W. Noblitt & W. T. Pink, 93–118. Norwood, N.J.: Ablex, 1987.

Whyte, W. F. "Interviewing in Field Research." In *Field Research: A Sourcebook and Field Manual,* edited by R. G. Burgess. London: Allen & Unwin, 1982.

Whyte, W. F. *Learning from the Field.* Newbury Park, CA: Sage, 1984.

Wilford, G. *Doing Sociology of Education.* London: Falmer Press, 1987.

Williams, S. B. *Hassling: Two Years in a Suburban High School.* Boston, MA: Little, Brown, 1970.

Williams, T. R. *A Borneo Childhood: Enculturation in Dusun Society.* New York: Holt, Rinehart, and Winston, 1969.

Williams, W. A. *The Tragedy of American Diplomacy.* New York: World, 1959.

Willis, G., ed. *Qualitative Evaluation: Concepts and Cases in Curriculum Criticism.* Berkeley, CA: McCutchan, 1978.

Willis, P. E. *Learning to Labour: How Working Class Kids get Working Class Jobs.* Westmead, UK: Saxon House, 1977.

Wilson, S. M. "A Conflict of Interest: The Case of Mark Black." *Educational Evaluation and Policy Analysis 12*(3) (1990): 309–326.

Witherell, C., and Noddings, N., eds. *Stories Lives Tell: Narrative and Dialogue in Education.* New York: Teachers College Press, 1991.

Wohlberg, K. "The Teacher as Missionary: Teaching as Moral Imperative in Papua New Guinea Schools." In *The Community School,* special issue of the *Papua New Guinea Journal of Education 15,* edited by D. F. Lancy, (1979): 120–136.

Wolcott, H. F. *Kwakiutl Village and School.* New York: Holt, Rinehart, and Winston, 1967.

Wolcott, H. F. *The Man in the Principal's Office: An Ethnography.* New York: Holt, Rinehart, and Winston, 1973.

Wolcott, H. F. "The Elementary School Principal: Notes from a Field Study." In *Education and Cultural Process in Modern Societies,* edited by G. D. Spindler, 176–204. New York: Holt, Rinehart, and Winston, 1974.

Wolcott, H. F. "Criteria for an Ethnographic Approach to Research in Schools." *Human Organization 34* (1975): 111–127.

Wolcott, H. F. *Teachers vs. Technocrats.* Eugene, OR: Center for Educational Policy and Management, 1977.

Wolcott, H. F. "How to Look like an Anthropologist Without Being One." *Practicing Anthropology 3*(1) (1980): 6–7.

Wolcott, H. F. "Adequate Schools and an Inadequate Education: The Life History of a Sneaky Kid." *Anthropology and Education Quarterly 14* (1983): 3–32.

Wolcott, H. F. "On Ethnographic Intent." In *Interpretive Ethnography of Education,* edited by G. D. Spindler and L. Spindler, 37–57. Hillsdale, NJ: Erlbaum, 1987.

Wolcott, H. F. *Writing-Up Qualitative Research.* Newbury Park, CA, Sage, 1990.

Wolcott, H. F. "What Qualitative Research has Revealed about Education's Researchers." Paper presented at the annual meeting of the American Educational Research Association, San Francisco, April, 1992.

Wolfe, J. F. "Effects of a Developmental Guidance Curriculum on the Interpersonal Cognitive Problem Solving Skills and Social Behavior of Elementary Pupils." Paper presented at the fifth annual meeting of Northern Rocky Mountain Educational Research Association, Park City, Utah, October, 1987.

Woods, P. *The Divided School.* London: Routledge & Kegan Paul, 1979.

Woods, P. *Inside Schools: Ethnography in Education.* London: Routledge, 1986.

Worthen, B. R., & Sanders, J. R. *Educational Evaluation: Theory and Practice.* Worthington, OH: Charles A. Jones, 1973.

Worthen, B. R., & Sanders, J. R. *Educational Evaluation.* New York: Longman, 1987.

Yin, R. K. *Case Study Research: Design and Methods.* Newbury Park, CA: Sage, 1984.

Zerby, C. "John Dewey and the Polish Question: A Response to the Revisionist Historians." *History of Education Quarterly 15*(1) (1975): 17–30.

Index